W9-BKZ-996

Spearheading Debate

Spearheading Debate:
Culture Wars & Uneasy Truces

Steven C. Dubin

Steven C. Dubin is Professor and Coordinator of the Arts Administration Program at Columbia University, New York, and an Associate, Research Centre, Visual Identities in Art and Design, University of Johannesburg.

This edition published by Jacana Media (Pty) Ltd in 2012

Jacana Media
10 Orange Street
Sunnyside
Auckland Park 2092
South Africa
(+27 11) 628-3200
www.jacana.co.za

© Steven C. Dubin, 2012

All rights reserved.

ISBN 978-1-4314-0737-8

Cover design by publicide
Set in Goudy Old Style 10/12pt
Printed by Mega Digital (Pty) Ltd., Cape Town
Job no. 001892

See a complete list of Jacana titles at www.jacana.co.za

They can come in different shapes and guises, but always wars come in increments.

Dave Eggers

In such uncertain times, our only certainty is that everybody gets to be an enemy of somebody, sometime.

Maureen Isaacson

Contents

Acknowledgements

Umberto Eco's medieval whodunit *The Name of the Rose* (1980) revolves around the question, "Who is ruthlessly killing monks in a 14th-century Benedictine abbey, and why?" The only obvious fact is that the bodies of holy men are piling up and all of them bear a telltale black stain on their tongues.

A maverick ecclesiastic detective is called in and uncovers duplicity, deep suspicions and rivalries in this holiest of places, and gradually unravels the mystery. The victims shared a curiosity for a category of knowledge that the Church has forbidden: Aristotle's fabled treatise on comedy. Indulging in such literary pleasures would, of necessity, deflect their attention from more spiritual matters. But simply locking this volume away has not curbed the interest of some of them.

To punish transgressions as grave as these, Church officials have smeared the pages of the illicit manuscript with poison. Readers who cannot temper their inquisitiveness pay the ultimate price, becoming unwitting accessories to their own deaths: as they wet their forefinger to turn each sheet, they steadily deliver a fatal dosage of the toxin to themselves. So much, then, for deviation from accepted doctrine.

A South African acquaintance who spent the bulk of her academic career in a legally mandated black university – it was the only type of place she could secure a position due to her own racial classification – muses on the fact that under apartheid certain books in the school's library were banished to a separate, locked room. Marx was an occupant of long standing of this intellectual ghetto, joined by other thinkers at the whim of heavy-handed officials as they got wind of what they believed were seditious ideas. But this set-up became an unexpected boon to her particular programme: many of the most radical students became attracted to the joint Philosophy/Political Science department partly because this course of study entitled them to relatively trouble-free entry to the restricted zone.

Today she speaks about the apartheid era with some wistfulness. It was a time of great hardships, to be sure – students were swallowed up by the repressive machinery of the state or disappeared into exile; careers such as hers were needlessly thwarted – but ideas were taken seriously, and intellectual thought was believed to have tangible consequences. It is a bitter irony that throughout history the critics of free expression typically attribute more weight to ideas and images than even their creators or staunchest defenders do.

Spearheading Debate is about the power of expression in its many forms in contemporary South Africa, as well as about those who seek either to expand or constrict this realm. Within the freedom of my own time and place, I have been fortunate to be able to conduct this inquiry unfettered. This book germinated from research I began under sponsorship of a Fulbright-Hays Faculty Abroad Research Fellowship in 2003. That investigation culminated in *Mounting Queen Victoria: Curating Cultural Change* (2009, Jacana). *Spearheading Debate* can be considered a companion volume.

I salute two people in particular. Jo Burger, librarian at the Johannesburg Art Gallery, has assembled and oversees an invaluable collection of books and research materials that I have utilised continuously; my personal and professional debt to her is immense. And stateside, James Boyles has been the most loyal of friends, habitually lending an attentive ear, a sharp eye and good cheer.

I have been a regular visitor to South Africa for 12 years. Along the way I have amassed a circle of friends and professional contacts who have provided encouragement, critical feedback, companionship, shelter, and immensely memorable experiences. It is, in every imaginable way, my second home, due to the kindness and generosity of people such as Carol Brown, Willem Boshoff, Leora Farber, Marisa Fick-Jordaan, Bronwen Findlay, Tjeerd Flentge, Wouter Gildenhuys, Fée Halsted, Juliette Leeb-duToit, Nessa Leibhammer, Alan Lieberman, Andrew Lindsay, Annette Loubser, Julia Meintjes, Elza Miles, Philip Miller, Natalie Knight, Sean O'Toole, Beverley Price, Andrew Putter, Fiona Rankin-Smith, Helene Smuts, Nikki Swanopoel, Ulrich Suesse, Colleen and Jeremy Wafer, Mary Wafer, Gundi and the late Wolf Weinek, Jean Westmore, and Sue Williamson. Thanks for sharing so much, and *mea culpa* if I've inadvertently left anyone out.

What a delight (and rarity) it is for an author to work with an editor of the calibre of Bridget Impey. She unfailingly "gets it", intuitively, personally and professionally. A heartfelt thank-you for championing my writing. And it's been a privilege to be associated with Jacana, a publishing house whose motto aptly declares "We publish what we like". Its booklist makes an invaluable contribution to the quality and depth of public dialogue in South Africa. It has also been a pleasure to meet and work with Maggie Davey, Shay Heydenrych, and the rest of the remarkable Jacana staff.

Finally, I acknowledge the work of my research assistants over the past several years: Caroline Babson, Joanna Sheehan, Ann-Marie Lonsdale, Julia Malta-Weingard, Amanda Bell and Lisa Le-Fevre. By ably managing my always expanding clipping files they have learned a great deal about South Africa through osmosis, opening a portal for them to catch a glimpse of a place that has transformed my life.

How Do You Sing "Happy Birthday" to a King?

All eyes were on the praise singer as he entered from the rear of the hushed room. He could be heard before he was seen, precisely tracing his sovereign's royal lineage and reciting a lifetime of celebrated accomplishments chalked up by the man. The *imbongi* activated a declamatory, singsong rhythm that has been refined over generations.

The audience of black Africans, a significantly smaller number of Indians, and a scattering of whites was rapt, either out of respect for a familiar ritual, or with fascination over something that for them was a novel performance. No matter the background of any of the nearly 300 individuals in attendance, the group as a whole appeared enthralled by this ceremonial prologue.

But for all the traditional trappings of the moment, the praise singer looked like any hip young black man you might see on the streets of one of South Africa's bustling urban centres – excepting his leopard-skin cap, with strips of fur that dangled in front of his handsome face. It was in sharp contrast with the appearance of His Majesty King Goodwill Zwelithini kaBhekuzulu, elegantly decked out in a dark double-breasted suit, complemented by a gold-and-black silk tie.

This moment provides a revealing snapshot of post-apartheid South Africa, circa 2002: steeped in tradition yet liberally sampling from a globalised culture; predominantly black yet multiethnic, with significant minorities boasting long histories in the region; and democratic, to be sure, yet wracked by a surfeit of social problems – in many respects stemming from the legacies of colonialism and apartheid, but emerging from the deficiencies of the current majority-led government as well – that threaten at times to compromise the egalitarian ideals conceived in struggle and formalised in the country's deservedly famous liberal constitution.

But what was the event that would draw the Zulu king to a Holiday Inn conference hall on the Durban waterfront a day before his 54th birthday? And what mobilised people from markedly different backgrounds to spend a winter weekend at an indaba ("meeting", "summit") dredging up old wounds, lobbing accusations at one another, engaging in withering debate about what it means to be a South African in the 21st century? And, in a few precious instances, inching towards a sense of reconciliation with one another.

The simple answer: a song. But the complexities of the situation demand a more thorough-going investigation of how and why a tune penned by the legendary Mbongeni Ngema of *Sarafina!* fame could crystallise so much anger and fear, and spark a national debate. How, in other words, does cultural expression expose the contours of national identity, replete with warts, blemishes, wrinkles and beauty marks? How does it draw people together and likewise pull them apart? How does a wide variety of expression – songs, artworks, films, even contemporary T-shirts as well as traditional attire – and the reception it is accorded reveal the history along with the future of a society?

That audience in Durban was thoroughly coached in advance as to the protocol governing the Zulu's king's appearance. "Men have no option but to stand," they were informed by Siyabonga Memela, the initial moderator and a staff member of Idasa, the Institute for a Democratic Alternative in South Africa, an NGO that co-sponsored the weekend's events. Moreover, attendees were told that the king could not be addressed directly; questions would have to be relayed through an intermediary. But, Memela further explained, that was likely a moot point: because of time constraints dictated by the king's hectic schedule, the audience would probably not be afforded that opportunity anyway. "We've reached this [decision] democratically," he quipped, although this offhand remark hinted at a pattern of rhetorical guarantees undercut by procedural heavy-handedness that would mark events throughout the two-day KwaZulu-Natal Dialogue Initiative Symposium. "People from the media are free to do anything, but report responsibly," they were cautioned. "You do it at your own risk."

The king weighed in on the controversy over Ngema's song "AmaNdiya" (isiZulu for "The Indians"), robustly endorsing it as fitting within an African tradition of singing as a vehicle for expressing either positive or negative sentiments. With a trace of unintentional irony, Zwelithini remarked that despite black Africans being numerically dominant in South Africa, they have "always had to play second fiddle in economic matters", alluding to a number of controversial claims voiced in "AmaNdiya": that the widespread poverty of Africans is due to mistreatment by Indians; that Indians are more oppressive towards black Africans than whites have been; and that Indians are infiltrating the country in steady numbers. Moreover, he cited his longstanding desire to "try to bring harmony to our kingdom", referring to this South African province saddled with a reputation for recurrent violence stemming from a variety of sources.

Zwelithini's appearance was capped by an acknowledgment of his imminent birthday. But moderator Memela informed the gathering that singing "Happy Birthday" to the king had not been authorised in advance. Nor did it jibe with the conventions of royal protocol. He therefore proposed "bending the rules", although he quipped he "didn't want to lose his head" by doing so. In an exaggerated charade of etiquette – played out within earshot of the king, as well as everyone else in the room – the request passed through a series of underlings until an aide with sufficient authority queried the monarch directly. And to the delight of the audience, the king assented.

Many in the crowd stood, and a rousing rendition of "Happy Birthday" rang out in English. As the final notes of the song were still resonating in the air, a woman stepped into the aisle and began to ululate loudly – a gesture taken up by others in the room. And then, in a powerful, crystalline voice, she initiated a second version of the song, this time in isiZulu. She thereby expanded the tribute but at the same time pointed up differing degrees of comprehension and participation that would dog events throughout the conclave.

My goal in what follows is to examine a seemingly disconnected assortment of ephemeral yet attention-grabbing incidents in contemporary South Africa to discover what relationships and larger truths they might divulge about its post-apartheid re-emergence into the world. Chapter 1 critically examines the "culture war" concept, demonstrates how it has not been broadened to factor in globalised dynamics, and assesses its usefulness for analysing controversies erupting worldwide. Chapter 2 provides a multilayered analysis of how the song "AmaNdiya" expressed interethnic tensions, commandeered public discourse in South Africa, and revealed social fissures as well as social affinities. Chapter 3 looks at clashes between tradition and modernity, subject and citizen, as customs are modified to accommodate present-day demands, and cultural residues from the colonial and apartheid eras are reshaped to continue the democratic struggle in new ways. Chapter 4 examines how essentialist views of race, nationality and sexuality shape arguments and institutions in deliberately exclusionary ways, from hate speech to same-sex marriage to race-based think tanks. Chapter 5 investigates how the freedom of expression enjoyed by the South African media during the post-apartheid era has gradually become more constricted as a consequence of a series of controversial episodes and the cumulative effects of an evolving series of official decisions. Chapter 6 explores how artists working in a variety of disciplines have run afoul of public opinion, institutional constraints or government regulations, in sometimes predictable and in other instances surprising ways, from Zapiro to Steven Cohen, Zanele Muholi to Brett Murray. Chapter 7 "bookends" the discussion of "AmaNdiya"; in this instance the song "De la Rey" became a highly charged declaration of Afrikaner pride at the same time that it raised widespread fears of a resurgent racial nationalism. The conclusion wraps up the book's arguments, reassessing the suitability of the culture wars concept for understanding the dynamics of contemporary South African life.

CHAPTER 1

The Battle Within, Without, and Beyond: Culture Wars in a Globalised Perspective

Popular culture often bushwhacks a trail that politics then follows.

David Carr, 2007

In 1992 I published *Arresting Images*, a comprehensive investigation of the acrimonious debates that had broken out in America over art and that demonised countless artists during the late 1980s and early 1990s. Such instances propelled the names of Robert Mapplethorpe and Andres Serrano into the national consciousness; infused everyday conversations with references to sadomasochism and profane body fluids; and introduced performance art – frequently chided as attracting an audience hovering somewhere between the fingers on two hands and a baker's dozen – to a broader public. This intersection of art with politics, spectacle and debacle turned sectors of the art world into a conflict zone; it forced artists and their advocates into becoming quick-thinkers who were battle-ready, media savvy, and ever more clued into legal matters and consequences. It was, by any measure, a heady time.[1]

In *Arresting Images* I reflected upon significant power shifts that resulted from the many civil rights movements that gained momentum from the 1960s onwards, and about a "seemingly endless array" of domestic issues such as "AIDS, homelessness, crime, drugs, a seriously overburdened healthcare system, the persistence of poverty". These matters had prompted beleaguered public officials to activate *the politics of diversion*, that is, to attack symbolic targets in an effort to deflect attention away from their failure to effectively address the most pressing concerns of their constituents.[2] These were proxy battles, but they pursued real victims and inflicted perceptible damages.

In the main I cited domestic causes for what had commonly became known as the culture wars. The major exception was my reference to the fall of communism and the termination of the Cold War, which deprived Americans of an unmistakable external enemy and forced them to readjust symbolic boundaries that had been salient throughout the post-World War II era. I followed this up with *Displays of Power*, a volume that argued that the culture wars shifted over the decade from targeting relatively marginalised and vulnerable artists to attacking venerated institutions, namely museums.

How clear cut it seemed; and, in retrospect, how narrowly conceptualised. Typical of most Americans at the time, my perspective did not extend appreciably beyond continental borders. Nor had my social science training done much to expand my gaze. But international events and momentous social changes over the intervening decade and a half have altered that.

The world has been transformed: globalisation has evolved from a relatively esoteric academic concept into the lived reality of workers from Manhattan to Mumbai (née Bombay). Technology has notably contracted the world and generated previously unimaginable linkages between people and places. Furthermore, terrorism, sizable displaced civilian populations and ecological catastrophes have all demonstrated the porous nature of national borders and the interconnectedness of communities of far-flung and diverse religiosities, ethnicities, and ideologies.

And I, too, have changed.

My perspective has been significantly enlarged by gaining a substantial amount of international experience, particularly in South Africa. Since 2000, and throughout more than 20 visits (the longest spanning 13 months) I have become a witness to the day-to-day chaos, crises, fears and governmental missteps that characterise life in contemporary South Africa. But, thankfully, I've also viewed the triumphs of ordinary citizens, against the odds, in the task of constructing a democratic society on the rubble left by a succession of oppressive regimes and from a multitude of destructive conflicts. Most importantly, I have been confronted with being a perpetual stranger: apart from the breadth and depth of the personal relationships I've developed here, I have been forced to reassess nearly every taken-for-granted assumption about the motives and behaviours of individuals, about cultural beliefs and communal institutions, that each of us bears as a social being moulded from the experiences of a specific time and place.

The comprehensive process of both shared and personal re-creation occurring in the New South Africa, embodied by the ubiquitous catchphrase *transformation*, bears a significance out of proportion to the insular experiences of a single country at the tip of the globe, however. South Africa is both a symbol and a laboratory. It represents one of the ultimate and most dramatic anticolonial struggles, which was closely monitored, encouraged and in due course celebrated throughout the world. And as it turned out, its democratic rebirth in 1994, along with its societal coming-of-age, has coincided with many of the major global trends that have shaped this millennium.[3]

At the same moment that South Africa prepared to restructure itself, a host of fresh ideas was bursting into global consciousness. For better or worse, South Africa's response to the postcolonial, transnational and information-based world into which it was thrust with the demise of apartheid serves as a surrogate, a prototype for the probability of the success or failure of egalitarianism, non-racialism and cultural renaissance elsewhere.

South Africa's transformation has been beset by fits and starts, follies and substantial accomplishments. And how could it be otherwise given the compound legacies of oppression to which the majority of its people have been subjected?

Africa in general has been ignored as a site of the culture wars, except as a reference point: on occasion the brutal ethnic and religious conflicts in numerous countries on the continent are held up as models of a *genuine* clash of traditions.[4] But how useful might this concept be, derived as it is from the American experience, to analyse a large number of rancorous confrontations between different social factions in South Africa? Do these blow-ups reveal fundamental fault lines and expose sensitive social nerves in the same manner they have in the US? And do these internecine struggles signify how conflict is now shaped and expressed generally across the world?

The Culture Wars Concept

The ascent of the "culture wars" concept paralleled the demise of the Soviet Union and the dissolution of the East–West impasse of the Cold War years. The phrase surfaced in the American media in the late 1980s and entered academic debates by way of a much-discussed book bearing that title by sociologist James Hunter in 1991. Conservative politician/commentator Patrick Buchanan exploited the idea to rev up delegates to the 1992 Republican National Convention by declaring an urgent "war for the nation's soul", and from then on "culture wars" became instantly recognisable, endlessly invoked and politically divisive.

The original formulation has become canonical. James Hunter defined culture wars as public conflict based upon incompatible world views regarding moral authority, or what he differentiated as "*the impulse toward orthodoxy*" from "*the impulse toward progressivism*".[5] In other words, divergent moral visions have supplanted economics as the critical factor driving a wedge between groups. Furthermore, internal divisions within religions are now more important than differences between denominations, allowing fundamentalists to find common cause across what were formerly impenetrable doctrinal lines. Evangelical Christians and certain Catholics, for example, who once carefully kept their distance from one another, now jointly rally against issues such as abortion and same-sex marriage, and have mutually embraced cultural creations like Mel Gibson's blockbuster movie *The Passion of the Christ* (2004). This perspective is now characterised as "the ecumenism of the trenches".[6]

The titles and subtitles of many of the volumes published on this subject invoke allusions to military campaigns or disease, increasing the sense of impending crisis. Hunter himself leads off with a series of vignettes, "stories from the front". Leaving aside the issue of how accurately these writers have reflected the actual state of affairs, their discursive style has unquestionably heightened the public's feeling of alarm.

Culture wars most commonly refer to the impassioned confrontations between groups within the same society, polarised over hot-button issues falling within the realms of race and ethnicity; the body, sexuality and sexual orientation; religion; and patriotism and national identity.[7] They are a consequence of social change as well as political shifts and realignments, both nationally and globally. Once culture wars commence they develop in directions that their instigators, actors and audiences cannot necessarily anticipate.

In the case of the United States – which heretofore has been virtually the exclusive scholarly focus of these debates – the increased strength and visibility of people who were once marginalised because of their race, gender, or sexuality have initiated struggles between those reaching for power or losing it, exercising or resisting it. A reallocation of political muscle has indeed occurred to some degree over the past several decades, eroding the monopoly once held by established constituencies. In effect, every skirmish of the culture wars within the American art world, for example, has been set off by work created by these former outsiders, confirming that these are contests over status and class.[8] Culture wars are dust-ups about

what can be seen, under what conditions;
what can be said, within what situations;
whose voices can be heard, whose are silenced;
what is meaningful, and who determines it;
what is remembered, and who dictates it;
what becomes history, and who constructs it;
what can be thought, and who prescribes it;
what is believed, and who imposes it;
where social boundaries are drawn, and who patrols them;
what is a citizen, and who is thus embraced;
what is valued, and who is entitled to it;
who and what merits respect, and how do they ensure it?

While "culture wars" has entered the popular lexicon, some academics have argued that James Hunter's definition was excessively broad and has provoked overheated rhetoric; they also dismiss his depiction of average citizens feeling split by social issues as inaccurate. These critics have raised both theoretical and methodological concerns. Most reject the notion of a bipolarisation of attitudes that is either stable or growing.[9] One sceptic took up Hunter's own point that 60% of Americans hold moderate positions to ask, "Can one have a proper war when two-thirds of the army are noncombatants?"[10]

Hunter countered by noting that "public discourse is more polarised than Americans themselves".[11] This acknowledges that the culture wars become a source of energy for particular interests: they generate good news copy and exciting sound bites; plump up individual reputations and inflate organisational membership rosters; and confer the illusion of popular support and moral authority onto particular spokespeople and their groups.

But the positions embraced by Hunter and his critics may not, in fact, be so contradictory. Hunter's challengers, especially those emphasising empirical measurement, concentrate upon precisely gauging unity and diversity, cohesion or disarray. Hunter, on the other hand, finds this to be a reductionistic enterprise; his hypothesis is a broad-spectrum one that captures the regularity of these explosive yet short-lived cultural skirmishes, which may not be dependent upon fundamental social cleavages or sustained political campaigns in order to occur.

A fair précis of the social science evidence would point to the fact that measurable phenomena are not necessarily the most salient causes of human action; perceived realities may well be. Cultural conflicts do not require rock-solid divisions to exist between world views. Individuals often bear contradictory impulses; political progressives can be culturally conservative, for example. Actual clashes depend upon both the exploitation of people's fears and the successful mobilisation of public support for or against some specific contentious issue. Once mustered, and their energy expended, individuals may return to a variety of social positions and standpoints, only to be potentially reassembled in different alliances, over diverse matters, at some future moment.

During the two decades that have elapsed since Hunter initiated this discussion, several significant developments must be factored in: some outlooks and beliefs have become increasingly hard-edged, hard-lined, and antagonistic; their reach has expanded globally; and culture wars are therefore no longer confined within a specific society: their scope transcends all manner of boundaries. But Hunter failed to foresee or has underestimated the significance of large-scale, transnational trends such as the extent to which religious orthodoxy can become a vector capable of carrying provincial concerns onto an international stage. And he also did not envisage wars of words escalating into actual body counts.

War Everlasting

Culture wars are inherently protean. Long before the "war on terror" became a household phrase, culture wars were shapeshifting, oscillating in intensity, striking without warning, breaking out anywhere. They are indomitable as well; rumours of their demise have invariably been premature.[12] "All of a sudden," one foolhardy writer imagined in 1997, "the phrase is beginning to seem out of date. 'Culture war' is starting to sound a little like 'leisure suit' – a throwback to a bygone era." But the cessation she predicted has yet to arrive.[13]

Following 9/11, pundits again envisaged an end to cultural hostilities. American television and film executives brainstormed how to tone down conflict and emphasise common values, while moral entrepreneurs intentionally moderated their rhetoric as well (especially after Reverend Jerry Falwell raised ire across the political spectrum by fingering liberals, homosexuals, feminists and others for presumably initiating a slack moral climate that had angered God and thereby allowed the attacks to occur). One observer weighed in at the time, "Like so much cultural noise and chatter and froth pre-Sept. 11, most of what passed for the culture wars was a luxury of peaceful and prosperous, fat and happy times."[14] Perhaps unforeseeable at that moment was how tightly interwoven all these battles, global as well as local, would become with one another.

Fast forward to the headline of a *New York Times* feature article in 2004 that claimed "Poet brokers truce in culture wars", about self-described right-wing Republican Dana Gioia, chairman of the National Endowment for the Arts (NEA). His operational strategy was distinguished by an emphasis on venerable arts institutions and canonical pieces – not individual artists or work that gets under the skin – an approach that, to many in the arts community, has defanged the NEA and made it largely irrelevant to their interests. Yet merely days before, the realities of a presidential campaign had intruded into public discourse, and familiar oratory was resurrected. A Midwestern Republican senator resolutely decreed then, "We must win this culture war."[15]

The article on the NEA summoned up the agency's knotty history of funding an exhibition of the work of controversial homoerotic photographer Robert Mapplethorpe. The other report discussed the opposition to such issues as abortion and same-sex marriages. Same war; different battlefronts. Should it be surprising, therefore, that an editorial writer would frame his arguments in 2007 under the rubric "The next culture war", highlighting the continued viability of this popular way of conceptualising contemporary debates and conflicts?[16]

Postcolonial theorist Gayatri Chakravorty Spivak has written of "the hot peace" that supplanted the Cold War. She argues that "in the New World Order – or hot peace – the hyphen between nation and state has come looser than usual ... [and] in that gap fundamentalisms fester".[17] It is precisely in those breaches and fractures that we should now expect culture wars to propagate.

A Gathering Storm

The culture wars are nothing if not raucous. That makes performance a useful frame of reference with which to view them. Adapting the perspective of Emile Durkheim, culture wars represent a ritualised quest for symbolic targets in order to clarify social boundaries and underscore communal membership. Moreover, public punishment of transgressors represents expiation, reuniting an atomised group with a restored sense of common cause.[18]

In a Foucauldian sense, the power dynamics are intricate: antagonists become entwined in what he perceptively characterises as *"perpetual spirals of power and pleasure"*[19]; exercising authority can be as gratifying as challenging or evading it. And once this relationship becomes conventionalised, neither party easily lets go; dialogue quickly congeals into disputes, drowning out moderate voices in high-stakes, extremely polarised, take-no-prisoners struggles. Moreover, Mikhail Bakhtin's perceptive dissection of the carnivalesque and containment capture the dual nature of the transgressive, both the fear and the fascination it generates.[20]

Culture wars display characteristics similar to moral panics (mobilisation by elites, interest groups, or the grassroots against targets of exaggerated or misplaced fears), as well as millennial movements (a sense of hyperbole, apocalypse and panic).[21] The fruits of such crusades are vivid displays of *who* belongs in a community, and *what* behaviours are deemed permissible at a particular moment. Victor Turner's discussion of social drama, liminality and communitas has relevance for understanding the experiences of iconoclasts as well as defenders of the faith.[22] And the concept of the public sphere – as originated by Jürgen Habermas and subsequently debated and enlarged by a host of critics, especially by those working from a feminist or queer theory perspective – compels us to consider the ways by which various publics (and marginalised counter-publics) bring their needs and opinions to the attention of representatives of the state, other groups to which they are opposed, or possible converts to their cause. In contemporary South Africa, such publics are as likely to use established sites and channels to communicate their desires as they are to take to the streets.[23] Notwithstanding these multiple affinities, culture wars have remained conspicuously under-theorised.

Stripped of their particularities, the manifold examples of culture wars occurring since the late 1980s suggest that they unfold in a multistage, snowballing manner. The idea of "a perfect storm" – the fortuitous and successive merging of a variety of critical factors – is an apt prototype.

A sense of alienation, discontent or frustration must provide the fuel for their eruption, likely stemming from social, political or economic change. These developments commonly result in the loss of power, status or resources for some, and a sense of uncertainty for most. We are speaking here of an unsettled, and unsettling, recent communal history.

These feelings must alight upon terrain that is subject to being contested because it is a highly visible and symbolic site of collective meaning and representation: museums, monuments, heritage spots, ceremonies and rituals, works of art (paintings, photographs, songs, films, plays), school curricula and place names are some of the most familiar examples. But a multitude of sometimes surprising sources will also suffice. Collective memory, cultural capital, and multiple forms of social value are generated at nodes such as these; they are both signifying and significant.

Amplification is subsequently necessary to advance the cause, by special-interest groups (for self-aggrandisement), elites (to distract attention from their failures as leaders, or from looming, tangible problems for which there are no simple or swift solutions), or the masses (giving vent to emotions that cannot easily find other outlets of expression, such as discontent regarding perceived discrimination and mistreatment). So while culture wars focus upon express targets, they are generally a surrogate for broader issues.

Elites or special-interest groups may justify their involvement in culture wars as being conducted "on behalf of" the grassroots, whether or not people have requested such support or were consulted. Even so, the general public may incur many of the social, physical, and financial costs of these battles.

Manipulation by the established media may be vital; exploiting new technologies can provide a competitive advantage as well. But the importance of traditional channels of communication, based upon intricate networks of social bonds, should not be underestimated.

This is the basic template, which is applicable far beyond the American experience. Local characteristics and peculiarities flesh out the evolution of specific skirmishes in distinctive ways.

Burqa or Bikini?

The brilliance of apartheid – if it's even possible to ethically incorporate such ostensibly incongruous terms within the same phrase – was the determined quest its engineers undertook to make the illogical seem logical, the contrived look as if it was natural, and oppressive policies appear to be reasonable and mutually advantageous. An example of such linguistic sleight-of-hand was the parsing of beauty to ensure that national misrepresentation could not occur. At one time South Africa insisted upon putting forward two representatives to the Miss World pageant: a white Miss South Africa and a black Miss Africa South. Such cunning did not prevent the country from being expelled from the competition altogether after 1977, however.[24]

It's easy to dismiss such pomp as antediluvian, irrelevant and insignificant. But its symbolic importance, and its power to attract both appreciation and derision, cannot be underestimated. When the competition was hosted by Nigeria in 2002, bloody riots linked to the event reduced churches and mosques to ashes in the city of Kaduna, left an official death toll of over 200 in their wake, and prompted an emergency airlift of the beauty contestants to England. This became a culture war of unprecedented intensity.

The clash was sparked by the cheeky comment of a Christian journalist that if the Prophet Muhammad were around, he would likely select a new bride from the contestants.[25] Repeated printed apologies failed to mollify the situation: the newspaper's editor was arrested for what was considered blasphemy; a fatwa[26] was issued against the young reporter, who quickly turned heel and fled the country; and the newspaper's satellite offices in Kaduna were burned to the ground.

The back story reveals significant pre-existent social clefts that produced the unrest, however. Nigeria is split into a predominantly Christian south and a principally Muslim north. It is a country rich in oil, but the population in general is desperately poor. In 2000, over 3000 people died in the northern city of Kaduna during riots in reaction to the decision by state officials to impose shari'a, Islamic law. And in 2002 Amina Lawal, the mother of a young child born out of wedlock, was thrust into international awareness after being sentenced to be stoned to death under shari'a regulations for adultery (at least five contestants boycotted the Miss World competition out of solidarity with her plight, including [the now-inclusive] Miss South Africa).

Islamic clerics and scholars had called for the pageant to be cancelled months before it was to be staged, reportedly out of respect for women's modesty. Organisers did, in fact, respond to protestors and changed the date of the event to avoid it coinciding with Ramadan. On the face of it, the debate and civil disturbances would seem to be religiously based, providing a classic exemplar of Hunter's clash of orthodox and progressive world views, as represented by shari'a law on the one hand, and Western jurisprudence on the other.

But the situation is considerably more layered. The British colonial policy of indirect rule endorsed existing institutions such as shari'a; "Koran and Sunna conformed to Pax Britannica",[27] so that the reinstitution of shari'a under the present democratic regime – it was suppressed during a military dictatorship lasting until 1999 – "represents decolonization".[28] Furthermore, postcolonial Nigeria is caught in the crosshairs of the larger struggle between the West, for whom the country is an important source of oil, and the East, seeking to enlarge the orbit of global Islam.[29]

A few commentators saw the pageant as a pretext for agitated rhetoric and interethnic violence, and not the root cause. One pointed out that five days elapsed between the publication of the offending remark and the inauguration of unrest, labelling the bloodshed and destruction as "premeditated".[30] Others noted that unemployed youth or *almajirai* were paid to strategically wreak havoc on certain targets, including property owned by the local governor.[31] Moreover, some protestors bore police and military uniforms and weapons,[32] thereby casting this as a political clash as much as anything.

According to one analyst of the Miss World competition, "In terms of the pageant's flexible and hybrid production, its massive and culturally diverse audience, it is clearly globalised. In terms of its rules of competition, its reliance on the nation-state for its organization of representation, it is postcolonial. In terms of the race and gender norms it celebrates and inculcates, it is modern and colonial."[33] The loci of culture wars are not simply sideshows, therefore, but are vitally connected to significant sociocultural trends. Even so, this does not preclude them from containing paradoxical and droll elements. In the 2002 Miss World competition, the American hopeful sang the mawkish African-inflected tune "Kumbaya".[34] But this didn't whisk her to victory. It was Turkey's entrant, a Muslim, who ultimately triumphed in the crisis-relocated London venue.

Rot in Denmark and 'round the World

The potential for a culture war to erupt on a truly international scale was dramatically realised a few years later. The target, somewhat surprisingly, was a set of cartoons.[35] But these were far from commonplace. Rather they were caricatures that lampooned the life of the Prophet Muhammad and the deeds of his followers. And the responses to them were deadly.

The epicentre of the dispute was Denmark, 2005. But its aftershocks reverberated across several continents. The list of places affected reads like an inventory of (once-exotic) ports of call; an abbreviated sample includes Azerbaijan, Chechnya, Kashmir, Sri Lanka and Bosnia-Herzegovina. By the time the hubbub faded after more than six tumultuous months, protests had occurred in dozens of locations, from Afghanistan to Austria, Indonesia to Ireland. The most sensational reports centred on Syria, where mobs burned down the Danish and Norwegian embassies in the capital, and Lebanon, where a similarly chaotic, volatile scene resulted in at least one death, multiple injuries, and the torching of the Danish embassy there as well.

In Pakistan, protestors deliberately homed in on a conspicuous symbol: an outsized statue of Ronald McDonald, iconic personification of Western capitalism, free enterprise, and cultural (together with dietary) hegemony, was toppled and incinerated.[36] Local outlets of KFC, Pizza Hut and Holiday Inn were likewise torched, stoned or ransacked, events that the tabloid *New York Post* mischievously trumpeted in the boldfaced headline "**MUSLIM MADMEN IN MAC ATTACK**".[37] That pushed one *Post* reader to retort, "junky fast food is *my* religion. What I hold sacred is the flame-broiled Whopper, the ten-piece Chicken Nugget bucket and the Double-Bacon Cheeseburger. I will fight till the end for my right to freely hit the drive-thru at 2 a.m."[38] Given the source, it's not clear if these remarks were tongue-in-cheek or an authentic *cri de coeur*.

The toll of death and destruction peaked in Africa.[39] As was the case with the hullabaloo over the Miss World competition, violence broke out in the northern region of Nigeria, but it spread to the primarily Christian south. The central mosque was burned in one city and scores of Muslim residents were murdered. In one instance, a man was the victim of a gruesome "necklacing", the notorious punishment meted out by black Africans to suspected government collaborators during South Africa's struggle for freedom, and that has been revived by communities frustrated by soaring crime rates and inadequate responses by the police.[40] One journalist attributed the ferocity of the carnage to the particularities of the political atmosphere, superimposed upon a lengthy list of internecine confrontations over the preceding decades. "Nigeria is entering a period of great political uncertainty in which it must elect a new president," she explained.[41] The final toll: one hundred people were left dead.

Protests swept the continent. Elsewhere in West Africa, tens of thousands of people marched in Niger. In North Africa, soldiers gunned down 11 protestors during a demonstration in Libya, and demonstrations were staged throughout Egypt, in Morocco, and Sudan. In East Africa, protests in Kenya were disorderly and resulted in some injuries, and Somalis took to the streets as well.

In South Africa, the issue became a rallying point for the country's Muslims, estimated by the 2001 census to be 1.5% of a population of nearly 45 million people.[42] Street protests occurred in Durban, Pretoria, and Cape

Town, where 30 000 people marched, reportedly one of the biggest political demonstrations ever seen in that city.[43] Here, too, local history and politics imbued the proceedings with a distinctive flavour: a poster read "One oppressor, one bullet",[44] referencing the infamous slogan "One settler, one bullet": a battle cry during the anti-apartheid struggle aimed against supporters and beneficiaries of the repressive system. It is a phrase that has been recalibrated time and again to fit the contours of successive battles (see Chapter 3). The controversy also launched a noteworthy debate about freedom of expression, hate speech and the social responsibility of the press – as well as its right to remain independent from government control.

The politically progressive *Mail & Guardian* reprinted a single example of the Danish cartoons next to a news story. It depicted a queue of suicide bombers eager to enter heaven, only to be informed by Muhammad that the supply of virgins from which they expected to be rewarded had been exhausted. The negative response to this editorial decision included delivery trucks being held up in a predominately Indian township outside Johannesburg, and editor Ferial Haffajee and her family, themselves Muslim, receiving abusive communiqués.[45] It also elicited this lament in a published letter-to-the-editor: "We have lived side by side in peace and harmony in South Africa, tolerating each other's religious and diverse cultures. Now you are destroying that peaceful coexistence." This writer punctuated her comments with the motto "Proud to be Muslim" alongside her name.[46] The newspaper subsequently issued an apology for the distress it had caused.

The cabinet also weighed in on the debate, cautioning that freedom of speech need be balanced by responsibility and sensitivity to the feelings of various communities, a declaration full of hyperbole but ultimately ambiguous and hollow. Some parliamentarians concluded that publishing these cartoons constituted incitement to violence against Muslims.

An Islamic advocacy group then picked up the cue, seeking an injunction against other South African newspapers that might feature the works, although none had intimated doing so. And in a late-night, end-of-the-week decision, Johannesburg High Court Judge Mohamed Jajbhay ruled that freedom of the press is not absolute, and accepted the plaintiffs' arguments that this material constituted "incitement to hatred". He barred any further reprinting of the cartoons, much to the distress of journalists and free-speech advocates who felt they were being muzzled. They decried the decision as tantamount to pre-publication censorship, and as setting a dangerous precedent.

One lawyer charged, "The cartoon furore [is] the first SA case to weigh the issue of human dignity against freedom of expression",[47] foundational democratic concepts whose definitions are still evolving in a country whose constitution was only adopted in 1996. In effect, the edict validated the concepts of group defamation and hate speech, moral grey areas that other controversies in South Africa would address as well.

More than Meets the Eye

At first glance, this uproar appears to be a straightforward case of editorial insensitivity, or perhaps even deliberate provocation, unleashing a violent reaction. When the Danish newspaper published the dozen satirical cartoons under the caption "Muhammads ansigt" ("Muhammad's face") in 2005, they proved to be razor-sharp, not simply farcical. It was a serious miscalculation.

But for the controversy to truly sizzle on a global stage, it became necessary that individuals with specific agendas commence deliberate manipulation and exercise political opportunism, tapping into a communal sense of anxiety. Moreover, it required time. Significantly, an incubation period of over four months elapsed between debut and disaster. One observer noted, "[T]he more we learn about this episode, the less it looks like spontaneous combustion", while another highlighted "the new Molotov cocktail of technology and incendiary art".[48] In today's world, images can be globally transmitted with ease, and cellphones become an extremely efficient means of mustering up demonstrators.

The cartoons were published at the end of September 2005 by *Jyllands-Posten,* by all accounts a small Danish publication with right-wing and anti-immigrant sympathies. It had also commissioned them. The editor's declared motivation was to openly confront the fact that the writer of a children's book about the life of Muhammad hit a creative dead end when he sought drawings to accompany it. Potential illustrators, it seemed, feared reprisals from Muslim extremists should they depict the Prophet – an exploit that is anathema to many, but not all, followers of Islam – and therefore engaged in self-censorship.[49]

The images were varied, from the aforementioned scene of suicide bombers approaching heaven, to the portrait of an angry Muslim whose turban has transmuted into a bomb with a lit fuse, and even some metacommentaries on the artistic challenges of representing the unknowable and the sacred. They ranged from spoof to spike.

Government officials rebuffed requests by local Muslims to discuss the matter, stoking their frustration and anger. An attempt by a coalition of Danish Muslim groups to press a criminal complaint was similarly stymied. And only a small symbolic jab was inflicted when some Muslims dubbed Danish pastries "Roses of Muhammad".[50]

Thus snubbed on their home turf, a group of Danish Muslim leaders later beat a path throughout the Middle East and North Africa, bearing a dossier with the offending cartoons. They carried three supplementary, ultra-provocative images with them as well: Muhammad depicted as a paedophile, being mounted by a dog, and represented in a photo by a bearded man wearing a snout mask. Some reports attributed their source as being hate mail received by Danish Muslims who had been outspoken on the issue,[51] while others pointed a finger at the imams as the creative culprits themselves.[52] Whatever the truth regarding their origins, these extra images lacked any subtlety or cleverness. They were unambiguously derogatory.

The file received wide exposure when 57 Muslim nations gathered for a summit of the Organization of the Islamic Conference in Mecca in December 2005. But not everyone rose to take bait as vile as this. Neither the Muslim Brotherhood in Egypt nor Hamas from the Palestinian Territories joined the campaign; they were preoccupied with upcoming elections.[53] Nevertheless, negative sentiment continued to ferment and swell.

In January, leaders from 17 Muslim countries sent a joint message of protest to the Danish prime minister, and Saudi Arabia initiated a boycott of Danish goods. In the meantime, newspapers in a number of European countries reprinted the cartoons, thereby reiterating the original cause of distress and broadening their public exposure. In early February, the controversy reached full boil with the destruction of the Danish embassies in Damascus and Beirut, and widespread chaos elsewhere.

A number of observers coupled the location and intensity of the negative responses with the need of disparate groups to score political points regarding pressing social concerns. Protestors customised their exploitation of the material to suit their particular requirements. In Iran, attacking the cartoons deflected attention away from the country's nuclear programme.[54] Interestingly, Denmark was earmarked to assume the presidency of the UN Security Council, so lobbing a preemptive accusation of racism at that country was a sly defensive move.[55] Syrian officials undertook a similar line of attack, to divert attention away from their alleged role in the assassination of the former Lebanese prime minister.[56] Factions opposed to President Pervez Musharraf in Pakistan used the cartoons as a way to criticise his alliance with the West (read: freedom of expression = disrespect for the beliefs of others) and solidify support for radical Islamic forces (defending the best interests of their brethren).[57] According to one journalist, "What we're seeing in the Middle East is *strategic theater* benefit performances for the Syrian government (now playing the Islam card), Hezbollah, Hamas and every tough customer in the neighborhood."[58]

Notably, the protests in India, a country boasting the second-largest Muslim population in the world, were peaceful. Adherents there do not share the marginalised position their co-religionists living in Europe do. Moreover, they are potential beneficiaries of a society where capitalism and democracy are offering a range of possibilities far beyond the reach of many Muslims living in the Middle East or Africa.[59] "[I]t is no accident," noted one South African journalist, "that the worst violence took place in countries where Muslim leaders are known for stirring up latent resentment that owes more to globalism than to religion. It's the same *verkrampte* ['hard-line', 'narrow-minded'] mentality that gave rise to apartheid."[60]

Clearly, therefore, the cartoons were a necessary but not sufficient condition for generating a culture war. The celebrated American cartoonist Art Spiegelman of *Maus* fame, no stranger to controversy himself, astutely called them a McGuffin, the Hitchcockian ploy to set a story in motion.[61]

Fertile Ground

South Africa is an exceptionally bountiful place within which to examine present-day cultural warfare. The foremost reason is South Africa's shedding of its pariah status and re-entry into the international community, after the first democratic elections held in 1994. With transformation such a pivotal byword, South Africans are critically assaying what has been done in the past, casting off unwelcome baggage from both the colonial and apartheid experiences, and fabricating anew – at every level of experience, from the personal to institutional. And this pertains to everyone, victor and vanquished, the formerly disadvantaged and the newly befuddled.

Not surprisingly, this is a fraught process: people are forced to let go of habitual ways of thinking and acting, and must continuously readjust to new definitions, new procedures, new expectations. The complex interplay between traditional belief systems and contemporary modes of thought and behaviour, the conflicting allegiances of "subject" versus "citizen",[62] the tension between birthright and democratic selection, as well as issues regarding authenticity and autochthony, freedom of expression, and group self-determination are commonly in the public eye.

The version of the culture wars concept most relevant to this aspect of the South African experience is one suggested by Hunter himself in a later elaboration: conflict between "a world view that seeks to maintain the normative ideals and social institutions" and "a world view that seeks its transformation".[63] But that fails to capture the whole story.

On par with the specifics of its fledgling status in the world, South Africa's reemergence has occurred against the backdrop of cultural controversies convulsing societies worldwide. As we have seen, at times these battles have pulled South Africa into the fray. So the timing of South Africa's rebirth has proven consequential, paralleling the emergence of globalised movements and developments that are impacting countries internationally, and at every stage of social development. The depth of feelings of social anxiety, the breadth of situations needing to be renegotiated, and the frequency and intensity of cultural battles in South Africa are, accordingly, over-determined. Engagements that can be exhausting, hurtful and disorienting to inhabitants become an unintentional windfall for the investigator.

No researchers have understood the local impact of global trends on South African society better than anthropologists Jean and John Comaroff. In a series of trenchant and insightful articles they have dissected phenomena as seemingly disparate, marginal or trivial as zombies, madmen, witches, magic, fears over organ harvesting, museum practice, customary law, and non-indigenous flora, and have demonstrated their significance as superbly coded markers for the resistance or accommodation to contemporary social, economic or political change. The term "culture wars" is virtually absent from their studies;[64] "moral panic" surfaces only occasionally.[65] But the essence of their approach shares an obvious affinity with these concepts.

The thread that weaves through much of the writing by the Comaroffs is that people make sense of major world trends by calling up understandings that have hitherto served them well in understanding their circumstances. They attribute the fervour of witch hunts and the belief in zombies in post-apartheid South Africa to envy of the sudden prosperity the beneficiaries of a service- and information-based economy whose workings are much more concealed than the production-based markets of the past. The Comaroffs do not view the turn to magic as both an explanation and an intervention as a retreat from the present day, but rather an ingenious example of "retooling familiar technologies as new means for new ends",[66] a form of adaptation occurring throughout the world in different guises. "Enchantment," they note, "far from slipping away with the resolute march of modernity, seems everywhere on the rise."[67]

To explain the zeal of the campaign against "alien invaders" – non-indigenous flora – especially after a catastrophic fire in South Africa's Western Cape in 2000, the Comaroffs focus on the ways global capitalism has forced a rethinking of national boundaries. Borders have become increasingly permeable to enable countries to participate in the world economy. This brings benefits, to be sure, but also means relinquishing a significant measure of the control that formerly existed over the movements of people and goods.

They argue that the debate over invasive aliens stands for much more than protecting fynbos, the distinctive and beloved vegetation of that region.[68] "The anxiety over foreign flora gestured toward a submerged landscape of civic terror and moral alarm," they argue. "[W]hile real enough in and of itself, [the tumult] was, at the same time, also a metonymic projection of more deep-seated questions facing the postcolonial state about the nature of its sovereign borders, about the right to citizenship within it, about the meaning and the passion inherent in national belonging."[69]

And in yet another paper the Comaroffs explore what they characterise as clashes between the "Rule of Law" and the "Kingdom of Custom". What happens, they ask, when the rights of a *citizen*, as guaranteed by the Constitution, come into conflict with the duties and expectations of being a *subject*, of traditional leaders, customary law and ethnic identities and affinities?

On the individual level, this can mean feeling torn between incompatible sets of obligations. On the communal level, both traditional and legal courts mediate these contradictions; specific rulings commonly privilege one set of principles over another. These judgements, and the personal actions that result from them, may be extremely combustible sources for new culture wars. "The received notion of polities based on cultural homogeneity and a sense of horizontal fraternity, real or fictive," the Comaroffs argue, "is rapidly giving way to imagined communities of difference, of multiculturalism, of ID-ology."[70]

The Social Construction of Acceptability

While the culture wars have taken on some new angles as they have breached the 21st century, certain attributes are as apparent as ever. One primary characteristic is the social construction of acceptability.[71] Art and all manner of cultural expressions are neither innately offensive nor inherently controversial. Hypothetically, any particular example could become so; their meanings are indeterminate and contingent. An example that strains credulity comes from 2005, when Burger King pulled ice cream from its menu in England in deference to Muslim complaints that swirls on its packaging bore a resemblance to Arabic script denoting the name of Allah.[72]

Building upon the earlier discussion, in order for a cultural uproar to take place, an array of players must first conjure up a disapproving interpretation of something such as art; next, successfully promote it to people with social weight, be it derived from positions of authority, an abundance of resources, or by dint of sheer numbers; and then organise and channel the open expression of their distress. The meanings of artistic works and cultural constructions change as they move through time, are brought before different audiences, and especially when they cross borders, whether cultural, linguistic, or geographical.

For example, Wagner's music stirs emotions among Holocaust survivors in Israel differently than it does with listeners in other places. Passions are so intensely negative in the Israeli situation, centring on the alleged connection between the composer, Nazism and the Holocaust, that there is a long and discordant history of opponents preventing the performance of his works in public. Likewise, Chris Ofili's painting *The Holy Virgin Mary* generated immense controversy when it was displayed as part of the exhibition *Sensation: Young British Artists from the Saatchi Collection* at the Brooklyn Museum of Art in 1999. But it had failed to raise ire when it appeared previously at a venue in London (where another painting did).[73] And as the photographs of the late Robert Mapplethorpe have toured the world, different images have set off varying reactions, demonstrating cycles of reception of the same material in various locales.

A museum director in Tel Aviv in 1994 feared that the image of a man's genitals, bleeding and ensnared in a mechanical contraption, would remind Holocaust survivors of torture. It was, therefore, removed. A picture of bodybuilder Lisa Lyon, to whom Mapplethorpe once devoted an entire volume, came into the spotlight in Germany in 2004. Although Mapplethorpe produced many nude photos of this woman, she wears a bathing suit in the work in question, and leans against a wall with her arms raised. Included within an exhibition nearby the birthplace of the reigning pope, it called to mind the crucifixion for some people. Moreover, it spawned a hunch that Christianity was being ridiculed, an association no one had previously drawn. And when a broad selection of Mapplethorpe's work was mounted in a groundbreaking exhibition in Havana in 2006, some locals were shocked by a photo of a badly battered American flag. They admitted they would be frightened to exhibit a Cuban flag in a similar condition; they thought of such a display as "forbidden". According to a veteran consultant to the Mapplethorpe Foundation who has witnessed a wide array of objections to this man's oeuvre, "You never know which image is going to trigger a cultural reaction."[74]

When the culture wars first erupted in America, photographer Andres Serrano was commonly billed as Mapplethorpe's evil co-twin. Senator Jesse Helms described the photograph *Piss Christ*, where Serrano submerged a plastic crucifix into a vat of his own urine, as a "sickening, abhorrent and shocking act by an arrogant blasphemer".[75] Helms consequently proposed legislation limiting the discretion of the National Endowment for the Arts to fund individual creative works. At the time Serrano quipped, "The [initial prohibitive] wording was 'obscene and indecent'. I always assumed that Mapplethorpe was the obscene one and I was the indecent one."[76]

When *Piss Christ* was included as part of a Serrano exhibition at the National Gallery of Victoria in Melbourne, Australia in 1997, the Catholic Church attempted to obtain an injunction from the supreme court to prevent it from being shown, and the catalogue was referred to the national censor to determine if restrictions could be imposed upon it. But a judge rejected this bid to shut the exhibition down, arguing that "in a multicultural, pluralistic and increasingly secular society, many groups have to accept the jibes of others".[77]

One of the groups in the forefront of the crusade was the Coalition for Prevention of Public Blasphemy. Regular prayer vigils were organised outside the museum, but they were ultimately overshadowed by two attacks on the photograph that took place over as many days, which seriously damaged it. Museum officials, also citing bomb threats, capitulated to the tumult; they closed down the exhibition, arguing that they could not guarantee security. An editorial in a Melbourne newspaper had asked, what if it "were [instead] a Star of David, a text from the Koran or an Aboriginal artifact [such as a rainbow serpent on a bark painting] ... As a mainstream belief, Christianity has no such protection."[78] The writers raised the same sort of protestation that beleaguered believers had done some years before in the US, but this time reflecting the distinctive ethnic and religious blend of their own society.

A decade later in Sweden, vandals propelled iconoclasm into the frontiers of new media. In the small university town of Lund, where Serrano's explicit *History of Sex* exhibition was being featured, four masked vandals armed with crowbars and axes stormed the gallery. Smashing works as they tore through the space, by the time they cleared out they had destroyed about half the photos. Self-proclaimed neo-Nazis, they were evidently accompanied by their own videographer. Within days of the incident the group posted an edited version of their escapade on YouTube, complemented by a thumping death-metal sound track and editorial comments about the alleged immorality of Serrano's work. These felons, members of a global generation that has cut its teeth at the intersection of electronic technology, relentless self-revelation and self-promotion, converted vandalism into performance art, mayhem into media spectacle.

Blurring the Borders

One of the significant lessons from the initial outbreak of the culture wars was that images that oftentimes raise the public's ire are those that smudge the boundary between separate but widely recognised and respected categories. *Piss Christ*, for example, combines the sacred and profane; it remains Andres Serrano's best-known and most controversial work. Serrano's *Heaven and Hell* – the title is obviously noteworthy – mixes the spiritual and the carnal, as does Chris Ofili's painting *The Holy Virgin Mary*, featuring a black Madonna surrounded by butterfly-like cutouts from pornographic magazines and with a shellacked clump of elephant dung representing one breast.

And the reason Serrano's series *The History of Sex* triggered such a negative response was likely not only because of the explicitness of his large-scale photographs but because some of them pushed into the outermost taboo regions of sexual expression, such as intimate contact between partners of widely varying ages and between human and animal, or pictured a person with female breasts and male genitalia. Anthropologist Mary Douglas's insights made several decades ago regarding "natural categories" are as pertinent today: it is fundamentally disarming to see distinctions such as masculine and feminine, sacred and profane, traditional and modern, or public and private folded into one another.[79] And that is precisely what many transgressive artists relish doing.[80]

A superb example from the South African context is Brett Murray's public sculpture *Africa*, comprising a tribal figure sprouting colourful Bart Simpson likenesses from its body: the developing world meets the media-saturated industrialised world head-on (see Chapter 6).

Elsewhere, two entries of this composite sort within a prestigious art competition in Australia sparked controversy in 2007. The theme of that year's Blake Prize for Religious Art, interestingly enough, was cultural diversity. But *Bearded Orientals: Making the Empire Cross* (a lenticular or holographic image where Jesus morphs into Osama bin Laden, depending upon the spectator's position in relation to it), and *The Fourth Secret of Fatima* (a statue of the Virgin Mary wearing the type of blue burqa that women dressed in under the rule of the Taliban), drew condemnation from the highest echelons of (Christian) religion and the government downward (both the prime minister and the opposition leader condemned the pieces). The artist of the "double vision" work hoped to juxtapose good and evil, as well as express concern about Bin Laden attaining a certain cult status, but many viewers judged her to be drawing a moral equivalency between the figures in this Christian–Muslim fusion.[81]

An Australian bishop obviously understood the power inherent within the double image by noting, "it's arresting".[82] The artist herself, Priscilla

Bracks, recognised this vitality as well. "[I]t is a very loaded work," she said, "which means that there's [sic] so many different meanings."[83] But others grasped the opportunity to turn this art and the reaction it had evoked into political capital. An editorialist touted the moral superiority of Christians with their embrace of the decree to turn the other cheek, and condemned the cockiness of contemporary creators like Bracks as "another artist to show 'courage' by mocking the one faith too nice to hit back". Commenting further, in an undisguised dig at Islamic fundamentalists, he declared, "Safer to crucify Christ again for the sins of others. How easy it is to slander the guy whose followers don't shoot back."[84] His was not a lone voice.[85]

Such examples are legion. Two works included in the 1998 exhibition *Pictura Brittanica* at the Museum of New Zealand, Te Papa, had proven to be controversial as well: *Virgin in a Condom*, a seven-centimetre statue of Mary covered in a condom, and a large-scale photographic version of *The Last Supper* by Sam Taylor-Wood, where a semi-naked woman substitutes for Christ, mixing a Baroque-like setting with people from the hip London art scene, combining sacred and profane, elite art and pop. When a version of the statue was exhibited in 1997 in Sydney's Museum of Contemporary Art, it was stolen and never recovered. But when shown in Europe, there was "barely a ripple of controversy".[86]

A familiar array of methods of condemnation was unleashed against the pieces: an appeal to prosecute them as "blasphemous libel" (failed); a request to the chief censor to restrict the catalogue (failed); and weekly protests. Two weeks after the show opened, one man resorted to vigilante justice: he kicked over the display, slightly damaging the statue, and breaking the Perspex case enclosing it. Found guilty of wilful damage, he was not remorseful, declaring "There is an element to modern art that is simply satanic".[87] Significantly, he had been convicted twice before, on the charge of trespass during anti-abortion protests,[88] underscoring how crusades against culture are part and parcel of larger pitched battles in which fundamentally opposed world views are being engaged.

And, to cite just two additional examples, in 2007 a British-born teacher working in an elite private school in Khartoum, Sudan became embroiled in a brief but volatile situation after a cultural misstep. She had asked her class of seven-year-olds to name a teddy bear they would be using in a class project; the kids overwhelmingly endorsed "Muhammad". When the story became public, it outraged some observers as combining blasphemy and idolatry. The affair became an international cause célèbre, generating daily news coverage; the woman was arrested, and could have been sentenced to a public lashing and up to a year in jail. Noisy street demonstrators called for her execution, but a presidential pardon (negotiated through the intervention of two Muslim members of the House of Lords) allowed her to return home after serving a brief jail term. And in a story reminiscent of the Danish cartoons incident, a cartoon image of the head of Muhammad set on the body of a dog appeared in a Swedish newspaper in 2007. "The entire Muslim race [sic] is angry," a Bangladeshi declared.[89]

Statements such as these, joined with the memory of past events, put Swedish companies on high alert in several locations worldwide, sent diplomats scurrying to defuse tensions, and generated a reward for the murder of the artist – with a promised 50% bonus if he were "slaughtered like a lamb".[90] An explanation of sorts is possible for the image: homemade sculptures of dogs are placed on traffic roundabouts as a guerilla art activity in Sweden, a practice that the cartoonist was lampooning.[91] But since dogs are viewed as impure in Islam, this transgressive amalgamation was deeply insulting to followers.

The Politics of Diversion

As we discovered when the Danish cartoons sparked a firestorm, many of the places where the flames burned white hot were ones where public officials were deflecting attention away from other, nagging problems. Shortly before protests broke out in Egypt, for example, more than 1000 passengers had died after an Egyptian ferry sank in the Red Sea. The grief of the families was matched by their anger at the government's inability to either prevent such disasters from occurring, or to competently manage such crises when they occur. According to one report, "Leaders often call attention to external enemies – most often the Israelis – as a device to allow their own subjects to blow off steam. The anger itself is almost always home grown."[92]

Prime Minister John Howard took up the ethical crusade against the disputed works of religious art in Australia in 2007 while he was trailing his opponent in an upcoming election. Moreover, President George W. Bush – whose Iraq policy Howard supported – was about to visit the country, a political liability with an Australian electorate that was highly critical of the war. His supposedly principled showboating became a failed strategy; Howard lost the balloting. And in Sudan, Muhammad the teddy bear became a pawn in a much larger drama.

Sudan, of course, had been under increased world scrutiny for the mass atrocities committed against its citizens in the Darfur region. Shortly before, the government had refused to allow peacekeeping troops from Scandinavia to be dispatched there, citing the cartoon controversy two years earlier. To those familiar with the situation, it was a diversionary ruse.[93]

And just five years after blood ran in the streets of Nigeria because of the Miss World competition, and two years after 100 more had died in riots over the Danish cartoons, an investigative report revealed that shari'a law was not being enforced in a Draconian manner and had not reshaped Nigerian society. Moreover, some of the same politicians who had most heartily supported the reinstitution of shari'a law found themselves the target of investigations into having embezzled millions of dollars of public funds.[94]

So rather than signifying a "clash of civilisations", the turmoil in Nigeria reeks of political opportunism, grandstanding and averting blame. "Many early proponents of Shariah," one journalist reported, "feel duped by politicians who rode its popular wave but failed to live by its tenets, enriching themselves and neglecting to improve the lives of ordinary people."[95]

New Spins, Old Themes

The culture wars were recognised as beginning in the late 1980s and early 1990s. But it is obvious that despite the scholarly critique launched against the concept, new episodes recur, and the label is continuously invoked in thematic and geographical territories that are both fusty and fresh. Notwithstanding the preponderance of episodes I have cited involving Muslims, the inventory of contemporary incidents is best described as (little "c") catholic in nature.

For example, hard rock/heavy-metal band Lordi represented Finland in the celebrated Eurovision music competition in 2006. The band members' outlandish appearances mirror the kitschy stock characters of horror flicks, such as zombies, ghosts and mummies; profuse make-up, claws and horns make them more Freddy Krueger and less the urbane, benign (and relatively obscure) dwellers of a land sandwiched between Scandinavia and the former Soviets. With Nordic national identity at stake, particular religious leaders and politicians preferred that a traditional folk singer represent the nation. Some even appealed to the president to derail the group's official participation. But in the end, what some Finns fretfully judged to be satanic wannabes rather than devotees of Saint Nicholas, trounced all the other entrants and glided to victory. In the New Europe, where people of different races, ethnicities and religions coexist in ever-greater numbers, Finland now stands for reindeer, the Aurora Borealis and "Hard Rock Hallelujah".[96]

The runaway hit documentary *The March of the Penguins* was unexpectedly drawn into the culture wars in 2005 after religious and political conservatives embraced these compassionate animal pairs as embodying such virtues as monogamy and parental sacrifice. Film critic Michael Medved hyped the film for audiences with traditional values: "This is the first movie they've enjoyed since 'The Passion of the Christ.' This is 'The Passion of the Penguins'."[97] But these same behavioural ideals were also advanced to support the opposition: a bonded pair of male penguins at New York's Central Park zoo was immortalised in the kid's book *And Tango makes three*, where they incubate a fertilised egg and then raise the chick. This non-traditional tale did not pass without fault-finding, however: the American Library Association declared it "the most challenged book" of 2006.[98] As Jean and John Comaroff demonstrated with the campaign against "alien invader" plant species in South Africa, critical and divisive social issues are "naturalised" and fought out in a manner that's less objectionable than direct confrontation between the parties in actual opposition to one another.

The Iraq War has also raised a number of issues that demonstrate interesting affinities with past events. There has been a general effort on the part of government and other officials in the United States to limit information and stifle any hint of dissent, such as disallowing photos of bodies of slain service personnel being returned stateside to be publicly broadcast.[99] In 2007 in Wilton, Connecticut, a group of high school students planned to present *Voices in Conflict*, a series of monologues assembled from the words of Iraqi citizens and American soldiers serving in Iraq, but it was cancelled by their principal because he feared audience members might potentially perceive "bias" in the points of view expressed.[100] Moreover, the Pentagon restricted access for troops serving in Iraq to internet sites such as MySpace and YouTube, and supervised participation in blogging or writing personal emails. All of these actions represent defensive attempts to preempt the possibility of dissent and controversy, efforts that do not raise as much outcry during a time when an actual war is being fought as they otherwise might.

When Technology Meets Ideology

One way to thwart the outbreak of culture wars within a democracy, then, is to strictly control information, thought and behaviour as systematically as possible. Conflict is unlikely when orthodoxy triumphs, as in a totalitarian society. But the present-day interconnectedness of different parts of the world – highly facilitated as it is by technology – can now implicate one society in the regulation of the internal affairs of another in ways that were unimaginable not so long ago. But this can also generate considerable fallout regarding freedom of expression in those places where there is a broader range of choices.

In 2006, Pulitzer Prize-winning columnist Nicholas Kristof suggested this disturbing hypothetical: "Suppose that Anne Frank had maintained an email account while in hiding in 1944, and that the Nazis had asked Yahoo for cooperation in tracking her down. It seems, based on Yahoo's behaviour in China, that it might have complied."[101] He was referencing the charge that Yahoo had handed over information to Chinese officials identifying who had sent certain unorthodox electronic messages; that data proved vital to convicting these cyberdissidents.

This and other revelations emerged from congressional hearings convened by the House Subcommittee on Africa, Global Human Rights and International Operations whose members questioned executives from the so-called "Internet Gang of Four": Yahoo, Google, Microsoft and Cisco.[102] Google has supplied a compressed version of its search engine, which builds in censorship by assiduously funnelling the user's attention to information supporting one point of view, while purging others. Clicking on "Tiananmen Square" while logged on within China does not yield the dramatic images of the phalanx of tanks and the lone, daring protester who stood them down in 1989, but instead brings up images of tourists and children releasing balloons in the plaza. Googling throughout the world produces "dissident group" in association with Falun Gong; if you call up the same subject in China, however, you discover "dangerous cult". There are distinctive slants on

Taiwan and Tibet as well, aligned with the government's outlook.[103] It is also possible to monitor blogs, and use filters to exclude certain words – the same gadgets that corporations or parents can use to restrict access or exposure, but of course implemented in a less expansive way than by a totalitarian society.

The technology companies defended themselves by arguing that entering the Chinese market, even with restrictions, is better than staying out. In other words, they provide a capacity whereby citizens can potentially use the technology to their own ends (the government can't patrol everything; one report states that China has been able to block 90% of websites regarding the Tiananmen Square massacre, and 82% with a derogatory name of the former president – significant, but not total control).[104] The counter argument is that companies need not conform to conditions dictated by the countries with which they do business, and some people have suggested the need for guidelines addressing fundamental protections of the rights to privacy and free speech, akin to the voluntary anti-discrimination Sullivan Principles,[105] which were one way that corporations worldwide took a stand against apartheid in South Africa, beginning in the mid-1970s.[106]

This controversy centres on the Chinese people, but does not actively engage them. That's the nature of a dictatorship. And so it demonstrates that while experiencing the turmoil of culture wars, it may seem as if the world is disintegrating from contrapuntal forces. But on the contrary, it shows that a society where culture wars occur is one where there is still space for debate, resistance and dissent. And the possibility of generating new ideas and understandings.

Culture Wars: Expanding the Scope

Have I unjustly found fault with James Hunter's formulation of the culture wars? In all fairness, the subtitle of his breakthrough volume in 1991 was "the struggle to define *America*" (emphasis added). His intention was therefore clearly stated, making his lack of comparative material beyond the borders of the United States reasonable at that time. Is this a classic instance of setting up a straw man and gloating over the ease with which it can be knocked down?

Not so: in the most recent explication and defence of his ideas, Hunter continues to demonstrate a peculiar silence. He remains oblivious to what is happening in the rest of the world, as well as ignoring America's growing interdependence with it. Amazingly, he makes no reference to globalisation, to 9/11, or the "war on terrorism", all of which have yanked Americans in general out of their cultural and political isolationism.[107] This deliberate refusal to look beyond one's own backyard is a glaring oversight on Hunter's part and ensures that he misses the opportunity to expand the application and relevance of his fundamental concept.

Furthermore, for someone whose formulation rests upon the conflict between orthodox and progressive world views, wouldn't it be logical to expect that the emergence of a militant version of Islam as a frequent factor in conflicts worldwide would have become a central concern for him? How, for instance, would this phenomenon relate to his thesis that fundamentalist perspectives unite believers across manifold doctrinal lines? Surely many of the episodes of cultural conflict that I've cited demonstrate an important qualification to this assertion; we have yet to see coalitions of orthodox Catholics, Protestants or Jews aligning with fundamentalist Muslims on social issues.

In the chapters to follow, my goal is to push beyond the limits Hunter has deliberately set for himself. The knowledge that can be gleaned beyond the American experience is intrinsically interesting and unquestionably valuable. It should be clear that to the extent we ignore global events, we are that much more impoverished in our understanding of the contemporary world, as well as of ourselves.

My focus therefore amplifies Hunter's work. From my standpoint, culture wars are trans*sensational* events, generating ferocious pageantries of drama and emotion. They are

trans*cultural*, overriding or assimilating parochial distinctions;

trans*national* and trans*continental*, disregarding manmade borders;

trans*portable* and trans*mittable*, shifting from place to place;

trans*historical*, surmounting the past and confronting the present;

trans*generational*, affecting young and old;

trans*gender*, engaging the sexes and challenging their meaning(s);

trans*mogrifying*, metamorphosing anxieties into actions;

trans*literative*, developing a conventionalised way of expressing disquiet and discontent;

trans*literate*, engaging symbols and forms of communication from a variety of sources;

trans*sisterised*, compacting vast quantities of material into singular representations;

trans*actional*, mediating the business of social change;

trans*fusional*, energising subterranean feelings and beliefs;

trans*gressive*, defying standard categories of experience;

trans*itional*, bridging different phases of social action and evolution;

trans*itory*, packing a big punch into a brief episode;

trans*parent* and trans*luscent*, uncovering veiled ulterior motives;

trans*cendental*, pulling participants beyond the mundane routines of life;

trans*figurative*, disrupting and altering the status quo; and thereby trans*formative*, leaving a legacy that may result in change, but can also include lingering attitudes that could provide the catalyst for new conflicts to break out.

To view the culture war concept more narrowly than this is a deliberate denial of its theoretical potential and a purposeful diminishing of its applicability.

* * *

To my surprise, and as a further example of how untested assumptions can frequently reveal one's own myopia and distance from reality on the ground, I was gobsmacked to discover that South Africans have greeted my explanation of this book-in-the-making as an examination of the culture wars in their country with a uniform, "Huh?" My first clue that this term, which may be ordinary to Americans but is essentially unfamiliar to South Africans, came when a prominent art museum director visiting New York asked me to clue her in to the meaning of "culture wars": she was expected to speak about the concept at a conference on art and AIDS and had no idea what it meant.

When I next travelled to South Africa I queried other people I knew who were generally savvy about cultural matters: curators and assorted museum personnel, artists, musicians, writers, political commentators and academics. Not one, from my admittedly limited and non-representative sample, was familiar with the idea of culture wars. My quest for information evolved into an emotionally charged game: in one regard I didn't wish to spoil my "no hitter", but I also felt compelled to keep trying to discover a person for whom the term rang true.

I failed to discover such an individual, which confers an unexpected dimension onto this book. Not only does my evidence extend the culture wars concept to new terrain, it also alerts South Africans to the understanding that struggles on their local turf are related to global concerns in fundamental ways. It's another means of heralding them back into world affairs, with its manifold messes along with its opportunities.

CHAPTER 2

Lost in Translation: What's in a Song?

Marginality invested the Asian with an odd kind of invisibility – "They only see us when they want to hate us".

Shiva Naipaul, 1980

The [Soccer] Match of the Year!

Natal Indians vs Natal Africans Poster, n.d., Durban Cultural and Documentation Centre

In food lies revelation. With the most humble of foods, even more so.

Visitors to South Africa, most particularly to KwaZulu-Natal's vibrant, multiethnic city of Durban, are undoubtedly perplexed when they first see signs advertising bunny chow, a local speciality. It originated as working man's fare, a self-contained meal-in-itself. At its most basic, a plain loaf of white bread, is halved, the core is scooped out, it is filled with some variety of savoury curry, and then the residual bread is used to seal it in. The loaf becomes a convenient take-away container, and pieces of bread can be dipped into the juicy mixture and eaten. It's cheap and convenient, an imaginative version of fast food predating multinational chains.

And yet its fanciful title belies a serious social cleft. Story has it that in days past, Indian shopkeepers and restaurant owners – whether due to apartheid restrictions or individual prejudices – would not serve food to black African patrons inside their establishments. Packaging their cooking in an edible bowl was an ingenious resolution. Indians profited without transgressing legal statutes, community prohibitions or personal preferences; black Africans received a nutritious and low-cost meal. Bunny chow represented both shrewd business practice and good value.

But this novelty also underscored the social distance between these two groups who share a great deal of common history within South Africa. It could be experienced by black Africans as yet another way in which they were being exploited, by "cunning Indians".

Like so many relics of a bygone age, bunny chow has gone upmarket. A franchise of French-named hotels in posh Plettenberg Bay, Constantia and

Hermanus now feature a version of the dish that's been tweaked considerably, with a seafood curry comprising mussels, calamari, linefish and prawns spooned into bread that has been baked in flowerpots. This tendency to shroud history with an overly sentimental coating pervades the New South Africa, post-1994.

The same propensity underlies the development of The Kingdom, located on an old sugar estate north of Durban along the coastal highway that now offers food, lodging, entertainment and a (multi)cultural village experience. A promotional brochure touts "The original Indian cane cutters village has been lovingly renovated to provide 28 en-suite chalets decorated in a combination of colonial and Indian style". Zulu, Indian and colonial customs and experiences are blended together – "three cultures on one estate" – eliding significant distinctions, schisms, antipathies, and histories of conflict and pain with a gauche marketing ploy.[108] But deep, ethnically based fissures are not so easily covered over. They may be dormant at times, but can burst open with enormous fury, sparked by sometimes surprising triggers.

Brothers in Struggle?

The histories and life experiences of black South Africans and their fellow citizens of Indian origin are braided together in noteworthy and complex ways. Both groups were exploited by colonial interests. Both felt the weight of apartheid. They have faced pervasive discrimination, dispossession, imprisonment, impoverishment and violence: symbolic and real, physical, spiritual, economic, and environmental. And they have heroically resisted their fate in significant ways. But many such alliances have frayed in the post-apartheid world; former associates have drifted apart, whatever sense of shared fate that once existed between black Africans and Indians has seriously eroded.[109] Drawing analogies to the entangled relationship between African-Americans and Jews is unavoidable.[110]

When Mbongeni Ngema released his song "AmaNdiya" (isiZulu for "The Indians") in February/March 2002, it brought to the surface attitudes that are seldom aired in such a public fashion. "AmaNdiya" evoked a variety of responses. Predictably, Indians overwhelmingly condemned it; fellow Zulus came to Ngema's defence. The song became the focus of several regulatory bodies, and politicians of all stripes jumped into the fray. Kings (His Majesty Goodwill Zwelithini) and elder statesmen (Nelson Mandela) weighed in on the song's merits and transgressions. And it significantly impacted day-to-day interactions between the races on the streets, in stores, and in communities where black Africans and Indians live close by one another. It electrified debate, spurred self-reflection, and in the minds of many, intensified fears and suspicions that drove a bigger wedge between the two groups.

What, in fact, did "AmaNdiya" say? Even that is in dispute. Among the claims Zulus made on Ngema's behalf was that the lyrics had been poorly translated into English and that he was therefore misunderstood and unjustly attacked. To his supporters, this was another clear-cut instance of how whites, Indians and other South African minority groups fail to grasp their way of life or identify with their experiences because relatively few of them have learned to speak indigenous African languages.[111] A translation, which was carefully vetted through speakers of isiZulu, reads as follows:[112]

Prelude (in English): This song represents the way many Africans feel about the behaviour of Indians in this country. It is intended to begin a constructive discussion that will lead to a true reconciliation between Indians and Africans.

O! Men!
O! Guys!
[repeat 3 times]

A man of courage is needed to face Indians
This issue is complex, it needs to be discussed by men
Indians don't want to change
Whites were better because we knew it [*sic*] a political war
Even you leaders of our country don't want to address this issue
You have bought roti and bethel nuts from Indians

Indians don't want to vote, when they vote they vote for whites
But they are full in parliament

Buthelezi why are you queit [*sic*]?
As Indians play with the
Children of Ngqengelele, children of Mnyamana
Zulus are poor, they live in shacks
They are stooges of Indians.
Where is Ndebele?
Where is Prince Gideon Zulu?
O' Your Majesty? Stand up!

I've never seen a Dlamini emigrating to India
But here is Gumede in Durban without a place to stay
We are suffering this way in Durban because the Indians took everything away
Yet they oppress our people

Mkhize is complaining, he is looking for business premises in West Street, Indians prevent him saying there is no space to let
Even you Mbeki why are you queit [*sic*] as Indians make fools out of us

O! Guys!
O! Men!
O! Guys!

You don't want to listen to me when I say, Give money to African
people who live around your Indian shops

At Isipingo, Clairwood, Durban, Phoenix, Verulam, Africans buy
from Indians
But Indians don't even want an African school

I've never seen a Dlamini taking his whole family to go and settle
in Bombay, India
But Indians arrive daily in Durban, they are full of [*sic*] the airport

O! Men!
O! Guys!

According to this characterisation, Indians are mercenary, exploitative,
opportunistic interlopers. Was Ngema being inflammatory? Or, was he merely
"telling it like it is", as he claimed, giving voice to common sentiments, airing
the views of people waiting in boisterous taxi ranks or relaxing in shebeens?
And beyond whether it was an accurate or fallacious portrayal of South
African Indians, what did it matter? It was, after all, just a song.

These were some of the questions addressed by people attending the
aforementioned 2002 Durban indaba where the Zulu king consented to be
serenaded on his birthday, an event convened in order to vent grievances
between black Africans and Indians and to possibly diffuse fears spawned by
"AmaNdiya".

The Man behind the Music

Mbongeni Ngema attracts respect and scorn, praise and damnation in equal
measure. He is a luminary in the South African entertainment business who has
been dogged by controversy at the same time that he has snagged major kudos.

Ngema is a composer, musician, playwright and director, most widely
known for such stage hits as *Sarafina!* and *Woza Albert!*, but his list of
productions also includes *Asinamali!*, *Township Fever*, *The Zulu* and *The House
of Shaka*, a synoptic tale about the lives of eight Zulu kings from Shaka to the
present-day Goodwill Zwelithini.[113] The current monarch not only gave his
blessing to this 2006 play but also assisted in pulling together the funds
necessary for its production. Ngema's honours include FNB Vita and Naledi
awards in South Africa,[114] an Off-Broadway Obie, multiple Tony Award
nominations, and 11 NAACP Image Awards.

Ngema was once the director of musical theatre at Durban's Playhouse
Company, as well as heading up the Mbongeni Ngema Academy and the
Committed Artists theatre company in Durban. He is also the co-founder of
Shout Africa, a venture to produce movies and set up and operate cinemas in
townships and rural areas.

His initial artistic voice was a revolutionary one. *Sarafina!*, which propelled him to fame, highlighted the 1976 student uprising in Soweto that ignited the liberation movement that ultimately toppled apartheid. While the play is considered a local classic, some critics now view it differently than when it appeared. "In the cultural weapon arsenal of the anti-apartheid struggle," one detractor wrote, "exclamation marks in titles of what became known collectively as 'protest theatre' were almost obligatory."[115] Such reassessments are fostered by both Ngema's personal conduct as well as the artistic choices he has subsequently made.

Ngema's reputation was severely tarnished due to a scandal that ensnared him, along with the newly established African National Congress-dominated government. In 1995 the Department of Health funded him to mount *Sarafina 2* with an AIDS-education message, featuring the eponymous lead character having grown from a protesting teenager into a social worker teaching about unsafe sex. Pieter-Dirk Uys, a.k.a. Evita Bezuidenhout, the beloved comic drag queen/social commentator, quipped that Ngema is a theatrical genius: he was paid more than R14 million "for a musical that doesn't exist".[116]

The play premiered 1 December 1995, World AIDS Day. But it was engulfed in controversy before, during, and long after its limited run. AIDS activists objected that some of the information in the play was inaccurate and that its message was muddled. Moreover, Health Minister Dr Nkosazana Dlamini-Zuma (then-wife of Jacob Zuma) had to fend off a number of accusations. Questions were raised about improper financial procedures, including suspicions of corruption, cronyism and a lack of fiscal accountability. Investigators charged that "an irregular tender" had passed from friend to friend, the health minister to Ngema.

At first the minister denied that her department was funding the production, claiming that the European Union was. That proved not to be the case. Eventually a "mystery benefactor" stepped forward to help bail the department out of a byzantine maze of commitments and arrangements.

Many other officials, including President Mandela, robustly defended the beleaguered minister. But in the end, the credibility of both the government and Ngema were seriously compromised.

Some now view him as the co-opted voice of the establishment. His pan-African musical *Sing Africa Dance* (2005), a large production spanning 500 years of history and featuring performers from about ten African countries, was backed by Nepad (New Partnership for Africa's Development) and the South African Department of Arts and Culture. Furthermore, one well-known cultural gadfly claims that the selection process had not been transparent when the Department of Arts and Culture funded a revival of *Sarafina!* that toured South Africa in celebration of ten years of democracy in 2004, underwritten with several million rands of government support.[117] Once again this led to the charge of cronyism. Others simply dismiss Ngema as a conman.

Even before tabloid celebrity journalism became such a familiar feature of the media, Ngema's unsavoury exploits have been surfacing regularly. He has been accused of beating and taking sexual liberties with the young protégées he has mentored in his productions. In one instance he married a woman he first met when she was a star-struck 13-year-old, but later abandoned her in New York City. She was subsequently deported as an illegal immigrant. Her enraged father, a chief, demanded reparative justice: he insisted that Ngema pay the balance of cows owed to him on the woman's lobola, along with a "fine" for dumping his daughter. It tallied to 39 animals.[118]

And his actress wife Leleti Khumalo, whom he also met when she was a teenager (he featured her in the starring role in *Sarafina!*), complained about her position within their polygamous marriage.[119] He and Khumalo later divorced, and Ngema declared insolvency in 2003. At the time of the controversy over "AmaNdiya" in 2002, a critic stamped him as "something of a has-been in bottom-line terms today", and concluded, "The idea that Mbongeni Ngema could, as he claims he's done, stimulate serious debate about racism through his 'AmaNdiya' lyrics or anything else, would be laughable if it wasn't so unfunny."[120]

Whose Side are You On?

Ngema recalls that he first became aware of the potential for controversy erupting around "AmaNdiya" after he was invited to appear on a public affairs radio show on Ukhozi FM, which broadcasts in isiZulu in Durban, some weeks after the song was first released. The moderator juggled simultaneous telephone hook-ups with both the minister of arts and culture and a well-known Indian leader, sparking a spirited exchange of opinions among the group. The next day, Ngema reports, he was characterised in the press as "bedeviling the Indians". And thereafter, the debate grew and grew.[121]

Positive responses to "AmaNdiya" barely surfaced in public. The people for whom Ngema was supposedly speaking did not readily have access to the media (see Chapter 5). Nor were their sentiments – whatever they might, in fact, have been – directly polled, or well represented by individuals in a position to react in official ways. But the negative responses were manifold, and the punitive actions that were taken were stringent.

Both the ANC and the opposition Democratic Alliance condemned the song. The SA Jewish Board of Deputies did as well. So, too, did Anglican Bishop of KwaZulu-Natal, the Rt Rev. Rubin Phillip, who called for it to be banned. And the late renowned sociologist Fatima Meer raged that the song was "a disgusting bit of racist diatribe which has no truth to it. As far as I am concerned," she declared, "with this one song, he [Ngema] wipes away whatever glory he has earned over the years".[122]

Nelson Mandela was also agitated. While he praised Ngema's previous artistic accomplishments, the former president's unwavering commitment to interracial harmony and justice led him to deem "AmaNdiya" "poison" because it resorted to stereotyping and ran the risk of discomfiting a significant minority group.[123] Mandela summoned Ngema to his home for a tête-à-tête.

The upshot? He asked Ngema to extend a public apology. But Ngema refused the old man's request. "I told Madiba that this is one time I am going to disappoint him," Ngema explains, offering this rationale: "I had a feeling that the Indian community has a tendency to run to Mandela for every little thing that happens; mine was not the first one … The issue was to fix race relations. Me apologising was not going to mean anything. It was not going to change the status quo."[124]

At the indaba, Ngema asserted that he had been "crucified" and publicly shared his logic for resisting Mandela: "Song is Godly," he asserted. "How can I apologise to God when God gave me the melody and lyrics? They do not come from me. Who am I to apologise for that?"[125]

Many people judged this to be a cynical ploy. Sue Brittion of the Diakonia Council of Churches (a Durban-based ecumenical organisation addressing economic justice and empowerment, peace, and related social issues), and an attendee at the indaba, countered, "That must give God a laugh. His motive was to get himself in[to] the limelight. Ngema loves the limelight. And he is a person who loves controversy. I think he made a much bigger issue out of it [interethnic tensions] publicly than is the reality on the streets."[126]

Father S'Thembiso Tshongase, a black African Anglican priest leading a predominantly Indian congregation who also participated in the indaba, concurred. In his estimation, the song was "probably business inclined".[127] And Joy Ellappen, a community activist in the largely Indian township of Phoenix, simply calls Ngema's assertion a lie. "His intention was to bring about hostility and bring about hatred," she argues.[128] An article in a popular magazine hit much harder, calling Ngema a "greedy racist" and charging that the controversy was "executed with gold and platinum discs in mind".[129]

For his part, Ngema gloats that "AmaNdiya" "almost overshadowed the World Cup". He views himself as a "victim of the press", explaining, "If you are in the forefront of the liberation struggle in any country and that struggle is won, you will always have people who have bitter feelings about you." Referring to the previous controversy over *Sarafina 2*, he notes, "I was on the front page for almost four years. And they couldn't break me down. The 'AmaNdiya' thing was an easier one for me because I knew I was right. They also gave me free publicity for all these years".

"AmaNdiya" did not fare well on the official front. The South African Human Rights Commission declared it to be hate speech. That body then forwarded a complaint to the Broadcasting Complaints Commission of South Africa (BCCSA), which banned it from general public broadcast, the exception being forums intended to stimulate public debate.[130] The South African Film and Publications Board banned sales to those under 18, requiring it to carry a warning sticker. "AmaNdiya" thereby earned the dubious distinction of being the first song to be censored in the post-apartheid era.[131]

South Africa's much-celebrated, politically progressive constitution of 1996 broadly guarantees freedom of expression, including protection of the press and media, artistic creativity, scientific research, and academic freedom. But Human Rights Commission (SAHRC) head Jody Kollapen explained at the indaba that there are also three significant limitations on free speech in South Africa: propaganda for war, imminent incitement of violence, and advocacy of hatred toward groups based upon race, ethnicity, religion, or gender. And in the SAHRC's estimation, "AmaNdiya" violated that third tenet.

Ngema thought that the ruling by the Human Rights Commission was "a big joke". But many of the people responsible for the various decisions to restrict the song emphasised that artistic expressions such as "AmaNdiya" were divisive and discordant at a historical moment when art should instead promote reason, reconciliation and mutual rapport.

Console Tleane, head of the Freedom of Expression Institute's media policy research unit at that time, felt that banning "AmaNdiya" set a dangerous precedent, even though the lyrics were "crude and racial and ethnic", and Ngema is "a loose cannon at times, controversial and ill-informed".[132] Tleane did not believe the song was hate speech, and saw this regulatory action as part of a pattern on the part of the Human Rights Commission and other regulatory and watchdog bodies of becoming increasingly conservative, and "rushing to close down certain debates that they do not agree with".

Moreover, he feared that another factor might have been in play: the head of the Human Rights Commission and the head of its legal department – the chief complainant in the case – were both Indian. "Did they take the matter on a platform of principle," he wonders, "or was it personal, because they were feeling aggrieved as part of the community that Mbongeni is talking about?"

Ngema had the crowd in his pocket at the indaba, however, where the atmosphere was tilted favourably toward him. When speakers referred to the pitfalls of translation, the crowd murmured loudly in agreement.[133] After Professor Herbert Vilakazi, of the Independent Electoral Commission,[134] and one of the panelists at the indaba remarked that "different communities must learn African languages – Indians, as well as upper-class black children," vigorous clapping greeted what he had to say. And the audience delighted in the seductiveness of conspiracy theories when presenters purposefully drew attention to the fact that the chairman of the BCCSA wielded similar censorship powers when he worked under the apartheid regime.[135]

The audience was also pleased with a number of statements made by King Zwelithini. The king declared that whenever Zulu people are upset about something, "we sing about it", validating Ngema's effort. He announced that Ngema "can rest assured of my complete support", and further asserted, "My people cannot be expected to be spectators of the economic development in the land of our forefathers". And then-Deputy President Jacob Zuma tacitly endorsed his friend Ngema when he spoke in political generalities and cannily avoided any indictment of "AmaNdiya". The songwriter had done a thorough job of cultivating the support of his allies beforehand, and the indaba consequently took on the atmosphere of a pep rally jumbled with a religious revival service.

Origins and Outcomes

The Indian community in South Africa is the largest outside the subcontinent. It numbered 1.2 million people in 2002, accounting for between 2.5 and 3% of the country's population. A significant proportion of South African Indians live in KwaZulu-Natal, as they have historically, where they outnumber whites and coloureds combined.[136]

Indians have deep roots in this part of Africa.[137] As psychologist, academic, and political activist Dr Saths Cooper proudly declared at the indaba, "This Indian is a fourth-generation African. His great-grandparents came as indentured servants to work the cane fields."[138] For the bulk of his compatriots, India is a mythic homeland. South Africa is home.

Indians were first brought to South Africa as slaves by Jan van Riebeeck in the 1650s.[139] Their numbers swelled significantly between 1860 and 1911, when over 150 000 indentured workers, largely impoverished and landless peasants, were lured by desperation to the Indian Ocean port of Durban. One contemporary newspaper article noted the "swarthy hordes came pouring out of the boat's hold", and with a supreme sense of condescension declared, "Master Coolie seemed to make himself perfectly at home, and was not in the least disconcerted by the novelty of his situation."[140]

Many "coolies", the derogatory label Indians shouldered, were put into backbreaking service on the sugar-cane estates that thrived in the steamy climate. Others laboured on tea or wattle plantations, on the railways, and in coal mines.[141] By all accounts their working conditions were brutal; their living situations fetid.[142] Local Zulus were considered unreliable labour. These Indians, far from where they'd been born, had little choice at the time but to endure their wretched circumstances.[143]

A different type of influx began in 1871 with the arrival of the so-called passenger Indians. These people paid their own fares and were under no contractual obligations to others. Many launched businesses, some catering to those who were indentured. In her classic account of South African Indians, Fatima Meer noted that they even called themselves "Arabs" so they wouldn't be confused with their poorer countrymen.[144]

Significant differences distinguished these groups from one another. The indentured Indians came from southern India, many were peasants, they were predominantly Hindu, and tended to be darker than the passenger Indians. The latter group originated from central and north India, were urban dwellers, mostly Muslim, lighter skinned, and felt socially superior.[145] Whereas the two groups did not mix,[146] their shared classification by successive white-dominated governments mediated the salience of differences in occupation, religion and origins among them somewhat.

A portion of the Indian community has achieved remarkably, rising to the highest echelons of business and government. Yet success has eluded many, many others. Referring to the "Indian community" is inaccurate; there are, in truth, Indian communi*ties*, widely separated by education, attainment, and opportunity. In 1969, Meer reported that 64% of Indians existed below the poverty line, and 28% just above it. She noted further that 60% of Indians were unskilled and semi-skilled, while 23% were white collar, although she qualified that by saying they received "poor wages". Less than 4% were said to "live comfortably", and 1% were described as wealthy.[147] And a book written nearly 30 years later pegged 60% of Indians as working class, demonstrating that the most obvious Indian success stories reflect the experience of only some.[148]

Meer's impassioned description of a "tin town" (squatter camp) occupied by Indians was infused with the same sense of indignation as the depiction of working-class Manchester, England, provided by Friedrich Engels in the 19th century. She explained that girls do not attend school, "So they hover around the yard, eating a slice of bread for breakfast, and for lunch some herbs picked from the wasteland, carefully flavoured with a few condiments … Sometimes the mother buys fowls' legs, or a sheep's head, or trotters, spending hours cleaning them. They never buy fresh milk." She continued her heart-wrenching observations, "Children, pot-bellied and unhealthy, with festering sores and running noses, play in the puddles left by the rain, or jump about on the wood piles."[149] While this description is dated, life in South Africa remains meagre for many Indian families.

As the 20th century progressed, Indians found themselves the target of a barrage of government regulations and restrictions, as did other non-whites such as black Africans and coloureds. At times, the interests of Indians coalesced with these different groups and they joined efforts. But at certain junctures the government granted Indians greater privileges than to others, and community self-interest prevailed. Moreover, Indians had a determined advocate who championed their rights over two decades spanning the turn of the last century, none other than Mohandas Gandhi, who developed his doctrine of satyagraha, non-violent resistance, on South African soil.

Uneasy Footing

Two events took place in Africa in 1994 that are etched into the world's consciousness. The first egalitarian elections heralded the establishment of a democratic South Africa. And an interethnic bloodbath claimed between 800 000 and a million lives during a one-hundred-day eruption of terror in Rwanda.

Democracy and genocide: one exemplifies immense promise, whereas the other regrettably confirms the image of catastrophic self-destructiveness that has wracked many parts of Africa during the postcolonial era. Ironically, the global sense of joy over the demise of apartheid actually may have deflected some attention away from the horror occurring some 2000 miles away.[150]

In the wake of that tragedy, the Rwandan government has outlawed ethnicity. The labels Tutsi and Hutu have disappeared from schoolbooks, identity cards, government documents. Mono-ethnic political parties have been banned. Furthermore, a new category of crime has evolved: "divisionism", or speaking about group differences – especially comparing the level of power, success, or political representation of one group relative to another.[151] A restraint on expression as severe as this is more tolerable in a society that has endured sorrow of such magnitude than the prospect that forthright dialogue could amplify rivalry and resentment. Or, even trigger a repetition of violence.

The memory of that genocide hangs heavily over Africa. It activates fears of the potential of a similar slaughter when strife breaks out elsewhere on the continent. And that's how the Rwandan genocide became a point of reference regarding "AmaNdiya".

For many Indians, Ngema's song evoked memories of one of the most troubling aspects of the Rwandan tragedy: the well-publicised role of the media in whipping up the fury that energised the slaughter there. Radio Télévision Libre des Mille Collines (RTLM) has been the focal point of criticism; two of its executives were ultimately brought up on charges of genocide, incitement to commit genocide, and crimes against humanity.

In the lead-up to the violence in 1994, radio commentators routinely spouted anti-Tutsi rhetoric, generating a negative climate of opinion. While deeply disturbing, it's doubtful that this rhetoric would be actionable in a legal sense. Once the carnage began, however, they provided specific information to the marauders, such as where Tutsis were hiding and the licence plate numbers of cars in which they were riding. Moreover, they repeated the mantra "kill the *Inyenzi*" ("cockroach" in Kinyarwanda, and slang for Tutsi), as well as the exhortations to "go work", "go clean" and "the graves are not yet full". A judge later denounced the broadcasts as providing a "drumbeat" and "petrol" for the atrocities – a direct incitement to violence.[152]

After a trial that stretched over three years, a United Nations International Criminal Tribunal for Rwanda found the two media executives mentioned above guilty in 2003, along with the editor of an extremist newspaper.[153] It was the first such international trial of journalists for hate crimes since the prosecution of the Nazi editor Julius Streicher, who was condemned to death in Nuremberg in 1946. The same court also indicted popular singer Simon Bikindi (dubbed "Rwanda's Michael Jackson" and the "government's hired cheerleader") on genocide-related charges.[154] His music is now banned in the country.

A Rwandan writing in a South African newspaper drew explicit parallels between Ngema's song and Bikindi's "Bene Sebahinzi" ("Sons of the Father of the Farmers"), which was aired unremittingly during the slaughter.[155] Bikindi questioned the authenticity of the origins of Tutsis to the region; Ngema likewise highlighted the foreign roots of South African Indians. Bikindi derided the character of Tutsis and distrusted their willingness to share with others; Ngema, too, underscored the self-interest of Indians. And both seemed to be exhorting their cohorts to take action. This writer concluded, "Take it from a Rwandan: in the right circumstances, a song intended to call on one ethnic group to confront another can be extremely effective in driving home the message of genocide."[156]

These legal convictions took place after Ngema's song was released in South Africa. However, the role that the media had played in the mass murders in Rwanda was well publicised, and many people endorsed a lower threshold of responsibility and guilt for influential journalists than the one that the courts ultimately employed. It's not difficult to understand how Indians in South Africa would connect the dots between their own situation and a litany of episodes throughout postcolonial Africa, which have resulted in Indians being dispossessed of their homes and businesses, expelled, or killed.

Indians have become targets in places such as Kenya, Tanzania, and Malawi, and most notably in Uganda in 1972. There Idi Amin demonised and drove 75 000 of them out of the country. In fact, this dictator's name was invoked by an editorialist in a major isiZulu-language newspaper in South Africa in 1999 who chillingly declared, "Blessed be the day when a new Idi Amin is born from the womb of a Zulu woman."[157]

The sense of vulnerability, tenuousness and dread that South African Indians felt due to "AmaNdiya" is easily comprehensible in light of such utterances and events. Ela Gandhi, a granddaughter of the Mahatma, a peace activist in her own right, and a former member of the South African Parliament, strongly believed the song should be banned, partially based on her memory of how important media, such as alternative, underground broadcasts from the ANC's Radio Freedom, had been to South Africa's anti-apartheid struggle.[158]

Herbert Vilakazi spoke at the indaba about the wide gap existing between the races apropos income and life expectancy, and alluded to the "gathering storm, like Germany in the 1930s". Others ominously referred to a sense of "crisis" at numerous points during the two-day affair. The print media sounded similar alarms, referring to Indo-African relations as "a ticking time-bomb", drawing parallels with Nazism, and condemning Ngema as being on a "witch-hunt".[159]

Moreover, black Africans and Indians have experienced previous flare-ups of violence in South Africa, and such episodes remain extremely sensitive subjects decades later. The cumulative weight of this evidence made Ngema's lyrics extremely worrying.

A Winter of Discontent

If Indians nervously inflated the importance and potential consequences of "AmaNdiya", it's easy to understand why: their anxiety was stoked by several alarming stories in the media. Following the release of the record one writer opined, "In yet another attack on people of Indian origin here, an eminent South African playwright has accused them of exploiting the country's masses."[160] Shortly thereafter, another article particularised the situation and confirmed their worst fears: an Indian supermarket owner was shot dead after being robbed in his store by 15 men. Eyewitnesses reported hearing them shout "Ngema, Ngema" as they fled.[161] Although the police attributed the motive purely to robbery, and prominent Indian businessman Vivian Reddy later confirmed that a police investigation found the claim about the chant to be unsubstantiated,[162] it was disquieting nonetheless.

As the winter dragged on, more reports appeared. One story described retaliatory attacks by Indians on black Africans at taxi ranks and on sports fields.[163] And another feature ratcheted up the sense of unease by disclosing that five Indian women had been murdered in the Durban area within two months. All the victims were in their late 50s or 60s. And although there was no evidence to link the unsolved crimes to black African perpetrators, the implication was clear: the article also described "Zimbabwe-style invasions by squatters" north of Durban in Nonoti and Inanda. Some Indian-origin families were vacating their land as a result. One man testified, "We have now become the targets and sitting ducks."[164]

Politicians, for the most part, refrained from escalating the rhetoric. But a top organiser for the Zulu nationalist Inkatha Freedom Party (IFP) rashly declared, "We have good Indians as brothers, but 90% of Africans support that song by Ngema. There have been threats that they want to drive the Indians here south of the Tugela [River]. I'm not interested in that but Indians have taken employment from Africans and they breed like flies ... The day Africans revolt, there will be a bloodbath."[165] Political scientist Courtney Jung boldly concluded in a book published in 2000, "Zulu identity, which divided Zulus politically in the 1980s, had grown less politically salient in the postapartheid period."[166] But subsequent events – such as the furore over "AmaNdiya" and the surge in Zulu identity politics in support of Jacob Zuma's presidential aspirations and in defence of his honour (see chapters 3 and 5, for example) – have proven her to be sorely off the mark.

The Past Haunting the Present

When Indians found out about the ethnic turmoil in Rwanda in 1994, they did not have the comfort of knowing "it can't happen here". Two defining moments in their own local history simmer with anguish caused by racially targeted killing and wholesale dispossession.

One Indian man's moving testimony during an open microphone/

audience response segment of the 2002 Durban indaba represented an emotional apex of that two-day meeting. The man precisely elaborated the horrible events that unfolded during the 1949 riots in Durban's Cato Manor district, and their enduring consequences. He declared that the wounds inflicted over half a century ago were still festering, and that any reconciliation between Indians and black Africans would necessarily have to be prefaced by an honest discussion of what had transpired back then.

Go to any gathering of Indians, he cautioned the audience, and the conversation will inevitably drift to memories of people forced to hide in attics or in manholes for dear life. The horror of seeing babies smashed to death against the wall by marauding black Africans. Or hushed voices will whisper about the awful repercussions months later, of young Indian girls who had been raped and became pregnant, and who then committed suicide out of a sense of revulsion and shame.

The speaker's point was not to assign blame. He hoped, rather, to provoke an open dialogue. He unwittingly embodied a remarkably prescient remark made in the immediate aftermath of the mayhem: "The generation that lived through that night of terror, January 14–15, will never forgive the Africans. For two generations at least the embers of hate will smoulder."[167] But despite its dominance over the memories and imaginations of Indian South Africans, surprisingly little analysis of the riots has been forthcoming.

Cato Manor lies not far from Durban's city centre. But, significantly, it was beyond municipal jurisdiction. Over the years the land had been occupied by Zulus, then the British, and subsequently by wealthy Indians. As the elegance of the area started to fade, Indians rented out portions of their properties to black Africans (the former were entitled to own land; the latter were not); shanties sprung up near market gardens. "Some Indians found it more profitable to become 'shack farmers rather than banana farmers'," one scholar noted.[168] Mid-century Cato Manor hosted a blend of people and activities (illegal pursuits such as home brewing were commonplace). Another scholar characterises it at this time as being "an unhealthy yet vibrant slum".[169]

Even today, the particulars of the incident that set off the unrest are somewhat muddled. It was midsummer, 13 January 1949. All versions concur that an Indian shopkeeper in central Durban struck a black African youth. Had the youngster been a thief? Had the boy first assaulted the shopkeeper's helper? Was the victim an employee himself? Whatever the exact circumstances were that day, black Africans saw the bloodied young man and became enraged. Significantly, the incident occurred at the end of the workday, it was hot, and there were crowds of black Africans waiting for buses or frequenting a municipal beer hall.[170]

Violence erupted, fuelled by rumours flying throughout the city. One tale claimed the youth had been killed, and his head placed in a mosque.[171] There was chaos over two additional days, much of the violence shifting to Cato Manor. Homes and businesses were destroyed, and the death toll broke down as follows: 50 Indians, 87 "Natives", one European, and four of undetermined race. Over 1000 people had been injured.[172] A writer at the time described a "human cyclone" on a "savage march" of "barbarous destruction".[173] Participants included black African workers, shack dwellers and tsotsis.[174]

Government authorities appointed a commission of inquiry to investigate, but in spite of the wishes by Indians and black Africans to be included the panel was all white. Indian and black African leaders stormed out of the hearings when it was announced that cross-examination of witnesses would not be allowed, guaranteeing that testimony would be accepted at face value.[175] The official report was therefore viewed with scepticism, and dismissed as "an essay in failure".[176]

A persistent belief among Indians is that the police escalated the bloodshed by transporting black Africans to the scene of fighting.[177] Some think that whites, possibly policemen, even disguised themselves as black and joined the tumult.[178] A fictional character proclaims, "Much of the violence was clearly orchestrated by unseen forces." And a community leader reflected on that time, "From newspaper reports it was becoming abundantly clear that there was an official conspiracy to paint Indians as black marketers and dishonest traders exploiting Natives, and thus deserving of their wrath. The Natives were doing no more than teaching the Indians an overdue lesson." He continues. "We had solid evidence of how the riots had been influenced by racist incitement from the cabinet level downwards."[179] But what would have been the rationale for promoting such lawlessness?

For one thing, the ANC and Indian political organisations had joined efforts in 1947, providing a united front of resistance to racist regulations.[180] And Cato Manor demonstrated that different races could coexist in the same area. The Nationalist Party had recently swept to power, and this was anathema to its belief that the races must be kept apart. Encouraging political violence between potential allies and thereby sowing mistrust between them served the Nationalist strategy of "divide and rule".

A year after the riots occurred, an Australian historian recorded these impressions: "It seems clear that the rank and file of Africans resent the somewhat privileged position of the Indians, who do not have to carry a pass and who do own certain property in municipal areas in Durban. The Zulu, moreover, is traditionally a fighter and is said to despise the peaceful and allegedly cowardly Hindu."[181] The government would soon undertake the drastic step of relocating both groups en masse to different places.

Like Cape Town's legendary District Six and Johannesburg's celebrated Sophiatown, Cato Manor could not be allowed to survive. And that became the second assault on its residents: under the authority of the despised 1950 Group Areas Act (the GAA), the government was empowered to declare that a locale could be reserved for the exclusive use of one racial group. And people of colour – black, brown, yellow, or shades in between – were the obvious losers, packed up and shipped out to dreary, remote areas, along with people only like themselves.

Family ties were strained; neighbourhood bonds broken. By 1966, 160 000 people had been removed from Cato Manor: 40 000 Indians and 120 000 black Africans.[182] Significantly many Indians also experienced the decline from being proprietors to becoming employees, compounding the trauma.[183] Cato Manor eventually became a vast wasteland.

After the Indians were uprooted, their presence remained written like an elegy on the landscape. Many of them had brought native seeds with them when they left their motherland: "In time … it was possible to tell where they had once lived by spotting mango and paw-paw trees."[184]

Continuing Concerns

The riots of 1949 and the massive displacements of people carried out under the jurisdiction of the Group Areas Act are not the only major incidents affecting South Africans of Indian descent that were, as Sue Brittion, strikingly notes, "stored in memory quite deep in their guts".

In 1985 violence broke out in the shanty town area of Inanda, next to Durban. Indian shops, businesses and houses were looted and destroyed, and most Indian residents fled to neighbouring Phoenix, thereby minimising the odds of suffering physical harm. The underlying causes were, as in 1949, a complex mixture of economic and political factors, with Indians being the clear losers.

An unfortunate symbolic target was the Gandhi Settlement, a place where peace meetings had been hosted that attempted to bridge the gap between racial groups. It was destroyed. But Ela Gandhi knows of instances where interpersonal bonds trumped racial exclusivity during the disturbances, with black African families sheltering Indians in their own homes during the disturbances and thus shielding them from harm.[185] Beyond such major conflagrations, people of different races can also rehash numerous incidents of one-on-one cross-racial violence that has affected many of them.[186]

When Fatima Meer published her book on Indian South Africans two decades after the 1949 riots, the memories of that event remained extremely fresh. She quotes one housewife who is "dubious" about "natives". Another informant talks about *"Crooked hair and crooked brain"*.[187]

A symposium held with Indian community leaders another two decades on in 1989 revealed much the same thing. One participant reported "complex feelings towards blacks, a mixture of solidarity, suspicion, fear, sympathy, etc." and many of them voiced anxiety about the transition to a majority government. Another of them stated, "As far as blacks are concerned, they [the Indians] have not forgotten the 1949 Riots and what has happened to Indians in the rest of Africa and, therefore, have fears and trepidation for the future, if black majority rule becomes a reality."[188]

Those inchoate fears found tangible form in 1993 when black Africans took over 800 newly built, government-subsidised cottages in Cato Manor that had been earmarked for Indians previously displaced by the GAA. The squatters resented the apparent favouritism being extended to one constituency.

They secured their claims by scratching their names onto the entrances. According to one report, "'They wrote down on the doors, remember the 1949 riots ... Cato Manor taught Indians a lesson that we'll never forget,' [a] Mrs Rajoo said. 'We have to look after our own interests first'."[189]

And a newspaper article published the day of the first open elections in South Africa reported that households in Phoenix were visited by young black African men with a "12-cent 'deposit' – 10 cents for the house, 1 cent for the car and another cent for their furniture – which they said they would take over after an ANC victory".[190] Headlines described Indians at the time as "fearful", "wary" and "fearing domination". [191]

It should come as no surprise, therefore, that according to a comprehensive survey conducted in 2000 and 2001, Indians were more likely to perceive themselves as victims than were black South Africans or coloureds; close to half of the Indians polled claim to have lived better under apartheid; of all the groups, they were the most aware of apartheid controlling crime; and their optimism regarding the future seriously trailed the attitudes of black Africans and coloureds.[192]

This is confirmed by other studies, such as one that reported that the perception of crime having increased was highest among Indians, and that their feelings of personal safety were the lowest,[193] and another survey done at the end of 2002 regarding how people perceived their prospects in 2003 that discovered that Indians were the most pessimistic racial group regarding the upcoming prospects for themselves, the country and the international scene.[194] Indians were therefore more acutely attuned to a disparaging depiction of themselves in the media than others with more power, comfort or security might be.

Across the racial spectrum, however, "apartheid nostalgia" has surfaced because of high unemployment and crime.[195] The ANC has fallen short of meeting the expectations that many South Africans held when the party took charge of the country in 1994. Daily life seems more unstable, and significant divisions remain between people. For Indian South Africans, who have been scapegoated before, an atmosphere such as this feels extremely ominous.

The Indaba: Chalk and Cheese

On the first day of the indaba, held 26 to 27 July 2002, I estimate that of the approximately 300 people in attendance, 75% were black African, 22% were Indian, and 3% were white.

Attendance slipped markedly the second day. Conspicuous then were three mute and blank-faced Indian men, probably in their 60s, clad in suits. They looked like schoolboys huddled at a required school assembly or an obligatory religious service they plainly didn't want to be at, boredom and incredulity as clearly etched upon their faces as the decades of hard work they'd obviously borne. Less than a handful of other Indians were present; less than a handful of whites, as well.[196]

The summit became "Africanised" as it progressed. What had been touted as an Indo–African dialogue increasingly narrowed to a monologue, as the intervals devoted to audience questions and comments were progressively dominated by members speaking isiZulu. Some Indians and whites nodded in comprehension with what was being said. But many were left out because they were not conversant in this language. The atmosphere became ever more exclusive.

Whereas panelists typically spoke from their particular professional expertise, audience members spoke primarily from their hearts. One type of comment proved to be a crowd-pleaser: *mea culpas* by Indians expressing regret for the way their brethren had treated black Africans in the past. During one audience participation period an Indian man prefaced his remarks by saying that South Africa had been very good to him. He patted his substantial stomach for corroboration, an emphatic, comical gesture that hooked his listeners.

He proceeded to offer a heartfelt apology on behalf of members of his family who had discriminated against black Africans in the past, offering a simple but potent example of indignities: domestic workers were always offered a drinking cup reserved expressly for that purpose, and never used by the members of his household. He expressed regret for not speaking up about such insults and instances of injustice that he'd personally witnessed.[197]

His public confession was met with enthusiastic applause, completely the reverse of the silence that followed people who testified about the 1949 riots and their continued impact on the Indian community. The bulk of this audience was disposed to accept expressions of contrition but was not amenable to discussions that might prick their own consciences.

When tea was served the hotel staff was black African, their supervisors, Indians. For those who noticed, this recapitulated and confirmed in miniature the status hierarchy that many black Africans had been disapprovingly referring to during the sessions. For others it may have seemed so "natural" as to go unremarked. In contrast to this glimpse of entrenched social reality, one Indian man had donned a tie bearing the likeness of former President Mandela, a conscious nod to multiracialism, non-racism and goodwill.

The indaba was co-sponsored by Ngobamakhosi (a group newly formed by Ngema to promote black African interests), the Institute for a Democratic Alternative in South Africa (Idasa, an NGO committed to sustainable democracy and social justice), and the KwaZulu-Natal Church Leaders Forum. This coalition of groups provided a broader representation of people and interests than some earlier plans for a meeting would have, but it also meant that people came with markedly different, and at points contradictory, agendas.

Shortly beforehand, billionaire Indian businessman Vivian Reddy was preparing to bankroll a gathering of black African and Indian business people. His primary concern was that the two groups were not making the most of Broad-Based Black Economic Empowerment (BBBEE, commonly referred to as BEE, the government initiative to diversify ownership and management of companies, heighten opportunities to procure government contracts, and facilitate skills development) by Indians partnering with black Africans to secure lucrative government contracts. He was alarmed that the tensions exacerbated by "AmaNdiya" "could shake investor confidence and fuel greater antagonism reminiscent of the 1949 tragedies".[198]

Reddy was reputedly the man who bailed out the government after its *Sarafina 2* fiasco, and his plan to facilitate interracial cooperation in business had the support of two high-ranking officials: Deputy President Jacob Zuma and Foreign Affairs Minister Nkosazana Dlamini-Zuma, formerly Zuma's wife and also the health minister in 1995, when she championed *Sarafina 2*. This was, unmistakably, an elite level of activity and concern, orchestrated by a small network of individuals with shared histories and interests.

At the same time, Ngema had announced the formation of Ngobamakhosi, named after Zulu King Cetshwayo's most trusted regiment – a title befitting the call to warriors in "AmaNdiya". He envisioned this as a forum for "indigenous" academics, artists, politicians, businessmen and others, an "unofficial commission" to listen to testimony regarding ill treatment of black Africans, and concerned with their cultural, social and economic enhancement. It was also envisioned as a means to counter Reddy's proposed initiative for interracial dialogue.[199] The mobilisation of these people supplemented what eventually became the indaba with a nativist perspective.

Ngema took his idea of a public forum to Idasa, which agreed to oversee the indaba, thereby including people from the private and public sector advocating issues such as human rights and freedom of expression. And with the addition of religious groups, the scope was broadened even more. A meeting of organisations was called prior to the indaba, and a half-day preparatory meeting exclusively for the religious community was held the day before the indaba, adding social justice to the agenda. When the indaba began on the morning of 26 July, it was the locus of varied expectations – social, political, economic and spiritual – on the part of people representing both elite interests as well as the grassroots. And business networking mixes with reconciliation like chalk and cheese.

Some prominent academics and religious leaders boycotted the event precisely because it was organised by people wielding considerable power and would be focusing upon the song, to their minds a peripheral issue and not the root cause of inequality and inter-group tensions. Sociologist Ashwin Desai was the most outspoken of this faction, charging that to feature Ngema was equivalent to "asking a rapist to be a reconciler in a rape case".[200]

Vivian Reddy expressed satisfaction with his investment of planning and money into the indaba. "People were able to start talking business deals," he proudly reported. "I am aware of several business deals that were concluded at the symposium." For Reddy, who hobnobs with leading politicians and captains of business and has grown his own fortune from a variety of sources – energy, casinos and healthcare (he holds the exclusive franchise on the oral

HIV test in Africa) – suspicions based on race are detrimental to business success in the 21st century. An apocryphal story about this ambitious and indefatigable entrepreneur claims that "When the activists of the Natal Indian Congress were picketing the House of Delegates he was busy securing contracts to electrify Truro House, headquarters of the House of Delegates".[201]

Reddy rejects the prevailing model of Indian family businesses as outmoded and irrelevant; good economic decisions must be made without fear of offending kin who are also partners. So Reddy sees opportunity, not calamity, in bringing others in. And in today's South Africa, that means black Africans. "Indians and Africans are growing together," he says, and it's a good time "to capitalise on business opportunities". Reddy ended up firmly in Ngema's camp; "maybe the song was a wake-up call," he concludes.

But for those who do not operate in such rarefied realms, for whom the sentiments of the most influential public figures who made an appearance unfairly tilted the indaba in the direction of supporting Ngema, and whose day-to-day efforts involve deftly bringing people together to work through emotionally sensitive issues, the gathering was a disappointment. As community activist Joy Ellappen reviews it, "I feel that justice was not done." Diakonia Council of Churches resource specialist Sue Brittion recalls, "I was frustrated. I thought that a lot of people that spoke were trying to make mileage out of things for themselves. I wasn't sure that a big meeting like that was the best way to really help with the fundamental questions." This was a feeling that was shared by others in the religious and social service communities. "People were looking for business and political advantages; I think that was quite alarmingly clear," she concluded. And Mpendulo Nyembe, a reconciliation project organiser at Diakonia, wrapped up his experience by saying, "I think nothing much has happened."[202] A news headline reporting on the indaba seemed absurdly off the mark when it touted, "Indaba helps heal rift between Africans, Indians".[203]

Throughout the two-day meeting, both black Africans and Indians referenced unhealed wounds and scars remaining from racist incidents they had endured. An idea that surfaced repeatedly was the need for a new stage in the liberation struggle, a continuation of the process initiated by the Truth and Reconciliation Commission hearings in the 1990s. Those investigations rivetted the nation, as victims painfully detailed the outrages they had endured under apartheid,[204] and perpetrators confessed their wrongdoings. But what was being called for in 2002 was somewhat different: community-based mini-boards of inquiry, where all manner of historical offences and grievances could be aired and sympathetically grasped. The subjects could range from micro-aggressions to major assaults. Pointing fingers at specific people, or exacting retribution, would not be at issue. Healing, moving forward, and building bridges between groups would be.

But efforts such as these require slow, sustained and painstaking work. The indaba was not able to address the deep-seated fears of its participants, nor establish the foundation for undertaking ongoing reparative work.

Gandhi: A Disputed Legacy

Mohandas Gandhi was called to South Africa in 1893 to represent an Indian merchant in a court case. The 24-year-old lawyer prevailed, and although he had not intended to stay in the country, his fate became bound up with his fellow Indians in South Africa until he returned home for good in 1914. The racism he witnessed and personally experienced in South Africa changed the course of his life, and emboldened the resistance that Indians demonstrated toward injustice in their adopted land.

An exhibition that opened in 2006 in the former Number Four Prison on what is now Constitution Hill in Johannesburg, *From Dandy to Dhoti*, showed Gandhi's evolution from a cultured and stylish lawyer to the self-effacing leader of the passive resistance movement, which had its origins in South Africa. Although he is revered worldwide, and he has been widely memorialised in South Africa, his reputation is also contested and demeaned here. This then becomes more evidence leading Indians to question and reassess their own contemporary circumstances.

For example, a sculpture of Gandhi was erected in Pietermaritzburg in 1993 to commemorate the 100th anniversary of his eviction from a whites-only train compartment, an event that radicalised him. But its spectacles are regularly stolen, and people disrespect his memory by leaving their beer or cola cans on his head.[205] And in the KwaZulu-Natal town of Dundee, prison cells where Gandhi was detained in 1913 for organising mineworkers were discovered to have been turned into toilets and a storeroom. Some of his outraged supporters were saddened that this historical episode had faded from memory and hoped the place could be turned into a monument instead.[206]

In 2006 a memorial to Gandhi outside a mosque was vandalised twice within the first month of its installation in the Newtown section of Johannesburg, the place where in 1908 he orchestrated the first mass burning of mandatory identity passes by Indians.[207] That same year the 100th anniversary of satyagraha garnered lukewarm support in South Africa, even though Gandhi's teachings were influential in the formation of the African National Congress, and the tactic of choice for the first mass anti-apartheid action, the Defiance Campaign of 1952.[208] At a festival held in his honour in Durban, and attended by Indian Prime Minister Manmohan Singh and President Thabo Mbeki, 200 supporters of former deputy president and political rival Jacob Zuma were forced to leave after they broke out singing his trademark song "Umshini Wam" upon the arrival of Mbeki.[209]

The boldest attack on Gandhi's reputation has come from the book *Gandhi: A stooge of the white South African government*, by US-based Indian academic Velu Annamalai, an updated 2007 reissue of a volume originally distributed in South Africa in 1995. Annamalai alleges that Gandhi was an imperialist, an elitist and an "Indian Hitler".[210] His discursive strategy highlighted small quotes from early in the man's career, devoid of context, which appear to represent prejudice and a desire to keep Indians separate from those Gandhi derogatorily referred to as *kaffirs*.

Whereas Gandhi did use *kaffir* and called Zulus "very lazy", he was a young man then, and reflecting the dominant sentiments of his times. His actions demonstrated a sincere concern for black Africans, however: the first black newspaper in KwaZulu-Natal was initially printed on Gandhi's press, and he worked as a stretcher bearer during the Bambatha Rebellion in 1906, tending to wounded Zulus.

Finally, a proposal was presented in 2005 to rename Durban's Point Road in his honour. But what was intended as a tribute sparked an outcry instead. The street runs through what was then a dodgy area, associated in the public mind with drugs, criminals and prostitutes. Like many cultural battles, this one became a Rorschach test for appraising the range of community sentiments.

Some Indians deemed this an insult, even though it was an apt fit in a basic regard: Gandhi's deepest sympathies always lay with the outcast and downtrodden. Ela Gandhi, the Mahatma's granddaughter, was miffed that the family was not consulted, and that a more central roadway was not chosen to honour her kin. And Ashwin Desai, who had boycotted the indaba because of its backing by certain elites, rejected this proposal using similar reasoning once again: the area was undergoing a residential building boom with glitzy new flats bearing expensive price tags – hardly a suitable tribute to a man who dedicated much of his life to advocating for the poor.[211]

Is Brown the New Black?

In 2005 the Johannesburg Art Gallery hosted *A Place Called Home*, an exhibition of contemporary art from the Indian/South Asian diaspora. The work of artists hailing from places as far-flung as Guyana, the Philippines, Trinidad, and of course South Africa, was included. Indian food was served up, and Indians were well represented in the opening crowd. The show was launched by Ferial Haffajee, then editor of the *Mail & Guardian* (a year later, she would endure threats after her paper reprinted one of the controversial Danish cartoons). She was an eloquent speaker, elegantly turned out in traditional Indian garb.

But Haffajee's remarks during this afternoon get-together were somewhat incongruous with the situation. She punctuated her comments with references to herself as a black woman, perhaps half a dozen times. Minorities who suffered under apartheid find it politically expeditious nowadays to self-identify as "black"; it most certainly opens economic opportunities. But it was surprising to hear such strategic positioning occur during an event that was celebrating and catering for a distinct ethnic group. She was "among family", in other words, not posturing before an impersonal public audience.

What might seem to be offhand remarks in fact succinctly capture the dilemma of marginality that South African Indians have long experienced. During apartheid, they were somewhat better off than black Africans, yet not deemed worthy enough to claim the respect and rewards accorded to whites. And in the post-apartheid era, they are not necessarily considered "black enough" to claim the rewards that are now available to those who were previously disadvantaged.

To return to the epigraph that opens this chapter, writer Shiva Naipaul prefaces the phrase I quoted by remarking, "The African was taught – and eventually came to believe – that his destiny was inextricably linked with the destiny of the white man. Marginality was thrust upon the Asian. Both black and white could regard him as an outsider intruding into *their* special relationship."[212] Regardless of the changes wrought by the new political dispensation in South Africa, many Indians remain uncomfortably betwixt and between, socially, economically and politically. As one Indian commentator noted during the battle over "AmaNdiya", "[j]ust over 140 years after arriving in South Africa as indentured labourers, Indians appear no more secure about their future in the country than when they first arrived".[213]

Mbongeni Ngema was spot on about one thing he wrote in "AmaNdiya": South Africa remains a place where people come to improve their lot in life. Tens of thousands of Zimbabweans regularly flee over the border to escape the political turmoil and economic collapse in their own country. Refugees from many other African countries do so too. The Chinese are streaming in as well: Africa is a lucrative trading partner, and a rich source of raw materials for China's expanding economy. And in Durban's Grey Street area, nicknamed "the casbah" for its concentration of Indian-owned businesses, new immigrants peddle all manner of goods, including the illegal and the counterfeit, to the dismay of old-time traders.[214]

A significant proportion of the newest arrivals from South Asia are from Bangladesh and Pakistan, not India. But many locals draw no distinction between these groups. They instead reify the apartheid-era classification of "Indian" as a catch-all term.

One newspaper article boldly declared, "Poor of Asia find paradise in SA".[215] And, indeed, that has been the case, as many have sought their fortune in the same way that generations that preceded them did: as general merchants or purveyors of food or fabric, in rural towns or black African townships. Between 500 and 1000 Bangladeshi immigrants have settled in the Free State, where people similar to them were once banned. They quickly learn to speak Sesotho, establish mosques and madrasas, and frequently marry local black women. One man who met his future wife at a taxi rank reflected, "That time I didn't have much money to pay *lobola*, but over time I gave her mother what I could."[216] On the surface, this appears to represent the promise of the New South Africa and the potential of non-racialism.

But there is a disheartening side to the story as well. Belying the optimistic headline, these immigrants maintain an uneasy coexistence with their neighbours. They can become a target of resentment. And oftentimes they are victims of crime. One Bangladeshi tried to minimise the tension by attributing problems to "local naughty boys".[217] Yet the difficulties are larger and deeper than that.

In community after community, South Asians have been harassed, attacked, or driven out of business by black Africans. In Limpopo in 2006, 43 people were arrested for attacking Pakistani shopkeepers whom they accused of abducting a child,[218] an incident that recalls the anti-Jewish blood libel of long historical standing. In a small community in KwaZulu-Natal in 2005, two primary school teachers who were Indian were warned "either leave the school or leave in flames". Some local people accused the teachers of using "bad English", and spicy Indian food was being served at the school – very unlike what the students customarily ate at home.[219] And as protests have heated up across the country against the government's failure to deliver basic services, South Asian businesses are typically trashed in the civil disturbances that frequently break out on these occasions.[220]

Perhaps the most wrenching episode of conflict between South Asians and black Africans occurred in a township outside Bethlehem, in the Free State. The target was a place with the buoyant name of Kahn's Let's Live Together Store, the sort of place where one extended family's dreams of stability and success were invested. But it was looted and destroyed after a fight between an employee and a local youth, a scenario that echoes Cato Manor in 1949 on a small scale. Compounding the tragedy, a family member was killed and one of her daughters was seriously injured when the car in which they had taken flight was involved in a crash.

"Coolies have got it coming for them," remarked one bystander to the violence. "Indians are unacceptable," another declared, "especially those young boys, the Pakistanis, who engage in affairs with our young schoolgirls. The general mood is that all Indians must go." And a statement made two years after the controversy over Ngema's work alarmingly affirmed the fears of his loudest critics; one local asserted, "We adhere to old values and beliefs and respect one another. But these Indians ... you've heard Mbongeni Ngema's song, 'AmaNdiya'. It's all true. You can't run away from that. These makula [a derogatory isiZulu term for Indians] ..."[221] While Ngema certainly does not bear responsibility for originating anti-Indian sentiment, his name and his most infamous composition have hardened into ciphers for hatred and intolerance.

Ngema asserts, "As much as 1949 is still on people's lips to this day, this song will always be." He believes that in the main Indians have not come to terms with the new reality of a majority-run government dominated by black Africans. And in his estimation, that is deeply problematic: "I think that white people have adjusted much faster," Ngema declares, "far better than Indians have. I think that the more Indians believe that they are a community on their own, and have nothing to do with African people, the more problematic it is going to be for them. Whether they like it or not they are in an African country."[222]

* * *

The indaba was long on words but short on action. The most eloquent of the speakers was Khaba Mkhize of the SABC, who movingly told the delegates,
    "Animals have tongues, but no language.
    Animals grew horns – that's *their* dialogue.
    Animals grew claws – that's *their* dialogue.
    Our mandate is simple: we have to communicate.
    The end of life," he concluded, "is the end of stories."

Chapter 3

Strange Brew: Stirring Colonialism, Apartheid and Tradition together in the Same Pot

[My father] believed in education as a way to revolution. Books, he'd say, are the great topplers. Tromp the Boers with Tristram Shandy! The poor man. For my mother, it was one settler, one bullet.

Peter Orner, 2006

Ela Gandhi's belief that "AmaNdiya" was hate speech did not deter her from teasingly adding, "I think it had a nice dance beat."

The lyrics of this song were clearly at odds with her core values as a public servant, a human rights activist, and a South African proud of her Indian descent. Nevertheless, Gandhi cheerfully acknowledged the seductive power of the medium of music. Needless to say, our reactions to culture are complex, and frequently contradictory.

The "AmaNdiya" episode brought two opposing notions of cultural production into focus. From the perspective of Ngema and those who supported him – whether due to a sense of shared identity, or from a deep commitment to unfettered speech – culture is a channel for expressing personal and collective histories, sentiments, exploits, anxieties and aspirations. Culture does not create these phenomena; it simply provides the means through which they can speak. Therefore, banning a song is folly: it wipes out the perceptible trace of certain ideas without questioning what actually spawned them.

But for a majority of Indians, and others who espoused restrictions on artistic expression in this instance, culture possesses a power and agency that is *sui generis*. It shapes the social environment rather than simply reflecting it. Culture is, therefore, something that must be continuously monitored because of the prospect it might generate dangerous ideas. The sense of peril is linked, of course, to one's social position and interests.[223]

Culture as passive object or active creator of reality: each perspective attracts proponents, and each side is disposed to advocating particular defensive or preemptory actions. This becomes especially interesting when someone who is inclined to support one viewpoint converts to the other, once a particular issue jars their sense of decency, reality, or security. And lest we become smug, each of us is capable of flipping our position, given the right set of circumstances.

A Call to Arms

Song has played a significant role in liberation movements worldwide. In America, "We Shall Overcome" was inextricably bound up with the civil rights struggle. But as powerful an anthem as it is, the lyrics convey righteousness, perseverance and serene confidence more than raw anger. So, too, is the case with many additional hymns and rallying cries that became popularised throughout the 1950s and 1960s. They were an apt fit: a movement grounded in religious faith and nonviolence was more about moral suasion than violent confrontation. "If I Had a Hammer" – philosophical and utopian to a greater degree than blatantly aggressive – could rally devotees, but hardly dispirited the souls of those in power.

Although "We Shall Overcome" was heard in South Africa as well, the soundtrack to the struggle here was more wide-ranging and generally harder hitting. This situation played out differently; many songs and chants were openly hostile and unambiguously threatening.[224] South Africans particularised their enemies, specified how to combat and destroy them. Moreover, toyi-toying literally shook the earth and fundamentally unsettled its targets. It compressed and metamorphosed throngs of people into pulsating, unpredictable, menacing human barricades and congealed their emotions into a colossal, seething, ominous presence.

A white southern African memoirist addresses how sound has been integral for black Africans in confrontation with their opponents over the ages. Describing the Battle of Isandlwana, where the British suffered a crushing defeat in 1879 at the hands of the Zulus, he recounts, "As the warriors advanced ... their places on the ridge above were taken by thousands of Zulu women, urging on their army in the traditional way by ululating, an eerie high-pitched keening that filled the air." Their yowls must have deeply disturbed and confounded the British troops. Thereafter, "[O]nce the battlefield fell quiet, a great wail was heard from the retinue of the Zulu women, as they mourned their dead. And this wail moved like a ripple through village after village until finally it reached the Zulu capital, Ulundi, fifty miles distant."[225]

The struggle may have been won, but this expansive vocabulary of sound, words and movement remains powerful; it can be mobilised whenever South Africans take to the streets to express their discontent, and adapted to present-day needs and concerns. A book that reveals the ways in which HIV/AIDS infects every part of the body politic in rural communities describes how support groups respond when one of their members succumbs to the illness. After obtaining permission from the family of the deceased, members attend the funeral en masse, wearing T-shirts inscribed in large letters with mottos such as "HIV-positive". But theirs is not a silent vigil: "They assemble under the funeral tent and they sing old freedom songs, the lyrics no longer about guerillas and machine guns, but about blood tests, CD4 counts, ARVs, and viral loads."[226] Specific songs and slogans retain their vitality, even though the enemy has changed.

In certain instances, however, forms of expression that were tailored to a period of civil warfare become subversive in new respects when they are invoked after open hostilities subside. What was once explicable becomes, well, awkward and potentially destabilising to the new order. Shifting from conflict to coexistence means traversing a particular type of symbolic minefield.

Dialling Out

One of the strangest episodes of calling for a ban of music in South Africa's recent history emerged as a bizarre footnote to another significant instance of interracial conflict. It was related to a far right-wing conspiracy to disrupt the nascent democracy and attempt to restore minority white rule. The plot was exposed in 2003 once the clandestine deliberations of its members were discovered, and after they had actually executed some violent actions.

Their rage had fuelled fever dreams of supremacy and destruction. For starters, the group known as the Boeremag ("Boer Force") proposed shooting down a plane over Khayelitsha, the vast township outside Cape Town, and opening fire on a bus in central Pretoria, creating panic.[227] They would commandeer military bases. Destroy all non-Christian places of worship and deflect the blame onto Muslim fundamentalists. Assassinate "race traitors" such as FW de Klerk, the final minority-race president who oversaw dismantling of the repressive apartheid-era infrastructure.

And when their megalomania reached full flower, they envisioned marching millions of black Africans into exile to Zimbabwe and driving all Indians by force to the KwaZulu-Natal coast, where they would supposedly be loaded onto ships bound for India.[228] This repatriation, a scheme bandied about for decades, would finally be realised.

With all that accomplished, potentially financed through cash-in-transit heists, they could reinstate the idyll of the *volkstaat*, the former Boer republics of the Transvaal and the Orange Free State. They progressed as far as planting a bomb on a road where former President Mandela travelled (the plan was foiled when he flew in a helicopter instead), and they set off bombs at a bridge, an airport, and in Soweto, destroying property and causing injuries and one death. In the end, 26 men were arrested and 22 were charged with high treason, terrorism, sabotage and murder.

Enter culture, via the sound system in the prison where they were held that transmitted Metro FM, loudly, from early morning through the evening. This station targets the urban market, featuring "black music": kwaito. It drove these men to distraction, and more. One of their attorneys called this "an instrument of torture", and complained, "We have men sitting here in tears and who are busy cracking … Some of my clients have suffered breakdowns, which affect their ability to stand trial".[229] It was also characterised as "psychological warfare" and "voice pollution".[230] One defendant was reportedly contemplating suicide. For these hate-driven men, who scorned anything not originating from their own specific heritage, it was the ultimate form of ironic, cultural payback.

Their trial eventually took place in Court C of Pretoria's Palace of Justice. Years earlier the Rivonia Treason Trial had been held there, involving 150 defendants who represented the leadership of the major anti-apartheid organisations. But before the Boeremag proceedings played out, the power of music as an important reflection of cultural identity – and, perhaps its use as a weapon – had been aptly demonstrated.[231]

A Singular Phrase, Multiple Meanings

Apartheid may have collapsed, but some of the weapons mobilised against it still resonate fiercely within memory, imbued with an indomitable sense of hatred. One slogan in particular seethes with singlemindedness and rage: "One settler, one bullet": the catchphrase of the Azanian People's Liberation Army, the armed wing of the Pan Africanist Congress (the PAC, a group that broke with the ANC over its policy of non-racialism). The men who stoned Fulbright scholar Amy Biehl to death during an infamous incident in 1993 were PAC partisans, and one of them openly admitted they saw the young American woman as a "settler", and thereby automatically deemed her to be an enemy.[232] Its rhetorical counterpart was "Kill the Boer, kill the farmer", attributed to Peter Mokaba of the ANC. These twin expressions condensed grisly sentiments into a few words, certain to chill people of European descent.

The PAC remains a small political party, and for nearly two decades the ANC has faced the challenge of transforming itself from an organisation dedicated to liberation into one entrusted with effectively managing a complex and continuously developing country. But the force of these slogans, and variations of them, continue to reverberate. Recall, for example, that during the protests against the Danish cartoons in 2006, demonstrators in Cape Town carried a sign declaring "One oppressor, one bullet".

Furthermore, the chant "One Boer, One bullet" was heard in 2005 during an anti-Afrikaans language protest by black African students at the University of Pretoria, echoing similar demonstrations nearly 30 years earlier by school children in Soweto.[233] Protestors representing the ANC, the South African Communist Party (SACP), and the Congress of South African Trade Unions (Cosatu) displayed signs declaring "Enough is enough – Kill the farmer, kill the Boer" outside a court building where a notorious murder case was being tried; the defendants were charged with severely beating a farmworker and then tossing him while he was still alive into a lion reserve, where he was then killed and eaten.[234]

"One rapist, one bullet!" became the mantra of protestors against a particularly heinous incident where several white women were raped by black African men.[235] "Een Taxi, een koel [*sic*]" ("one [black] taxi, one bullet") accompanied a spate of shootings at vehicles by white men in the Northern Province (now Limpopo).[236] And "Tata-ma-chance, tata-ma-bullet" emerged as a slogan after a car hijacker died in a shootout with the police – a forewarning that crime would be dealt with harshly.[237] The basic format is thus reconfigured to fit different circumstances, with the positions of antagonists and their targets permuting in countless surprising ways. The slogan has lost none of its fury.

One of the most talked-about invocations of the apartheid-era expression occurred in June 2002, at the same time that the controversy over Mbongeni Ngema's "AmaNdiya" was raging. At the funeral for the charismatic former ANC Youth League president, deputy minister, ANC strategist and "young lion" Peter Mokaba, ANC supporters repeatedly chanted "Kill the Boer, kill the farmer". Although President Thabo Mbeki, most of his cabinet, and former President Nelson Mandela attended the event, no one condemned it or did anything to stop it.

For all his popularity, controversy also swirled around Mokaba. He was an AIDS dissident, denying the significance of HIV, although he apparently died from complications of the disease (a fact that went unremarked at his funeral). And he endured allegations of being an agent for the apartheid government, charges directly at odds with his status as a hero of the struggle. Reiterating the ethnic split that was so apparent during the Ngema controversy, Mokaba attributed these accusations to "an Indian-led, Natal-based 'cabal' within the UDF [United Democratic Front, a major multiracial coalition of organisations that fought apartheid]".[238]

After the funeral, several groups condemned the chanting, including the Democratic Alliance, the Freedom Front, and the Afrikaner Eenheidsbeweging (Afrikaner Unity Movement). ANC spokesperson Smuts Ngonyama dismissed their complaints, however, reversing responsibility for any harm done by remarking, "People are making an issue out of nothing. If they continue to do so they will polarise society."[239] But President Mbeki was much more conciliatory, declaring in Parliament, "Those farmers and Boers are as much South African and African as I am, entitled to the same rights and privileges that are enjoyed by any other South African. Nobody anywhere has a right to call for the killing of any South African, whatever the race, ethnic origin, gender or health condition of the intended victim."[240]

This situation provided an ideal counterpoint to the Ngema affair. In that case, his words were declared to be hate speech, even though no solid or direct connection could be made to actual violence being incited by "AmaNdiya". But Mokaba's funeral was held against the backdrop of a substantial amount of documented violence taking place against white farmers in the post-apartheid era. Websites, especially those with a far-right political perspective (bearing names like stopboergenocide.com and genocidewatch.org), have characterised the brutality as a "pogrom" or "ethnic cleansing", taking place in what amounts to "killing fields", and even drawing a parallel to the slaughter that occurred in Rwanda. In fact, at the same time the Mokaba funeral was taking place, a white farm couple was being murdered in KwaZulu-Natal. One report asked, "What will be the reaction of ANC leaders if farmers start chanting 'Kill the Xhosas, Kill the black man' during the[se] funerals …?"[241]

Farmers' organisations dismiss the premise that the large tally of rural murders are simply criminal, citing the extreme viciousness with which they are often committed, and the fact that oftentimes nothing of value is taken from the victims. They see this rather as a sustained campaign of terror with the goal of driving whites out of the country. To cite simply one instance, an elderly couple was killed in 2006, and the old man's hamstrings were severed, the same way African poachers incapacitate game they capture in the wild.[242] A website boldly declares, "The death rate for South African farmers is 313 per 100 000, perhaps the highest for any group of people on earth who are not at war."[243]

The results of a two-year inquiry reported in 2003 attributed only 2% of such murders to political motives, however, and cited robbery as the intention in 90% of the cases.[244] But such accounts are dismissed by many people on the ground. In Limpopo, for example, a group erected a memorial called *Plaasmoorde* ("farm murders"). It consisted of a large cross made from many smaller white crosses, surrounded by scores and scores of additional markers planted on the hillsides: a dramatic visualisation of their sense of victimisation and loss.[245]

People who feel they are the target of slogans such as "Kill the Boer, kill the farmer" believe these are unequivocally an incitement to violence. But on the other side of the issue are free speech advocates who dismiss these sorts of linkages. Jane Duncan, former executive director of the Freedom of Expression Institute (FXI), argues that slogans such as these are metaphorically based and are about killing "the system" that white people represent, not necessarily about killing particular white people. She believes that "the Boer" or "the farmer" in these instances is a symbol of apartheid, and therefore does not qualify as hate speech.[246] And Console Tleane, an FXI employee at the time of the Ngema affair, believes that the South African liberation lexicon was "full of very robust language". Songs and slogans were meant to inspire people, to mobilise and psych them up, but not to guide specific actions. He also confides that "Kill the Boer, kill the farmer" has become infamous largely due to the fact that it was recited in English rather than in a black African language.

There were a number of songs that were "cruder" than that, according to Tleane. He cites one, which loosely translated says, "My mother rejoices when I kill a white person." He recalls the emotional charge it generated: "I remember when we used to sing that song, whee! And we'd even sing it in front of white comrades." Tleane alludes to other phrases that were explicable in the context of the times, such as "Your joining fee is a white man's head". But he insists that these phrases were never meant to be taken literally.

Section 16(2)c of the South African Constitution states, "hate speech is regarded as the advocacy of hatred that is based on race or ethnicity and which constitutes incitement to cause harm". But when the Human Rights Commission first considered whether "Kill the Boer, kill the farmer" was hate speech in July 2002, it decided that the phrase did not qualify as such, and was simply an example of free expression – much to the amazement and consternation of those who feared its potency. But the decision was reversed on appeal almost exactly a year later, a ruling FXI condemned as not being based on empirical evidence of a connection between the motto and present-day killings.

The later ruling means that invoking the phrase could result in civil suits under the Promotion of Equality and Prohibition of Unfair Discrimination Act. And public opinion also broadly condemns it: according to a 2004 report, 74% of respondents agreed that "Kill the Boer, kill the farmer" was hate speech. Whites gave this position the strongest support (86% saying "yes"), followed by Indians (83%), black Africans (68%), and coloureds (63%). And when the survey asked if "Because of freedom of expression … it is okay to call anybody any name", 91% of respondents disagreed.[247]

Yet "Kill the Boer, kill the farmer" continues to be used, as cited in some of the examples above, as well as in an incident in which school pupils protested against their white teachers by using the chant. They set tyres alight as well, echoing tactics that were customary during the struggle years.[248] Moreover, ANC Youth League President Julius Malema rekindled the debate by singing it in public in 2010, spawning a controversy that eventually led to a banning order being placed upon him and a court decision that the phrase is unconstitutional and a possible incitement to murder.[249] In 2011 he was found guilty of hate speech for singing "Dubul' iBhunu", isiZulu for "Shoot the Boer". The cultural legacy of the anti-apartheid struggle thereby retains its viability across generations. And the definition of hate speech continues to expand to incorporate the possibility of "psychological harm", a notably difficult matter to assess.

Counting Cows

In the opening years of this new century, age-old traditions are also being remoulded to suit contemporary realities. Take the custom of lobola, or bride price. One enterprising soul has realised that time-honoured rules of negotiation are not as binding as they once were, when all parties were firmly rooted within easily identifiable and mutually respected social systems. The labour market, migration and urbanisation are responsible for much of the erosion of these ancient ties. The orchestrated depredations of apartheid are an obvious factor as well.

To address these changed circumstances, this man has created a contract to be signed after negotiations have been successfully concluded, a much more formal and comprehensive understanding than the sort of simple note that previously sufficed. It includes the names and identity numbers of all the partners; the amount of money to be exchanged; and space is also provided to enumerate goods to be handed over, such as cows and blankets. A graduated agent's fee scale has been formulated as well: R250 for a monogamous relationship, R350 when a man is taking a second wife, and then rising in increments of R100 up to a maximum of R650 for a fifth wife, or any larger aggregate. This agreement balances alternative sets of conventions: the consent of the other wife or other wives is required (all the women must agree, and sign on), and court permission ("taking into consideration his customs") must also be secured.[250]

Moreover, qualified lobola negotiators are available at R1000 for those who need them (if one of the parties lacks elders who are capable of satisfactorily representing their interests, for example). Customers have included a white man marrying a black woman, a scenario that neither the ancestors, colonial rulers, nor the architects of apartheid formally (or formerly) endorsed.[251]

This is a noteworthy example of a legal system continuously adapting to changed circumstances, accommodating what might otherwise be incompatible wishes. This process was referred to in the opening chapter as the interplay between traditional beliefs and contemporary modes of thought and behaviour, the conflicting allegiances and demands of "subject" versus "citizen". Tussles such as these surface at the interface between traditional medicine and indigenous knowledge systems, as opposed to Western-based, allopathic remedies and techniques;[252] the assertive or defensive use of witchcraft, involving conduct that may violate legal statutes protecting individuals from bodily harm; or when the practice of ritual slaughter for ceremonial purposes contravenes present-day standards of hygiene, public health and humaneness, especially when this formerly rural-based behaviour is transposed to an urban environment. More than particular activities are at stake; people's sense of themselves as social beings is very much at issue in all these instances.

This last example is especially meaningful. As some residential areas that were once exclusively occupied by people of European origin are gradually becoming home to a mixture of people, the possibilities of exposure to seemingly exotic behaviours are heightened, as are the prospects for misunderstandings to occur. The city of Johannesburg agreed to allow ritual slaughter in backyards in 2003, contingent upon celebrants giving their neighbours notice of the event seven days in advance. Credo Mutwa, the famed writer, sangoma and president of the Gauteng Traditional Healers Association, applauded the decision. He reflected, "It is only when our culture starts to be respected that other nations will see humanity and the beauty in us."[253]

The slaughter of animals accompanies the reverent observance of milestones within black African traditions, including marriages, funerals, or the celebration of a young man's return from initiation school. It links the living with their ancestors to ensure that benevolence and protection will come to the descendants. Such rites bestow continuity, security, and an enduring sense of identity.

Many black Africans are reclaiming such observances as an affirmation of ancient values and bonds, with the vision that they are now potentially liberated from the type of prohibitions, restrictions or intrusions imposed by previous systems of government. But assertion commonly meets resistance. And debate can be enjoined between people bearing different cultural values, as well as among those who claim the same cultural heritage.

One instance where these issues came into the spotlight was the revival of the Zulu First Fruits ceremony, or *Umkhosi wokweshwama*. Such renewals have become a priority for King Goodwill Zwelithini. In olden times, when a king formed a male age cohort into a new regiment of warriors, the young men proved their strength and cohesion by killing a bull, barehanded. The intention was that this be done as swiftly and humanely as possible. An academic with a Zulu birthright asserted, "Africans were denuded of their essence; their ceremonies and beliefs were distorted. By reviving some of these ceremonies and customs, the king hopes to re-imbue us Africans with our pride and self-confidence ... [T]hrough these ceremonies," he argued, "we reclaim our essence as a people."[254]

But what is tradition for some represents torture and cruelty for others. One person's custom becomes another's regulatory crusade. Cultural expression becomes a target for suppression. "Which war are they fighting?" a letter-to-the-editor writer implored, when the ritual was reenacted in 2006. "They are not warriors in any sense of the word, they are a bunch of brutal, bloodthirsty thugs."[255] Such frank speaking out is somewhat tempered by fear of running the risk of being labelled insensitive at best, racist at worst. Another letter writer declared, "South Africans have exchanged racist tyranny for the tyranny of political correctness."[256] And an SPCA spokesperson who has challenged the practice for a decade pointed to the complication of politics and ethnicity in the present era: "A lot of magistrates are not prepared to take on the Zulu monarchy",[257] once again highlighting how the tug of one's position as a subject can intersect with, and complicate, one's status as a citizen.

A journalist who is also a Zulu represents the difficulty of mounting a critique from within a community; the pressure to sustain tribal loyalty is immense. Fred Khumalo remarked that he has been labelled a "Zulu in denial whenever I question practices that have been rammed down my throat in the name of Zulu culture".[258] He admitted his shock over the report of the ritual slaughter of a bull, which included strangling and gouging its eyes out. He also pointed out a predicament that native peoples around the globe have broached in the postcolonial period: is culture a static entity, freezing people in historic time, or is it a dynamic and shifting creation?

Indigenous groups have steadily challenged their depiction in museums around the world, for example, such as the prolonged debate over the Bushman diorama at the South African Museum in Cape Town.[259] In such instances they have bristled at being encased in a sort of cultural amber. And, according to one scholar, "indigenous identity is the condition of participation in a global political dialogue ... it is the international language of rights and the existence of international meetings and organisations that establish the very meaning of indigenous identity".[260]

In other respects people clutch onto cultural practices precisely because of their supposed sense of eternalness. Khumalo warned his fellows against the latter strategy. "[T]ime marches on, dear people," he declared. "Cultures evolve and some customs get jettisoned along the way. Today, there are many other ways of expressing one's gallantry rather than killing a beast with one's own hands." He concluded, "Zulus of today cannot be like the Zulus of King Shaka's time."[261]

Purity or Cruelty?

King Goodwill Zwelithini embodies the esteemed and powerful line of Zulu monarchs. He is the present-day arbiter of custom among his people; his authority prevails in matters of tradition. Zwelithini has referred to a particular ritual as "an umbilical cord between modern Zulus and their ancestors",[262] a remarkably vivid articulation of how his community of believers sees itself inextricably linked to the past. The ritual in question is virginity testing, which has been growing in popularity due to its active endorsement by traditional leaders, and as a response to the spectre of that most modern of global phenomena, the AIDS pandemic. But it has also collided head-on with a growing, universalised culture of human rights, and its embodiment within the contemporary state.

Virginity testing is conducted by female specialists among both the Zulu and Xhosa, women who vocally defend the practice and their execution of it. Such examinations have been on the rise since the mid-1990s, and may be conducted throughout the year in a variety of private and not-so-private settings. One practitioner defiantly stated, "They may as well arrest me. [Nelson] Mandela went to jail for what he believed in and, when he got out, everybody accepted his views were not so strange. Maybe they will realise virginity testing is meant to build our nation, not destroy it."[263] And Nomagugu Ngobese, the "doyenne of testing" in KwaZulu-Natal, expressed the feeling that rituals dear to her people are being unfairly singled out for censure, without people like herself being sounded out for their perspectives: "The question is why is the government targeting our culture when other races are allowed to practise their own cultures freely? We're not going to stop this culture [-al practice] particularly because we were not consulted about it."[264]

The specific source of her wrath was a proposed Children's Rights Bill that would ban the practice. A subsequent compromise with critics imposed the restrictions that those submitting to the testing must be 16 or over, and also consent to the inspection. The bill was passed by Parliament in 2007 and implemented in 2008. The basis of the legislation is that virginity testing violates the right to privacy and bodily integrity and that it is unsafe as routinely practised. The Commission on Gender Equality supports this perspective, as does the South African Human Rights Commission, as a possible violation of human rights. But while these government bodies have opposed virginity testing, one ministry supports its execution in conjunction with the annual Reed Dance (see below) wholeheartedly: the KwaZulu-Natal Arts and Culture Department both organises and financially underwrites the event, with a massive budget in 2007 of R2.5 million.[265]

One of the primary sources of official criticism is that the examination is conducted by women using their bare hands – sometimes with men looking on – and is thereby invasive and potentially a source of spreading disease. Even when plastic gloves are worn by the testers, they may be used again and again. Moreover, girls as young as five are sometimes examined, raising doubts about their capacity to grant informed consent.

The "coming-out" rite for virgins is the Reed Dance (*Umkhosi woMhlanga*), where throngs of young women dance bare-breasted for their king, and each deposits a long reed that she carries throughout the ceremony as she approaches him. If it should break before the girl reaches that point, this signals that she has already engaged in sexual intercourse. Revived by King Zwelithini in 1984, some 20 000 girls participated in the event in KwaZulu-Natal in 2005. Two years later, the number had swelled to 30 000. It is also celebrated in Swaziland, where it can attract upwards of 75 000 young women, and has become a feature of the yearly First Fruits Festival as well.[266]

But the reliability of such tests is questionable. According to one source, girls sometimes stuff meat or lace into their vaginas to deceive the testers;[267] they may also squirt toothpaste inside themselves to suggest the appearance of an intact hymen.[268] Testers carefully look for additional signs of sexual activity, however. "[C]ertain lines below a girl's eyes, behind her knees and on her breasts" reportedly signal such behaviour;[269] aspirants are graded from "A" to "C" on the degree to which their virginity is betrayed by highly subjective "folk constructs" about the desired appearance of their genitalia, and the "innocence" of their eyes.[270] Passing the examination brings respect; failing it draws scorn.[271]

Within the current social climate of South Africa, being certified a virgin also creates dangers. If a girl is marked with a white star or dot on her forehead, she may fall prey to rape due to the widespread and insidious belief that an HIV-infected man may be "cured" of the virus by having sex with a virgin; certificates are often issued now instead. They could also become a target of envy by other girls who "might be inclined to encourage their brothers, friends or neighbours to rape them".[272]

And in yet another demonstration that South Africa has been drawn into global developments, the Reed Dance has become an event of note for sex tourists coming from places as widely scattered as China, the Netherlands and Chile. Some of them have made this an annual pilgrimage. These voyeurs intrude into rites leading up to the public event and photograph experiences such as the maidens bathing nude in the river. Selected shots have made it onto the internet.[273] A markedly divergent perspective was offered by a journalist who characterised the participants as resembling "disoriented refugees rather than any male strumpet fantasy", however. He dismissed the ceremony as being "as fascinating as watching cow-dung dry", and concluded "to find even a sliver of sexual arousal in the affair is near impossible".[274] Still, salacious outsiders eagerly appear.

Critics also see virginity testing as discriminatory since it only involves girls. But King Zwelithini has sought to silence this opposition by proposing virginity testing for boys as well. An expert asserted that the practice was "ancient", involving the questionable criteria that a young man must display a tight foreskin, and be able to urinate as high as he is tall, or even over his head, by holding his penis upright.[275] The king believes the government would be better advised to supervise male circumcision than virginity testing; initiation rites result in scores of deaths and mutilations each year (not incidentally, circumcision is a Xhosa rite, but until quite recently, not a Zulu one). He declares, "We cannot apologise about our tradition. There's no department that we'll ask permission from to uphold our culture and tradition … As a nation, we'll not be forced out of our culture."[276]

This statement points to the fact that all parties to this debate are arguing from their distinctive social positions, and that power, legitimacy and resources are at stake for each one. At the grassroots level, for older rural women who are bearing the brunt of the AIDS epidemic by caring for the sick and orphaned, virginity testing is a way to validate the standards with which they were inculcated as girls – even as it simultaneously reproduces social arrangements that narrowly constrict women's sexual behaviour.[277] It helps reestablish the legitimacy of these women within a world where social controls seem to have seriously eroded. According to an anthropologist who has studied the phenomenon, "A gendered epidemic requires and demands a gendered response."[278]

For traditionalists like King Zwelithini, and others holding strong tribal identities, revivals of this sort can buttress their claims as a political force to reckon with, a centre of power existing apart from official governmental decrees. It is also easy for such people to interpret measures proposing to regulate virginity testing or other behaviours dear to their constituencies as signifying tribal rivalries: the governmental ANC hierarchy was strongly identified with people of Xhosa heritage from 1994 until the end of 2007, and one of their central customs – the abovementioned male circumcision rite – has largely been left unfettered, even though it garners sensationalistic headlines about kidnappings, injuries and deaths every winter when initiation schools are operating (typically June to July).

To an advocate of virginity testing who is already sceptical of the government, its fiddling with matters such as this bespeaks a willingness to let the AIDS epidemic continue its deadly march through local populations, without concern for its devastating consequences. For people whose authority has been eroded as democracy has supplanted customary rule, this has become an important cultural battleground. So to members of royalty and rural women alike, the revival of interest in rites like virginity testing parallels the resurgence of behaviours attributed to witchcraft, as people recycle, refashion and reuse the various elements in their time-honoured cultural inventory to understand and address contemporary challenges.

But for many politicians, government bureaucrats, and workers in certain NGOs, invoking the language of human rights becomes a priority (although as Petchesky [2000] makes clear, the topic of sexuality was a relative late-comer to the human rights agenda). Not only does it express values that are deeply important for them; it also heightens the prospect that South Africa can enter the orbit of nations within which personal freedoms and individual choices, guarantees of legal rights and safeguards, are fundamental. Customs that in their eyes victimise and discriminate against the most powerless members of a society cannot be tolerated, and condemn their advocates to a realm of superstition, inequality and oppression. Moreover, the sad fact is that there is no evidence that virginity testing has had any positive impact at all on stemming the tide of new HIV infections.

Choosing Sides

Out of the dozens of plays on offer at the 2003 National Arts Festival in Grahamstown, South Africa's premier performing arts extravaganza, one stood out by the controversy it provoked. The concerns emanated from at least three different sources. The first entailed competing images of women; the second, the locus of control over a group's history; and the last, the impact and reception of artwork that crosses familiar dramatic borders. In each respect, offence was taken even before the curtain went up.[279]

The piece was *Thuthula – Heart of the Labyrinth*, written by well-respected poet and Rhodes Scholar Chris Mann. He based his script on books by a Xhosa historian, J. Henderson Soga, and an epic poem written by J.J.R. Jolobe, a Xhosa by birth as well. The story was rooted in historical events from the early 19th century; the setting, the Eastern Cape frontier, where the Xhosa, British colonialists and Trek Boers (descendants of other European settlers) were gripped by a complicated rivalry for dominance over land and other resources.

The lead character, Thuthula, spawned comparisons drawing from classical as well as contemporary culture: she was dubbed an "African Helen of Troy" and a proto-feminist, but also dismissively portrayed by Xhosa traditional leaders as a dissolute temptress like a character on the television soapie *The Bold and the Beautiful*, who married a father and his sons in turn (interesting that at the same time that they are guardians of tradition, these leaders are also clued into pop culture offerings such as soap operas).[280] Was she a seductress who undermined social stability, or a woman who defiantly followed her heart and thereby resisted patriarchy?

The basic story unfolds as follows: the beautiful Thuthula falls in love with Xhosa prince Ngqika who, because of his youth, is not yet permitted to rule. His uncle Ndlambe, from a related clan, steps into the position of chief. Moreover, he chooses Thuthula as his bride, and her family assents to the marriage.

As time passes, not only does the prince chafe under his uncle's continued exercise of power, his longing for his beloved (and, possibly, a desire to provoke his adversary) leads him to have her kidnapped so that they may elope together. This triggers a new episode of clan warfare, and when Ngqika finds his forces being crushed, he appeals to the British for support. But this provides only a short-term advantage: internecine fighting had weakened the Xhosa, and they were eventually conquered by the British in 1818 at the Battle of Amalinde.

Objections were raised by present-day Xhosa royalty who called for a boycott of the production, echoing an aspect of the resistance of virginity testers to the Children's Rights Act: they resented not having been consulted over the play, an oversight that they claimed rendered them "faceless".[281] Moreover, they feared the potentially negative impacts of *Thuthula*. On the one hand, they considered it "immoral", "disgusting and disrespectful" – the chairman of the House of Traditional Leaders calling it "a blow against our efforts for moral regeneration".[282] On the other, they feared it could re-trigger clan rivalries between present-day descendants, the Ama-Ngqika and Ama-Ndlambe, a concern that obviously would not be raised had the ancient enmities been resolved, not merely be lying dormant. But one facet of the story that *Thuthula* made clear was that the defeat of the Xhosa was not simply due to the invading colonists, but their own civil war made them more vulnerable – not a flattering detail for those trying to burnish their historical legacy.

The larger question became, "Who is qualified, and entitled, to narrate and interpret a group's stories?" Spokesman for Rharhabe, King Maxhobayakhawuleza Sandile, declared, "As custodians of this heritage, we always welcome initiatives that seek to promote awareness of our history and heritage … but we are smelling a rat." They challenged the abilities as well as the motives of the people behind this production: "They are adamant they would never allow the writing and interpretation of Xhosa history to be usurped by 'whites who were out to make money and were not concerned about the restoration of the dignity of the Xhosa people'."[283]

In this regard, such critics were joining the ranks of some African-Americans, Jews, First Nation peoples and others who have chafed at artists who do not share their DNA, yet who represent their experiences and seemingly speak for them. But playwright Mann roundly dismissed any transgression on his part. He countered, "I felt I was a writer in a democratic society, not a clan's *imbongi*, and believed that history was not owned and should not be vetted or controlled by royalty."[284] He also railed at the *City Press* for "playing the race card" by publishing the quote about whites allegedly profiting off the heritage and experiences of black Africans.

Artwork that crosses boundaries provokes discomfort, and *Thuthula – Heart of the Labyrinth* drew liberally from the cultural archive. The play blended Xhosa culture with Elizabethan drama, and injected other classical allusions into the story. This pastiche also included a scene with a distinctive postmodernist spin, where the dialogue between Ngqika's men and a British representative humorously highlighted the pitfalls of translation, an issue central to the controversy over Mbongeni Ngema's song "AmaNdiya". One reviewer gushed that the director had "achieved an African play where the dancing and chanting become an integral part of the action and not an extraneous addition. She has melded theatrical aspects beloved of African audiences most effectively with drama as it is appreciated by western audiences, thus creating *a transitional drama* of high significance."[285] But those who patrol and defend traditional boundaries, be they spatial or cultural, are more at ease with material that stays within established limits, not those that blur them.

The Xhosa royalty who were outraged threatened legal action if necessary to halt the play, another instance that demonstrates how in today's world they oscillate between the primordial and the contemporary, as needed. The impasse was broken after the Eastern Cape Department of Arts, Sport and Recreation sent the chairman of its arts council and a professor with a Xhosa background to meet with the king and his retinue. From that point forward, it was "thumbs up".

All in all, the intensity of this opposition is curious – it may even seem to be misplaced, on first glance – given that the primary audience for the play would likely be urban-dwelling, black and white art aficionados, not the sort of people over whom traditional leaders hold sway. But its symbolic weight was enormous, and the anger it elicited offers a glimpse into how profound the colonial impact was, and still is. Untold numbers of Xhosa were lost in battle with the settlers; their cattle were confiscated; Xhosa women were abused; Xhosa autonomy was constricted; Xhosa identity, seriously battered over time. On the whole, kinsmen were stripped of their dignity and pushed into a subordinate status from which they are only now able to emerge. Tribal history thus has an immediacy, weight and preciousness that can be difficult for outsiders to grasp.

Moreover, the status of traditional leaders has been in flux since the demise of apartheid, making it important for them to fight to retain control over some domains. The distribution of land and many other matters of life in rural areas remain under their authority; history, and its retelling, is important to them as well. But their power is circumscribed in other respects, although they are rewarded heartily by the present-day government in the form of salaries, security and luxury vehicles (BMWs have become virtually obligatory).

In 2006 to 2007, for example, the royal house of KwaZulu-Natal received R31.4 million for palaces and the maintenance of the Zulu queens (in 2008 there were six of them). As one traditional leader defensively argued, "How can people be proud of their kings if they walk? How can people be proud of their kings if they're poor?"[286] But these royal houses are becoming more and more an echo of the past, out of sync with the democratic drift of the rest of South African society,[287] going through the motions of rituals largely for the benefit of one another. One observer notes, "All the world over, surviving royal families are strangely loved and generally ignored."[288]

Paralleling the debate over this play was the announcement of another new work, whose explicit motivation was to avoid some of the difficulties raised by *Thuthula*. Just before the National Arts Festival commenced, a Xhosa playwright honoured a legendary figure of his group's history with the musical drama *Makana*, about the life of a Xhosa warrior who courageously fought the English colonialists at the Battle of Grahamstown in 1819. He became one of the first political prisoners on Robben Island, and reportedly drowned while attempting his escape from there.[289] The pull quote of an article featuring the project was forthright in its description: "The Rev. Mzwandile Maqina's new play is an African interpretation – as opposed to a European misinterpretation – of the life of Makhanda."[290]

This was an opportunity to tell the story in a way that had been denied, suppressed or distorted in the past, and to build community solidarity (it was strategically staged at a church in New Brighton, a black African township area of Port Elizabeth central to the liberation struggle, a venue where anti-apartheid plays were once presented). The author described his mission in the following way: "This is to challenge the view that Makana was a liar who said the whites' bullets would be turned into water and his army would suffer defeat at the hands of European colonialists. For instance, in African culture, a hero's martyrdom is not regarded as defeat but as a permanent victory over the forces of evil."[291] To those who feel they have suffered so much, hagiography was preferable to a questioning reassessment.

The politics of representation – the quandaries and consequences of who has the right and opportunity to tell a group's stories – is hotly debated in South Africa, as it is elsewhere. Feminists worldwide have been particularly engaged in discussions about the legitimacy of speaking for oneself or speaking for others, and the complications of establishing distinct boundaries of legitimacy in these regards, whatever one's social position. Many black African artists fervently argue that they have fewer opportunities to produce work about the experience of people like themselves than others do, especially in such intensely market-driven creative industries as filmmaking. They speak of this situation as another instance of being colonised; in this case, history becomes the scarce and sought-after resource.

One South African director complained that white producers "numb our stories", while another asked, "Why do the whites have to heal us?"[292] Many white artists counter these objections by arguing for an unrestricted marketplace of ideas. Writer André Brink, for example, rejects what he fears as an "apartheid of the mind", and explains, "Voices may speak: but unless they are informed by tongues of fire they can only babble. *This* is the real issue – not whether the artist chooses, through an act of the imagination, to speak in one voice rather than another."[293]

Black artists seem to be arguing as much about structural limitations within the arts as about an imbalance in perspectives within what gets produced. At the end of the day, of course, in a country with the racial entanglements of South Africa, there is no patently "black" or "white" experience. Each group has continuously impacted the fate of the other in profound respects in spite of the labyrinth of restrictions that also may have kept them apart in many ways.

Goring Someone Else's Bull

Controversy turns upon more than a particular act or expression. *Who* engages in the behaviour, how it is perceived within its social context, and its mixture with seemingly contradictory conduct all enhance the potential for public debate. And in South Africa, a wily politician's encounter with a particular beast fulfilled all the requisites for a cultural squabble.

Tony Yengeni is a former chief whip of the ANC, a flashy party loyalist whose forte has been the sort of in-the-trenches work of mobilising and aligning support so crucial for successful political dealmaking. His (fleeting) fall from grace happened in 2007 when he was convicted of fraud for trying to conceal information from parliamentary investigators: he had received a munificent discount of nearly 50% on a new Mercedes-Benz from DaimlerChrysler, a side story to a scandal-ridden arms deal (see below). He also garnered headlines when his cadres defiantly marched with him to the gates of Pollsmoor Prison to begin his four-year sentence; again when he was released less than five months later due to a radically trimmed term, and chauffeured home in a Mercedes-Benz; and especially after a photo of his ritual sacrifice of a bull at his father's house in Gugulethu, outside Cape Town, as part of a cleansing and welcoming home ceremony ended up on the front page of the *Saturday Star*.[294]

The paper also opted to append a sensationalistic headline, "Bloody welcome home for Yengeni," to its coverage.[295] One reader rebuked it for reproducing such an image as "tasteless". Others blasted both the publication, and the behaviour it had depicted, as "horrific" and "barbaric".[296]

Yengeni's credibility problem rested upon the feeling many people shared that his under-the-table wheeling and dealing was being punished with barely a slap on the wrist. This then encouraged an interpretation of his invocation of tradition as gimmicky and insincere, thereby dictating a closer examination of its ethical acceptability. A young white radio host remarked, "Tony Yengeni amuses me – there is something incongruent about someone who likes animal sacrifice and appeasing the ancestors on one hand – and ML500 Mercedes-

Benz cars, Armani suits and Johnnie Walker Blue on the other."[297] Another account disparaged him by noting, "When the women finished singing traditional songs, Yengeni was first to drink the traditional beer. He became very upset when his father passed around his designer Tommy Hilfiger golf shirt for the family to wipe fat from the slaughtered animal from their hands."[298]

A trendy sense of fashion and revered ritual practices do not easily mix; Yengeni became a poster boy for political arrogance, excess and corruption. And not only did his behaviour engage public opinion; the Cape of Good Hope SPCA, the South African Human Rights Commission, government ministers, the Commission for the Promotion and Protection of the Rights of Cultural, Religious and Linguistic Communities, the Icamagu Institute,[299] and the Congress of Traditional Leaders all jumped into the fray.

The SPCA was enraged because the bull was trussed, and Yengeni was pictured with his clan's ceremonial spear. This made the group question the degree of discomfort and trauma the animal experienced before it was killed. But a key element of the ritual is that the animal must bellow or "burp" before it is slaughtered, a signal that a connection has been made between the ancestors and the supplicant. If the animal does not do this on its own, it may be jabbed with the spear. The SPCA received a complaint from someone who saw the published photo, and instigated an investigation.[300] Animal rights activists, and others whose sensitivities were violated, faced off against advocates of traditional Xhosa rites.

In his zeal and fury, one critic misconstrued a key aspect of the practice: "Yengeni's inherited view that a speared bull bellows to communicate with its ancestors [sic] as opposed to a psycho-physiological response to pain is as absurd as believing his Range Rover starts not by the turn of [the] ignition, sparks and mechanics [sic] but by some god throwing down a lightning bolt."[301] The significance of the bellowing is to suggest that the animal is summoning the human's ancestors, not its own, however. Another detractor played a game of "Can you beat this?" (or, "How low can you go?"), pushing the embrace of cultural relativity to the point of absurdity: "[I]f, hypothetically, a tribe of cannibals were to join the throng of refugees and fortune-seekers to South Africa and demanded the right to perform cannibalistic rituals, would you condone it?"[302]

But many black Africans rallied behind Yengeni. The Department of Arts and Culture stood up in his defence, saying it was his constitutional right to practise his religion, and that targeting him for participating in this rite amounted to "selective racism".[303] Nokuzola Mndende of the Icamagu Institute declared, "The SPCA should leave Yengeni alone and back off from our culture. We as black people in this country have to explain ourselves every time we need to do what is sacred and important to us."[304] And Congress of Traditional Leaders president Phathekile Holomisa accused the media of disrespecting black African beliefs and concluded, "It is funny that we as black people never criticise other people's cultures and we don't even poke our noses there, but we must be apologetic to foreigners [sic] in our land."[305] The resolute conviction that certain assumptions and activities are authentically African, and also in constant need of justification and defence, profusely seeps through such statements.

Yengeni's legal conviction did not discernibly stain his reputation in the eyes of his supporters, nor did the subsequent controversy his release from prison aroused. To the contrary, this all amplified his repute as heroic, a tenacious individual who triumphed over undeserved persecution. He returned to what he knew best, networking and manoeuvring through complex political terrain, at this stage of his career on behalf of his friend Jacob Zuma.[306]

But the way ANC members embraced and even honoured Yengeni was deeply disturbing to those who saw him as simply another member of a growing roster of public officials whose behaviour has flouted morality and good judgement, without receiving much official admonishment or substantial punishment, significant shaming or shunning. "Morality has been abandoned: if it's legal, it's good," one distressed observer wrote. "[I]gnoble behaviour," he argued, "threatens to become our social norm."[307]

The (Mis)interpretation of Cultures

During the debate around the revival of slaughtering a bull for the First Fruits ceremony, one commentator observed, "'It's our culture' has become a phrase top leaders in the ANC use to justify their sexcapades."[308] In other words, "culture" can be claimed as the restoration of authentic links to the past. Or it may be invoked as an unimpeachable excuse for certain sorts of behaviour, and a diversion from present-day shortcomings and misdeeds.

On that latter score, politician Jacob Zuma has distinguished himself. If Frank Sinatra had his emblematic "My Way", the anti-apartheid struggle song "Umshini Wam" ("My Machine Gun") is Zuma's trademark. This association is common knowledge in South Africa and is frequently referenced. When Indian businessman Vivian Reddy launched a casino in the KwaZulu-Natal town of Newcastle, a gossip columnist joked about Zuma's benediction, "In his speech, he made reference to his trademark song, 'Umshini Wam', saying he couldn't wait to play the slot machines, since he's always looking for his machine!"[309]

When Zuma was imprisoned on Robben Island, he became a cultural commissar of sorts, organising a choral group to perform struggle songs and assembling troupes to perform traditional dances – a melding of the time-honoured and the contemporary to build and sustain a sense of solidarity. He also had an Indian cellmate, one of the many instances during the apartheid era where members of different ethnic backgrounds were thrown together in common cause.[310] Like his friend Mbongeni Ngema, Zuma is wildly popular. He has also been at the epicentre of some notable scandals.

President Mbeki removed him from his position as deputy president of the country in 2005 after the conviction of his financial advisor Schabir Shaik on fraud and corruption charges. That trial focused on a huge and controversial arms contract with a French arms company worth R60 billion, Shaik's exploitation of his relationship with Zuma to procure a share of it for himself, and a reported R500 000 bribe paid by the French to Zuma. Further revelations brought to light Zuma's financial interdependence with certain powerful dealmakers: Shaik paid substantial amounts of money to two of Zuma's former wives; Zuma's traditional homestead in rural KwaZulu-Natal was allegedly bankrolled in part by kickbacks from the French company; and Vivian Reddy helped Zuma secure a bond for the complex of houses there, and then paid the monthly instalments.

Zuma was indicted on corruption charges in 2006, an episode dubbed South Africa's "Watergate",[311] but the case was thrown out for procedural reasons. Inside the courtroom, an assembly of Zulu chiefs, wearing their customary leopard-skin loincloths, shouted their delight at the termination of the proceedings. Outside, thousands of supporters rejoiced as well. A witness described the jubilant scene as follows: "Scantily clad Zulu women, some waving cardboard machine-guns, danced in celebration." Zuma, too, threw himself into the merriment, dancing and singing.[312]

"Umshini Wam" can be interpreted in different ways. On the one hand, it's a call to armed action against the enemy. But the "machine" in the refrain also carries a sexual connotation, one that emerged more clearly when Zuma was prosecuted earlier in 2006 for raping a woman. Tragic in its own right, the act was even more repugnant for several additional reasons. It was perpetrated by a top public official in a country burdened with a record incidence of sexual crimes (by some accounts, it has the highest rate of rape in the world). Moreover, Zuma once headed the National AIDS Council and the Moral Regeneration Movement, a campaign that emphasised monogamy. And the victim was someone he'd known since she was a girl, and she looked up to him as a parental figure and mentor.[313] Khwezi (a pseudonym) had been a victim of multiple previous rapes, is HIV-positive (a fact that Zuma knew), and his admission of showering afterwards as AIDS "risk reduction" or "prevention" brought howls of ridicule and contempt from his critics.

The crowds that gathered to support Zuma during the trial, many of whom were bused in from rural KwaZulu-Natal, Zuma's birthplace,[314] created a spectacle in the streets, borrowing from a repertoire of elements popularised during the struggle years. They chanted, sang, and loudly blew vuvuzelas. Khwezi describes being the target of threats and harassment by the crowds: some bore placards saying "Burn the bitch"; they stoned a woman they mistook for her, burned panties, and also burned an effigy of her;[315] and some of those supporting her were subjected to gestures of having their throats slit or having a pistol fired at them.[316] On one occasion a man "parading in chains like [*Roots* protagonist] Kunta Kinte" carried a poster reading "Zuma raped". And some women even called the victim "ungrateful" for having had the opportunity to have sex with such a great man.[317]

The throngs of both men and women backing Zuma sang sexually explicit songs to intimidate the plaintiff throughout the trial. A journalist reflected, "'You should be glad you do not understand Zulu'. He said this in reaction to Zuma's supporters' never-ending chant of unprintable names referring to a woman and her mother's sexual body parts."[318] A gender activist who wrote a book on the episode concluded that these demonstrators "turn[ed] our mother tongue into a traditional weapon of mass destruction".[319] On at least one noteworthy occasion counter-demonstrators braved chilly weather clad in kangas, and boldly declared that a woman could not be held responsible for any sexual abuse she might receive, notwithstanding the way she dresses. They used a customary form of style to underscore a very modern point.[320]

Zuma's defence was unadorned: he pleaded guilty to being a bearer of Zulu culture. Although fluent in English, he testified in isiZulu. Zuma interpreted the fact that Khwezi was wearing a kanga (a length of cloth traditionally wrapped around the body, from above the breasts to the knees, of East African origin) to be a sexual come-on. In other words, his victim "wanted it". As a Zulu man, he claimed that tradition dictated he could not leave a woman in an aroused state without having sex with her (he had massaged her with baby oil).[321]

In the end, Zuma was acquitted. He testified that he was willing to "do the right thing", offering to pay lobola for the woman, another nod to traditional beliefs and practices. Even so, a prosecutor stated that the assertions the politician had made about "cultural imperatives" dictating his actions were bogus. "[R]ather than Zulu-culture," she argued, his behaviour represented a self-serving "Zuma-culture".[322]

And when the verdict came down, Zuma's supporters rejoiced wildly once again, "Umshini Wam" the showpiece of their rowdy demonstrations. Zuma celebrated by belting out the song on the courthouse steps.

One explanation for the fervour expressed by Zuma's supporters was the amount of suspected political intrigue underlying the cases. His advocates were suspicious that he may have been "set up" by his accuser in order to discredit him – sentiments simmering since Zuma's corruption charges came down, the hunch being that President Mbeki, a Xhosa, was determined to disgrace his Zulu rival.[323]

Zuma's machine gun has become so integral a part of his political and social identity that a group called the Friends of Jacob Zuma Trust offered the song as a ringtone in order to raise defence funds for him. The promotion promised that "polyphonic and monotones can be downloaded at a cost of R5. The truetone bearing Zuma's original voice can be downloaded at a cost of R10."[324] So, just as traditional rites are reinvigorated with fresh meanings in a democratic South Africa, apartheid-era rallying cries become protective gear and marketing ploys.

Launching his own volley in this cultural war, Zuma subsequently filed defamation claims against a multitude of defendants, from publishers down through reporters, and targeted the well-known editorial cartoonist Zapiro against whom he took particular umbrage for what he considered relentlessly unfair (read: unflattering) coverage of his legal difficulties. As one journalist noted, "It ain't over until the fat lady sings. The song could well be Umshini wam".[325]

* * *

"Umshini Wam" gained renewed exposure and achieved increased notoriety during one of the most disturbing episodes in the post-apartheid history of South Africa: the outbreak of xenophobic violence against African foreign nationals in May 2008. The song was sung by marauders who displaced tens of thousands of people, burning their homes, stealing their meagre possessions, and beating and killing them. The official tally was 62 dead, some of them the victims of torturous cruelty (and, as it turned out, nearly a third of those casualties were actually South Africans).

According to one account, "'Umshini Wam' is a song of revolt and xenophobic attackers believe they are in revolt against President Thabo Mbeki's administration. There is a perception that Zuma is more sympathetic to the plight of ordinary South Africans and understands the threat foreigners allegedly pose to their livelihoods."[326] Such attacks, it noted, have increased since Zuma was elected ANC president in December 2007.

CHAPTER 4

Culture Club:
Moffies, Baboons and Natives

... the tracing of colonial original sin is a bit like uncovering the
abusive mother behind a serial killer: it explains everything and nothing.

Alessandra Stanley, 2005

In 2003, an 18-year-old white South African man touring Zimbabwe with his family was tragically murdered during a robbery. A particular detail in a news report stands out: "one of the suspects was found in possession of a pocket knife, a spark plug and a hyena's tail"[327] – the latter to supposedly protect him from being detected by the police. Stories such as these are commonplace and often convey a sense of surprise by black African criminal suspects when they are apprehended; their use of muti to (reputedly) render them invisible to the authorities, or impervious to bullets, seems to have inexplicably miscarried.

Simon Moyo, Zimbabwean High Commissioner to South Africa, saw a larger significance in this incident. He decried, "It is unfortunate that some media in South Africa have found it appropriate to exploit the issue and bring in their usual obsession with [social problems in] Zimbabwe ... Such conduct [the reporting, not the crime] is deplorable in the extreme. It is insensitive, un-African and inhuman."[328] As an apologist for the regime he was representing, Moyo was engaging in the ploy of metaphorically shooting the messenger, thereby diverting attention from the actual offence. Moreover, he was throwing down an intimidating gauntlet: it is a serious breach of racial solidarity, he was in effect saying, to speak publicly of misdeeds or questionable behaviour coming from your fellow black Africans. To do so signifies breaking ranks and raises serious questions regarding *your* authenticity, trustworthiness, and sense of ubuntu. It is a transgression that is "un-African".

Just what it means to be genuinely African is very much contested nowadays in South Africa. One accrues bona fides by behaving in some ways, but refraining from other activities. Believing in certain principles, but rejecting alternatives. Embracing selected forms of cultural expression, but snubbing different options. When the various credits an individual has amassed are mentally tallied by his or her peers, one either embodies the *essence* of Africanness or one does not.

This is a way that culture is hemmed into very narrow definitional zones.

And, perhaps, ossified. If someone cannot either gain entry into or retain a legitimate right to operate within these constraints, they risk condemnation and ostracism by those who guard such an essentialist point of view.

Contemporary discussions make it clear that identity can be thick like impasto or as thin as a diluted pigment. A particular identity is central to some people's sense of self; it becomes their essence, their *raison d'être*. But it may only be incidental to others who could, hypothetically, adopt the same spirit. Identity may develop into body armour, or be lightly draped as a jacket. It can be blatantly worn on your sleeve or simply used to accessorise. Those who seize a particular identity most fully – be it racial, cultural, religious, national, gender, or sexual – may expect it to bear a similar significance for others. If it does not, the apostates may have hell to pay.

When Mugabe Met Sally

To a habitué of the gay male scene in the Johannesburg suburb of Melville or Cape Town's De Waterkant and Green Point quarters, news of a "Mugabe" in the vicinity would likely elicit a mixture of anger and alarm. But not literally, in this instance, Robert Mugabe – the freedom fighter turned ever-more despotic leader of Zimbabwe – but what he represents. In Gayle, a subcultural argot initially generated among Cape Town's coloured "moffies" during the repressive 1950s, a Mugabe is a homophobe, someone who despises Zelda (a gay Zulu), Golda (a gay Jew), Irma (a gay Indian), and Gladys (a gay man in general). He especially loathes Hazel (sex between men), and more specifically, Sally (to fellate someone). And the last place he would want to be caught visiting is Betty's house (engaging in male-to-male anal sex).[329]

Like other forms of slang, Gayle provided an important reference point for a group of social pariahs. And it remains the lingua franca in certain situations, among particular constituencies. Invoking this vocabulary bestows a common sense of identity, clarifies the boundaries between outsiders and insiders, and provides an opportunity to comically skewer one's own personal sense of oppression as well as assail one's oppressors – like the camp sensibility also does.

As much as Gayle represents a distinctly local idiom, the ontological status of homosexual behaviour among black Africans remains disputed. Homosexual men and women become a habitual soft target for autocratic African leaders who use anti-gay diatribes and campaigns to deflect public attention away from their personal blunders, profligacy, outrages and inadequacies. In southern Africa that has included Namibia's Sam Nujoma and Zimbabwe's Robert Mugabe.

The opposition to homosexuality expressed by African leaders and segments of the general public parallels many of the quarrelsome contours familiar in other parts of the world. But with the addition of one significant component: the frequently heard claim that same-sex behaviour is not indigenous to the continent, but an unfortunate, unwelcome and scummy residue of colonialism. Before Europeans arrived, so this argument goes, Africans were strictly heterosexual. Homosexuality "belongs" to the white man. It is "un-African".

Scholarly research repudiates such claims: a book about South Africa and Zimbabwe reveals that same-sex behaviour is relatively common, even in rural areas, and oral history indicates that this reflects a record of activity going back many generations.[330] Moreover, a book detailing female same-sex practices uncovered a broad range of experiences with a lengthy history throughout the continent, even documenting the exchange of lobola.[331] And gay advocates in Namibia note that "nearly all indigenous languages – including the Oshiwambo spoken by the majority of Swapo [South West Africa People's Organisation] supporters – have a word for homosexuals".[332] Gay proponents argue that rather than white colonials being the conduit for same-sex behaviour, they actually imported the condemnatory attitudes of Victorian thought and moralising religious belief and imposed them onto their African subjects. But information and reasoning such as this has minimal impact upon those who have a cultural axe to grind.

Under the rule of Sam Nujoma, a Swapo resistance leader and then president of Namibia from 1990 to 2005, officialdom orchestrated an unremitting attack on homosexuality. In 2000, for example, the home affairs minister told police recruits that "gays and lesbians are to be eliminated from the face of Namibia" and claimed that "the only gay people in Namibia were Europeans".[333] In 2001 Nujoma's homophobia was dramatically revealed when he raged, somewhat contradictorily, "Definitely it's against God's will. It is the devil at work ... They must keep it in Europe. Which god is responsible for these homosexuals? Is it the god of the Africans or the god of the Europeans?"[334] He also equated priests who condone gay marriage with missionaries who had abetted the colonialist agenda of controlling native peoples and seizing their land.

Earlier that year, at the University of Namibia, Nujoma had declared that homosexuals should be "arrested, imprisoned and deported", adding that "We in Swapo have not fought for an independent Namibia that gives rights to *botsotsos* (criminals), gays and lesbians to do their bad things here".[335] He also denounced women who fall in love with foreigners. Members of the Namibian Special Field Force (SFF) meanwhile raided a township area of the capital, Windhoek, and ripped earrings out of the ears of native men. One of the officers decried, "When did you see men wearing earrings in our Oshiwambo culture? These things never happened before independence."[336] He was suggesting that the freedom that came with democracy was abrading the potency of traditional values. And in 2003 Nujoma proclaimed, "We are no longer going to tolerate those who continue to despise the African people and their culture ... Homosexuality is against nature and our culture in Namibia." He then slipped in an appeal to demographic reasoning to help justify his prejudicial perspective: "We have a small population, we need to multiply."[337]

Nujoma has been dubbed "Mugabe lite", mockingly noting the similarities between the men's attitudes and deeds. As a leader anxious to sustain his authority, the challenges he faced clarify both the timing and tenor of his rhetorical crusades. Nujoma routinely amplified his anti-white and anti-gay oratory whenever questions about his leadership were in the public eye.

While Namibia is a land of great natural beauty, its desert starkness leaves little arable land. And in a country where the rates of poverty and unemployment are sizeable, land redistribution is a burning issue. It is, perhaps, *the* issue, particularly in light of the invasions of white-owned farms by "war veterans" beginning in Zimbabwe in 2000, and the forcible confiscation of land there. Sam Nujoma's Swapo-dominated government made many promises that it would purchase and then reallocate land to the general populace. But progress has been glacial; inept bureaucrats have been dreadfully deficient in fulfilling those pledges (except in the case of providing for high-ranking officials who have bought land for themselves courtesy of cheap loans).

Whenever Nujoma initiated questionable new policies, he commonly cranked up his attacks on "foreign influences" as being the genuine enemies of the people, thereby deflecting attention from his own machinations. For example, this became Nujoma's method as soon as he set about amending the constitution to permit himself to run for president for a third time. And it was the same story when he expropriated private property in order to build a lavish and phenomenally expensive new presidential state house. This pattern is clear, dating back to anti-gay tirades in 1996 that elided homosexuality with "foreign and corrupt ideology".

At that time Nujoma's secretary for information and publicity backed him up by declaring, "It should be noted that most of the ardent supporters of this [sic] perverts are Europeans who imagine themselves to be the bulwark of civilisation and enlightenment. They are not only appropriating [sic] foreign ideas in our society but also destroying the local culture by hiding behind the façade of the very democracy and human rights we have created."[338] Namibia's National Society for Human Rights saw through the ruse, however, and countered, "The move appears to be the tip of an insidious, much wider and protracted strategy spearheaded by and or run from State House and such campaign is apparently aimed at stemming the tide of a rapidly growing civil society in Namibia."[339] Under Nujoma's rule, the coming of elections, insinuations that he might be deficient in fulfilling the demands of his job, or potentially scandalous conduct on his part were all excellent predictors for his lashing out at Gladys and her cohorts.

The Rise and Fall of Non-Western Civilisation

At the Zimbabwe International Book Fair in Harare in 1995, Robert Mugabe launched a culture war against gays in unequivocal terms: his government forcibly banned a display by the Gay and Lesbian Association of Zimbabwe, and threatened to withhold financial support from the event if homosexual literature was put on view. Moreover, he brayed that gays were "a scourge planted by the white man on a pure continent" and "worse than dogs or pigs".[340]

Likening someone to a dog denotes enormous contempt throughout Africa, and this became the opening volley in a sustained campaign of hatred. As in the case of Namibia, this crusade has been couched in terms of cultural integrity and autonomy. But when politicians accuse gay people of being "the 'festering finger' endangering the body politic",[341] the motives are surely more complex.

Nicknamed "Uncle Bob", a moniker that sounds suspiciously and creepily perverted, Mugabe revived colonial-era sodomy laws, even though his conflation of homosexuality and colonialism reveals his intense disdain for that earlier era. Mugabe has attributed the country's financial woes to the legacy of British colonialism, and through what can only be characterised as a rant, fumed that Tony Blair was leading "a gay government of the gay United gay Kingdom".[342] He also accused Blair of using "gay gangsters" to attack him, a reference to OutRage! activist Peter Tatchell's attempt to arrest him in London for human rights violations.[343] Furthermore, at a public celebration of his 82nd birthday in 2006 Mugabe, speaking in Shona, "denounced homosexuality … 'Leave whites to do that,' he declared". He also threatened to jail clergy who might conduct gay marriages.[344]

Mugabe has become a prime target for artists. Local writer Dambudzo Marechera has been critical of the regime, as has Bongani Madondo, painting large-scale canvases akin to the style of Jean-Michel Basquiat, depicting Mugabe with flaming and spiked hair, apropos the devil. The cheeky and controversy-beset South African design company Laugh it Off Promotions (see Chapter 5) created a satirical T-shirt superimposing Mugabe's likeness onto the iconic mascot Lion Man of Simba brand snacks, replete with a little crown balancing on his head. Mugabe's "muzzle" is drawn in white, giving him a grizzled look, and an appearance that resembles reverse-blackface. The caption read, "Ruled by Terror" (instead of "Roarrring with Flavour") along with "Zimbabwe"; the symbolic crown appeared as well as the "dot" over the "i". And the president's remarks at the 1995 Book Fair motivated South African artist Gordon Froud to create *A False-Bottomed Suitcase for Robert Mugabe* (1995), a mixed-media assemblage that contained male clothing and heterosexual pornographic magazines such as *Hustler*. But when a hidden compartment was exposed it revealed a homoerotic male torso made of fibreglass, insinuating that just below the surface of heteronormality lurks suppressed desire. It was included in the first national lesbian and gay art exhibition, which sparked controversy in the city of Bloemfontein in 1996 (see Chapter 6).[345]

Zimbabwe asked South Africa's Broadcast Complaints Commission to ban a record and a music video of a kwaito song, "Zimbabwe, Zimbabwe". The video showed a man vomiting into a toilet, and criticised the "war veterans", the ragtag cadres of men who terrorised white farmers and their families and took their property by force. Zimbabwean officials objected that "it was detrimental to the 'cordial and excellent relations' between the two countries".[346] The South African Broadcasting Complaints Commission did not agree to proscribe the piece, but conceded that it should only be shown late at night. Moreover, the South African Broadcasting Corporation apologised to the Zimbabwean high commission. Within the country itself, people must exercise extreme caution: a man was arrested under the Law and Order Maintenance Act after he remarked that Mugabe had a rubber penis made in China. He was referring to the speculation that Mugabe suffers from tertiary syphilis, which might explain his fanatical behaviour.[347]

Mugabe's assault on expression has been an attempt to prop up a government that is bankrupt in all senses of the word: Zimbabwe's economy has declined precipitously (inflation reached an unfathomable 2.2 million per cent in July 2008, and the central bank issued a Z$100 billion bank note),[348] and the government has demonstrated a patent disregard for human rights. The bulk of the population has been forced into desperation, or exile. This societal freefall was prompted by the land invasions in 2000, which turned highly productive farms into wastelands.[349] Not coincidentally, Mugabe pumped up the volume of his anti-gay attacks at the same time his alleged comrades were terrorising the countryside. This classic case of playing the politics of diversion has been little more than a transparent sham, with homosexuality becoming a scapegoat for megalomania and misrule.[350]

Which Team Do You Play For?

At first glance, the situation in South Africa appears to be quite different. In 2004, for example, two young black male actors made pop culture history when they shared a kiss on the wildly popular soapie *Yizo Yizo*. And in 2006 another media milestone was recorded when two white male characters exchanged vows on *Isidingo*, another soapie staple. It is unimaginable that either episode could have originated in Namibia or Zimbabwe; or anywhere else in Africa, for that matter.

But for all the differences between South Africa and the rest of the continent, important similarities and shared beliefs link it to its neighbours.[351] The gay kiss on *Yizo Yizo* brought extreme hostility down upon one of the actors. And a journalist, aiming to display his nonchalance about what he saw, unintentionally corroborated a stereotype instead. He wrote that growing up in a coloured community prepared him for such behaviour. He was not shocked, he explained, because he'd been taught that "white people tend to do crazy things".[352] Now by extension, non-whites do, too.

And while the breakthrough episode of *Isidingo* came on the heels of the legalisation of gay unions in South Africa, the show's writers and producers were deliberately discreet in how they handled the matter. They were careful to keep the event out of a church, a secular person officiated at the ceremony, and the men exchanged only a very brief on-screen kiss.[353]

One critical factor *does* distinguish South Africa on this matter, however: the equality clause in its much-lauded, highly progressive constitution made it the first country in the world to prohibit discrimination based upon sexual orientation. That should have smoothed the progress of legalising gay marriage. Nevertheless, the struggle was protracted and at times generated offensive remarks. Homophobia and hate crimes remain prevalent. And people holding traditional views of varying kinds continue to resist the spirit of the law.

A study by the Human Sciences Research Council (HSRC) reported, "in many instances we are more conservative than Britons or Americans ... The survey revealed that more than three-quarters of South Africans are opposed to same-sex relationships and abortion, and that the same proportion supports the death penalty." Only 5% of respondents believed that same-sex relations were not wrong. The highest proportion of negative responses came from those provinces with the greatest number of people living in traditional, tribal areas.[354]

One man struck all the familiar anti-gay chords in an impassioned letter-to-the-editor published in a South African newspaper. He warned that homosexuals possessed "spoiled identities" and their behaviour was potentially "genocidal" for Africans. And he laid the responsibility for the threat at the door of European culture. "The sexual confusion of whites, as demonstrated in their history and culture," he argued, "is another indication that white people are uncomfortable in relation to the rhythms of the natural world." He ended his screed with this call to arms: "The Afro-renaissance must be a transforming power that helps black homosexuals to capture the true essence of their souls. Let us overcome the demons from the west!"[355]

The notion of "spoiled identities" speaks in an interesting way to some essential beliefs within black African culture, and Zulu culture in particular. Zulu men identify with powerful animals such as bulls and lions. Their individual exploits summon this recognition: when they engage in traditional stick fighting, for example, one man yells "*Nansi inkunzi*" ("Here is the bull"), to which his opponent replies, "Here is another bull". But a "mental shift" takes place when men must act in unison, within situations such as warfare or ceremonial dancing. In these instances Zulu men refer to themselves as oxen, because "inspanned oxen work as a team, in common purpose". In other words, individualism recedes when collective needs are paramount.[356] For a man to declare himself homosexual within such a patriarchal, masculinised and mutually interdependent culture would obviously cloud his identity as a recognisable, conventional and reliable cohort.

At the annual Reed Dance, in 2005, the aforementioned event where thousands of maidens dance before their sovereign (Chapter 3), Zulu King Goodwill Zwelithini declared, "The Zulu nation would not be this big, with millions of people, if there was the problem of gay people that we have today. This new behaviour [sic] is quickly becoming a threat in our nation because it encourages people not to have proper families that have children."[357] In response, the manager of the Durban Lesbian and Gay Community and Health Centre noted, "You can go to places like Ulundi [the capital of traditional Zululand] and talk about human rights, but there the Constitution is a government document – the king's rule is considered supreme."[358]

Another facet of the opposition to homosexuality is represented by an assortment of religious groups that formed the Marriage Alliance of South Africa to protest the legalisation of same-sex marriages. Including both the Catholic Church and the Evangelical Alliance of SA, it was a classic case of coalition building à la James Hunter, an instance of people uniting in common cause across doctrinal lines against what they perceived to be a threat to their essential beliefs.

Moreover, when Mcebisi Xundu, president of the Eastern Cape Council of Churches, came out in favour of same-sex marriage, many churches withdrew from the council and there were calls for him to quit. The deputy president wondered, "Why he chose to be politically correct instead of Biblically correct we don't know." And another minister declared, "If he can't stand for the Word of God, then he should rather step down."[359]

The tone was considerably less civil in the letters-to-the-editor page of *The Star*, where a black African churchman carried on an extended and extremely acrimonious exchange with other readers whom he had enraged with his opinions. In one of his dispatches, printed with the unfortunate headline "Rape better than same-sex intercourse", he argued that rape may be unlawful but homosexuality is unnatural. "It is far better for a virgin to suffer rape," he reasoned, "rather than for one to engage in homosexuality." In a country with an appalling incidence of gender violence, including unimaginably young victims, it was an unconscionable declaration. He also applauded the conservative and controversial African Anglican Archbishop Peter Akinola who has split from the mother church over homosexuality.[360] But employing a markedly different attitude, Njongonkulu Ndungane, Archbishop of Cape Town, published a passionate plea for mutual tolerance and understanding in a major Sunday newspaper.[361]

Various South African politicians and leaders have also revealed an anti-gay bias. For example, the mayor of Durban commented in relation to the desire to grow tourism in the area, "We should stop comparing ourselves to cities like Cape Town. In fact, Cape Town can stay with its moffies and its gays."[362]

And at a 2006 Heritage Day celebration, Jacob Zuma declared, "When I was growing up, *ungqingili* (a gay man) would not have stood in front of me. I would knock him out."[363] Many of Zuma's staunchest supporters distanced themselves from this insult, however. One person struck back by citing a struggle song, and reflected on its changed meaning: "Today, just as I was under an impression that we are all enjoying the fruits of freedom borne by our protest song 'Se nzeni na?' ['What have we blacks done?'], I'm struck by a bitter reality. The tables have turned [blacks are now oppressing gays; what have gays done to deserve this?]."[364] Not surprisingly, in a social climate such as this, the complement to the HSRC research quoted above was a study that found that only 31% of the gay people surveyed felt comfortable being "out", and merely 25% "felt their constitutional rights were being put into practice".[365]

Priscillas in the Platteland

The sole married gay couple in the small South African town of Klerksdorp is a pair of Priscillas. But it's not what you may suspect. In Gayle, Priscilla denotes a cop. In this case, it is two men who met on the first day of police training and held their wedding in a police hall. They report having encountered little resistance to their relationship in what is described as "a conservative platteland dorp".[366]

It's difficult to know how much weight to attribute to a tale such as this. As unexpected as it may be, the story also makes a good deal of sense: because small town residents must interact with one another frequently, they are forced to look beyond the abstraction of stereotypes. Furthermore, these guys embody the law, an archetypal masculine role (in spite of advances women may have made in the field). What is clear is that the struggle over gay marriage in South Africa was not put to rest after the requisite legislation was passed. Individuals personifying other types of authority have guaranteed that the implementation of legal regulations butts up against significant resistance.

There is more than a little irony in the fact that traditional beliefs unexpectedly provided an important opening for the accommodation of non-traditional marital arrangements within the framework of South African law. In 1998 Parliament ruled that customary polygamous marriages were legal, thereby setting a precedent for marriage not being defined exclusively as the union between a man and a woman. A year later, a court ruled that unions under Islamic law, which may also include a man and more than one woman, were legal as well.

In 1999 the Constitutional Court also struck down sodomy laws that had remained on the books from previous regimes; previously it had been a Schedule 1 offence like murder or rape, punishable by life in prison. While seldom enforced, it could be, at the whim of particular officials. And a series of rulings incrementally recognised the legitimacy of enduring gay relationships. The military and police banned anti-gay discrimination (2002); the Constitutional Court declared it legal for same-sex couples to adopt children (2002); and same-sex partners were granted inheritance and survivors' benefits identical to heterosexual couples (2003).

In 2005 the Constitutional Court found that the Marriage Act was unconstitutional, and ordered that a new one must be enacted by Parliament by 1 December 2006. If it did not do so, rights guaranteed under the Marriage Act would automatically be extended to heterosexual and homosexual couples alike. Parliament put forward a Civil Unions Bill, rather than declare that marriage was an option for all people regardless of their sexual orientation, and that triggered an association in many people's minds with a form of oppression that they knew all too well.

That system, of course, was apartheid, which offers a surfeit of odious doctrines and emblems for comparison. A South African law professor objected that limiting gays to civil unions epitomised the discredited strategy of "separate but equal". By the terms of the bill, same-sex unions could not be called marriages, except at the ceremony; marriage officers would have the option to refuse to participate; and the arrangement was only to be available to same-sex couples. This scholar characterised the proposal as a "second class form of legal recognition", humiliatingly crafted "apartheid-style".[367] And a professor of law at Cambridge reflected on the past and declared, "I can already picture the park benches, sprayed with a twist on that old hoary prohibition: Straights only."[368]

In another instance, this measure afforded a self-identified heterosexual woman the opportunity to reassess her country's history, as well as that of her own family. As a child growing up on the racially privileged end of apartheid, she contemplated the ways in which her parents may have been complicit in sustaining an oppressive regime. She questioned, for example, whether her parents should have taken her to a racially restrictive beach when she was a child. The Civil Unions Bill forced her to engage in some post-apartheid soul-searching, from which she concluded, "[F]or me, personally, getting married can no more be justified in 2005 than sitting in a WHITES ONLY train carriage could be in 1980."[369]

Of course words as bold as these were written from a relatively comfortable social position, and it's impossible to know how this person (or anyone else for that matter) would conduct themselves at the coal face in a morally ambiguous situation, where their sense of wellbeing or economic and personal security might truly be at issue. Nevertheless, it represents a munificent show of emotional support from someone who need not say anything at all.

The issue was visually condensed and skewered in an editorial cartoon by Zapiro, whose work is well known on the editorial scene in South Africa. The drawing entitled "What religions want …" (*The Star*, 21 September 2006) depicts a male–female couple along with a man outfitted in a religious frock, standing on the front steps of a church. All of them are beaming, and facing a throng of well-wishers. A banner strung overhead between two trees reads "Apartheid Grand Reopening". On the church itself, signs announce "marriage", and "no gays". Meanwhile, a scowling bureaucrat sits at a table set up at the rear of the church and calls forward same-sex couples. The signs there decree "separate but equal (ho ho) civil unions", and "gays only".

Apartheid, and its demise, is still relatively fresh in the minds of many South Africans. Drawing overt links between life before and life since is, therefore, a powerful rhetorical strategy. No one wishes to be tarred with that oppressive brush today, or to have anything that they are doing be pigeonholed in this manner. When people condemn their opponents by creating such analogies, eradicating the taint becomes a tall order.

All these rulings took place on a political level far removed from the grassroots. But the sentiments of a key segment of the public were aired elsewhere. For example, attendees of a three-day conference hosted by the National House of Traditional Leaders (NHTL) predicted that homosexual couples risked being ostracised as pariahs, and ran the danger of becoming victims of violence in rural communities. Spokesperson Sibusiso Nkosi declared, "Traditional leaders have vowed to make it their mission for the coming five years to campaign against this wicked, decadent and immoral western practice." Moreover, they argued that only a man can pay lobola for a woman, while simultaneously lamenting escalating lobola costs in general.[370]

The Congress of Traditional Leaders of SA (Contralesa) played the trump card of communal tribal land, which continues to be doled out by traditional leaders. The organisation balked at the Civil Unions Bill, and its president Patekile Holomisa declared same-sex couples would not be eligible for land because "it was not humanly possible for same-sex couples to have children". That seemed consistent with customary beliefs (albeit a fallacy), whereas his statement that "same-sex marriages are undemocratic" is simply puzzling.[371] A letter-to-the-editor writer, representing a religious perspective, put a fine point on the argument by declaring, "[T]he South African constitution ... is only 10 years old, and cannot prescribe mankind's behaviour shaped over millennia."[372]

In the end, Parliament passed the Civil Unions Bill into law on 30 November 2006. The Civil Unions Act allows any two people over the age of 18 the choice of entering into either a civil partnership or a marriage partnership; this, of course, includes same-sex couples. Heterosexual couples are additionally covered by the Marriage Act and the Customary Marriages Act. So while sex-same couples are now legally recognised by the state, a residue of parallel or inferior status still lingers.

You can't Pick your Family

Humankind's relatives in the animal kingdom span a broad and diverse chain of interconnections. We may not be able to pick our families, but we can choose to acknowledge and honour some species more than others.

Gay activists have rallied behind penguins: as noted in Chapter 1, a pair of males in New York's Central Park Zoo successfully incubated a fertilised egg and then raised the chick, certifying an alternative family configuration. And some have embraced an example of closer kin, the bonobo, or pygmy chimpanzee. Their gentle, cooperative ways and blissful ambisexual activity provide a striking option to the usual way we characterise modern life in beastly terms, such as "dog-eat-dog" and "running a rat race".

But equating human and animal behaviour is more typically a way to put someone down rather than to praise them or identify with them. In a well-publicised American incident in 1993, an Israeli-born student at the University of Pennsylvania hollered, "Shut up, you water buffalo [*behema*]" at a group of female African-American students, after his studying was disturbed by shouting beneath his dormitory window. The women took it to be a racial slur; he countered that this was an insult commonly used in his society for someone who is being rude. Nevertheless, he was accused of racial harassment and subjected to a campus disciplinary procedure. An interesting example of cross-cultural misunderstanding, some people cited this at the time as evidence of a climate of "political correctness" run amok, particularly on campuses.[373]

South Africa's version of this sort of racial sniping occurred in 2005, when Malegapuru Makgoba, vice chancellor of the University of KwaZulu-Natal (UKZN), published a caustic critique of what he branded the wrath of the country's white men who have been unseated from their exclusive positions of power during the post-apartheid era. Purportedly drawing upon the work of Harvard psychologist Howard Gardner, and comparing white men to baboons, Makgoba declared, "The dethroned male becomes depressed, quarrelsome and a spoiler of the new order until he gets ostracised from the colony to lead a frustrated, lonely and unhappy life. This is our 'primate heritage'."[374]

Makgoba mentioned the Boeremag conspirators (Chapter 3) as an extreme case of this phenomenon, but cited the more commonplace exemplar of white men who are unenthusiastic and resistant to Black Economic Empowerment, critical of black executives, or who emphasise any negative economic consequences they may have personally experienced since 1994 rather than recognise and appreciate a broader perspective on current conditions. Makgoba predicted the eventual triumph of African values and sentiments throughout the population, and issued the following challenge to disgruntled and retrogressive individuals of European origin to undergo a cultural makeover: "He should learn kwaito, dance like Lebo [Mathosa], dress like Madiba, enjoy eating 'smiley and walkies' and attend 'lekgotla' and socialise at our taverns."[375] Makgoba was issuing a manifesto, a behavioural and attitudinal litmus test that could parse to what degree any person, white *or* black, embodied "Africanness". The cultural battle was thus engaged.

Makgoba is no stranger to controversy. In 1995 his appointment as the first black vice chancellor at the University of the Witwatersrand polarised academics along racial lines. In 2006 he banned sociologist Ashwin Desai, one of the outspoken critics of the 2002 Afro–Indian dialogue over Mbongeni Ngema's song, from attaining a post at the University of KwaZulu-Natal. That same year the Freedom of Expression Institute claimed Makgoba was responsible for a "climate of fear" there.[376]

Because of the unique history of that province, Makgoba's bristling over the sluggish progress of black African achievement was actually more complicated than he articulated. "Makgoba's problem does not really lie with white males, but with Indians," one report stated. "[T]he largest group of staff as a whole is of Indian descent. Whites dominate academic staff and professorships. But the lower you go down the rungs of the academic staff, the more disproportionate the Indian dominance becomes ... The future is Indian."[377]

But since Makgoba framed his argument in black and white, that's how it subsequently unfolded. One UKZN academic feared that Makgoba's outlook could instigate witch hunts within universities, or prompt white academics to passively withdraw from participation in campus life, a development that a "skills-short society" could ill afford.[378] Others clucked their annoyance and disillusionment that a prominent black African like Makgoba was projecting a prototype of power that duplicated the authoritarian dimensions of the previous regime – chest thumping rather than exploring ways in which power might be shared collaboratively.[379]

Still others were indignant that a double standard was at play. The author of one letter-to-the-editor remarked, "If I were to write a full-page article about similarities between baboon behaviour and the thought processes of black people, I would be called an extreme racist."[380] In fact, prior to this occasion the Human Rights Commission had decided that labelling someone a baboon was a human rights infringement, after three white men had called a black African petrol attendant by that term. But the SAHRC did not weigh in during this debate, underscoring the rather widespread feeling that different rules may apply to different racial groups.[381]

Just how complex this becomes is illustrated by a legal tussle between a local government official and another woman in the Eastern Cape in 2004. Nosimo Balindlela, provincial minister for sports, arts and culture, filed a civil claim of R100 000 "against a [presumably white] woman Erika de Beyer, who called her a baboon in the parking lot of an East London shopping centre".

De Beyer had previously apologised and paid a fine of R1500. A journalist explained, "What is interesting about this particular incident is that the baboon jibe was uttered, they say, in impeccable Xhosa – meaning that both women were operating in the same language system ... It is not unusual to find Xhosa-speaking whites in the Eastern Cape (or Tswana-speaking whites in the North West Province, or Zulu-speaking ones in KwaZulu-Natal, for that matter)." This raises knotty questions regarding racial licence and legitimacy. The writer concluded, "If you call a black person a monkey or a baboon in Afrikaans or English, the implication is clear. If you call them a baboon in their own language, which has effectively become your own, what then?"[382]

Makgoba's prescription for authenticity riled those who reject essentialist notions of race. "Eating 'smiley and walkies'," wrote one man, "might, to the confused and angry mind, seem authentic expressions of African culture. In reality, they are no more than the unfortunate legacies of apartheid and the severe economic repression."[383] And another questioned Makgoba's experiential relativism and conjectured, "Will there be special cultural police to ensure, in his [Makgoba's] words, that 'more racist white males are being caught, fingered out, and revealed'?" And might the net of enforcement be cast even wider, he wondered: "What if a black man likes Mozart, ballroom dancing, French cuisine, and Sandton socialising?"[384]

Makgoba's critique seemed to be addressed to social and intellectual elites:

businessmen, academics, and other knowledge workers. But populist-oriented spokesmen from the Afrikaner community spoke out against him as well, including popular singer Steve Hofmeyr (who berated him for not choosing to take part in traditional Afrikaner rituals) and rightwing leader Dan Roodt (who countered Makgoba's apparent social Darwinism by cynically arguing that if black Africans were as superior as the vice chancellor was claiming, they would not need compensatory measures like BEE and affirmative action).[385]

For the most part, however, Makgoba's outlook seemed to be a cautionary tale for anyone – liberal whites or "sell-out" blacks – who would dare criticise the performance of newly empowered black Africans, be they in the boardroom or the president's retinue. One familiar political commentator deplored what he feared could be interpreted as "a symptom of something we might call a little wave of new black South African reactionary fascism".[386] Were this true, adherence to party lines, both literally and figuratively, could quash independent action and free inquiry.

Joining the Club

As president, Thabo Mbeki characterised post-apartheid South Africa as the era and setting for an African Renaissance. Furthermore, he put himself forward as the philosopher king to reign over what he envisioned as a vibrant efflorescence of ideas, art and design reflecting indigenous knowledge and experience. This, according to him, was the potentiality that the freedom from colonialism and apartheid had brought forth.

And what might this distinctively Africanised theorising sound like? Mbeki provided a first-rate example in one of his weekly online communiqués, published in 2007. A scandal had broken out during the preceding weeks over medical care in the impoverished Eastern Cape after a local newspaper published the results of its two-month investigation into conditions at the maternity wards of Frere Hospital in East London. The findings were shocking: 2000 babies were stillborn over a 14-year period, in a place that reporters described as woefully under-staffed and under-equipped and where the standard of care was inadequate, even bordering on negligent in some respects.

Prompted by these findings, Deputy Health Minister Nozizwe Madlala-Routledge made an unannounced visit to the hospital and declared that conditions there represented a national disaster. But when her boss Minister Manto Tshabalala-Msimang conducted her own inspection, she concluded that the earlier assessment was inaccurate. One report revealed, "her [Manto's] flunkies raided another Eastern Cape hospital ... That way, when the Minister arrived, she [saw] spruced-up wards full of incubators and fluffy bedding. Mysteriously, pot plants arrived out of nowhere for the ministerial visit and, just as mysteriously, disappeared soon afterwards."[387] Equipment, ranging from heart monitors and blood pressure machines to new refuse bins, was put in place as well, according to an article with the acerbic title, "Quick! A broom! Manto's coming!"[388]

Within a month of the story's release, the Health Department announced a major infusion of new equipment and personnel into the hospital. Moreover, the deputy minister was fired, as were the hospital's medical superintendent and two of its senior doctors, for backing her. The president and his health minister, meanwhile, closed ranks against all critics, denying that there had been a problem in East London.[389]

Mbeki's account of the claims and counter-claims drew upon an idiosyncratic array of sources, ranging from Charles Dickens to Marx to miniskirts – all of his references bearing suspiciously Western pedigrees.[390] Mbeki contrasted the objectivist, fact-based position represented by Thomas Gradgrind in *Hard Times*; the conundrum of short skirts of the 1960s (did they reveal a woman's sexiness, or merely provocatively hint at what remained covered?); and the postmodernist predicament: reality consists of multiple "truths", and the astute observer must thoughtfully deconstruct the motives and vested interests that lie behind each version before accepting any of them.

This pastiche of ideas might sound extremely clever. But Mbeki used this argument to privilege the perspective of his minister, and discredit the validity of the perspectives presented by critics. "Here we have a clear demonstration of the problem our country faces," Mbeki claimed, "when are facts, facts and a truthful representation of objective reality, or should we resign ourselves to the notion that we live in a post-modern world, which includes permissible 'rejection of truth as correspondence to reality'!"[391] The president and his followers faced a similar challenge when they bucked the global medical perspective on HIV/AIDS and insisted upon a distinctively African therapy for those stricken by the pandemic.[392]

But cleverness such as this holds the worth of a substantially devalued currency in a country where a majority of people would likely respond that the country's problems are less semantic and philosophical than Mbeki alleged, and much more unadorned – issues such as poverty, unemployment, lack of basic services, and crime, for instance. And invoking postmodernism seemed exceedingly inappropriate and insensitive to the feelings of the hundreds of mothers who had lost their offspring in that East London facility.

Mbeki wrote off the *Daily Dispatch*, the newspaper that broke the distressing story, as imagining itself to be "virtually oracular". And he tried to shame people who condemned his leadership and his officials by declaring, "The simple truth is that the DA [the Democratic Alliance, that challenged the government's findings], perhaps taking advantage of the liberties afforded by postmodernism, is making the statement that everything is Fact – truth corresponding with reality – if it communicates a negative message about the ANC and the government."[393] In the end, for all his invocation of trendy terminology and literary allusions, Mbeki was the one falling back on grand narratives and insisting upon dividing the world in Manichean terms.

Native Intelligence

In March of 2006, about a year and a half before the hospital scandal broke, an announcement heralded a conference with the provocative title "Where are the natives? The black Intelligentsia today". It concurrently introduced a new enterprise, the Native Club, to be based at the Africa Institute of South Africa (AISA, an independent think tank). The logic behind both ventures was the "full de-colonisation of the African intelligentsia", the revalorisation of indigenous knowledge and values, and the development of a distinctive South African cultural identity. All these activities were deemed to be necessary given the obliteration of local cultures due to the twin onslaught of colonialism and apartheid. These endeavours were designed to offset centuries of spiritual and cultural damage.[394] And by invoking "native" they exploited the increasingly familiar strategy by previously marginalised people to embrace terms of oppression and redirect their meaning to something affirmative.

Statistics that proponents of the conference and the Native Club offered were impressive in demonstrating the need for amplifying public debate and boosting the range of participants within it. Only 5% of the South African population buys books other than for educational purposes, and merely 21 out of 123 members of the Publishers' Association of South Africa is headed by someone who is black.[395] Moreover, black Africans represent nearly 80% of the population and yet author only 3.6% of scientific publications. Whites, who make up approximately 10% of the country's total, produce 92.5% of scientific work.[396] And whites fill at least two-thirds of the positions at leading universities.[397] "Do they [black intellectuals] enjoy imparting knowledge that has been produced by 'others', when they have the capabilities to be the masters of their own story?" one person asked. Appraising the racial imbalances within the publishing industry in particular, he concluded, "somebody else is talking and black people are listening".[398]

To justify the Native Club, its chairman Titus Mafolo, also an advisor to President Mbeki, repeated the argument marshalled by traditional leaders who decry Western contamination of customary practices, or the objectionable situation whereby one group continually speaks for, and represents, another's experiences. He lamented, "Though we are Africans, many South Africans seem to have an identity crisis. Through our dress, music, cuisine, role models and reference points we seem to be clones of Americans and Europeans."[399]

While there is a broad consensus that the racial imbalance in knowledge production, distribution and consumption in South Africa is acute, the proper way to counteract this remains very much an open question. And as advocates and opponents of the Native Club squared off, both sides revealed how heavily saddled nearly everyone in this society is with the baggage of past struggles, historical disparities and mutual suspicions, and infected by bad blood.

The Natives are Wrestling

Just as some of those who were offended that Malegapuru Makgoba's vision of leadership was both stale and demonstrably harmful from an historical perspective, critics of the Native Club were repulsed by what they imagined to be its resemblance to a now-discredited group, the Afrikaner Broederbond ("League of Brothers"). A secret society with roots back to 1918, the Broederbond promoted Afrikaner nationalism following their demoralising defeat in the Anglo-Boer War, and sought to counterbalance the power of English-speaking whites. Throughout three-quarters of a century the Broederbond was the incubator for racially restrictive policies, a source of backroom economic dealmaking, and a place for nurturing national leadership; its roster boasted every prime minister during the apartheid years of 1948 to 1994.[400]

The idea of a "Native Broederbond" was frequently invoked during the Native Club debate, with great apprehension regarding what it could devolve into. One man wrote, "They will eventually become drunk with arrogance and power, and end up being unacceptable ... All my life I have seen how organisations like the Native Club and the Broederbond end up becoming morally corrupt with self-enrichment and jobs for pals."[401]

Another concern revolved around who would be eligible to participate. Some notable black personalities were conspicuously left out, such as *Mail & Guardian* columnist John Matshikiza, radio and television commentator Tim Modise, and freedom of expression advocate Console Tleane. A spokesperson for the Department of Arts and Culture bluntly delineated where he thought the line should be drawn: "I am troubled by the rise of a hand-picked bunch of black commentators and public intellectuals who opine on freedom of thought, speech and independence and who diss the government at every opportunity. They are coconut intellectuals: black outside, white inside."[402]

He was describing what is commonly written off as "Afropessimism", an attempt to sidetrack criticism of government officials by focusing on the alleged negativity and betrayal of their detractors instead. "If you listen carefully," the Arts and Culture spokesperson wrote, "they reinforce racist assumptions about ... non-existent threats to freedom of expression by the government ... they limit their role to throwing stones at the government ... For them, it is all about corruption, Zimbabwe, Zuma and the alleged shutting down of space [for open debate]."[403] From this individual's perspective, the government was functioning just fine, thank you very much, save for the poisoned pens and wagging tongues of some wearying critics.

But a person who proudly wore the coconut label responded, "To qualify for this club you must be black black. How do you determine that? Do you use the pencil test, the nose test, or the head test?"[404] She was citing some infamous techniques of apartheid-era racial classification boards that relied upon putatively "scientific" criteria to categorise people. For example, if a pencil stuck through a person's hair became caught by its texture, this "confirmed" his or her Africanness. And that had profound consequences for his or her identity and opportunities.[405] Once again, it also brought to mind Malegapuru Makgoba's constricted vision of cultural Africanness. And invoking yet another historical precedent, the same writer remarked, "They remind me of Sabra (the South African Bureau of Racial Affairs), the apartheid government's think-tank of non-Natives, who thought about the Natives all the time, to the point of wanting to control them."[406]

The issue of control surfaced in another respect: concern that members of the Native Club would be kept on a short leash by the government. Minister Pallo Jordan at first refused to answer whether or not the Department of Arts and Culture was financially underwriting the conference and the group. But he eventually admitted the fact in a popular Afrikaans-language newspaper. For many this cosy arrangement represented a fundamental clash between intellectual work (predicated upon an expansive exploration of ideas without a predetermined interest in the outcome) and government service (with the expectation of loyalty to particular policies and incumbents). Both the Democratic Alliance and Cosatu opposed the Native Club on the belief that it was essentially a "front" for or branch of the ANC.

Sceptics, both black and white, continually referred to the danger of participants becoming praise singers and propagandists for the power structure, yes-men, apologists and ideologues for the status quo, hired hands (and minds) to maintain hegemony. From this perspective, the integrity of the participants would inevitably be compromised, corrupted and co-opted. The self-proclaimed "coconut intellectual" cited above further wrote, "[Y]ou need only write what we tell you to write, then you'll be admitted. You see, that is what is meant by black."[407]

Never one to pass on the opportunity to skewer the foibles of people with power, or aspiring to it, comedian Pieter-Dirk Uys voiced support via his alter-ego Evita Bezuidenhout, with tongue firmly in cheek: "[W]hy shouldn't blacks have their own place? In the past it was called the township, a Bantustan or a jail. But now it is a beautiful, elegant venue that has all the best in catering facilities, comfort and security. They deserve it, *siestog*." She did not whinge or wallow in self-pity for what she had lost; on the contrary, in the spirit of social transformation and reconciliation, she was willing to roll her dress sleeves up and contribute to the success of this new project: "Of course, as a white Afrikaner woman I won't be in the hallowed halls of black intellectual power. I will be in the Native Club kitchen. No native wants to have that job any more."[408]

One white commentator was particularly blunt in his assessment of the situation, however: "The natives get the goodies," wrote Robert Greig, "the rest – the niggers – stay outside."[409] And veteran journalist Max du Preez also refused to temper his anger and suspicions. He labelled the architects of this enterprise "a bunch of pompous, self-important fat cats" spouting "pure emotive victim-speak". Du Preez continued, "The Native Club appears to be dominated by men who see their calling as providing intellectual legitimacy to the present ruling elite. This is not surprising, because many of them depend on government contracts and handouts to pay their monthly instalments on their BMWs." In the final analysis, he rejected the principle of racial or ideological exclusivity wedded to analytical inquiry by posing a question, and offering the following prescription: "[W]hy do they have to hide behind a new apartheid? ... Keep the name. Keep the black leadership. Drop the apartheid."[410]

Black responses were equally as forceful. "[P]eople are still afraid whenever darkies meet on their own," wrote one man.[411] "White hysteria," claimed another.[412] And several people dismissed the idea that the Native Club could represent "reverse racism".[413] In such an overheated atmosphere, non-whites even became opponents of one another, citing the same cultural reference to different ends. One man offered up Steve Biko's Black Consciousness as the obvious model for the Native Club, while another remarked, "Steve Biko's motto was 'I write what I like'" – a staunch refusal to toe *any* ideological line.[414]

Important implications for life in the academy lay beyond this debate. In the past, access to higher education was severely limited for black Africans, and so-called "bush universities" produced technicians, not intellectuals.[415] But now, if the reflections and ideas of a select group of black Africans were being privileged by the government, people of different races and opinions would likely be marginalised in higher education. Frequent references to "settler intellectual domination" during this controversy made it clear that academic advancement will likely be increasingly tied to racial membership and ideological acceptability in the future.

Moreover, sectors of government seem to be at cross-purposes on the subject of the production of original knowledge. Only a year later, Education Minister Naledi Pandor announced a radical restructuring of South Africa's universities, flipping the ratio of students pursuing the humanities (including social sciences and the arts) in favour of business, engineering and technology. Social sciences graduates more than doubled from 1994 to 2004. But under the new policy, humanities enrolments would be slashed and thereafter strictly limited; the goal "to produce more job-ready graduates" in more applied fields would be foregrounded.[416]

On the one hand, a rapidly developing country like South Africa has a glaring need for technically trained professionals. But on the other hand, a campus with fewer students pursuing courses of study that are inherently questioning, namely the humanities, social sciences and the arts, are potentially less volatile places. And a society where a smaller proportion of people have received an education that values open inquiry is one where the population would also be less questioning and easier to manage. A former dean of education critiqued the new guidelines by declaring, "If you have only the sciences, you run the risk of creating engineers without ethics and doctors without values."[417]

But if a government wishes to reduce critical scrutiny of its policies and practices, this is an adroit strategy.

CHAPTER 5

The Sounds of Silence:
Media Rights and Wrongs

Sooner or later those who try to falsify reality to achieve partisan
objectives discover that lies have very short legs.

Thabo Mbeki, 2007

One writer noted during the controversy over the Native Club, "We have witnessed a fierce ideological struggle for control of the media. Its products remain largely [E]urocentric."[418] And after Jacob Zuma successfully escaped prosecution in his trials for corruption and rape (both in 2006), he turned against what had become an irritating thorn in his side: the media.

Zuma filed multimillion-rand defamation lawsuits against publishers, editors, writers and the cartoonist Zapiro, each of whom had taken him to task for his alleged criminal behaviour, as well as for his public conduct inside the courtroom and beyond. For someone who has been so strongly identified with a particular song, perhaps it's not surprising that another of his targets became radio station 94.7 Highveld Stereo, for playing the satirical tune "My Name Is Zuma" by Darren "Whackhead" Simpson.[419]

These episodes and others have raised important issues about the functions and limitations of the media and open dialogue within a newly democratic society. The ways in which these debates have been shaped and how they have played out have been consequential for what gets reported, the range of opinion and material available for public view, how freedom of expression has butted up against the law, and the ways in which professional journalists, artists and others have learned to conduct their business.

Style Wars

Some of Zuma's supporters sported "100% Zulu Boy" T-shirts during his rape trial, but Cape Town-based Laugh it Off Promotions (LIO) broadened the stylistic war by creating another design, one which was decidedly uncomplimentary. In a manner that has become the company's signature, it chose a corporate logo and subverted its original meaning. In this instance LIO selected the distinctive typeface used by Puma brand shoes, plopped in the name Zuma, and swapped the big cat with the silhouette of a

93

provocatively-posed nude woman, resembling those that commonly decorate the mud flaps on trucks. It constituted one more critical strike against a public figure who had disgraced his office with sleazy behaviour.

The people behind Laugh it Off have been labelled brand terrorists, ad busters, trademark rebels and culture jammers. And that is by their admirers. Representatives of companies that have been targeted by LIO's makeovers are more prone to invoke such terms as parasites, counterfeiters or thieves. And these detractors include some of the world's largest multinational corporations, such as Coca-Cola, Nestlé, Colgate-Palmolive and Pfizer.

A young entrepreneur with a background in journalism and media studies named Justin Nurse heads Laugh it Off.[420] He and his university buddies started engaging in guerilla marketing when they were students. He explained the meaning of the firm's name during an interview: whenever someone in the group decided to skip a class, it was a case of "laughing it off". That phrase became "like a battle cry for apathy". But over time the expression evolved to represent its opposite: "Get your ideas off the couch, no use sitting at home and saying 'this is fucked'. Laugh it Off is about effecting change, doing something about it."[421]

The company's modus operandi reflects the do-it-yourself ethic of twenty-something, media-savvy activists. Its general formula weaves together a fresh sensibility with a keen sense of satire, frequently amplified with a touch of the risqué. In Nurse's words, the inordinate amount of power that corporations wield within the media environment "really grates my carrot". His goal is to be "an independent media voice".[422]

Unless you're a target of LIO, you'll more than likely crack a smile when you see its products. One of LIO's early T-shirt designs spun off the corporate logo of a well-known South African bank. LIO substituted a phallus for a flagpole, and retained the motto "Simpler. Better. Faster". But it changed "Standard Bank" to read "Standard Wank" instead. In 2001 police raided a store in Johannesburg to seize its inventory of the shirts, only to discover that the stock had already been sold. The bank registered a complaint with the Department of Trade and Industry for trademark infringement, a precursor of trouble to come in the future.

An article in the investigative publication *Noseweek* claimed that a search-and-seizure warrant was "improperly issued" in this case because it was authorised by a section of the Trade Marks Act that refers to counterfeit goods, which LIO's T-shirt was not. Moreover, the article questioned the priorities of police who were poised to mobilise six teams of inspectors in this case yet seem so woefully inadequate in responding to the country's notably high rate of violent crime.[423]

At the hands of LIO, the motto of telecommunications giant MTN, "Hello the Future" transmogrified into "HIV – Hello the Future"; the National Lottery's slogan was changed from "Tata ma'chance, Tata ma'millions" to "Tata ma'change", with one stick figure holding up another at gunpoint (who is generally seen leaping for joy) in "National Robbery"; "Enjoy Coca-

Cola. You Can't Beat the Feeling" became "Enjoy Corruption. You can't beat the stealing"; Husky brand dog food was altered to Horny, accompanied by a picture of two dogs humping one another; the Black Like Me cosmetic line gave way to Blacks Like Me; and Lego became Legover, with two figures made from the popular plastic playthings shown in a sexual position.

Although some companies have "laughed off" these corporate caricatures, many others have had lawyers send letters demanding that LIO desist. Up to 20 have threatened to pursue legal relief.[424] The first to actually carry through was SABMiller.

By any measure, SABMiller is a corporate colossus. Operating 111 breweries in 24 countries, it is the second-largest brewer in the world. It dominates the market in developing regions such as Central America, Asia and Africa. South African Breweries (the SAB in SABMiller) was established in 1895 and controls 99% of the South African market.[425] Its top three brands – Carling Black Label, Castle and Hansa – account for more than 80% of local sales, and they all command loyal followings and broad brand recognition.[426] SABMiller's corporate profile has been heightened through its sponsorship of all manner of sporting events. In both 1999 and 2000, the company invested R20 million in advertising,[427] propelling its numerous brands of beer into the pantheon of South African icons.

So when LIO spun off a stinging T-shirt parody of Carling Black Label ("America's lusty lively lager since 1852"), it pricked the giant and roused it into fighting mode, triggering a legal clash that took three years to conclude. LIO changed Black Label to Black Labour, Carling Beer to White Guilt, and "Brewed in South Africa" to "No regard given worldwide", while retaining the distinctive design, colours, and typescript of the original packaging. The re-engineered motto then read "Black Labour/White Guilt/Africa's lusty lively exploitation since 1652/No regard given worldwide". SABMiller is Dutch-owned, so the citation of 1652 refers to the arrival of Jan van Riebeeck at the Western Cape coast, the inauguration of colonialism in this part of the world, and the commencement of racial inequities that persist to the present day.[428] (A later version read "Black neighbour/White fence/Africa's lusty, lively land reclamation".)

SABMiller filed a notice of motion against Laugh it Off Promotions in May 2002, the established company pitting itself against a fledgling enterprise and its 25-year-old director, Justin Nurse. The company contended that it had been portrayed in a racially prejudicial and inflammatory light, and that LIO intended to harm its reputation. SABMiller was adamant in enumerating its efforts to treat its workers fairly, and felt that LIO's take-off was distasteful and potentially quite damaging.

Nurse, on the other hand, argued more philosophically, taking the position of the iconoclast: he asserted that the reverence accorded this brand of beer made it subject to open debate. This confrontation pitted a maverick proponent of unrestricted freedom of expression against the privileges of legally protected commercial speech. Nurse advocates "'ideological' jujitsu, a

Japanese martial art that uses the opponent's weight against him, in an anti-brand war".[429]

LIO's spoof had clearly touched a nerve. Not only were financial interests at stake for SABMiller, Nurse had dared to insert the issue of race into public dialogue, raising thorny issues of how business interests have perpetuated and profited from the racial exploitation of labour throughout South Africa's difficult history. And SABMiller, it seemed, was being singled out for scrutiny.

Moreover, alcohol is not simply the basis of many a jol; its production and distribution are closely entwined with race relations in South Africa. White-dominated governments maintained a monopoly on the manufacture of beer offered for sale to black Africans in urban areas, and operated the only legal drinking establishments for them. Farmworkers were compensated using the "dop" system (legal from 1928 to 1961), which forced them to accept part of their wages in alcohol or allowed them to buy it on credit, and thereby contributed to rampant alcoholism, perpetual impoverishment, and a staggering rate of foetal alcohol syndrome in succeeding generations. And while the legacy of residential segregation is still obvious throughout the country, one notably enduring example of separate commercial amenities are the side doors that still cater to black Africans at many liquor stores. These lead to a small area stocking mostly beer and a few types of cheaper liquor favoured by this clientele, in marked contrast to the more expensive selections on offer in the main store. SAB is particularly implicated in this history: 80% of its sales come from quart bottles sold in black African townships, and 90% of the company's sales overall come from the black African market.[430]

Nurse's personal biography and his subsequent professional endeavours are inextricably tied up with events of a national magnitude, such as the end of apartheid. He characterises it as "nothing short of what September 11th did to New York".[431] His social and artistic sensibilities were shaped by the dramatic experiences that unfolded around him as a child, and the dissonance he discovered between the way his parents' generation understood the world and acted within it, and how political changes destroyed established assumptions and patterns of behaviour, discrediting much of the past. He was coming of age just as his country was being reborn. He reflects, "For me growing up, as a thirteen-year-old just starting high school, suddenly I had black kids in my class. And it was great, cool. [And he and his classmates realised] Well now, this political prisoner Nelson Mandela, who you sort of read about, and this whole history that we learned, all of that [as it turned out] actually isn't true."

Nurse, like other socially conscious young adults, has been acutely aware of the privileges his race and class position have afforded him. At university he readily detected the disparity between the impoverishment of local black Africans and the relative comfort he and his friends enjoyed. He recalls, "We were doing our part, as it were, and sort of easing our white guilt by employing a maid three times a week. Hey, we could have had a maid once a week and washed our dishes ourselves, but that was sort of doing our part, and that is how white South Africans feel a lot of the time."[432] To his dismay, even today white South Africans make small conciliatory gestures without addressing the core issues around racism, or fundamentally moderating its pervasive and lasting effects.

At the most basic level, Black Labour/White Guilt was an attempt to raise an issue of great consequence that is all-too-often ignored. The T-shirt was less a smart-aleck prank and more a call for collective soul searching. The prospect that LIO might be legally impeded in its campaign to address the country's racist legacy is what fired Nurse's determination to fight back. As he sees it, the issue of race "is very often swept under the rug in South Africa, and I am not sure how far we are prepared as a country to go beneath the surface. Because with all the things that we've had, including the TRC, it is always skimmed over, on the surface. [Archbishop Desmond] Tutu never really pushed it; I mean, he is a very gentle man." Nurse concludes, "I guess that as a country you have to look at how far do you need to go into the past to properly address it and make peace with it?"

Barbie to the Rescue?

When SABMiller's showdown with Laugh it Off Promotions appeared before the Cape High Court in February 2003, LIO's supporters expanded the satiric repertoire to agitprop by displaying placards in the gallery reading "SAB=South African Bullies". Given the behaviour the corporation displayed on many fronts, it was an assertion that would be difficult to refute. For example, Justin Nurse claims that three television producers wished to present his story but were afraid that corporate sponsors would object, and they did not wish to run afoul of them.[433]

One of the legal strategies that LIO adopted was to cite an American precedent from 2002 whereby the Dano-Norwegian pop group Aqua and MCA Records Inc. won the right to continue to market its 1997 hit song "Barbie Girl" without interference from Mattel, Inc. The toy giant had argued that the song violated its trademark, but a court ruled the musicians' right to freedom of speech trumped that protection. LIO's attorney was astute to recognise the resemblance between the intimidating practices of both mega-companies, as well as the similar impulse on the part of creative parties in each case to peel away some of the layers of sanctity that enshroud the signature products of these firms. In the South African instance, a corporation with a near monopoly within the local market came out with guns blazing against an upstart, three-person operation. In the American example, Aqua was but one of the targets in a succession of legal assaults that Mattel has unleashed against artists who have dared to depict Barbie – an obvious target because of being an icon of femininity – in ways that contravene corporate gospel.

For example, Mattel helped block distribution of the film *Superstar: The Karen Carpenter Story* by Todd Haynes and Cynthia Schneider (1987), which used Barbie to represent the popular singer who succumbed to anorexia nervosa (the corporation was joined by A&M Records, for unauthorised use of copyrighted material, and the Carpenter family). In 1999 Mattel sued Canadian stripper and nude model Barbie Doll Benson for trademark infringement; in 2007 it likewise pursued adult entertainer China Barbie. And in 2008 the company was awarded a $100 million judgement against MGA Entertainment, whose wildly successful Bratz line of dolls has made more significant inroads into Barbie's domination of the market than any previous contender. Mattel claimed Bratz were designed by one of its former employees, who later joined the rival company.

In my own run-in with Mattel as one of the curators of *Art, Design and Barbie: The Evolution of a Cultural Icon* (1994), the corporation did not care for references I made in the show's exhibition catalogue to such things as the obvious gay subtext to Ken (especially evident in the model Earring Magic Ken), the legal difficulties faced by the company's founders (indicted on multiple counts of fraud and conspiracy), and the activities of the Barbie Liberation Organization (whose members famously kidnapped Teen Talk Barbies and Talking Duke GI Joe dolls from store shelves, surgically removed their recorded voice boxes, and then gender switched them and snuck them back into stores, to great comic effect).

I wrote at the time how Mattel reminded me of the sort of possessive husbands and boyfriends who are ubiquitous on American talk shows and control everything their wives and girlfriends do, including how they dress and who they associate with. In my essay "How I got screwed by Barbie" I argued, "Mattel acted like a bully with me. But like most bullies, while they may hold a physical advantage, they're acting out of great insecurity."[434] In all these instances an extreme imbalance of resources has generally allowed Mattel to get its way.

Justin Nurse staked out important expressive territory by stating, "Our T-shirt is a piece of art and it's up to the interpreter to interpret it how they want to."[435] In this way he joined the long lineage of South African artists who have imaginatively critiqued oppressive aspects of the status quo, particularly apartheid. Furthermore, it placed him under the umbrella of the freedom of expression clause of the South African Constitution, which specifically guarantees freedom of "artistic creativity".

An interesting precedent to LIO's activities was the work of art student Benz Kotzen, who launched a poster campaign in 1981 depicting a range of faux everyday goods branded with the term "apartheid". The ubiquitous Lion Matches box and logo became Apartheid Doos ("box"; colloquial for a woman's genitalia)/White Elephant brand. The image of a bull and the title Apartheid Twak (Afrikaans for "tobacco" or "bullshit") were emblazoned on a cloth bag of tobacco. And a fabricated can of Apartheid Lager beer was photographed alongside a curbside bearing the actual stencilled street name Laager.[436]

But legal counsel for SAB wished to puncture any attempts on LIO's part to inflate its activities into selfless social criticism. From the company's perspective, LIO was practising bloodsucking, pure and simple: "This feigned altruistic intention [on the part of LIO] is no defence to trademark infringement," a lawyer for SAB declared. "Laugh it Off is using the SAB trademark to generate income for itself. They are piggy-backing to sell their products and there are millions to be made."[437] SAB feared its brand was being diluted.[438] SAB saw harm, not humour.

Aggravation

When the decision was handed down, the court sided with SAB, and LIO was ordered to pay court costs. The judge could not establish that SAB was directly harmed by the slogan Black Labour/White Guilt. Nonetheless, he ruled that the T-shirt was prejudicial toward the brand and violated its protection as a trademark. But he went further, to the surprise of many people. The judge stated that the catchphrase exceeded the boundaries of protected expression and bordered on hate speech, a rather remarkable decree given other allegations where hate speech have either been validated or denied.

SAB's lawyers had claimed that LIO was playing the race card. Justin Nurse wondered, "If you are calling a spade a spade then how can it be deemed hate speech?" A letter-to-the-editor jumped to his defence: "In the Laugh it Off judgement, racism is being confused with anti-racism. It is not hate speech to state publicly that colonialism and apartheid exploited black people in Africa any more than it is to state that Nazis murdered millions of Jews." The writer continued, "The constitutional provision against hate speech should never be used to silence robust statements that draw attention to reality – in fact, that approach simply entrenches the subordination of black people."[439]

What is more, in a declaration that almost seems to be a caricature of justice, the judge further stated, "LIO committed a form of '*aggravated lampooning*' by introducing the race factor, 'something which our constitution and our new democracy are at pains to avoid'."[440] Justin Nurse was puzzled by the concept of "aggravated lampooning" and somewhat at a loss to define it (can there be soothing or sympathetic lampooning?). He reflected, "I guess with aggravated lampooning there is some sort of malicious intent behind it. But it wasn't like we set out with any malicious intent. It was just literally 'Black labour, white guilt'; 'this is a cool idea'."

Many journalists, for whom freedom of speech is sacrosanct, predictably came out in support of LIO in a David-versus-Goliath struggle such as this. The publication *Noseweek* proclaimed, "some multinationals now consider themselves theocracies empowered to have 'non-believers' tried and burnt at the stake," and blasted patent lawyers as "priests of the New Inquisition".[441] A columnist in the *Mail & Guardian* spoke of "corporate fascism" and asked, "Why does it use a steamroller to crush an ant?" Writing before the verdict was announced, Robert Kirby cautioned, "Should the court's decision go against Laugh it Off its precedent will provide business concerns both large and small with a shield behind which they may hinder and obstruct even nominal criticism of themselves or their products. That's a dangerous possibility."[442]

Kirby's rage intensified after the decision had been rendered. In a follow-up opinion piece he remarked on the court order that LIO be held liable to cover substantial legal costs. He characterised SAB's stance as "the baseball-bat approach ... to redress what, in essence, was a minor dig in its ribs," and concluded, "When South African Breweries smashes you in the mouth, you stay smashed in the mouth." Rather than understanding the T-shirts as "aggravated lampooning", Kirby saw "fairly mild parody". He was disturbed by the precedent this decision could set and characterised it as being "close to the point of prescriptive censorship".[443]

But Kirby saved his deepest wrath for an attack on corporate hegemony: SABMiller's culpability for abusive and unethical business practices, and its rather lame attempts to redress past wrongs. Kirby believed that Laugh it Off must have struck an extremely sensitive nerve in the corporate headquarters of SAB, and compared those executives to the Krok brothers, the powerful South African entrepreneurs whose fortune was built upon skin-whitening concoctions sold to black Africans. The columnist wrote, "The Kroks bought off the national conscience by erecting an Apartheid Museum to serve as a sort of moral car wash and valet service to repenting honkies – and we all thought Black Label had cornered the market on white guilt."[444]

Despite the tenor of objections such as these, SABMiller had scored a broad and decisive victory in round one of the legal proceedings. When Laugh it Off raised the question of the extensive history of the white exploitation of blacks in South Africa, SAB was singled out as the exemplar. But a reconfigured logo that was clever in conception ended up running smack up against the limitations of legal language and reasoning.

Barbie Redux: *A Luta Continua*

Laugh it Off was down, but not out: Justin Nurse opted to appeal the Cape High Court decision to the South African Supreme Court in Bloemfontein.

Straight away SABMiller tried to derail LIO's quest: it petitioned the High Court to require Laugh it Off to post security of R350 000 before additional litigation could go forward. That would have proven to be a significant financial hurdle for Nurse and his allies. But the court ultimately sided with LIO in this instance, reasoning that the right to proceed with a case should not be stymied simply because one party was significantly undercapitalised in relation to the other.[445]

Once again, Barbie became a touchstone for legal strategising. This time the precedent that LIO's attorney cited was the case of Tom Forsythe, an American artist who ran afoul of Mattel with his photographs of *Food-Chain Barbie* (picturing the doll skewered and roasting in an oven, included as an ingredient in a wok stir-fry, in a blender, and with her butt positioned at the wrong end of an electric mixer). Forsythe was using Barbie as symbolic shorthand to comment on the objectification of women.

The doll's brand recognition is as well established in America (and worldwide) as Carling Black Label and Castle are in South Africa, thereby "inviting" send-ups. After a five-year-long battle, Forsythe won his fight with Mattel over copyright and trademark infringement. The company was ordered to pay legal costs of nearly $2 million for initiating a frivolous lawsuit.

In round two Laugh it Off argued that SABMiller must satisfy the burden of proof that its trademark had suffered from being parodied. But when judgement was announced in September 2004, LIO was once again the loser. The court upheld Laugh it Off's right to express itself but drew the line at doing so for commercial purposes, in other words, selling T-shirts. LIO was guilty of committing commerce, in other words, not of using proscribed speech.[446] In the court's judgement harm *was* done to SAB's reputation, and it did not believe this ruling would seriously impede freedom of speech. Moreover, LIO was ordered to pay the court costs of SABmark, the division that owns the company's trademarks.

An editorial in the *Mail & Guardian* bemoaned, "If the question is whether big business and lots of money can buy silence, the unequivocal answer in this judgement is yes. And that is a great shame. Secondly, the judges seem to say that even if such harsh criticism would be allowed – one must be careful not to make jokes about race, especially in South Africa." It concluded, "We the people, the judges seem to suggest, are too frail for barbed humour."[447]

SABMiller and Laugh it Off continued to spar with one another: in 2004 SAB forced LIO to remove the company's image from a calendar and a publication, resulting in significant additional production costs.[448] LIO also shut down its website for a time over fear of further lawsuits.

The Supreme Court decision could have ended the saga. But Justin Nurse was determined to see this through to the end. And that meant one additional appeal, this time to the Constitutional Court in Johannesburg.

By then it was 2005. A spokesperson for SABMiller characterised LIO's marketing its products as being comparable to "a person walking into a store and helping himself".[449] A journalist later rallied to LIO's defence by arguing that SAB had "overreacted" and was guilty of "hogging public space". Thinking about the shelter that the courts had guaranteed to corporate interests, he observed, "Mickey Mouse has more protection than Jesus Christ or Muhammad" – an opinion that many fervently religious people would affirm (Chapter 1).

He went further, however, arguing, "We need to reverse the priority currently given to possession of private property over freedom of expression, to money over ideas, to bread over spirit."[450] This opinion highlights how significant LIO's critique actually was: after all, it's not such a radical gesture in a prosperous and democratic society such as the United States to launch an anti-corporate attack. The relative wealth of the country enables such dissent without fear of drastic social consequences. But in South Africa, where the futures of millions of impoverished people depend upon the economy taking off (plus distributing profits in a somewhat equitable fashion), and the democracy is quite young, speaking out against corporate conduct is akin to bad faith at best, heresy or treachery at worst.

Justin Nurse abhors what he sees as a distinct coziness between government officials and corporate heads, one hand washing (and feeding) the other. A spate of corruption scandals confirms this comfortable alliance between elites, yet there is relatively little public outcry against it. Nurse lamented, "South Africans are very keen to just turn a blind eye to things, and to just get on with their lives. They are very ambivalent and apathetic."

Kings, Queens and Pawns

Laugh it Off's confrontation with SABMiller was not anomalous. This conglomerate, like Mattel, is regularly drawn into struggles in which its business and advertising practices are dissected and challenged. It is also not above using satire or taunts itself.

In 2002, for example, SAB found itself on the defensive over one of its ads that irked the Milk Producers' Organisation. It pictured three men dressed in white, drinking milk at a cricket match. But once the guys switched to beer their fun and sense of camaraderie escalated. The trade association did not share SAB's sense of humour and complained to the Advertising Standards Authority that SAB had denigrated its product.[451]

In 2004 SABMiller went head to head with rival Anheuser-Busch in the United States via duelling commercials. The quarrel deteriorated to a level of name-calling worthy of a schoolyard spat. Anheuser-Busch is known as the King of Beers, but Miller dubbed it the President of Beers in a mock political campaign. Anheuser-Busch countered by calling Miller Lite the Queen of Carbs, and mentioned it was owned by a South African, not an American, firm. Anheuser-Busch then boasted that it is "American-born and American-brewed". With national reputations at stake, SAB filed suit to stop Anheuser-Busch's ad campaign, alleging it was sexist and homophobic.[452]

Back home, organisers of the June 16 Roots Festival in 2005 – an alcohol-free talent show held in Soweto for under 16-year-olds on Youth Day, commemorating the uprising that invigorated the anti-apartheid movement in 1976 – also lodged a complaint with the Advertising Standards Authority against SAB for its Pay Your Respects campaign. The ad in question featured a young man pouring a bottle of Castle Lager beer onto the ground as a libation. Beer is, indeed, used to honour the ancestors in this way, but it is *umqombothi*, traditionally brewed beer, made in homes. The image that SAB presented therefore mixed the sacred with the commercial.

Festival personnel blasted the image as "a blatant abuse of drunken profits and an insult to our history". SAB tried to deflect criticism away by noting the campaign was thought up by a black African creative director, and the company felt it showed no disrespect. But the festival manager condemned it nonetheless and countered, "It was SAB-stocked bottle stores that were one of the main targets of public anger in the 1976 uprising."[453]

And an exposé reportedly based on documents provided by an SABMiller employee charged, "SAB evaded revenue services during the apartheid years, exploiting 'black beer consumers and apartheid's "black homeland structures"'." SAB subsequently denied those charges, and fell back on the fact that it had recently been cited as the best employer in South Africa.[454]

Victory at Last?

Laugh it Off's luck finally changed when the Constitutional Court heard its appeal in 2005, the first time that body had heard a trademark infringement case. The Constitutional Court overturned the Supreme Court decision, ruling that SABMiller had not proven that LIO caused material damage to its brand, and noting that LIO was not selling beer but offering a social critique. According to Judge Dikgang Moseneke, "In the court's view, the expression of humour was not only permissible, but necessary for the health of democracy." And Judge Albie Sachs castigated SABMiller by charging, "Simply bringing proceedings against Laugh it Off risked tarnishing Carling Black Label ... more than the sale of 200 T-shirts could ever have done."[455]

The victory was a cause for celebration by those who support freedom of expression. But the lengthy saga was also a cause for concern. Playwright and arts commentator Mike van Graan lamented, "In 10 short years we've become a democracy for the few, for the relatively wealthy. It is those who have resources who may express themselves ... economic forms of censorship (or self-censorship) may yet come to replace apartheid-style political censorship."[456]

Console Tleane of FXI – an organisation that had strongly backed Laugh it Off's legal battle – was troubled by trends he has noted since 1994. Reflecting on the Mbongeni Ngema case, Tleane stated, "It tested the extent to which this country is able to deal with controversial speech. And I think that we failed that test. Rather, we resorted to a quick fix." Asked to characterise the status of freedom of expression in South Africa, he responded, "I'd say it's thriving, and I'd say it's still being framed, and I would also say it's a bit threatened."[457] And former FXI executive director Jane Duncan divided the post-apartheid period into two, stating that between 1994 and about 2000 there was an expansion of freedom of expression from a combination of purging apartheid legislation from the statute books and open debate about the meaning of democracy. But since the millennium, "spaces have started to contract".[458] One of the primary factors she cited was the wide-ranging centralisation that Thabo Mbeki implemented while president.

The battle against a corporate giant did not vanquish Justin Nurse's spirit. His unrepentant, rebel stance remained strong throughout. In a statement that might be considered his personal creed, Nurse revealed "I've always believed that it's easier to get forgiveness than permission."[459] When asked whether he believed there were any sacred cows, any issues that he would not tackle or personalities he would not take on, he replied with an emphatic "no". Even former President Nelson Mandela might ·be fair game. Nurse speculated, "You could look at the things that he has done and say, 'Well shit, we can never go there.' But if it is warranted, then you should. I think that is the nature of satire and comedy: there is always going to be a victim."[460]

The Red and the Black

When Console Tleane noted in 2003 that freedom of expression was flourishing in South Africa, he expanded upon what he meant with an unintentionally prescient statement. "I'd say that it is thriving," he explained, "in the sense that unless I call [President] Mbeki a baboon, I do not have any fears of people coming, or the police coming to my house. Saying 'Mbeki is losing the war on HIV/AIDS,' or 'Mbeki doesn't care about the poor' – we are free to criticise, to engage in things like that." He concluded, "So there are spaces, unless one uses libelous or defamatory language." Just two years on, the use of "baboon" as an epithet became a contentious issue (Chapter 4), and after that the eleventh-hour cancellation of a television screening of a documentary about President Mbeki became the source of a struggle between South Africa's national public broadcaster, the filmmakers, and a public eager to view for itself what the hubbub was about.

The South African Broadcasting Corporation (SABC) put out a call for proposals for a series of documentaries about significant South African personalities. The SABC left it to the creative community to decide who such figures might be, and after sorting through proposals it approved a list of nine subjects, including media personality Felicia Mabuza-Suttle; Supreme Court of Appeal (and subsequently Constitutional Court) Judge, author and AIDS activist Edwin Cameron; opposition party leader Patricia de Lille; and businessman Schabir Shaik, whose conviction for corruption in 2005 implicated his friend Jacob Zuma in wrongdoing as well. The SABC also endorsed a pitch by Broad Daylight Films whose co-producers, radio journalist Redi Direko and filmmaker Ben Cashdan, suggested examining the personal life and career of President Thabo Mbeki.

The idea for the series *Unauthorised* was to present entertaining documentaries that were "quirkier" than mainstream. programming. The mandate was to surprise viewers as much as to simply inform them. In the words of SABC group chief executive Dali Mpofu, these features were intended "to deviate from the routine and documentary format but also to provide the public with information about prominent figures which was provocative, no holds barred, controversial, hard-hitting, and 'unauthorised' by these personalities".[461]

Despite such a bold pronouncement, Ben Cashdan remains a bit puzzled that Broad Daylight's proposal was successful: as an investigative journalist and a self-declared political leftist, Cashdan's stock in trade is dissecting issues around power, economics and ideologies. His professional inspiration comes from the work of others who specialise in "taking the mickey, taking the piss out of people in high office",[462] not from those who uncritically fawn over their official accomplishments. In hindsight, Cashdan sees the conflict with the SABC as somewhat inevitable; its commissioning him to make such a film was "asking for trouble".

The SABC had slotted the Mbeki instalment for broadcast on 17 May 2006. But to the surprise of Cashdan and Direko – as well as untold numbers of ordinary viewers who relied upon the printed schedule – the film was not presented on television that evening. Nor was it until nearly a year and a half later. At a public screening and forum organised by the producers in between those dates, SABC executive Mvuso Mbebe offered a cryptically lyrical rationalisation for the network's decision. Mbebe declared, "he had wanted 'a long red dress', but had received 'a small black mini'."[463] But "Can you make a film or write a book to order?" questioned Cashdan. "I don't think you can."[464] What, then, was *really* bugging the SABC? What did it find truly objectionable?

The SABC claimed that the film implied Thabo Mbeki might be implicated in the assassination of popular South African Communist Party leader Chris Hani in 1993. And while this issue was indeed addressed in the film, it was in the context of Mbeki's revelation in 2001 of an alleged plot against himself, the conspirators purportedly spreading this rumour about illegal conduct in order to defame him. The filmmakers were not, however, pointing a finger at the president; in fact, Redi Direko spoke on camera, debunking the accusation against Mbeki.[465]

The real bombshell was actually a bit of archival footage uncovered by the producers. It featured President Nelson Mandela cautioning Thabo Mbeki at an ANC party conference Mafikeng in 1997 that "a leader elected unopposed may be tempted to 'use that powerful position to settle scores with his detractors' and may 'marginalise them and, in certain cases, get rid of them and surround himself with yes-men and women'."[466] The mark of true leadership, Mandela counselled, would be to resist such temptations and thereby allay the fears of one's opponents.

Mandela's words sounded uncannily prophetic, as if peering into the not-so-distant future and predicting such actions as Mbeki's dismissal of a health official who dared to point up shortcomings in the government's delivery of healthcare in the Eastern Cape in 2007 (Chapter 4). According to Cashdan, this film clip may have been familiar to a small number of political insiders, but was largely unknown to the general public. And it was stunning.

After the SABC balked at screening the Mbeki film, it sparred with Broad Daylight Films for more than a year over the ownership and suitability of the work. The SABC claimed that the work was "incurably defamatory", although that judgement was rendered by both in-house and outside legal consultants only *after* the SABC's failure to show it as programmed. Such a dismissive and blanket judgement was roundly disputed by other experts, including FXI's

Jane Duncan who condemned the characterisation as "rubbish". In fact, in the run-up to the originally scheduled screening, the producers and the SABC had negotiated a series of alterations to address certain concerns; Broad Daylight delivered a final edit to the SABC just the day before it was to air. Cashdan thus feels he repeatedly made sincere efforts to provide a satisfactory product.

Different explanations of the impasse surfaced. According to one scenario, timorous bureaucrats feared the official fallout from showing a potentially controversial documentary, and therefore backed away. Early on, Cashdan believed SABC executives may have been threatened not to proceed with it; he alleged, "one senior employee in a recorded cellphone message stated that somebody 'high up' had 'influenced' the decision'."[467] But there was scant hard evidence of such actual attempts to quash the film, and Dali Mpofu categorically denied that any such pressure had been applied to his staff.[468]

Cashdan and others later on realised the cancellation was likely due to internal confusion at the SABC, with some units striking out in adventurous directions while others were being more guarded – a classic case of the right hand not knowing what the left hand was doing. And Cashdan notes a dramatically different working style between the BBC and the SABC. In his own past experience, personnel at the BBC furnish precise criticism to commissioned artists and recommend specific changes to be made to their work, all of it in written form. Moreover, BBC staff lawyers review all material and append a note of legal explanation. Each party therefore understands the reciprocal expectations and responsibilities. But Cashdan claims that most of the feedback he and his partner received from the SABC was verbal, and there were not prescribed procedures for monitoring progress and providing clear-cut feedback. That heightened the opportunities for miscommunication and working at cross-purposes.

On reflection, Cashdan attributes the problems he experienced with the SABC to a corporate culture that demonstrated disorganisation, inconsistency, and insufficient attention to detail. A newspaper article at the time came to a similar conclusion, noting "The SABC's reasoning for not flighting the unauthorised documentary of Thabo Mbeki is so fraught with contradictions and muddled thinking, it's tempting to consider SA's public voice not so much responsible for censorship, but rather guilty of just being hopelessly, irresponsibly inept."[469]

Is That All There Is?

In basic respects, *Unauthorised: Thabo Mbeki* was not the film that Cashdan and Direko had originally envisioned. One reason was key: many Mbeki allies refused their requests to be interviewed on film. That did not surprise the producers a great deal. But some of the president's loudest critics declined to speak to them as well. Cashdan partially chalks this up to fear of retaliation by an increasingly paranoid and vindictive leader, but also to the desires of others to tell their own stories at a moment that is optimum for them. He explains, "People want to choose the time and place to fight their battles. Those who have really good stories to tell want to save them for their own autobiographies. People who have serious battles to fight with Mbeki want to be in exactly the right time and place to fight those battles, and not let bits leak out in somebody's documentary film."

Cashdan readily admits that the documentary was a bit shallow and overly earnest. He mordantly remarked, "It's not a great film … it won't cause a genocide."[470] When he introduced the as-yet-to-be-broadcast documentary to audiences on a "freedom of expression" tour of screenings in urban venues, township church and community halls, and in rural areas, Cashdan characterised the work as mediocre and rather boring.[471] And some critics savaged it. One dismissed it as "a short and apparently aimless film about a short and apparently aimless politician", and although only 24 minutes in length, he decried it had a "*Gandhi*-like bum-numbing quality".[472]

Nevertheless, it did provide an occasion for people to publicly discuss life under the current leadership and the status of South Africa's democracy. One man wrote, "The banning of a documentary seems a lot like the burning of books, and reeks of totalitarian style censorship. Is SA a democracy, or are we headed for a one-party dictatorship?"[473] And a critic nostalgically observed "It was a bit like the old days of the *Weekly Mail* Film Festival – a movie under threat of banning, an audience eager to see it, a contentious panel willing to discuss it and all the issues in detail."[474]

That jibes with a comment someone made to me after a showing in Johannesburg that it reminded him of pre-1994 gatherings that were exhilarating and opinionated free-for-alls where the dialogue really seemed to matter. At the event I attended, the audience was predominately made up of black Africans under the age of 30. Those who rose to speak during the post-screening discussion were forthright in their observations, highly critical of Mbeki, and many of them sharpened their remarks with a wicked sense of humour. Even people who openly declared their respect for Mbeki as "their leader" wondered aloud how he could be so thin-skinned to possibly care about such a depiction.

The SABC threatened to block the producers from exhibiting the film on their own – "unauthorised", as it were, with the ownership of the work in dispute – but backed off from pursuing legal remedies. In Cashdan's estimation SABC officials came across as "bully boys" and Broad Daylight Films was cast as "heroic". But SABC's Dali Mpofu also laid claim to a chunk of the moral high ground. In a full-page statement that the SABC ran in South African newspapers, he floridly remarked, "An independent national broadcaster is a very important part of any democracy and in fact is the oxygen without which a democracy cannot survive."[475] He even repeated his oxygen metaphor later in the same account.

Moreover, Mpofu portrayed the SABC as the victim in this complicated episode, claiming it had been the target of "an orchestrated campaign aimed at impugning our commitment to one of the fundamental values of public service broadcasting, namely editorial independence from political bias". He explained, "the producers ... have seen fit to conduct a media campaign aided and abetted by right-wing organisations and some like-minded fellow travelers", duplicating language he used elsewhere as well.[476]

Given Cashdan's usual ideological home turf, it was somewhat surprising to see him summarily shifted to the other end of the political spectrum. But it was undoubtedly a calculated strategy and not a faux pas. Recall the rhetoric attached to the debate over the Native Club (Chapter 4), where critics of the ruling party were condemned for their colonialist mindset (if they were white), or their ill-informed allegiance and obsequiousness to the status quo of former regimes (if they were black). In Cashdan's analysis, the term "right wing" "is a code word for counter-revolutionary, especially when it's used by a black person against a white person. It's a code word for undermining black leadership and the revolutionary objectives of the country."

It's necessary to understand this episode in its timeframe. Broad Daylight's tussle with the SABC happened in 2006, and the production company initiated its countrywide screenings in mid-2007. This was just before President Mbeki's leadership came under increased criticism because of a series of public relations catastrophes, inaugurated by his firing of the deputy health minister Nozizwe Madlala-Routledge. Up until that point, it made good sense for a public broadcaster to curry favour with the political incumbent. But as the political tides increasingly shifted in favour of Jacob Zuma during the waning months of 2007, it is unlikely that the SABC would have championed Mbeki's cause with such fervour had the documentary just been coming on line at that point.

The fate of *Unauthorised: Thabo Mbeki* brings the central dilemma of a state-sponsored public broadcaster into sharp focus. Should the SABC move toward a more commercial model, it becomes increasingly subject to the possibility of corporate executives dictating what it presents. This can manifest itself in a "dumbing down" of programming as well as a smoothing off of the edges of any commentary in order to create the most comfortable commercial environment in which its sponsors can make their pitches, to the most compliant consumers. But should the broadcaster play up the state-funded approach, it is prone to domination by political elites who wish to be presented in the most complimentary light. The SABC is in a precarious position at best, tossed and battered between the Scylla of supercilious politicians and the Charybdis of commercialisation.

Mbeki, Authorised

A different spin on Thabo Mbeki's presidential accomplishments and future legacy is the hallmark of *Fit to govern? The native intelligence of Thabo Mbeki* (2007), a book by a provocative and singular voice on the contemporary

South African scene, Ronald Suresh Roberts. London-born but raised in Trinidad, educated at Oxford and Harvard, this lawyer turned journalist and gadfly made a name for himself because of his brashness, combativeness, and his eagerness to have his voice heard on the most contentious social and political questions, without regard to how fantastical or offensive his opinions might be.

Whereas Ben Cashdan was forced to borrow against his house to complete his film, Roberts's project was sponsored by a stipend of more than a million rand, courtesy of ABSA bank and brokered by one of Mbeki's closest associates in the presidency, Essop Pahad. Roberts touted his own book while he dismissed other portrayals of his subject. He amassed a throng of enemies in the process.

He sparred with columnist John Matshikiza, who called Roberts "brattish" and "the snooty ex-Trinidadian [who] makes the rules wherever he goes".[477] One of Roberts's favourite ploys, however, was to deflect criticism by accusing his detractors of being flunkies of corporate interests, apologists for those whose power still derives from colonial or apartheid privilege.

He famously sued journalist Chris Barron for defamation over his article "The unlikeable Mr Roberts", which detailed Roberts's dismissal from a South African law firm because of a conflict of interest with one of its clients. Roberts maintained, however, that he left because he was not willing to be "the firm's 'smiling native'". Moreover, Barron described Roberts's ongoing feud with the SABC over a broadcast he found objectionable. Barron also cited the editor of the *Sunday Times* who called Roberts "an egregious West Indian carpetbagger", and explained, "Blacks who criticise the government are dismissed venomously by Roberts as whites' lackeys and slaves to Eurocentrism. Not for nothing has he been called the government's 'freelance hit man'".[478]

At the conclusion of a well-publicised trial, the judge ruled against Roberts in a fusillade of invective: "Mr Roberts, you were obsessive ... and also haughty, arrogant, self-important, a name-dropper, excessive, outlandish, vindictive, venomous, relentless, evasive, argumentative, opportunistic, un-convincing and untruthful". The judge characterised Robert's correspondence with the SABC as "unbalanced, paranoid and obsessed", and rejected the charge that Barron's article entailed "character assassination". Rather, the judge chided, "I consider that any harm done to the plaintiff's reputation was self-inflicted."[479] (Roberts finally paid the judgement of R1 million to the *Sunday Times* in 2009.)

Whereas an official scolding such as this would humiliate many people into silence, it simply confirmed Roberts's suspicions that a diminishing white power structure finds an outspoken black man such as himself to be threatening. Condemnation energised rather than vanquished him. Roberts referred to himself as the victim of a "media-lynching" and vowed, "the mining house liberals have not and will not destroy me, as the homophobes indeed destroyed [Oscar] Wilde". Roberts made it clear that his inner sense of righteousness counterbalanced any prospect that he would experience this as a setback. "The trope of the Despondent Native," he defiantly stated, "has no space near me. Outside the colonial media, there is an upsurge of support."[480]

That is a claim that is difficult to assess, not least of all because it's not clear what media sources Roberts would define as having moved beyond the "colonial mindset". The mainstream media, to be sure, broadly condemned him. He was labelled a "presidential *imbongi*",[481] and his book was dismissed as "an *apologia* for Mbeki".[482] What was clear is the extent to which Roberts racialised his every move, and those of his opponents as well. A rare example of the support Roberts claimed to command was represented by the following letter-to-the-editor, which seemed cut from the same cloth as Roberts's own declarations. Reacting to the denunciation of Roberts by John Matshikiza, one man wrote, "Roberts brings a fresh insouciance to our hypocritical and chickenshit public debate. The ad hominem attacks on him harbour the same old nauseating reality – the assertion by certain quarters of the population that polemics are no place for Bantus. How else are we to explain the fact that the most outspoken members of the intellectual lynch mob come from the white liberal posse?"[483]

Did this statement, coming from someone without a public profile or institutional affiliation, represent one voice or multitudes? Just how significant was it? What was more troubling was the declaration by someone endowed with impressive credentials, and for whom race supplanted all else in his reaction to Roberts's trial. Dumisa Ntsebeza, Western Cape chairperson of the Black Lawyers' Association, a commissioner of the Truth and Reconciliation Commission (TRC), and himself an acting judge, came to observe the proceedings in Johannesburg firsthand. His reason? "I heard from a colleague that it was a pleasure to sit there and witness how a black person can actually cut down an overrated white counsel to size," Ntsebeza explained.[484]

When a racial prism of this degree of magnification is used to view the media or the judiciary, much of the nuance, detail and zones of indistinctness that are so critical within these realms are obliterated – diminishing the degree to which the public is able to believe in their independence, sense of fairness, or quest for degrees of objectivity.

Dead in the Water

The SABC is obviously susceptible to government meddling and manipulation, thanks to its position as the state-sanctioned broadcaster. But what sorts of pressure can be exerted to rein in private forms of expression that take aim at official shortcomings? Earlier in 2007, a prominent South African corporation found out, after it met unexpected resistance over a public service campaign that exposed a vulnerable governmental flank.

First National Bank (FNB) announced an anti-crime campaign, "Help us help South Africa", targeting multiple forms of media: newspapers, radio and television. A significant prong of the plan envisioned placing 2.8 million copies of an insert into Sunday newspapers. Its text opened by expressing pride in the country and celebrated the fact that South Africa had been chosen to host the FIFA World Cup soccer tournament in 2010. But it expressed concern as well, noting "crime rates are the highest on the continent". Moreover, it included an appeal to the president, pleading for him to "please make crime the government's number one priority", which readers could forward to Thabo Mbeki in an envelope with prepaid postage. It also encouraged respondents to relate their own personal experiences with crime in their replies.[485]

The revelation of its proposed launch coincided with news of its demise. And reports of direct government interference were offset by emphatic denials. Nearly every news account reported a meeting taking place two days before the inauguration of the campaign at FNB's Johannesburg headquarters between bank officials and representatives from the president's office. Nevertheless, in an oddly worded pronouncement, presidential spokesperson Mukoni Ratshitanga declared, "It is difficult to hide a meeting of this nature to the public and we don't want to lie to the public. As far as I'm concerned, there was no such meeting."[486] Deputy President Phumzile Mlambo-Ngcuka echoed the denial.[487] For their part, FNB officials spoke of "refining" or "suspending" the initiative, although it was clearly stillborn, not merely postponed.

According to one report, the president's envoys expressed concern that FNB's plan would disadvantage Mbeki in his succession struggle within the ANC.[488] It was also slated to begin less than a week before the president's state-of-the-nation address, an obviously impolitic bit of scheduling. Another government spokesperson was forthright in his condemnation of FNB's stratagem, asserting "[P]ositioning themselves as an opposition party is not appropriate ... Trying to incite people to behave in a certain way towards the head of state cannot be condoned."[489] The government was clearly not pleased about airing this problem in such a public forum.

A guest columnist for the *Mail & Guardian* thoroughly condemned FNB's backpeddling, declaring it an "exercise in bootlicking, abject self-censorship" and a "gutless retreat".[490] And Democratic Alliance leader Tony Leon bemoaned, "It is strange that such a lion in the financial sector can turn into a mouse when pressure is put on it by government."[491] But *was* it so strange?

Some reports detailed the bank's substantial dependency on the government because of the business it receives from agencies such as the treasury and the revenue service, as well as from provincial governments.

And beyond such specific interconnections, other stories revealed that FNB had experienced pressure applied from within its industry as well. Business Against Crime represents corporate social responsibility in this domain,[492] and some leaders apparently felt that FNB's initiative could compromise the goodwill it has built up with the government over time.[493] An opinion piece was more pointed, alleging that "some of its competitors ... accused FNB of being opportunistic", and that "reports have suggested that the anti-crime campaign was canned because it threatened to destroy some hard-won trust that had been nurtured between white big business and the government".[494]

Fighting crime is one of many areas over which the government is routinely criticised for ineffectiveness. Its consequences affect citizens of every economic bracket, every race, and in every location. FNB's proposal to do something positive in this regard was viewed by the president's office as an attack, not as a potentially positive supplement to its own efforts. Its cancellation was yet another hijacking in this crime-weary society.

Gatvol

New media domains such as websites and the internet operate beyond the reach of institutional anchorage and governmental oversight in many respects. That enables people to use them to express points of view that could otherwise put their livelihoods at risk or jeopardise their freedom – if they were to express similar opinions as employees or as citizens subject to the regulations with jurisdiction over other forms of speech. New media thus provide a communications frontier where a person's word is still, largely, their unfettered word.

The sense of *gatvol*, feeling fed up, that led First National Bank to propose its ill-fated anti-crime campaign has spawned additional opportunities to publicly air such grievances, utilising technologies that are challenging the domination that newspapers, radio and television enjoyed throughout the 20th century. Such sites facilitate a no-holds-barred type of expression that might be out of bounds in more traditional forums. They provide the means for a grassroots response to a perception of governmental indifference to the general population's quotidian problems, personified by Safety and Security Minister Charles Nqakula's notorious 2006 statement to those "whinging" about high levels of crime to "Get a life!" and advising them, "There are two options: You can complain until you are blue in the face or leave the country so that the rest of us can get on with our work."[495]

Whereas FNB's scheme touted South Africa's successful bid for the FIFA World Cup soccer tournament in 2010, the website www.crimexposouthafrica. co.za used the highly anticipated event as a springboard for challenging the government's lack of success in curbing crime, as a warning to potential visitors, and as a cyberspace memorial to victims (a similar one was www. gatvol.co.za). And website developer Neil Watson strategically timed its debut just before the 2006 World Cup soccer tournament held in Germany in June and July. He planned to post crime statistics along with photos of murder victims (South Africa is commonly cited as ranking first in the world for rape and second for murder).

Watson boasted, "South Africans brutally murdered in the past will return from their graves, and via their families and friends tell the international community of their horror."[496] Furthermore, he seemed mindful of the potential of his venture to embarrass the South African government as well as subvert the success of the 2010 competition, which would be humiliating on the world stage. Watson expectantly noted, "A decline in international tourists will serve as a warning to the South African leadership to clean up their act."[497]

Watson offered a precise rationale for adopting such a strategy in a story that reported, "He doesn't believe in 'going with placards in front of the courts,' because the former regime didn't pay any heed when 'African people complained like that'."[498] One posting to the site compressed into a few words frustration with standard channels of communication, an example of how dissatisfaction with the perils of life in South Africa is inducing emigration (the so-called "chicken run"), and a sense of self-righteousness: "I am going to America soon," one person defiantly wrote, "Don't call me a traitor; call me an ambassador of truth."[499]

Before long a "cyberfight"[500] ensued when Pieter Boshoff established www. realsouthafrica.co.za to counter Watson's site. Boshoff slammed Watson for trying to undercut potential job creation and the economy. Boshoff, in turn the target of threatening calls, was dismissed as a *kaffirboetie*, a term of derision for someone who did not adhere to the racial status quo.[501]

The old SA flag had been posted on www.crimexposouthafrica.co.za, but Watson removed it; he believed that Boshoff may have "planted it" to discredit the website. It was one of several attempts to align him with right-wing sentiments and causes, which Watson claims to reject.[502] Nonetheless, comments on the site "have been slammed as bordering on hate speech because of the derogatory references to black people".[503] Another post called his website "treasonous" and threatened to murder Watson and rape his "moffie father".[504] Among the most extreme postings was one that contested the familiar slogan "One settler, one bullet" and magnified it to previously unheard-of proportions: "One gunship, one township".[505]

The Time Before (The) Man

British ex-pat David Bullard penned the weekly column "Out to lunch" for 14 years to the amusement and annoyance, delight and consternation of the *Sunday Times* readership. His enviable journalistic run came to an abrupt halt on 10 April 2008, however, four days after a column entitled "Uncolonised Africa wouldn't know what it was missing" ran in the paper. Bullard was summarily fired by editor Mondli Makhanya via a call to his cellphone.

Bullard had created a reverie about "simple tribesmen" during precolonial days, a time when people were supposedly unburdened by complex technology or evolved human sensibilities. The passage that most evoked the ire of critics read, "Every so often a child goes missing from the village, eaten either by a hungry lion or a crocodile. The family mourn for a week or so and then have another child".[506] The coming of European civilisation purportedly changed all that, for the benefit of all parties.

Such is the stuff of neoconservative rhetoric or "comic" interoffice emails. And it reverberated with the same brashness Bullard had expressed eight years earlier when he wrote "that visiting US president Bill Clinton's black entourage would be pleased that their ancestors were taken into slavery when they saw conditions in South Africa".[507] Bullard asserts, "Negativity sells. I'm an Afro-realist, not an Afro-pessimist."[508]

Was Bullard's writing hateful? No doubt. Was it racist? Quite possibly. But was it hate speech? Most likely not.

Jane Duncan argued, "I think there is an attitude that all racist speech in South Africa, because of our history, is automatically hate speech. And that's not the case. [In actuality only] a narrow area of racist speech qualifies as hate speech." For expression to meet the legal standard of hate speech, it must include the advocacy of hatred based upon race, ethnicity, gender or religion and incitement to cause harm.

In the months before he was sacked from the *Sunday Times*, David Bullard's hard-hitting style provided plenty of evidence that no topic was out of bounds for him, no insinuation unexpressed, no language taboo. He referred to the politicians and their cronies involved in the arms deal as "reptiles".[509] He used such cringe-inducing terms as "pale males", "darkies", and "our office Zulu".[510] Furthermore, he alleged that his phone had been bugged,[511] and openly wondered whether or not the ANC was involved when he was shot during a home invasion in Johannesburg in 2007.[512] He articulated a sentiment that was largely unexpressed in public at the time, but has since become commonplace, when he asserted "the great rainbow miracle has faded".[513]

Bullard took special aim at the ruling party. He mused, "At the tribal council in Polokwane last December [2007], the tribe spoke loud and clear and Thabo Mbeki was voted off the island."[514] But he was quite alarmed as well as he monitored the manner by which the party conducted its business. "The ANC," he asserted, "is run along the lines of a charismatic religion, and independence of thought is not encouraged."[515] What concerned him even more was that such repressive practices would seep into the general society.

Bullard seemed keenly aware that the type of investigative journalism that had repeatedly revealed the improper conduct of South African government officials could provoke a political backlash against the media. He ominously noted, "The vultures are circling and our freedoms don't look quite so guaranteed, particularly if they ridicule politicians or ask embarrassing questions about unusual money flows."[516] Bullard alleged, "There's a small but vocal group of people who believe that the media have run amok and need to be on a short leash."[517] And weeks before Bullard himself became a news story, he wrote "we slip back into the middle ages and become an agrarian society once again",[518] foretelling his infamous, career-changing column.

Not surprisingly, the incident stoked up letter-to-the-editor writers. Notably, their sentiments for and against Bullard closely paralleled racial lines: those with recognisably black African names condemned him, while others lamented the columnist's fate and its implications for free expression.

One enraged reader complained, "To imagine that Africa would have remained agrarian and not developed technologically without colonisation is out of an arch-racist manual ... to give column space to a man who holds such views is flabbergasting. Would you give space to Hitler's secretary?"[519] Another simply dismissed the column as "an adolescent display of failed satire",[520] counterbalanced by a man who condemned the response of the editor of the *Sunday Times* as "immature journalistic censorship".[521]

A somewhat surprising response came from Max du Preez, an acclaimed journalist who was the target of censors and sometimes condemned by a critical public during apartheid. He wrote, "South Africans should be forgiven for being sensitive, even hyper-sensitive, about racism." He lumped Bullard together with Dan Roodt, a writer known for his strong Afrikaner nationalist ideas, and argued that in regards to freedom of speech, "They are the ones undermining it, not we who ask for action against them." Du Preez then concluded, "It is racist writing such as Bullard's column on Africa and colonialism that leads to a closing down of democratic space for others to be forthright and robust in their comment."[522] One would expect a free speech advocate to argue in the reverse: deeply offensive remarks should spur a vigorous response, not close off dialogue. For a figure with the stature of Du Preez calling for restrictions provides a significant glimpse into how the legacy of race relations in the past hover above – and cloud – contemporary open discussions in South Africa.

Still others initiated a familiar scenario: the SAHRC received three complaints against Bullard, which prompted an investigation. Bullard's response was a combination of surprise, defensiveness and contrition. He grumbled, "I was personally staggered that a column that started with the word 'imagine' could ever be taken at face value."[523] In several public statements he stressed that his schtick was "show business", and that as far as he was concerned, the column in question was business as usual. He argued, "My brief is to be outrageous – a guy who upsets people on a Sunday and sells newspapers."[524] He linked his fate to those accused of witchcraft: racism was the new blasphemy.[525]

But Bullard also issued an apology that was generally perceived as sincere, even by his critics (including one of the complainants to the SAHRC, a body that dropped its plans to take Bullard to Equality Court once it heard his expression of regret). The columnist "took responsibility for having allowed 'poison to pollute' the newspaper".[526] Bullard sued the publisher in Labour Court for two years of potential income lost due to wrongful dismissal but the case was thrown out in 2009 because his apology seemingly annulled his claim that his free speech rights had been violated.

Drawing a Line

One of the more curious and unscrutinised aspects of this controversy is that critics honed in on one passage of Bullard's column and virtually ignored the rest of it. Extracted from the body of the piece, Bullard's remark about the absence of a fundamentally moral dimension to African tribal life is understandably insulting. But Bullard's column is as much a critique of Western capitalism and consumerism as anything else, enhanced by a sly reference to the acceleration of Chinese investment in Africa that many observers fear may signal a new brand of colonisation on the continent. Bullard was writing with extremely broad strokes along with subtlety, taking aim at a variety of targets. But the ambiguity of his motives and tone triggered multiple readings, many of them negative (a commonplace occurrence with contemporary art; compare many of the examples in Chapter 6).

Moreover, another declaration Bullard made in this column seems equally if not more offensive. He wrote that before the intrusion of the West, "the various tribes of South Africa live healthy and peaceful lives, only occasionally indulging in a bit of ethnic cleansing". Clearly it was more comfortable for critics to raise the issue of the European colonial exploitation of blacks than interethnic strife or black-on-black violence. Bitter ethnic rivalries had been in high relief during the ANC convention in Polokwane a few months earlier. These sentiments would move from enmity to actual violence just weeks after Bullard's controversial column when xenophobic attacks rocked South Africa in May 2008. Condemning historical injustices was easier for critics than confronting contemporary realities, however.

During the lengthy battle between Laugh it Off and SABMiller, a commentator from the BBC asserted that LIO's parody "crossed the line from humour to hate-speech".[527] Two magazine editors who regularly published Bullard and generally advocated for him boldly stated that, "A timid columnist is no columnist at all."[528] Even so, they averred that they would have never published his contested piece: "There is a line and that column crossed it." They continued, "As satire it failed miserably because it just wasn't funny." At the same time, they realised, "you can't push writers to explore the outer boundaries of their comfort zone and then nail them for it".[529] Bullard reported that his editor made a similar claim: "He talked of a line being crossed but where," Bullard wondered, "was that line?"[530] Such boundaries are both socially constructed and continuously shifting, their position buffeted by current events at the same time that they are anchored by racial, gender, religious, regional, and many other differences. In this instance Bullard miscalculated where the limits of propriety lay and found himself marooned in a cultural no-man's zone.

This controversy exposed some significant and simmering social divisions. Well-credentialled people took aim at Bullard, just as newspaper readers did. Justice Malala, an executive in the corporation that owns the *Sunday Times*, railed "What exactly does Bullard think we are? Animals who just fuck and forget about our children a week later?"[531] And Arts and Culture Minister Pallo Jordan displayed an unusual anti-foreigner twist: "we can't afford to import racists from other parts of the world," he cautioned. "[D]on't come to Africa and insult us – that's like coming to someone's living room and defecating on their carpet."[532]

Jordan struck another chord that could be interpreted as racist in its own right. "I was quite alarmed for a very long time," he said, "that Bullard could write like that in a paper edited by an African. I doubt if a Jewish editor would have allowed things like that to be written about Jews ... (but) this African editor allowed it."[533] Jordan simultaneously denounced the editor for not "acting African" enough – paralleling Robert Suresh Roberts's claim that Mondli Makhanya was "black" (his quote marks) and thereby a "colonial creature" or lackey[534] – as well as implied that Jews mechanically act in a predictable, uniform, and self-protective way. But he was not the only one to make such an allusion; "Imagine the uproar if Bullard had written the same racist drivel about Jews," Justice Malala speculated, implying that Jews are successful at demanding they be portrayed in positive ways, that they are a social force to be reckoned with.[535]

Another journalist challenged the line of propriety himself. Moshoeshoe Monare recounted an exchange he'd once had with a top aide to Zimbabwe's Robert Mugabe. In that instance Monare was advocating for the credentialling of some white journalists. The aide told him, "the problem with South Africa is that we have over-stretched the Mandela reconciliation ideal, thus sacrificing the dignity of the very people who were humiliated by apartheid". At the time of the encounter, Monare accused this man of being racist. Now, he admitted, the man "had a point".[536] It was a not-so-coded message to whites to be mindful of "their place".

Another unremarked feature of this controversy was the fact that the *Sunday Times* decided to publish Bullard's column, yet quickly condemned it in light of the public outcry it provoked. But where was editor Mondli Makhanya when the paper went to press? Surely he bears some responsibility for allowing the column to run. Either it measured up originally, or Makhanya was not executing his duties properly. According to FXI's Jane Duncan, Makhanya had *not* read the article until complaints started streaming in. The editor, in her words, had been "sleeping on the job".

One letter-to-the-editor writer wisely observed, "The wounds of the past have yet to heal, and 15 years into our constitutional democracy is still too early to venture into the terrain that Bullard dared to do."[537] One of the complainants to the SAHRC expressed similar sentiments, arguing, "When you are at the receiving end of a stereotype, no amount of creative expression can mask the pain or reduce the offence it causes each time it is uttered."[538] Bullard's blend of cynicism and satire, uncomfortable truths and unspoken issues can be difficult to swallow, particularly for people who have been demeaned and demoralised for generations.

Holy Cow(s)

Magazine editors Kevin Bloom and Phillip de Wet summed up this case with a vivid impression of the columnist's multiple offences: "Bullard slaughtered some holy cows (and then set them on fire before pissing on the flames)."[539] Shortly before David Bullard was dismissed from the *Sunday Times*, another columnist had met a similar fate.

The man in that instance was Deon Maas, a writer for the Afrikaans-language *Rapport*. Maas had written about Satanism as a belief system deserving of equal protection as a religion under the Constitution. He wrote, "If Muslims think they are having a bad time, they should look at Satanism. They really have a bad deal."[540] It was a serious miscalculation for this readership: the article brought down an avalanche of negative responses, including threats to boycott the paper and burn its distribution trucks. Because Maas was quite new in this position, and *Rapport* had been experiencing a significant decline in sales,[541] the newspaper had much less to lose by dumping him than the *Sunday Times* did by firing someone with the extended tenure that Bullard held.

Some people sensed a disturbing trend developing. Jane Duncan noted, "What we see now is a real attack on columnists. I think one has to distinguish between columnists and the spaces they should have to say what they have to say, and hard news. I think we are really losing that distinction." Her remark was shaped by an additional incident that followed closely on the heels of these others: a large outcry against the tabloid *Sunday Sun* columnist Jon Qwelane's "Call me names, but gay is NOT okay ..."

Qwelane sided with Robert Mugabe that homosexuality was "unnatural"; "wrong is wrong," he stated. Qwelane continued, "I pray that some day a bunch of politicians ... will muster the balls to rewrite the constitution of this country to excise those sections that give licence to men marrying other men, ditto women. Otherwise, at this rate, how soon before some idiot demands to marry an animal, and argues that this constitution allows it?"[542]

Qwelane was no stranger to controversy. He traded accusations of racism with the white farmers' group Agri SA. He was investigated by the BCCSA for possible hate speech against illegal immigrants when he suggested the Constitution be suspended in order to round up and deport them. And he became enmeshed in a dispute over possible financial irregularities within a publishing company where he once worked. When a forensic report failed to validate his claims he suspected a cover-up, and accused its board of "necklacing the truth".[543]

The mobilisation of people against Qwelane in his role as a writer for the *Sunday Sun*, and the intensity of their outcry, differentiated this from the preceding episodes. In the Bullard case, three individuals filed complaints with the SAHRC; but in this instance, nearly a thousand people jammed its email system with their objections. Moreover, public demonstrations were held in both Johannesburg and Cape Town, demanding that the paper apologise, and also sanction Qwelane.

The issue hit the letter-to-the-editor columns as well. One impassioned writer labelled Qwelane's sentiments "plain old ugly apartheid-style prejudice", cited the role of radio in the Rwandan massacres, and with an authoritative flair asserted that "there is evidence that when homophobic utterances by opinion leaders and public figures increase, so do acts of violence against gays and lesbians".[544] His arguments were emotionally appealing but theoretically wanting; the violence against gays and lesbians in South Africa, as elsewhere, is much more deeply rooted than sprouting from public pronouncements.

Bullard argued this should open up a discussion, not close it off. "Whether or not you agree with Qwelane," Bullard declared, "he has a right to tackle those issues in print ... Some intelligent debate would be preferable to all this hysteria."[545] And Jane Duncan suggested, "We do undeniably have these regressive, racist tendencies in our society. Are we saying that we shouldn't provide a platform to deal with the fact that they exist, so that we can get them out there and debate them and debunk them? Is that what we're saying?"

The Press Ombudsman ruled that this was not hate speech, but that Qwelane had violated the Press Code for publishing "derogatory references to people's sexual orientation". The *Sunday Sun* was ordered to apologise.[546] The case dragged out through 2011, by which time Qwelane was the South African ambassador to Uganda (a place where public condemnation of homosexuality has also occurred). He was found guilty of hate speech by the Johannesburg Equity Court and ordered to make an unconditional apology to the gay community; in addition, he was instructed to pay a R100 000 fine to the Human Rights Commission. Qwelane's continued disputation of any wrongdoing led some to demand that he be recalled from his governmental post.

Jane Duncan reflected on these attacks on columnists and concluded, "I think it is going to backfire on the editors in the long run, because then they are going to find their own space to publish controversial opinion diminishing. And they aren't going to be able to get it back very easily once it's gone."

These debates over editorial responsibility and the limits of acceptable speech coalesced in a spectacular way in 2011 when *Sowetan* columnist Eric Miyeni condemned *City Press* editor Ferial Haffajee as a "black snake in the grass" for her paper's investigation into the finances of ANC Youth League President Julius Malema, accused her of harbouring racial self-hatred, and threatened that she would have been a candidate for necklacing as a stooge for white interests in an earlier time. Heads rolled (Miyeni was fired and the acting editor resigned) and the definitions of hate speech and freedom of speech were once again tested.

A Big Scoop

The Bullard episode capped off a year of spiralling tumult between the media and the government, between the proponents of freedom of expression and those wishing to curb it in various respects. In the midst of this flurry of attempts to cut short the discussion of contentious issues, columnist Maureen Isaacson remarked, "Silencings and threats and outings spring up like weeds in our South African garden of paranoia."[547]

This continuing confrontation between editors, reporters and public officials was activated by journalistic revelations of malfeasance, misconduct and cronyism in the Department of Health. But these stories quickly implicated others, all the way up to the presidency. The significance of what began to unfold in August and September 2007 was recognised immediately. An editorial in the *Mail & Guardian* audaciously declared, "In the past seven days there has been a *tectonic shift* in South Africa's political landscape. Forces long held in check have started to break loose, and the consequences for President Thabo Mbeki and his legacy are ominous."[548] And an investigative magazine report published later chose the bold title "80 days that rocked the nation". Its writer, the famed Rian Malan, framed recent events as the struggle between "a government that prefers to remain unaccountable for anything [which] battles reporters who want to know everything".[549] The profession of journalism itself became front-page news.

Recall the July 2007 revelations of a seriously faulty medical system in the Eastern Cape (Chapter 4). That put one of President Thabo Mbeki's closest associates, Health Minister Manto Tshabalala-Msimang, under intense scrutiny. These two held a deep bond. Mbeki and Tshabalala-Msimang shared formative experiences during their exile from South Africa in the apartheid era; were politically linked through an important family tie within the ANC hierarchy (the minister's husband was ANC treasurer); and of necessity they became advocates for one another in the face of intense local and international criticism directed at their (mis)handling of the HIV/AIDS pandemic.

On 12 August 2007 the front page of the *Sunday Times* blared the headline **"MANTO'S HOSPITAL BOOZE BINGE"**. It was followed the next week with the startling banner **"MANTO: A DRUNK AND A THIEF"** in large-sized type one can imagine being reserved for the outbreak of war or a natural catastrophe. It was a clear pronouncement that the gloves were off between the media and the government.

The 12 August story carried revelations of Minister Tshabalala-Msimang's outrageous conduct while she was a patient in a Cape Town hospital for a shoulder operation. It disclosed reports of her drinking both before and after the procedure, being abusive to staff, and demanding that food be brought to her from an upscale market. The 19 August disclosures were even larger eye-openers: years earlier she had been dismissed from a hospital post in Botswana for drinking and stealing (blankets from the facility; a wristwatch from a patient); many episodes of erratic behaviour she had displayed in meetings or in public were likely due to her habitual drinking; and she opportunistically jumped to the top of the queue for a liver transplant, while endangering the success of the new organ by continuing to use alcohol. In other words, Tshabalala-Msimang abused her power, allowed personal demons to interfere with the completion of her official duties, and she offered a terrible role model in a country beset with medical problems.

These were explosive stories, raising serious questions of competency and highlighting decidedly unprofessional and incongruous behaviour. They were the result of rigorous investigative reporting and the use of stolen copies of the health minister's medical records. These published accounts set up a test of the constitutional guarantee of freedom of speech and the public's interest in knowing about the conduct of elected officials versus an individual's right to privacy. It took a judge to sort out the issues.

Tshabalala-Msimang noted that the National Health Act made the publication of information from personal health records illegal without prior consent of the individual; she never denied any of the allegations against her, however. *Sunday Times* editor Mondli Makhanya refused to back down, insisting that the stories were "200% correct". The minister and Cape Town's Mediclinic consequently sued the publisher, editor and two journalists at the *Sunday Times* for defamation, and demanded the return of the stolen records. They also insisted that an injunction be granted prohibiting the publication of anything further from the files. The case was argued before the Johannesburg High Court with Judge Mohamed Jajbhay presiding, the same man who ruled in two cases in 2006 that freedom of the press is not absolute, and had enjoined South African newspapers not to reprint the disputed Danish cartoons (Chapter 1).

Ronald Suresh Roberts was the rare public figure who rushed to Tshabalala-Msimang's defence. More than anything, the *Sunday Times* stories confirmed his pre-established hunches about South African journalism. He wrote, "The Great Hospital Records debate reveals the gross illiberalism of colonial discourse." Never content to issue an unadorned statement, Roberts linked what he viewed as the maltreatment of the minister by unethical members of the fourth estate to a chronicle of outrages against the non-white body, including the dissection of Sarah Baartman (the "Hottentot Venus") in the 19th century, and the intrusive search of the bodies of miners for stolen gems in later eras. He concluded, "The bizarre discourse around a minister's liver repeats this ancient and profitable contempt for native dignity".[550]

A professor of media studies took a different slant, noting how Manto Tshabalala-Msimang had become a favourite foil of the media, seriously eroding her credibility even before such specific damning revelations came out. He detailed the uncomplimentary nicknames she'd been stuck with, such as Dr No and Dr Beetroot; she had even been christened Frankenmanto.[551] Moreover, he noted that calling her by her first name only was a sign of disrespect to both her age and her stature.

Cartoonists routinely skewered her; photographs that editors chose to run were typically "unflattering" or showed her in a "combative mood". The professor likewise put all this in an historical perspective, albeit one quite different from the one Roberts used: "The strident tradition of journalism is partly informed by a modern-day media mindset in SA. It is aimed at making a decisive departure from the sycophantic practices of most of the mainstream media during apartheid SA."[552] Chris Barron's interview with presidential spokesman Mukoni Ratshitanga brought forth a great deal of evasion, but gave this official the opportunity to accuse the media of demonising the minister; it amounted to "character assassination" in his estimation.[553]

The court's decision was mixed, but displayed a discernibly favourable tilt toward the *Sunday Times* and its co-defendants. The judge ruled that because there was a prior debate about Minister Tshabalala-Msimang's fitness for office, the disclosures made by the newspaper were integral to that discussion. The public's right to know thereby won out over this individual's right to privacy. Jane Duncan concurred, arguing that there would have not been any other way for the *Sunday Times* to present these stories without the use of the stolen documents (for the record: the newspaper denied that anyone affiliated with it had removed the documents from the clinic, nor was there credible speculation that it had).

The judge ruled that Tshabalala-Msimang's personal behaviour contradicted and undermined the Health Department's campaign against alcohol abuse; questions about her past judgement and behaviour might be explained by these personal revelations; and her drinking while in the hospital was inconsistent with her professional position, regardless of how the information was obtained. He also concluded that she received preferential treatment for her liver transplant, an abuse of power.[554]

The judge ruled that the *Sunday Times* must hand over the minister's medical records to the clinic, and destroy any copies; he did not, however, prohibit the newspaper from commenting further on them. Although the *Sunday Times* was ordered to pay the costs of two of the three attorneys for the plaintiffs, the minister was not awarded the punitive costs she had requested. In all, the court only granted two of her eight demands.[555] An editorial that ran after the court case stated, "The *Sunday Times* respects the court's criticism and accepts the censure without reservation." Moreover, it stressed that "the information we published had nothing to do with intimate details of her medical condition. It was about her abuse of position."[556]

The intrigue extended beyond the courtroom. In retaliation for the revelations, the police assigned a top investigator to the case that took him as far as New Zealand to track down who stole, and then leaked, the medical records. The two journalists responsible for the stories believed their phones were tapped in order to discover anything that could be used to discredit them. And Essop Pahad threatened to withhold any future government advertising in the *Sunday Times*, a potentially significant monetary blow.[557]

Moreover, after the verdict was announced the Health Department spent R380 000 to run two articles as advertisements in five different papers. One was written by the Health Department's head of legal services; the other, by its director-general. The legal services chief attacked Judge Jajbhay, charging that his decision "constitutes a serious threat to one of the founding values of our constitution – the rule of law".[558]

The allegation was felt to be an assault on the independence of the judiciary, and potentially the basis for a charge of contempt of court against the writer. It is noteworthy that the Health Department paid for these ads even though Tshabalala-Msimang had sued the *Sunday Times* in her personal capacity. The agency justified this as a necessary expense in order to inform the public about the right to privacy and the sanctity of medical records.[559]

In the *Mail & Guardian's* end-of-the-year annual report card on government ministers, Manto Tshabalala-Msimang retained her usual position at the bottom: she received an "F". This echoed a 2006 national poll whereby the Health Department was "judged the least competent". Maureen Isaacson jibed, "the sinking ship of the health ministry is allowed to be steered by a drunken sailor".[560]

And while both Tshabalala-Msimang and her champion, President Mbeki, took significant hits as a result of these damning disclosures, the press came under heavy fire as well.

The *Mail & Guardian* lauded the *Sunday Times* for its exposé, crediting its editor with publishing "inconvenient truths" about a dubious public official. Its editorialists feared the broader implications for their profession, however. "Makhanya is a brave and principled editor," they wrote, "and the attack on him is clearly intended as a warning to the rest of the media. The purpose is to make all journalists think twice about critical reporting or commentary on the government."[561]

A letter-to-the-editor writer picked up the same theme, stating: "In the Far East there is a saying that the fish rots from the head and this is clearly the case with Mbeki and the government he heads." The man went on to argue, "the culture of debate that should mark a healthy and vibrant democracy is being systematically stifled … This, as I am sure many of my fellow countrymen and women will agree, is a dangerous step in the direction of authoritarianism."[562]

But Rian Malan offered the most devastating critique, understanding that the sense of exceptionalism that South Africans have enjoyed since 1994 had become more difficult to sustain, seen against some of the events of 2007. More and more, South Africans fear that negative trends they've watched unfold throughout Africa since the 1960s may be cropping up in their country as well. "Big-Manism is Africa's deadliest poison," Malan warned, "and … the best antidote is a free press."[563]

Hard-hitting Journalists

A veteran black African journalist wrote, "Today we are witnessing the ghastly consequences of the culture of violence that has become an integral part of the South African society. For a long time we have condoned and nurtured violence in the name of the liberation struggle. That violence hasn't abated."[564] The quote has a contemporary resonance, all-too-frequently embossed with brutal details in articles carried by South African newspapers. But this statement was published in 1991, when the country was anticipating a radical remaking, and not during the new millennium.

It came from a 1990 seminar hosted by the South African Institute of Race

Relations that brought together black African journalists along with a range of cultural workers to share professional experiences and brainstorm about combating threats to freedom of expression. The participants were less concerned about governmental controls at that historical juncture than the pressures and threats emanating from black African activists for them to tout specific political perspectives and downplay dissenting, or even alternative, points of view in their writing. The attendees were alarmed over being forced to become propagandists; editors of both the *Sowetan* and *Ilanga* detailed boycotts against their publications, violence against their distributors and buyers, up to the threatened necklacing of a reporter.[565]

They also bewailed the fact that certain white journalists were reluctant to report critically on black liberation organisations or their leaders out of fear of jeopardising their "liberal credentials".[566] And that sort of self-censoring and unofficial informational embargo extended into the earliest years of the South African democracy.

But no longer. Unstated but widely respected understandings have eroded as a new generation of journalists has hit its stride. Lacking the need to tout those liberal credentials, these journalists are not afraid to attack the failings of government and other officials.

Recall the earlier comment by Justin Nurse that he didn't consider any topic, business or individual, to be sacrosanct from critical scrutiny. He feels everything and everybody is "fair game", including Nelson Mandela. Furthermore, a young black African audience member at a screening of Ben Cashdan's *Unauthorised: Thabo Mbeki* made the same point: perplexed how a man could rocket from prison penury to fantastic wealth in a relatively short time like Mandela did, he too called for an end to any type of embargo on investigating public figures. Such voices represent a radically different stance towards black Africans holding public office.

Mondli Makhanya edited the *Mail & Guardian* between 2002 and 2004. According to Rian Malan, he continued that publication's "tradition of unabashed shit-stirring" when he subsequently took the reins of the *Sunday Times*. He is hated by the ANC establishment, condemned as a coconut, a reactionary, a race-traitor, even an askari ("a black who bears arms on behalf of the white man").[567] Makhanya's professional history partially explains the zealousness of the paper's pursuit of the Tshabalala-Msimang story. It accounts for the magnitude of the government's striking back as well.

Research conducted for an MA degree in communications by Onkgopotse J.J. Thabane characterised 35% of the *Mail & Guardian* editorials under Makhanya as "'mince-meating' the president". Onkgopotse concluded that Makhanya and the *Sunday Times* were engaging in "a campaign against the state" and put themselves "in the business of 'regime change'".[568] This increasingly adversarial relationship between the government and the press has called out a number of actions and proposals to intimidate, regulate and defang journalists during recent years.

Under apartheid the primary target of media censorship was reportage of the liberation movement that was contesting the white supremacist government for power. During the post-apartheid era, the focus has shifted to shutting out voices that contest the policies and practices that the former liberation party has implemented, and forces that threaten to coalesce into a new form of populist politics.

Courting Disaster

As mentioned at the opening of this chapter, Jacob Zuma – stung by being pummelled by the media over its coverage of his corruption charges, and even more so for its attention to the ways he and his supporters comported themselves during his trial for rape – launched a legalistic counterattack in mid-2006. He sued seven media organisations and individuals, representing a broad range of opinion, for defamation. The suits totalled more than an astonishing R60 million, a strategy condemned by the human rights watchdog organisation Reporters without Borders. Zuma claimed that the way he had been depicted was injurious to both his dignity and his reputation.

Cartoonist Jonathan Shapiro, a.k.a. Zapiro, responded immediately. And he took it a step further. As one of the defendants (in the amount of R15 million) he pictured himself at his drawing table facing down Zuma and wondering, "Would that be your reputation as a disgraced chauvinistic demagogue who can't control his sexual urges and who thinks a shower prevents AIDS?"[569] Zapiro dismissed the suits as a "cheap publicity stunt",[570] and declared, "It's a bit of a joke. I can't imagine how he thinks he is going to get a cent out of me."[571] Unbowed by the threat, one of Zapiro's recurring images has been a caricatured Zuma with a spigot sprouting out of his head, referencing his absurd version of AIDS risk prevention as taking a shower after unprotected sex; the image shadows the politician like a corona of idiocy and misinformation.

Zapiro sparked additional outrage over a cartoon he published in 2008. It depicted the leaders of the ruling alliance – the ANC, Cosatu, the South African Communist Party and the ANC Youth League – holding down a struggling woman. She is draped with a sash that reads "Justice System" and is blindfolded. The men forcibly stretch out her arms and her feet have been bound; her anguished writhing resembles the body of Christ on the cross. Zuma, in the meantime, is poised in front of the helpless woman. One of his allies shouts, "Go for it, Boss!" as Zuma unzips his pants. This shocking image referred to Zuma's recurrent criminal indictments, his successful avoidance of conviction, and the escalating intimidation of the judiciary by his supporters (see Chapter 8).

Zapiro dismissed charges of racism over this depiction although even some of his supporters believed he may have gone a bit far this time. The furore was reignited in 2011 when he published a corollary drawing: in this one a ravaged Lady Justice yelled encouragement to her beleaguered companion "free speech", a screaming and struggling figure who was being held down by the ANC (a caricature of party secretary-general Gwede Mantashe) while facing a leering, showerheaded "Govt" about to drop his trousers. Justice shouts "Fight, Sister, Fight" in solidarity, referring to the outcry over the ANC's campaign to muzzle the press through a proposed Protection of Information Bill and Media Appeals Tribunal. This cartoon spawned cries of both racism (allegedly reprising colonial stereotypes) and sexism (trivialising rape by using it as a metaphor) against an artist who clearly does not pull his punches.

Zapiro's career has straddled the apartheid and post-apartheid eras, and he personifies the shift from being an unwavering supporter of liberation ideals and struggle leaders to someone equipped with an equal-opportunity critical eye. He was detained during the apartheid era for his steadfast support of parties like the ANC and the United Democratic Front (UDF). But Zapiro notes, "As things have changed over the years, I've had to knock the stuffing out of my politically correct make-up." He admired Zuma at one time, but after the disclosures at the rape trial, Zapiro concluded, "that kind of chauvinist pig attitude is completely fair game".[572]

Politicians filing lawsuits such as these would stand little likelihood of success in most parts of the world. That is even more the case in South Africa where there is no concept of punitive damages.[573] And Zuma's chances for a successful outcome were handicapped further by the fact that most of the examples of expression he targeted were editorial observations and not the reportage of "hard facts".

Laugh it Off's ultimate victory in its case established the legitimacy of editorial comment and satire. Judge Albie Sachs asserted at that time, "humour should be protected as 'one of the great solvents of democracy', permitting opposition to power and convention to be articulated in a non-violent form".[574]

But winning a positive or profitable judgement may not have been Zuma's point. Retribution and intimidation were likely motives. However, after the ANC conference in Polokwane in December 2007, where Zuma succeeded Thabo Mbeki as ANC president, Zuma dropped the reputation portion of his lawsuits. His political triumph would make it difficult to argue that his reputation had been significantly damaged. He did, however, continue to sue on the basis of violation of his right to dignity.[575]

The impact of Zuma's threats is difficult to precisely measure. Mainstream publications with a national audience have sufficient resources and expertise to fend off harassment of this sort. But it can be much more of a threat to smaller, community-based media, for whom mounting an adequate defence could be challenging, and the threat of being ruined financially could feel quite plausible. In such instances, a politician's bark can be every bit as intimidating as his or her actual bite.

Tightening the Government's Grip

Another way to restrain the media emerged during an extended debate over proposed amendments to the 1996 Film and Publications Act. This act mandates that all films be submitted to the Film and Publications Board for pre-release review, as well as print media that include sexual images or written descriptions of sex. The board can ban child pornography, sexual violence, bestiality, and violence that constitutes incitement to harm; it may also restrict access to other material by age. And an amendment passed in 2004 empowered the board to add advocacy of racial hatred to the list of proscribed movie themes (religious hatred was already prohibited). But for the most part this legislation has largely exempted newspapers and broadcast media from the board's oversight.

Print and broadcast media are regulated by the Press Ombudsman, the Independent Communications Authority of SA (Icasa) and the Broadcasting Complaints Commission (BCCSA). A conference on child pornography in 2006 prompted activists to raise new concerns about protecting kids, however.

The new bill equates to prior restraint and pre-publication review, among the most insidious forms of censorship. All visual images would be treated as "film": documentaries, soapies, photojournalism – anything. But it would become a logistical nightmare to enforce if every bit of breaking news had to be evaluated in advance. The late ex-parliamentarian Helen Suzman noted that "the apartheid government did not have general laws censoring the media except during states of emergency,"[576] throwing this proposal into a very harsh light. A *Sunday Times* editorial also dredged up an apartheid-era memory, quoting the director of the Bureau of Information explaining in classic bureaucratese during that period, "We do not have censorship. What we have is a limitation on what newspapers can report."[577] Journalists were in fact subject to many laws at the time, and their work was constantly scrutinised; reporters and photographers were routinely harassed, imprisoned, tortured, and driven into exile.

The amendments were proposed by the Department of Home Affairs and approved in August 2006 by the cabinet. Film and Publications Board CE Shokie Bopape-Dlomo insisted "There is no need to panic",[578] and Home Affairs Deputy Minister Malusi Gigaba tried to allay concerns by stating, "We seek to protect the children, not muzzle the media!"[579] A journalist even argued that "[the] government has no plans to place impimpi (informers) in newsrooms, leering over editors' shoulders".[580] But the actual enforcement mechanisms were notably absent, generating a loud outcry from professional associations. That in turn gave officials pause, and they did not move forward with the proposal.

Parliament eventually followed up by holding two days of hearings in May 2007 at which many people expressed fears of the potential chilling effect of implementing this type of oversight. Someone remarked it was "tantamount to 'using a sledgehammer to kill a fly'", and there were other comments such as "Orwellian" or "bewildering". An African Christian Democratic MP went on record saying that his party is against child porn, "But, we are convinced that the bill goes way beyond child pornography and ... should it be passed in its present form, the provisions will result in an instrument of government control over the press."[581]

Jane Duncan was concerned about the broader implications of the bill on free expression. According to her, "Previously, the written word would be innocent until proven guilty, so you would only have to submit a publication if somebody complained about it. And yet, the bill actually reverses that, it places an onus on people who are producing controversial material." If implemented, she feared it would represent "a very profound shift for writers, artists, academics – people who trade in the written word and the visual image, on a daily basis".

The SABC: South African Broadcasting Crisis

As South Africa's national public broadcaster, the South African Broadcasting Corporation is the most contested media site in the country. But the SABC has a mixed institutional character. The state is its sole shareholder, and the SABC is under the jurisdiction of the minister of communications. Its board of directors makes recommendations to her regarding the appointment of three executive directors. Members of the board are themselves put forward by Parliament, but formally appointed by the president.

Even so, a mere 2% of the SABC's budget comes from the government. Approximately 80% is generated by advertising; the rest relies upon television licences paid by viewers. The SABC presents both radio and television programming, spanning the country's 11 official languages.[582] An SABC executive pithily stated, "Making profit is not what the public broadcaster is about; we are not Rainbow Chickens [the popular food outlet], we should be assessed on programming, and on educating and entertaining the public, not the profits we make."[583]

Recurrent turmoil at the SABC has seriously undermined the public's trust in it. A confidential market research survey commissioned by Snuki Zikalala, managing director of news, revealed in 2007 that only one of its programmes was seen as "credible". That was the weekly investigative show *Special Assignment*, and this finding was consistent across language groups. Additionally, viewers believed the broadcaster was subject to external political control, and some of them "experienced SABC presenters as 'apologetic', saying they should expose 'the truth without fear'". Tellingly, in light of Dali Mpofu's criticism of the hard-hitting investigative style of the *Sunday Times* in its revelations about the health minister, respondents to the study felt that the SABC was, rather, "inclined to attack government institutions and not government officials in charge of these institutions". Such an approach discounts assessing accountability and assigning responsibility while it also sidetracks devising schemes to fix what's wrong.[584]

Consider these quotations describing the atmosphere at the broadcaster, sampled from newspapers spanning merely four months during 2008. One journalist characterised the SABC board as a "cast of clowns [that] has run amok"[585] and noted, "The knives are out for Dali Mpofu."[586] Another alluded to the "weekly soap opera" at the SABC;[587] one more quoted an MP who compared the antics there to the Mad Hatter's Tea Party;[588] yet another referred to "The battle for the SABC" and "more drama" unfolding at the organisation. The title of that article declared, "SABC teeters on the brink."[589] In recent times the South African Broadcasting Corporation has become better known for crisis and controversy than for being an effective and trustworthy communicator.

After the debacle of *Unauthorised: Thabo Mbeki* in mid-2006, the SABC itself seemed to generate news as much as it reported it. A major story a year later was the appointment of new SABC board members. The practice of nominating and selecting the board was designed to be transparent, and exempt from political meddling. But politics has steadily crept into the process to an ever-increasing degree.

An unsuccessful nominee during the 2007 round used his personal experience to shed light on how procedures have evolved. Ryland Fisher, a former editor of the *Cape Times*, was informed by a sitting board member that he stood a realistic chance of getting appointed only if he had been nominated directly by the ANC. The party, he was told, "saw the SABC as one way of fighting against the 'reactionary media'." The ANC relies on the certainty that the board consists of people who can be depended upon to toe the party line. And as it turned out, the final list submitted by Parliament to the president was stocked by people with political bona fides but included no one with a media background (perhaps not surprisingly, a nominee by the Freedom of Expression Institute did not make the cut either).[590]

A chorus of discontent arose over the selection process that year; the Inkatha Freedom Party (IFP) and Cosatu loudly voiced their dissatisfaction. Several reports indicated that rather than the process proceeding from the Parliament to the president, Mbeki and Luthuli House – the ANC's central headquarters – managed the selections and pressured ANC MPs to march in step to its orders. An IFP MP described the selection process as a "toxic and a cynical political manipulation" whereby Parliament simply "rubber stamped" nominees linked to Mbeki.[591] A bold headline in the *Sunday Times* declared, "ANC's bullies ram through SABC board"; the accompanying story reported how "the iron hand of Luthuli House" had commanded, "This is the list – no discussion."[592]

President Mbeki authorised the appointment of his loyalists shortly after his failed bid to continue on as president of the ANC. As one journalist wisecracked, "Mbeki was widely seen as cocking a snook at his own party's new leadership" by installing people with ties to himself and black African business interests.[593]

That then provoked allies of ANC President Jacob Zuma to initiate a campaign to have the appointees removed. The attention of the board members was thereby sidetracked from doing the actual work of running the SABC to fighting to preserve their own positions instead. In 2008 Parliament passed amendments to the communications bill, allowing the entire SABC board to be removed by Parliament from what are designed to be five-year terms. That would place board members in a constant state of anxiety, perpetually second-guessing their own actions.

Pieter Mulder of the opposition Freedom Front Plus party announced, "Alarm bells should be sounding over the abuse of democracy when a ruling party finds it necessary to amend laws in order to solve short-term internal problems."[594] That was similar to a letter-to-the-editor writer who had lamented in an earlier round of crises at the SABC, "the public broadcaster has opted to wage a guerrilla war against our nascent democracy". However, he cautioned, "It would be a very sad situation if the SABC boards and staff were to be changed after every election to allow for party deployment by the winner."[595]

The previous reference to "The knives are out for Dali Mpofu" alluded to riveting personnel dramas affecting some of the highest ranking SABC officials as well. On 6 May 2008 CEO Mpofu suspended managing director of news, Snuki Zikalala. But the next day the SABC board rallied behind Zikalala and suspended Mpofu in retaliation. And it did so twice more in a month, after he successfully challenged the board's actions in court. Mpofu's seesawing legal dispute captured headlines daily.[596]

Zikalala had come under attack because of allegations of blacklisting of certain political commentators by his division (see below). And the stated complaint against Mpofu was that he had bungled two important contracts: domestic soccer broadcasting rights had gone to a private broadcaster, as did the local broadcast rights to the 2010 Soccer World Cup tournament. Moreover, when a group of senior managers demanded that the board be dissolved because of the disruption it was causing, they themselves were also suspended. The back story was that each party in these dramas had its respective allies, and SABC personnel became the public face of some very deeply entrenched battles.

This amount of turmoil had disastrous consequences for the SABC. Internally, morale was low; employees were fretful about the security of their jobs and the likely conditions of their work in the future, should they be fortunate enough to stay on. Externally, the public's perception of its national broadcaster had plummeted precipitously. The SABC's integrity and editorial independence had been severely compromised, its production capacity had diminished due to such a high degree of in-house squabbling, and its future direction become hazy at best. By mid-year 2009, the members of the controversial SABC board had resigned and it was dissolved by Parliament; the broadcaster was delinquent in paying scores of independent producers and in need of a multibillion-rand financial bailout; and investigations were underway into charges of fraud and mismanagement.

Making a List?

Coinciding with the SABC's refusal to screen *Unauthorised: Thabo Mbeki*, another scandal rocked the national public broadcaster, an episode that prompted drawing additional analogies with apartheid-era practices. The SABC was accused of maintaining a blacklist of commentators whom it would not call upon to make editorial remarks on its programmes. The common characteristic reportedly shared by those who were being banned was their critical stance towards Thabo Mbeki and his government. Alleged to be included on the list was William Gumede, one of the directors of Broad Daylight Films. He had had a previous experience with the SABC balking at airing one of his projects when a programme about his book on the president was axed from the television schedule.[597]

What began as a rumour erupted as a scandal when well-known SABC radio personality John Perlman directly challenged one of his guests on air, SABC spokesperson Kaizer Kganyago. Perlman contradicted Kganyago's denial that a blacklist existed by stating, "it is happening in practice". Perlman confirmed he knew this from personal experience. An article on the issue then wondered, "Will SAfm presenter John Perlman's head roll?"[598] And a letter-to-the-editor writer noted "some speculation that he might be fired for heresy".[599]

A further report stated that several SABC producers confirmed that they were told by Snuki Zikalala, the managing director of SABC news and current affairs, to snub certain voices, a list of people that overlapped with one that Mbeki himself attacked in *ANC Today*. Nevertheless, the SABC denied enforcing "any blanket bans".[600] The most Kganyago would admit to was circulating an in-house document to stimulate discussion about who would be "acceptable" talking heads and who would not.

One person who charged to the SABC's defence was Sandile Memela, the man from the Department of Arts and Culture who just a month earlier had blasted black Africans who criticised the government as "coconut intellectuals" during the debate over the Native Club (Chapter 4). Memela hailed Zikalala as a "patriotic journalist" and snickered at "non-existent banning orders", summoning apartheid era lingo. And he brushed away any imputations of importance to those who were supposedly banned by declaring, "the media itself ... has created the false impression that these personalities are 'know-alls' without whose subjective knowledge we would all soon be plunged into Middle Age-like darkness. This is a blatant lie." He charged, "[T]here is absolutely nothing breathtaking about so-called commentators: they are just replaceable pieces of the human experience." Memela wrote this off as a non-story. "[W]hat is happening at the SABC," he concluded, "is an attempt at precisely what takes place in every newsroom everyday: 'filtering' opinion!"[601]

But far more people believed this was a disturbing development.

An editorial in the *Citizen* cautioned that the likelihood of a blacklist "should ring alarm bells" and argued, "Following the axing of the Mbeki documentary, it is clear that the noose is tightening around critics of the government. And, with cracks in its tripartite alliance … the ANC is desperate to control the SABC and suppress independent voices." It was one of many articles that used the phrase "His Master's Voice" to describe the relationship between the SABC and the ANC president,[602] while another journalist derided the broadcaster as a "lapdog of the ANC".[603]

Dali Mpofu appointed a commission of inquiry to investigate the charge that there was an SABC blacklist. Done without the consultation or support of the SABC board, it would later came back to haunt him. The investigation reached a mixed conclusion. On the one hand, it revealed that certain individuals were indeed habitually ignored for comment, violating the Broadcast Act, the Constitution, and the SABC's own licence. On the other, the practice was inconsistent and did not reveal a clear-cut bias against particular perspectives, for example, being anti-Mbeki. As much as anything, decisions were made in accord with the personal prejudices of news director Snuki Zikalala and what he felt to be "acceptable" and "unacceptable". No smoking gun could be found: editorial preferences tended to be expressed verbally, rather than being written down.

Nevertheless, the stench of systematic bias remained strong. A professor of media observed, "Inheritors of a media apparatus designed to legitimise the apartheid regime, the ANC apparatchiks who control the SABC have faithfully continued the practice of seeing themselves as the PR arm of the state." He cautioned, "The irony is that the abuse of the SABC's public service mandate will as surely backfire on the ANC and its SABC hacks as it did on the apartheid system."[604]

During this 2006 controversy at the SABC, CEO Dali Mpofu pledged, "I want to get to the bottom of the allegations and any problems that affect us as a national public broadcaster … Within a year or so the SABC must be beyond reproach."[605] That promise was unrealised: the SABC instead became embroiled in ever more turmoil. The conjecture about John Perlman's fate after becoming a whistleblower was well founded, however: half a year after this saga began, Perlman resigned from SAfm, along with his co-anchor Nikiwe Bikitsha.

Taking Sides

One columnist, reflecting upon the South African media's many exposés of dishonourable behaviour on the part of government employees, quipped, "When a senior official is exposed as having had her hand in the cookie jar, it wasn't the editor who put it there."[606] Nonetheless, negative fallout has affected journalists who are responsible for making such disclosures, and some of their professional associations as well.

SABC head Dali Mpofu reacted bitterly to the articles the *Sunday Times* published about Health Minister Tshabalala-Msimang, as he did to the critical coverage his own organisation received throughout the press. He denounced what he saw as a withering of journalistic ethics, and in a stinging letter withdrawing the SABC from Sanef, the South African National Editors' Forum, Mpofu declared, "[We] will no longer stand idle whilst we are being made a whipping boy and a scapegoat by the profit-driven media. Even less are we prepared to associate with the enemies of our freedom and our people. We cannot remain quiet while our mothers [Tshabalala-Msimang] and our democratically chosen leaders are stripped naked for the sole purpose of selling newspapers."[607]

Mpofu was, thereby, once again staking out a prime position on the moral high ground. To solidify that claim, he chose the formulaic strategy of invoking a mythically unspoiled version of Africanness. "Shame on all of you," Mpofu charged, "especially those who have turned their backs on your own cultural values for 30 pieces of silver, pretending to be converted to foreign, frigid and feelingless [sic] freedoms."[608] He could have as easily been rebuking local advocates for gay rights.

Mpofu had thought of pulling the SABC out of Sanef before the Tshabalala-Msimang revelations, but those articles convinced him he no longer wished to be part of that professional association. Employing the same tactic he used against Ben Cashdan, Mpofu criticised media professor Anton Harber and veteran journalist and freedom-of-expression advocate Raymond Louw as "right-wing, conservative", and labelled *Sunday Times* editor Mondli Makhanya a "fellow traveller" and a "delinquent" for discourteously referring to the health minister by her first name. That, said Mpofu, "is foreign to our culture".[609] Harber's response was not the only one that characterised Mpofu's management style as being dictated "by tantrum",[610] and he lamented that "at a time when the SABC should be celebrating the fact that they had joined the world of independent journalism after 1994, it was retreating into a laager".[611]

At least one black African journalist challenged Mpofu's usurpation of the right to exclusively speak for his colleagues or to narrowly define what is "African". Thabo Leshilo, editor of the *Sowetan*, argued that support for freedom of expression is not a luxury of the privileged but a concern for all, and should have no colour requirements. He found it insulting that Mpofu believed freedom of expression to be a "foreign" notion. Furthermore, Leshilo characterised the professional practice that Mpofu was advocating as "patriotic journalism" – not a complimentary term, as it had been for Sandile Memela – an approach that meant that "reporting for the public interest is inhumane and inimical to the values of ubuntu".[612]

A white columnist likewise rejected Mpofu's stance, and used the man's own statements to discredit him. Andrew Donaldson did nothing to disguise his disdain for the SABC executive's perspective. Reporting on a Media and Society Conference hosted by Sanef and the SABC, Donaldson raged, "[Dali] Mpofu and [Smuts] Ngonyama [ANC information chief] know f*** all about press freedom. Nothing. *Niks*. Zip. Diddley-squat. *Ha a tsebe selo*." In a confusing pronouncement that obfuscated more than it explained, Mpofu purportedly referred to the stories published by the *Sunday Times* on the health minister by saying, "Freedom of the press and public interest were 'red herrings' … The press is a machine, it doesn't have any freedom. Freedom belongs to the people, they have a right to make a choice."[613]

Donaldson went on to describe a peculiar hypothetical allusion Mpofu made to "tradition". The journalist wrote, "He [Mpofu] then turned to his penis. In the South African context, he said, freedom of expression should also be the right to express culture. In his culture, for instance, he could not address gatherings, like the conference, if he was uncircumcised. 'So,' Mpofu concluded, 'from narrow Western eyes, [they] see it as a denial of freedom of expression.'"[614] With that declaration Mpofu joined the ranks of other South African public figures who have cynically invoked "culture" as a way to bludgeon others and dismiss a universalistic concept that could instead be "customised" to fit the most challenging encounters between tradition and contemporary life.

Pointing Fingers

At a time when the media become fall guys for beleaguered politicians and convenient scapegoats for complex problems, it should not be surprising that after xenophobic violence exploded throughout South Africa's major urban areas in May 2008, some people pointed to the media as a prime culprit. Sixty-two individuals died and tens of thousands were driven from their homes during the bloodshed. It was the result of pent-up frustration felt by South Africa's poor, which has obvious origins in the country's acutely unequal distribution of wealth, the government's deficient record of service delivery, and the enormous strain put on housing and jobs by the influx of political and economic refugees across South Africa's relatively unregulated borders.

Criticism erupted on a regional stage: at an awards ceremony in Accra, Ghana, for African Journalist of the Year, one speaker said, "There will be no accountability for the deaths in South Africa, Zimbabwe, Kenya. The media has the power to make people accountable but we don't because we are not independent." Amare Aregawi, an Ethiopian media specialist, argued more specifically, claiming that a "lack of thorough analysis fuelled both Kenyan and South African crises. 'Reporting in South Africa did not show the simmering hatred' after attacks on Somali immigrants in 2007."[615] However, an examination of press coverage shows that such incidents have regularly made the news. If no official ameliorative action followed, can the media legitimately be blamed?

The tabloid *Daily Sun* bore the brunt of the condemnation of the media in relation to the 2008 attacks. This paper proudly declares that its primary readership is "the guy in the blue overall", the ubiquitous uniform of (primarily) black African manual labourers. Critics call it "trash", "sensationalism", and claim it sometimes fabricates stories.[616] One profile of the paper observed, "Like sensational tabloids the world over it shrieks, groans, crackles and weeps with stories that extract every ounce of emotional juice from the daily freak show of life."[617]

But readers are delighted with it: the *Daily Sun* boasts the largest circulation in the country (its Sunday edition published the controversial column by Jon Qwelane). They relish the lurid reports of out-of-control human emotions and of the fantastical, such as the antics of tokoloshes. They also hungrily devour the regular reports of bumbling and deceit by business and government. More than any other source, the *Daily Sun* tutors the masses on how they are being ripped off or underserved. And it does so in language they can understand.

The *Daily Sun* came under fire for the lingo it used during the violence, particularly its labelling of immigrants and refugees as "aliens" with regularity in sensationalistic headlines. A study showed that the *Daily Sun* "had the highest number of reports on foreign nationals … and it was also guilty of the highest degree of slanting".[618] Some people therefore drew a direct line from such publicity to concrete actions, inflating what might be a contributing factor at best to being a root cause of the trouble instead. Complaints were made to the SAHRC and also to the Press Ombudsman by a coalition of groups including the Media Monitoring Project, the Consortium for Refugees and Migrants in South Africa, Lawyers for Human Rights and others, because the *Daily Sun* used derogatory references to describe non-nationals and routinely tied them to crime. Moreover, many critics felt the newspaper did not condemn the violence, but rather seemed to be a mouthpiece for the perpetrators. The Press Ombudsman's eventual rejection of these claims drew ire.[619]

Arts and Culture Minister Pallo Jordan's response to this issue was opportunistic and alarming. He felt the *Daily Sun*'s handling of these events was prima facie evidence for the necessity of a governmental watchdog agency: "Have you been reading the *Daily Sun* for the past three weeks?" he asked. "Do it and if after that you do not think we need a media tribunal then you are far more optimistic than most of us are." Moreover, he faulted the community of professional journalists for not watching over their own: "[There] is a single newspaper inciting the violence," Jordan noted, "and not a single one of the [other] newspapers, not even Sanef (South African National Editor's Forum), has taken it up."[620]

Who's at the Controls?

The South African media have been largely self-regulated. A Press Ombudsman, sponsored by the Press Council, responds to public complaints and investigates whether or not violations of the South African Press Code have taken place. While the ombudsman cannot impose fines, he can ask offenders to apologise. In light of many controversies regarding the media, however – especially the *Sunday Times* disclosures about the health minister

– the ANC has raised the possibility of imposing government oversight as well. Journalist Maureen Isaacson noted, "The government's already stretched tolerance went to hell after the *Sunday Times* expose."[621]

The idea of a Media Appeals Tribunal (MAT) first surfaced at a June 2007 ANC policy conference. This body would provide a place to appeal decisions made by the ombudsman, and would be accountable to Parliament. During the ANC Polokwane conference later that year, the ANC passed a resolution entitled *Communications and the Battle of Ideas* that stressed the need to balance freedom of expression with the right to privacy and human dignity. The text read, "It has to be understood as an initiative to strengthen the human rights culture embodied in the principles of our constitution and an effort to guarantee the equal enjoyment of human rights by all citizens."[622]

The ANC argued that an ombudsman working under the auspices of a professional association could not be an effective regulator. But a Media Appeals Tribunal raised fears that the ANC wished to tame the media because of what many party loyalists felt was its relentlessly adversarial relationship to government. President Mbeki, for example, had referred to the *Sunday Times* in an online letter as exhibiting "truly frightening behaviour, which, in reality, belongs to wild animals".[623] An appeals tribunal would ensure that freedom of expression could not be used to justify conduct such as publicising information from confidential records. But critics of the proposal feared the repression this potentially represented. One journalist claimed, "If an organ of state can sit in judgement over the media, they are no longer free … It's one of those touchstones that determine whether a country can call itself democratic."[624]

Pallo Jordan – perhaps intentionally, perhaps not – appeared to tip the ANC's hand by revealing that the MAT may have been an idle threat. Jordan stated, "The media tribunal is just an idea, no one has worked out what they are going to do. At the end of the day, they may think it is not a good idea. But one of the reasons why people are so fed up is the propensity of the South African media to try people in the press."[625] Yet in a country where a politician like Jacob Zuma can repeatedly evade punishment and a cabinet minister behaved in ways directly contradictory to her profession and policies, the media become the public's court of last resort.

Media and its Discontents

Some debates regarding South African media parallel those happening elsewhere in the world. Media concentration and editorial independence are a growing concern, especially when business conglomerates with particular political ties threaten to increase their holdings to include key media outlets. In 2007, for example, cash-heavy corporations with directors connected to the ANC made bids to take over both the *Sunday Times* and the *Mail & Guardian*, the newspapers that have had the most critical editorial policies and have become the biggest irritants to the ruling party.

A diversity of perspectives is a coveted public goal in a democratic society, and especially in a country with a plethora of languages and cultural traditions. But attempts to amplify "African" versus European-centred cultural offerings can mean that new programming forces out established, beloved programmes and personalities. Longtime viewers and listeners feel themselves being displaced in what seems like a zero-sum game of programming based on crude racial categorisation rather than journalistic quality, and the failure to recognise that audience preferences cross cultural lines and are not simply reducible to group membership.

And a proposed Protection of Information Bill laying out guidelines for the security classification of government documents threatens to limit the investigative reach of reporters. Critics are concerned that national security interests be balanced with transparency regarding journalistic investigations of official corruption or the abuse of power. Would regulations be legitimate informational firewalls, or simply shields held up to conceal official excesses and wrongdoing?[626]

At the end of the day, as important as these debates are philosophically, how do they impact the bulk of South Africa's citizenry? As a whole, media practitioners were out of touch with the sentiments of the rank-and-file ANC membership and had not foreseen Jacob Zuma's decisive defeat of Thabo Mbeki for the ANC presidency at the December 2007 national conference in Polokwane – what one commentator called a "Zunami".[627] Jane Duncan believed that a major reason Zuma downgraded his legal claims against the media afterwards was because he realised that all the critical media coverage of him had not significantly handicapped his rise to power. She argued, "I don't think that Zuma supporters necessarily give a damn about what Zapiro or others have had to say about Zuma."

This perspective is ratified by another media observer, Edwin Naidu, who states, "In the run-up to Polokwane, the media and political analysts got it wrong by assuming that the portrayal of Zuma as a sex-hungry person with loose morals and an inability to manage his finances was enough to consign him to the political scrapheap." That led Naidu to question, "In a country of almost 48 million, a paltry three to four million people read newspapers so, in essence, the media has to ask itself who it is talking to and on behalf of whom?"[628]

For obvious reasons, the commercial media focus on issues concerning audiences drawn from the higher economic groups. According to Duncan, "other people have exercised their freedom of expression in more popular and unmediated forms", such as public protests, as a result. There is an extremely high incidence of such events in South Africa: an estimate by the Centre for Civil Society at the University of KwaZulu-Natal puts the number of service delivery protests by black South Africans at 6000 per year; a 2009 newspaper headline blared the phrase "Burn, the Beloved Country".[629] For Duncan this is an indication that "people are using gatherings and demonstrations in order to claim a voice that they feel that they do not have through the media". She concluded, "[The] chattering classes have very little influence over politics in this country, and particularly politics within the ruling party. It [their talk] tends to just float over the surfaces" In Duncan's estimation, "I think people in South Africa practise freedom of expression in spite of the media, not because of it".[630]

So while politicians have reacted with predictable anger at pointedly negative media depictions of themselves, and have proposed various means of reining in free expression, the media are also in some basic respects peripheral concerns. That may help explain why Thabo Mbeki only granted the *Mail & Guardian* its first interview with him during his presidency in the run-up to Polokwane, and he consented to an extended conversation with Mondli Makhanya of the *Sunday Times* as well. Courting the media can have its benefits, such as burnishing badly blemished public profiles, but print and broadcast journalists do not seem to hold the power to make or break a career.

Contributors to the debates over the media have commonly invoked apartheid-era references to either dramatise their own perspective or diminish the magnitude of their opponents' grievances. Allusions to "necklacing the truth", *askari, impimpi,* and banning orders all point to the enduring resonance of experiences during that half-century of intense repression, especially as they impacted the free flow of ideas. The South African media will undoubtedly continue to be contested terrain, even if they primarily speak to an audience that represents a relatively small proportion of the population overall.

Alternative avenues for expressing underrepresented points of view – be they the streets or the information superhighway – will continue to attract attention as well. Black African discontent in the townships spills into the open; white Afrikaner disgruntlement has colonised certain websites. A distinctive corollary to the crime websites detailed earlier is the circulation of alarming rumours and speculation on the net.

In 2007 right-wing fear of widespread black-on-white violence occurring when Mandela dies – variously dubbed "Operation white clean-up", "the Night of the Long Knives", or "Uhuru" – fuelled a rumour that Madiba had died, but the government was covering up his death to forestall the inevitability of such carnage (Mandela was, in fact, on holiday in Mozambique). The stories were spun from the visions of genocide by Siener van Rensburg, the so-called Boere Nostradamus, from the Boer War-era.

Such hoax emails have prompted investigations into links between the Boeremag (on trial for treason, terrorism, sabotage and murder, a process that dragged on for years; see Chapter 3) and a group called the Suidlanders, whose spokesperson Tanya du Preez has adopted the nom de guerre Racheltjie de Beer, an Afrikaner folk heroine. But echoing the distrust of the mainstream media, some whites feel this is in fact a government disinformation campaign to expose whites' plans to mobilise post-Mandela.[631]

And at the time of Mandela's 88th birthday in 2006, a racist ringtone circulated in the Western Cape featuring a song that declared *kaffirs* should be dragged behind a bakkie and attacked with dogs. Unlike columnists accused of hate speech, whose names and professional homes are public information, it is much more difficult to trace the source of such messages. The ANC Western Cape provincial secretary Mcebisi Skwatsha denounced "these thugs who try to undermine our democracy, peace and stability, and at the same time, encourage violence against people".[632]

First National Bank executives may have backed away from launching their anti-crime media campaign, but a law firm initiated its own mini-crusade by publishing an advertisement in the *Beeld*, the Afrikaans-language newspaper. It read, in part, "We might not have an advertising budget like that of FNB, but we have De la Rey courage." A partner in the practice explained why they had invoked the name of an Afrikaner general from the Anglo-Boer War: "De la Rey courage is something that he had when he took up the struggle against the English colonialists in a peaceful way, not by way of arms … The new struggle is against crime." This sort of nostalgic search for leadership reveals a great deal about the feelings of pervasive social crisis held by citizens under South Africa's new political dispensation, and about the present status of Afrikaners in particular.[633]

CHAPTER 6

Shame and Disgrace: The Arts, their Publics and Would-be Censors

Censorship: ... a sort of forced removal of ideas into artificial homelands for the ideologically impure.

Chris Roper, 1998a

Apartheid haunts; censorship has gone to hell. It is not part of the aftermath of apartheid.

Nadine Gordimer, 2001

In recent years many autocratic leaders and powerful regimes have fallen, and so have the monuments erected to their glory. Influential ideas have been challenged; new paradigms and discourses have replaced them. And in the realm of popular culture, characters and stories that had been adored for generations have been called into question.

The *Adventures of Tintin* has come under fire by critics in a politically correct age as embodying racist and colonialist ideas, and thereby perpetuating pernicious stereotypes and beliefs. In the United Kingdom, as well as in Belgium, the home of cartoonist Hergé (Georges Remi), official commissions have investigated the appropriateness of continuing to publish some of his drawings of native peoples that do not align with contemporary reality and consciousness. And in South Africa, the publisher of the series in Afrikaans decided not to bring out *Tintin in the Congo* for those very (sensitive) reasons. Local cartoonist Zapiro urged the company not to ban the story but to contextualise it instead. "I would talk about it," he argued, "I wouldn't censor it."[634]

Zapiro's creative turf is the editorial cartoon, and his visual perspective on the controversy skilfully captured the essence of the dispute (*The Star*, 31 July 2007): a book cover reflecting the original design depicts Tintin, his dog (Milou/Snowy), and a broadly caricatured black child riding together in a motorcar, circa 1931. Boxes marked "racism" and "paternalism" are strapped to the vehicle's sides in this version, and a movie camera marked "colonial view" is mounted onto it as well. Their auto has been stopped at a security boom marked "2007". A puzzled officer asks, "What do we do about that baggage?" His colleague proposes, "Perhaps a warning label …"

But other voices were not so measured. An enraged letter-to-the-editor writer denounced the books and rejected Remi's depiction of natives: "Such obnoxious disparagement is not new and it will continue to prosper as long as there are fellow perverts who feed like maggots on the carrion of racist stereotypes." He concluded his harangue with a hypothesis: "Seemingly, due to a warped imagination and lack of talent, Remi resorts to scraping at the bottom of sewers to dredge the filth of racism." The headline that accompanied the piece – obviously not scripted by the same person – was jarringly at odds with this man's sentiments: "Freedom of expression should always prevail", it declared.[635]

Tintin has not been the only target of such hand ringing and invective, or even alteration. For example, children's author Enid Blyton, the creator of popular children's books including *The Magic Faraway Tree*, *The Enchanted Wood* and *The Folk of the Faraway Tree*, has been beloved in South Africa over generations, partly because of the country's connection with the Commonwealth. In recent years the names of three of the four children in these stories have been changed: Bessie to Beth, because of possible "connotations of black slavery", and Fanny to Frannie and Dick to Rick because of potential sexual associations. Furthermore, Gilbert the Gollywog has disappeared from the cast of characters altogether. The owner of the copyright stated, in a fashion characteristic of those who fiddle with an artist's original intent and also presume to be in touch with what audiences desire, "This is not about being politically correct, but about making the characters relevant to today's consumers."[636]

These revisionist episodes once again underscore how global events generate local reverberations. Nadine Gordimer's bold pronouncement that censorship has "gone to hell" during the democratic era in South Africa is, regrettably, wishful thinking. The roster of those endowed with power in the country may have changed since 1994, and the character of the controls at their disposal may have been altered, but significant efforts to restrict, rework or expunge expression from the public arena continue to occur.

Just as the local media have become the focus of attempts at regulation, artists of all types have also run up against noteworthy barriers to their exercise of freedom of expression. In the past few years even Gordimer's work has encountered such problems. And she herself has been accused of trying to censor a fellow writer. Such cultural wars are a barometer of the countervailing winds of change and resistance blowing across South Africa's cultural landscape.

Vagina Dialogues

In the early days of South Africa's democracy a student artwork plummeted from honour to infamy within a matter of days. Until recently, *Useful Objects*, a ceramic piece by Kaolin Thompson, was arguably the most notorious artwork produced in the post-apartheid era. It unquestionably helped shape the debate around what freedom of expression would look like under the new political dispensation.

Thompson's creation garnered the Martienssen Prize in 1996 for the best student work in an annual exhibition held at the University of the Witwatersrand. She was not yet 20 years old. A review in the *Mail & Guardian* praised the work, noting that it addressed sexual and political issues as well as raised significant questions regarding the intersection of art and craft. A picture of it accompanied the article.[637] Because of the attention this review drew to the piece, *Useful Objects* became the subject of a parliamentary debate less than two weeks later.

Useful Objects is a ceramic ashtray with a half-smoked Gauloise Blondes cigarette. In a follow-up to the original *Mail & Guardian* review, the same critic described it as "resembling a black vagina, lips or a turd".[638] In particular it raised the ire of Baleka Kgositsile, deputy speaker of Parliament, based upon what she'd gleaned from the initial article. She subsequently condemned the work in a critique that was featured in another major South African newspaper.

Kgositsile questioned whether a picture of an artwork such as *Useful Objects* would have been published had it instead depicted the genitalia of a white woman or man, or the organs of a black man for that matter. She argued, "While 'freedom of expression' is something we must guard jealously, especially because of the repression we have experienced under apartheid, it cannot be encouraged at all costs. People's pride and dignity," she stressed, "cannot be trampled on in the name of freedom of expression."[639]

If Kgositsile were a private citizen, her opinion would have been merely one of many. But it gained considerable weight because of her official position, and *Useful Objects* grew in significance because it materialised at the same time that new legislation was being considered. The proposed Film and Publication Bill would establish a Film and Publication Board, a Review Board and Classification Committees. As projected, this would have liberalised the incorporation of sexually explicit material within certain media, but did not cover television and newspapers.[640]

Thompson's artwork raised the concern that perhaps the bill needed to be expanded and strengthened, making it even more comprehensive than previous apartheid regulations. Kgositsile declared, "If need be, legislation must protect our people from degradation that is likely to continue in the name of trying to keep up with some arbitrary artistic ideals not set by the majority of those affected by these academic debates."[641] The lawmaker thus invoked a classic argument of would-be censors, that the acceptability of art should somehow be democratically determined. At the same time, she highlighted the immense gap in understanding between those operating in the art world or rarified intellectual circles, and others in the general public and the government.

Kgositsile's position drew both support and criticism. One letter writer asked, "How can we expose the negative images while at the same time strengthen the positive images? Thompson has failed to achieve this balance – if she ever attempted to."[642] As reasonable as this may sound on first consideration, it proposed a project different from the one the artist chose for herself. Moreover, it was calling for something other than art, an outcome that was more didactic than imaginative.

The writer continued, "Black women's bodies have been used as dumping grounds and 'useful objects' throughout history – but we are not victims. We have a history of struggle that goes back to the time of colonial conquest and slavery. Perhaps the vagina could have been shown contracting," she suggested, "therefore rejecting the cigarette … instead of lying there helplessly."[643] These sentiments recall the debate over the play *Thuthula – Heart of the Labyrinth* (Chapter 3), where one creation was expected to shoulder a heavy symbolic load due to a long history of racial oppression, and because of the relative paucity of opportunities that people who have been exploited have had to express themselves creatively in the public realm.

Members of the art community generally defended the work, one of the most repeated themes being that multiple meanings could be embedded within *Useful Objects*, and that depicting the oppression of women did not perfunctorily replicate their exploitation. Several critics of Kgositsile's position bemoaned the fact that the politician had missed the irony in the artwork, a fairly predictable situation given the barriers that black Africans have faced in furthering their educations and being exposed to arcane modes of expression.[644] Because of that historic imbalance in opportunities, one person's sly critique can easily become another's affront.

One writer, employing a large measure of satire himself, declared, "The old regime enacted censorship laws to perpetuate the unjust exploitation of the majority by a minority. These laws are to be scrapped," he noted, "but some artists are seizing the opportunity to produce works which do not subscribe to the artistic ideals of the masses, or which are open to many interpretations." This man mockingly cautioned, "To safeguard our country's newly-won liberty, we must support Kgositsele's [sic] campaign for laws which restrict the release into the public domain of art prioritising artistic expression above nation-building."[645] But just beneath the surface of such sarcasm was a distressing sense of déjà vu; had the yoke of old-style censorship been shaken off, only to be replaced by new forms?

In his inimitable style, Zapiro neatly capsulised the dual threat to art in contemporary times: Kaolin Thompson's *Useful Objects* is shown flanked by two markedly different-looking people squaring off against each another. On one side is a rather demented and enraged man wielding a hand stamp with the word "CENSORED" inscribed upon it. On the other, a somewhat schoolmarmish Deputy Speaker Baleka Kgositsile glares at the work disapprovingly. One is identified as "politically incorrect white male apartheid-era censor"; the other, "politically correct black female post-apartheid would-be censor". But for all their differences, they share the same dialogue balloon: "I don't know about art, but I know what I **don't** like!" they pronounce in unison.[646]

Kaolin Thompson's voice was barely heard throughout this debate. Soon after the story broke she was quoted as saying, "Even though I didn't intend it to be racially specific, I wanted the work to be about pain, to highlight the objectification of women and to place the personal in the public sphere."[647] Later on she reflected that *Useful Objects* represented self-exploration and was therapeutic for her. But rather than be saddled with the reputation of "infamous artist" or indulging in "arty-farty, up-its-own-arse art",[648] Thompson switched creative direction. She devoted much of her creative attention in the aftermath to music, especially with her band Naked.

Thompson's one opportunity to discuss her work in public was by leading a discussion group at The Body Politic conference at her school, Wits University, the month after the student show. According to an account of the conference, "[S]he seemed hurt, baffled and perhaps excited that it was so easy to wind people up"[649] – a reasonable cluster of feelings for a young artist who was caught unawares in the public eye to experience. But since this was a gathering focused upon *au courant*, renegade theories of the body, taboo and transgression, with the spirit of Foucault infusing the proceedings, the broadest sampling of opinion was not being voiced.

Nearly simultaneously, however, a more public airing did take place: the SABC presented a discussion of the artwork and the fallout it had generated on a programme called *Focus*, moderated by journalist Max du Preez. But the SABC was later called before the Broadcasting Complaints Commission for showing the work during that programme. A complainant attacked Du Preez as a "pervert" and "grinning idiot"; Du Preez countered, "Victorian fundamentalists should not be able to write anything they like about journalists".[650] For his part, Du Preez argued that a productive discussion of controversial subject matter required that viewers actually see *Useful Objects*. And he rejected the suggestion that a warning should have been appended to his broadcast; to his mind, that might have sensationalised the situation to an even greater extent.

More than a year later *Useful Objects* was also drawn into the discussion at "Speaking of Others," a conference held in Cape Town as part of the Second Johannesburg Biennale. With the politics of representation an overarching theme of the gathering, *Useful Objects* became an important case study in racial and class privilege, exploiting the experiences of Others, and artistic intentions and responsibilities. One artist characterised the event as a "mini-truth commission".[651]

Useful Objects was bought by the Spier Wine Estate in Stellenbosch and became part of its collection of work by South African artists. An exhibition of paintings Thompson presented in 2005 demonstrated her sustained interest in depicting women and their sexuality. But whatever she has accomplished, articles about Thompson throughout the years invariably bring up the one youthful work that has become her signature production. The moniker "vagina artist" shadows her.

A Visceral Reaction

Looking back, it's evident that immediately post-1994, South African artists were determinedly testing the limits of acceptability, playfully toying with the previously taboo, assertively addressing subjects that could only be explored covertly in the past. A prime example was a 1997 exhibition entitled *Purity and Danger*, curated by Penny Siopis and inspired by a book by anthropologist Mary Douglas, whose work on natural categories, taboo and transgression, order and pollution, provides tantalising clues into understanding contemporary artistic practice as well as the responses it elicits.[652] Academic Jane Taylor opened the show with the following query: "what are our taboos now, in a time in which our constitution in so many ways is more radical, for some even more transgressive, than much popular opinion?"[653] The artists in *Purity and Danger* chose the body as their site of inquiry, a space of secrecy and abuse that had been cloaked with the shame of repressive religious morality and politically conspiratorial silences.

Out of more than a dozen participants, the work of one artist in the show drew particular attention: *I'm King of the Castle*, a set of 39 photographs of her six-year-old son by artist Terry Kurgan, with him play-acting various roles such as warrior, cowboy or ninja. In some instances he was naked. These images brought childhood sexuality and the eroticised bond between mother and child to the fore. Viewers' opinions included reactions such as "chilling", "nauseating" and "pornography".[654]

One critic dismissed such charges, following a line of reasoning that echoed the strategy previously used by expert witnesses who testified on behalf of an American museum director who was charged with pandering obscenity for exhibiting the photographs of Robert Mapplethorpe in Cincinnati. She stated, "[They] are *not* pornographic, because their form is as impeccably restrained as their content is combustible."[655] Another reviewer saw parallels with Victorian-era images, representations that we now interpret as an elaborate mixture of innocence and unrequited desire. She concluded, "In South Africa, not known for tolerating a culture of radical sex, acceptance of difference, or patience with conceptual art, an exhibition like Purity and Danger is a snake's tail rattling in the grass of social propriety."[656]

In 1998 Kurgan curated *Bringing up Baby: Artists Survey the Reproductive Body*. Like the first gay and lesbian exhibition *Gay Rights Rites Rewrites* (see below), this show was a response to specific political developments: in this case the parliamentary debate over abortion, which propelled previously private matters of sexuality into the public eye. As Kurgan stated in her introduction to the exhibition catalogue, "Dramatic changes in our social and political context have created the necessary public space for this exhibition."[657]

Kurgan's subsequent work has explored topics ranging from the intimacy of the family to multifaceted explorations of urban communities, from memory to the here-and-now, yet more than a decade later people commonly associate her with this early controversy.[658] And while a significant component of the negative response to Kurgan's work obviously relates to the fact that she presented photographs of a real child, taken by his mother, just a month later another artist was attacked for exploring similar territory. But in this instance the person was conjuring images just from his imagination, through paintings and drawings.

University-based Mark Hipper was exploring the human body in his artwork before becoming embroiled in a significant legal fight, and continued to do so until his death in 2010. One critic remarked on his "stringent visual economy" and the vulnerability of his nude figures.[659] Another found herself "immediately impressed by the expressive power of fine draughtsmanship. Some of the line is reminiscent of Matisse," she noted.[660] Yet another favourably compared his work to Francis Bacon's.[661] And in an earlier show in 1997 a reviewer characterised Hipper's artworks in the same way that Kurgan's photographs had been described: "The confluence of diverting subject matter and confident execution," she observed, "lends them their resolution and intensity."[662] But others could not get past his subject matter, and therein lay the trouble.

Hipper presented an exhibition whose focus was childhood sexuality, concurrent with the National Arts Festival in Grahamstown in 1997. *Viscera* was presented at the Rhodes University School of Fine Art, where Hipper worked, and was not officially a part of the annual festival. Deputy Minister of Home Affairs Lindiwe Sisulu raised concerns over the exhibition after it had been sensationalised in a newspaper account, although she had not then personally viewed it. That put her at loggerheads with Film and Publications Board CEO Dr Nana Makaula, who emphasised the impressive credentials of her fellow board members, asserted the independence of this body, and resisted any intimation that interference by government officials into matters under its jurisdiction would be tolerated.

The board was a newly authorised entity under the Film and Publications Act, the legislation that figured into the debate concerning Kaolin Thompson's *Useful Objects*. Mark Hipper's work became the first test of it. This issue caught the board unawares, the legislation being a mere two months old. CEO Makaula explained, "These events have overtaken us. When we took office we were supposed to take the Act and revise it … to first of all put forward classifications of things that were banned in the past, especially erotic material".[663] But the board wished to proceed in both the letter and the spirit of the regulations.

Local law officials also proceeded prudently because this was relatively uncharted territory for them as well. They received complaints from Sisulu, the South African Council for Child and Family Welfare, and the area's National Council of Child Welfare. Meanwhile, two members of the Film and Publications Board flew to Grahamstown to see the exhibition for themselves. They determined it was not pornographic or sexually stimulating for viewers, even though paintings showed a boy masturbating, and other works depicted children's genitals. The board members did, however, restrict viewing to children over 12 and ordered that a warning be posted so visitors could know what to expect. A subsequent meeting was held with additional board members, hearing the testimony of a variety of experts as well as the artist. The outcome once again was that Hipper was within the bounds of the law.[664]

What Hipper intended to be candid portrayals of children coming to terms with their sexuality, others rejected as lewd. Hipper believed that honest depictions and discussions around sex were healthy; his opponents believed such activities were harmful and dangerous. Significantly, Hipper used no live models to do his work. Moreover, the importance of context was critical to interpreting what he had done. Some of his close-up drawings of children's faces were inferred to portray sexual pleasure, although he disclosed that they were modelled on drawings of an asthmatic in a medical textbook,[665] and a reviewer noted that others resembled kids with Down Syndrome.[666] Hipper's most thorough description of his motives came after he testified before the Film and Publications Board. He explained, "I never saw the work being about children; they were about myself or my wife," he said. "We all carry a child within us, and at the time I was painting them it was really about being fragile, and experiencing vulnerability."[667]

Deputy Minister Sisulu acknowledged that hers was "'a conservative African background' and [she] was strongly opposed to pornography".[668] Her outrage put her in the same camp as Deputy Speaker Kgositsile; both interpreted the work of young white artists as being offensive and dangerous to people whom they believed were the most vulnerable, namely women and children.[669] "It's most frustrating to act within the framework of the law," Sisulu tellingly concluded.[670]

Trojans: Danger or Protection?

The sort of concerns that the photographs of Terry Kurgan and the drawings of Mark Hipper churned up about paedophilia and child abuse were unashamedly exploited the year before by outré performance artist Steven Cohen during the 1996 annual Gay and Lesbian Pride Parade in Johannesburg. Carrying a banner reading "BRING US YOUR CHILDREN, WHAT WE CAN'T FUCK WE EAT", he enraged people across the political and sexual spectrum.

Gay art and artists have emerged gradually on the South African scene. Looking at two exhibitions that claimed to be "firsts", one during apartheid and the other after it had been dismantled, reveals a great deal about the creation of local gay expression. In 1982 – a year when photographer Robert Mapplethorpe's work, which helped establish an explicitly gay contemporary aesthetic, was surfacing in America – a private gallery in Cape Town hosted what was billed as the inaugural national exhibition of gay art. But what, exactly, did "gay art" mean? And who was a "gay artist"?

In retrospect it was an ill-conceived affair with a muddied viewpoint that barely skimmed the surface of possibilities. "Ironically," a journalist pointed out, "most of the artists were 'straight' and this might be the first and last time they did gay works."[671] One of the participants patronisingly remarked, "[T]he gay world is a mysterious world, and so it is fun to fantasise about it. I find it interesting and inspiring."[672] And another reflected, "I think it is important to stretch oneself a bit further into different areas." Trying to identify with gays, she adds, "has been almost a spiritual experience that has given her insight and has broadened her outlook".[673] The exhibition showcased a sort of vicarious roleplaying, which neither afforded artists who were gay the opportunity to explore the meaning of their life experience and their art, nor did it begin to define the field of gay expression. It was more frivolous than foundational.

But a great deal had changed by 1996. The impact of the gay rights movement had become global. A draft constitution was being debated; since it has been ratified, this South African document has become an exemplar of inclusiveness worldwide. And artists felt much freer to explore identities that had previously been vilified and criminalised. It was against this backdrop that *Gay Rights Rites Rewrites* became the first national gay and lesbian art exhibition. It was different from the 1982 show in key ways: this one included considerably more artists (60 as opposed to five), its scope was more comprehensive, its themes more explicitly sexual, and it was hosted by museums – public institutions subject to community and official oversight because of the involvement of public funds.

This was a politicised exhibition from the outset. It was initiated to become part of the discussion around the sexual orientation clause in the interim constitution, and as a rejoinder to the homophobic utterances of Robert Mugabe (recall Gordon Froud's *A False-Bottomed Suitcase for Robert Mugabe*, discussed in Chapter 4, and included in this exhibition). The show was underwritten by the Royal Netherlands Embassy, one of countless examples wherein overseas government and non-governmental agencies have sponsored cultural and human rights programmes in South Africa. One reviewer characterised it as "celebrat[ing] gay desire" and "yet a strain of angst also runs through the exhibition".[674]

The roster of participants represented "gays and straights-in-solidarity"; Steven Cohen and Penny Siopis both contributed work, thereby representing each sector.[675] The objective of *Gay Rights Rites Rewrites* was to influence policy while at the same time beginning to construct a canon of gay art. It was initially assembled for the Southern African Colloquium on Gay and Lesbian Studies, a group that was obviously receptive to its *raison d'être*. But the exhibition ran afoul of public opinion when it later opened at Oliewenhuis, a museum housed in the former residence of the governor general of the Union of South Africa, a formidable edifice built in neo-Dutch style and surrounded by lush and expansive gardens. It is located in Bloemfontein, known as a centre of Afrikanerdom. A journalist noted the stark contrast between the openings at the different sites: "If Cape Town was an exercise in exquisitely stylish networking (the crowds snacked on choux pastry swans) … Bloemfontein was a different kettle of *koeksisters* … The opening itself was as predictably tense as Cape Town's was trendy."[676]

Oliewenhuis is a place where art competes with people wishing to take tea outdoors and enjoy the natural surroundings. It is as much a cultural institution as a place for family outings. One of the curators reflected a few years later, "It was no accident that we chose to take *Gay Rights Rites Rewrites* to the Oliewenhuis – it was to be a kind of Trojan Horse within a bastion of white Afrikaner conservatism."[677] Their provocative gesture was not unrewarded. As one observer noted, it "got tongues wagging".[678]

And more: before the exhibition opened, the director of the National Museum (which oversees Oliewenhuis) selected out a number of works and ordered that they be displayed separately in a closed room and with a warning attached. This space was variously described as a "quarantined" area or a "chamber of horrors".[679] Co-curator Joan Bellis explains that what these pieces shared in common was that they featured nudity, and frequently male genitalia. She recalls, "These works formed a proportionally small but integral part of a fairly large exhibition: clustered together, however, and especially to those who subsequently visited no other room, they created a deliberately misleading impression."[680] This official intervention in effect concentrated the overtly sexual material in one place, thereby reinforcing the hoariest, most negative (read: deviant) stereotypes of the gay community.

Although a group of local clergy agitated for closing the show, it was not successful. At a critical juncture the deputy minister of arts and culture sent a warning to the director of the National Museum that "any such action taken against the exhibition would go against the grain of the interim constitution".[681]

Bellis provocatively argues that the end of apartheid created a psychological vacuum for people who had supported the previous regime, and that gay people provided a surrogate target for their anxieties and hatred. "Homophobia comes as easily to the practitioners of apartheid as does racism," she asserts. Exercising control over the exhibition, therefore, represented "a relocation of the political dynamic of 'otherness' from black to gay and a continuation of the apartheid mindset".[682]

Bellis also makes a valuable distinction between gay art and artists, and queer art and artists, a division that is possible only in light of theorising that has emerged during the intervening years. Because this exhibition was conceived as playing a part in a public dialogue regarding inclusion of gay people under the umbrella of legal protection, much of the art fell within the bounds of accepted and acceptable norms of expression. But some artists took a less assimilationist stance, celebrating queerness with a confrontational, devil-may-care attitude.

Steven Cohen was representative of this group, and his work was among the most talked-about. His *Pope Art* (1995) responded to a papal visit to South Africa.[683] A photographic screenprint on cloth, the repetition of a riotous array of disparate elements created unlikely, in-your-face combinations: a South African flag, a crying infant, a headless man who is positioned "bottoms up", condoms, the profile of a pope, and an erect penis mixed in a visual mayhem of sacred and profane. On the one hand works such as these defiantly flouted propriety and conventionality. On the other, they provided an obvious focus for official condemnation and attempts at containment, became the fantasised target of a clergyman with an urge to spraypaint,[684] and challenged the work of those who chose to "normalise" gayness rather than sensationalise it.

But Bellis observes that what may have been more unsettling than the provocative artists was the fact that people whose works were already in the Oliewenhuis collection were now revealed to be gay because of their inclusion in this show – unsettling because they had been there all along, but undetected. Revisiting her earlier allusion Bellis suggests, "[A] battering ram is easily recognisable as dangerous; a Trojan horse is towed unrecognised within the very walls of the beleaguered city."[685]

In the final analysis, *Gay Rights Rites Rewrites* provides a superb example of the social construction of acceptability. The selection of works remained uniform as the exhibition travelled through three South African venues: Cape Town, Bloemfontein, and finally Johannesburg (where celebrants at that opening sipped blue vodka). What differed was the reception. In Bloemfontein, where Afrikaner conservatism and Dutch Reform asceticism command considerable weight, religious groups were able to quickly mobilise against what they viewed as a grave moral transgression. The same images that some metropoles and certain subcultures welcomed proved to be anathema within a more provincial setting.

The Suppression Two-Step

If Bloemfontein is a cultural capital for Afrikaners, Stellenbosch University in the Western Cape is a crown jewel. Coincident with the brouhaha over the national gay and lesbian exhibition, a series of controversies regarding artwork incorporating male genitalia also sparked protest.

In 1996 Mark Coetzee was swept into "the storm of the loincloth", "the battle of the bulges".[686] Coetzee was a recipient of the Volkskas Atelier Award, which paid his way to Paris to study and paint. After returning home, recipients were required to present a show of their work in one of the affiliate galleries of the South African Association of Arts (SAAA). Coetzee chose the Bellville branch, which shared a municipally owned building with the Bellville city library. Moreover, the local council paid the salary of the gallery's curator.[687]

The town administrator balked, however, when he learned that Coetzee's work featured male nudes. "[A]ttitudes stiffened after Coetzee disclosed the content of his work," an art critic slyly reported. "While the Bellville members probably have no problem admiring pictures of naked women, pictures of men in similar states of unadornment are a different ball game."[688]

Coetzee was offered a way out of the crisis similar to the strategy enacted at the Oliewenhuis in Bloemfontein: to segregate some of the "stronger" works from the main part of the show, along with a warning. But it was a resolution that Coetzee could not abide, and he held a "protest exhibition" elsewhere.[689]

Merely half a year later, controversy broke out again in the same venue, and over work by the same artist. In this instance he was part of a group show entitled *Bad Books*, featuring the work of over a dozen students and lecturers at Stellenbosch University. A press release stated the show's aim was "to reveal the unknown, the unspoken and the undiscovered".[690]

The previously quoted critic gleefully dubbed what occurred as a "battle of biblical proportions".[691] The piece that drew criticism was Coetzee's *His Gaze Falls II*, which featured a model of a penis in an open Bible. Government officials were drawn into the ruckus: after the mayor toured the exhibition he declared some of the works to be blasphemous and concluded they should be removed. When Gregory Kerr, an art professor at the university, resisted, he was "branded an Antichrist".[692] As word spread a group called Christians for Truth angrily entered the gallery and made off with the Bible. Coetzee, in response, laid a charge of theft against them.

In the end, the mayor decided to close down the show at the same time that participants chose to withdraw their work in protest. The mayor acted on the basis of complaints of both blasphemy and pornography from his constituents, and felt he had to be sensitive to them. The government's financial support of the gallery was his point of leverage. But clearly, more was involved in this story. "Many students were battling with [what Professor Kerr called] a 'poignant and difficult' reappraisal of the '*verkrampte*' [hard-line, narrow-minded] mores and authoritarian values of the former government."[693] Students at this elite Afrikaans-medium university, it seemed, were openly rebelling against the core principles of their personal, intellectual and spiritual fathers. And while an "alternative" defiant culture did exist among Afrikaner youth (see Chapter 7), the idea that something like that could be flourishing at Stellenbosch was anathema.

A spokesperson for Christians for Truth felt called to root out this supposed evil. Gerhard le Roux decried not only what he had seen at the gallery, but took it to be evidence of a broader problem of the attrition of authority. He announced his group was next targeting the university "where it would seem 'students were allowed to question any value system. If students at Stellenbosch are allowed to question a Christian value system, we parents should know that. Do they see their right to freedom of speech as an absolute right that includes blasphemy?'"[694] The hegemony of religious and political values that had been buttressed by the elaborate infrastructure of apartheid was eroding, much to the dismay of groups such as these.

This episode was not the last time Mark Coetzee hit the headlines, however. He was embroiled in yet another controversy the next year, one that demonstrated additional features of the intricate dance that artists and their opponents often engage in. Unlike Kaolin Thompson, who refused to be drawn into the spotlight, Coetzee seemed to actively seek its ambit.

In 1998 a group of fine arts master's candidates held a graduation exhibition at a Stellenbosch University gallery. Just prior to its opening, Professor Gregory Kerr ordered that Coetzee's life-sized paintings of men with erect penises be removed from the show. In response, his fellow students removed their work as well.

The "culprit" in this instance was the same person who had taken the heat over the previous show, defending artwork against censorship by government officials. Could someone have morphed from a guardian of free expression into its foe in less than a year?

Kerr characterised his decision as the "most horrible of my career".[695] His explanation for what he had done was that he had agreed he would give university authorities a "heads-up" should he feel any works might become controversial. Their reasoning was that they could thus be prepared in advance to deal with any protests that might occur. But Coetzee only delivered his work shortly before the exhibition commenced; just 15 minutes before the show was to open, Kerr had the artworks taken down.

Kerr was clearly a man perched on the horns of a dilemma: his personal sentiments endorsed artistic autonomy, but his institutional responsibilities pulled him towards restraint. His public statements reflected his predicament. "I fully support the students in their decision to take down their work," he declared, "as I would have done exactly the same under these circumstances."[696]

As a journalist noted, "neither Kerr nor Coetzee should be typed as the villin or victim".[697] Coetzee was a veteran of controversial situations and obviously played a part in orchestrating what happened to him. Kerr, in fact, accused him of "publicity seeking tardiness" as a deliberate ploy to kickstart the regulatory machinery.[698] On the other hand Kerr, as department chair, refused to contest the constraints of his position or the conditions that his superiors had laid out. A person in his situation obviously has to balance urgent issues against longer-term considerations, such as the future viability of his department. And it's in spaces such as these where compromises often get made that result in censorious actions.

After hearing that the students questioned the legitimacy of "pre-censorship" of their submissions, Kerr reconsidered what he had done. He later expressed regret that he had not taken more of a proactive stance against his superiors.[699] Good people working within institutional contexts sometimes feel forced to act in ways counter to values they hold dear. The lesson in such instances is that individuals who try to restrict the exhibition of art can be conservative or progressive, well intentioned or malicious. Whatever the motives, however, the consequences can be the same for the artists involved.

A Dane, in Dutch, Again

Common to these disputes regarding the body, concern over depictions of the male body in particular was paramount. In South Africa, which regrettably has the most HIV-infected people in the world, it was probably inevitable that such dis-ease would coalesce with anxieties centred around black African sexuality in particular and discomfort with public representations of the pandemic as well.

Relatively early on – both in the democratic history of the country and with the progression of the disease through the general population – the Transvaal Museum in Pretoria designed a travelling exhibition in conjunction with World AIDS Day 1995. The display included information on the spread of the virus as well as condoms and instructions on how to use them. The director boasted, "[T]he museum had consulted widely on the issue to ensure the exhibit was not offensive, and that it was politically correct." It was something of a surprise, therefore, when an early visitor called what she'd seen disgusting and equated it with pornography. She declared, "As a ratepayer, I think it is utterly appalling that this filth can be mounted in a public museum where it can be seen by schoolchildren."[700]

Emotional responses such as these, stemming from deeply held moral convictions, become perfunctory and routine. But a much more complex debate erupted at the 13th International AIDS Conference in Durban in 2000, a place where it would be reasonable to expect that attendees shared a common concern and a basic stock of knowledge, and would be less apt to respond unreflectively. In question was the work of Dutch photojournalist Geert van Kesteren: images of people struggling with AIDS in Zambia. They had been published in *Newsweek* and a book, *Mwendanjangula! Aids in Zambia*, and many of them depicted hospices, mortuaries, or funerals – casualties, for the most part, who were either dead or dying. The work was not banned per se, but it was not selected as part of the cultural programme. Gideon Mendel's *Positive Lives* and Gisele Wulfsohn's *Living Openly* were chosen instead. Several newspapers labelled these decisions censorship nonetheless.

Van Kesteren's project did not align with the ideology of conference organisers as precisely as the others did. In other words, Van Kesteren did not present a public face of AIDS that was sufficiently positive or "empowering". He highlighted victims, not warriors fighting on their own behalf. His work could potentially corroborate stereotypes and confirm public fears of the disease. But it also had the potential to expose a situation that gets a pitiably small amount of attention.

Van Kesteren's visual evidence portrayed people with little agency, meagre support, and scant hope. Even the titles that Mendel and Wulfsohn chose for their projects betray an approach that is fundamentally uplifting. A committee coordinator wrote, "It is considered policy of the government and NGOs that shock tactics in the context of South African society and culture are counterproductive and we have avoided this approach … many South African audiences are unsophisticated and not used to this kind of realism."[701]

So while the authenticity of what Van Kesteren had captured was not in dispute, its imagined impact most certainly was. The theme of the conference, ironically, was "Breaking the Silence".

A parallel situation played out a few years earlier in the US, when

Nicholas Nixon exhibited a selection of photographs of people with AIDS (PWAs) at the Museum of Modern Art in 1988 (later published as *Bearing Witness: People with AIDS*). Nixon, too, concentrated "on the physical ravages of the disease: the ghastly skin lesions, the wan bodies and sunken spirits", as I once described this work.[702] But that perspective did not sit well with ACT-UP, the direct-action group that fought public ignorance and prejudice as well as governmental inaction and corporate self-interest. ACT-UP members picketed the museum, handing out pamphlets declaring "NO MORE PICTURES WITHOUT CONTEXT", and demanded portrayals of PWAs that were "vibrant, angry, loving, sexy, beautiful, acting up and fighting back".[703]

A scholar who examined the South African episode for her MA thesis presents evidence of a basic contradiction in the stance of the conference organisers who were responsible for rejecting Van Kesteren's work. To the objectors he represented "the longstanding, historical European tradition of white, middle-class male media practitioners who construct the non-Western 'Other' for their home audience".[704] In their view Van Kesteren, consciously or unconsciously, was shaping reality in harmony with his social position and cultural perspective for particular political ends. He was speaking on behalf of others, but what he was saying effectively trapped them into a subordinate position and perpetuated their relative powerless.

But were the organisers of the cultural programming acting much differently? One a white academic and AIDS activist, the other a black African AIDS activist, they likewise operated from a specific philosophical position. For example, they expressed concern for children from disadvantaged communities who might visit the conference, see Van Kesteren's images, and leave with the "wrong" impression or traumatised.[705] But their assumptions preempted the possibility of children (or anyone else) having the opportunity to look for themselves and form their own judgements.

Moreover, "In the opinion of the objectors, Van Kesteren's way of visually describing the Zambian HIV/AIDS pandemic contradicts, discredits and suppresses the way the portrayed subjects and the South African audience would prefer to describe themselves".[706] But here, too, the objectors presumed to understand in advance the desires of others, with no evidence of actually reaching beyond their own beliefs and prejudices. Who then was the most culturally arrogant and insensitive in this situation: a self-proclaimed activist artist who spent time with people and recorded what he saw of their predicament, or the conference gatekeepers who presupposed they knew what was best for attendees, and for PWAs in general? Was Van Kesteren following the colonial script of self-interest and exploitation, or was he affording a voice to people who are otherwise silenced?

The young scholar concludes with a remarkable display of partisan reasoning that rationalises what censors commonly do. She argues, "[T]his article ... suggests a juxtaposition of Van Kesteren's 'speech' (his photographic texts) against [Professor Lynn] Dalrymple and [Beverley] Motlhabani's 'silence' (the non-selection of the photographs …). Silence, in this case, represents a form of power and is mobilised as a means to articulate agency in that it decides over the 'invisibility' of Van Keteren's photographs by choosing not to have them exhibited."[707] "Resistance" in this case prevailed over the desirability of multiple perspectives, and the dialogue they might provoke.

Some similar issues came to the fore at the conference "Sex and Secrecy" held at the University of the Witwatersrand in 2003. In this instance pictures taken by Danish-born Ditte Haarløv-Johnsen of young black gay men in Mozambique, some of whom were naked, set off a heated debate about representation. In both these cases the photographers were not "drive-by shooters", but had invested significant time with the people whose lives they were recording: Van Kesteren had spent four months in Zambia collecting his images, with the assistance of a local AIDS activist; Haarløv-Johnsen knew the people she documented for three years.

During a plenary session a female delegate named Nokuthula Skhosana asked, "What is the fascination with the black body?"[708] She also openly wondered if this were not a continuation of abuse that goes back to the mistreatment of Sarah Baartman, who was publicly displayed to both the delight and revulsion of Europeans in the early 19th century. Baartman's remains were repatriated from a French museum in 2002; for good reason, her blatant exploitation carries enormous symbolic significance in contemporary South Africa. The delegate's remarks consequently stung, putting the organisers and the artist on the defensive.

Skhosana argued, "Displaying these pictures without even thinking of what they might mean to other people is a clear manifestation of white arrogance – the authority to display, to consume and to devour without regard." Paralleling the debate over *Thuthula* that was taking place in the press at the same moment, she demanded to know, "Why is it that at every conference one attends, white 'experts' present on black lives? Whites continue to present us, talk on our behalf and exploit us in the process," she stated. "They publish, define us as we are still trying to define ourselves and represent us."[709]

Haarløv-Johnsen countered charges of racism by explaining, "This is a hidden community and these people have been bravely open. This is a powerful thing to do in the midst of turmoil."[710] So rather than exploiting these men, Haarløv-Johnsen argued that she was facilitating their struggle for self-acceptance and social recognition in a highly repressive culture, and during a deepening political crisis. Conference organisers Graeme Reid and Liz Walker acknowledged the damage inflicted by racism and colonialism, but noted, "so too have black gay men been subject to … [the] insidious silence of invisibility and oppression". They also reported that the next stop for the exhibition was Maputo, "where it was received as a celebration of a new-found gay identity and became the touch pad for a new gay organisation in Mozambique – the first of its kind in the country".[711]

The criticism was not confined to the academic halls where the conference

155

took place. The *Mail & Guardian* came under fire for publishing a selection of the photos on its cover in conjunction with its coverage of the controversy, including a full-frontal nude. That next week the editors struck back strongly, claiming, "It is not the first time culture and ethnicity have been raised as barriers to artistic freedom in South Africa. It was a knee-jerk response of the apartheid censors, usually in defence of conservative Afrikaans or white South African sensibilities."

The editors wished to make their position clear: "We will not heed such complaints, and nor should the authorities. One of the key victories in the struggle against apartheid was that of free artistic expression over censorship."[712]

Reid and Walker later published an overview of the conference in a scholarly journal. They highlighted the centrality of "themes of secrecy, silence, and taboo",[713] and reflected, "In coupling sex and secrecy, we aimed to foreground the issues of power, stigma, and silence. We needed to understand when sex is secret and why."[714] Conspicuously absent, however, was any reference to the photographs, even though they provided a singular example of a project that successfully bridged the realms of scholarship and activism.

It's plausible that Reid and Walker did not wish for the controversy to divert attention from everything else that occurred during the event and possibly eclipse its overall accomplishments. But by excluding this important episode from their authoritative account, they effaced an important social divide between racial groups and their diverse experiences, expectations and desires.

Going to the Bush/Going to the Mat

African male initiation has provided a remarkably rich vein of material that has been mined by artists across media and colour lines. However, some of their varying portrayals have provoked vigorous debate.

Hitting the circuit in South Africa in 2008, *Son of Man* was not the first film featuring a dark-skinned Jesus, but the overlay of his story with modern-day political struggle in Africa – more liberation theology than doctrinal exegesis – lent it a particular resonance. Notably, Jesus hears his call to minister to the world while undergoing his traditional Xhosa initiation rite and encountering a black leather-clad Satan.

Several South African-made documentaries have tackled the contemporary meaning of this custom directly. *Umgidi* (The Celebration/Shadow Dancing, 2004), for one, relates the story of Sipho Singiswa (45) and his adopted brother Vuyo (27). The difference between their ages was sufficient to give them fundamentally different life experiences: Vuyo was born in the pivotal year of 1976, Sipho was then 16.

Sipho was secretly circumcised while a political prisoner on Robben Island. Instead of the conventional hut hidden away from everyday affairs, a bathroom was clandestinely used. It was illegal to do this, and had he been caught an additional six months would have been tacked onto his sentence.[715]

To be circumcised in the manner that he was constituted an act of defiance by Sipho, within circumstances that stripped individuals of their dignity and their heritage. It was an assertion of identification and continuity with the past, an instance of tradition defying the governmental powers-that-be. But this rite of passage was never fully completed because the announcement celebration that heralds the event to the family, community and the ancestors was never held. This omission had gnawed at the men's father, so 27 years later Sipho returns home to bring closure to the matter.

As the story unfolds it becomes clear that the family is split by additional issues: the younger son refuses to be circumcised. Moreover, he is gay. An uncle suggests that they kidnap Vuyo and forcibly circumcise him, but the father pragmatically notes, "The Constitution doesn't allow us this, we would be arrested for abuse. In our African culture, yes, but these days you would get arrested."[716] And Sipho's wife and co-director Gillian Schutte struggles with whether she will allow their mixed-race son to "go to the bush", "go to the mountain", or "go under the spear", as attending initiation school is commonly called, when he reaches a suitable age. A cluster of contradictions such as this is what good stories, and films, depend upon.

At the National Arts Festival in Grahamstown in 2007, a play picked up many of the same themes. *Ndiyindoda, I am a Man* recounted the experiences of four boys as they pass into manhood, combining poetry, traditional music and hip-hop. One of them becomes ill and is taken to the hospital, an all-too-frequent consequence of the rigours and the careless procedures that prevail in many of today's initiation schools. He is later chided that "real men" don't go for medical help. This group's questions about what constitutes a man are renewed when they reunite years later and one of them reveals he has a gay son. The masculinity of black Africans, cramped for generations by repressive laws, exploitative work opportunities and the weight of custom, is now in a state of expansion and flux, open to inquiry and new potentialities.

Dancers have taken up this theme as well, interrogating it through a contemporary viewpoint. *Abakhwetha – The Initiates*, choreographed by Musa Hlatshwayo, premiered in Durban in 2002. One reviewer hailed it as an instant classic within the South African repertoire, but noted the artist was greeted by a mixed reaction of "ululations, cheers and boos". She explained, "He was a hero to many for airing his views on this cycle of death, and a heretic to some who were offended at seeing this delicate, but powerfully articulate, theatrical impression of Xhosa initiation."[717]

The controversial element was, once again, the deaths and injuries that plague this practice. Like the aforementioned play, this work combined movement with elements as disparate as praise poetry, music and body painting. And in 2004 the Vukami Dance Theatre launched a performance at the Windybrow Theatre in Johannesburg. In this instance a boy is unwillingly taken to initiation and during a dance ceremony he is struck by lightning and killed. When the rest of the boys triumphantly return home, this boy's parents discover a white dish outside their gate, a signal that their son is dead.

Looking at an additional performance whose point of departure was also a traditional practice reveals another aspect of ritual practice in today's world. Sphelele Nzama created the dance *Umphafa* (2006) about his murdered brother. It was described as follows: "Based on the Zulu belief in which a family takes the dead person's restless soul to the *amadlozi*, the ancestors, through the Umphafa tree, this dance fuses Western theatrical performance with real religious practice."[718] The reviewer did not report any negative reactions, although it seems as if the performance was less literal or intelligible than *Abakhwetha – The Initiates*. Even so, the mixture of elements plus the public exposure of a typically intimate ceremony had the potential to produce discord. But, as it turned out, the dance was therapeutic for those whose lives were closest to the events: "Talking about this experience after the performance, the dancer-choreographer confirmed that after his brother's death the family had performed the actual ritual but regarded the stage experience as 'setting us free'."[719]

Moreover, when Sizwe Zulu of the Flatfoot Dance Company presented *Disturbance of the Inner Ear*, he declared he was "'the Jesus of my own crucifixion … the director of my own history … a man, a queer man' and … shed his boxing gloves and gown to dance nude to the accompaniment of a live cello".[720] Either of these works might have become controversial because of the volatile themes they explored. But that potential was tempered by the fact they played to self-selected audiences that would not only have a higher tolerance level for such innovation and exploration, but who have in many instances come to expect it within contemporary dance.

All of these productions were created and performed by black Africans, amounting to an insider's perspective, however idiosyncratic. But a broader range of visual artists has taken initiation as their subject. And at times they have not fared so well, setting off turf wars and ideological skirmishes.

Poetics or Polemics?

Award-winning artist Churchill Madikida describes the sense of risk involved for those who endorse certain cultural practices yet hold them up to scrutiny: "The respect and love I have for my culture is immense," he has stated, but "To begin to interrogate all that I am brought up to believe (as the ultimate rite of passage) feels like an insult towards those who groomed me to be what I am." His creative impulse has overcome any reticence to work within the realm of ritual, however. He explains, "Nevertheless I feel morally compelled and obliged to take a stand on what I feel is an unnecessary … sacrifice of young lives and also a delusion that is decimating our communities … [and yet] My objective is not to attack 'traditional' practices."[721]

In his show *Liminal States* (Johannesburg Art Gallery, 2003), for example, Madikida used video and performance art (*States of Limbo*) to reenact some of his own personal experiences; mixed-media installations (*Cuts, Skin and*

Blood) gave them material form. In his video *Lullaby for Saluka* the artist sang to a sculpture he had made, calling on the ancestors to take care of initiates who have been killed or maimed during initiation. *Struggles of the Heart* showed him eating and then disgorging mealie pap. The ingestion symbolises the general public's "swallowing whole" stereotypes of traditional practices as savage, or an individual in a traditional setting unquestioningly consuming his community's values. The spitting out represents rejecting those customs that are no longer relevant or which contravene constitutional rights to dignity and personal safety. Tradition, in other words, can both nourish and suffocate, a possibility accentuated by a soundtrack that includes heavy breathing and gagging noises. He admits that by straddling these positions, "I feel like I am walking on thin ice".[722]

As autobiographical as Madikida's art is, one critic shrewdly locates him as "speak[ing] to a wider contemporary concern with the traumatically zoned and coded body". But such parallels are not an exact fit: "Euro-American artistic practice of this sort is of course tinged with neo- or post-primitivisms," this commentator argues, "and betokens a rather theatrical crisis of self and other-identification sited on the body."[723]

Madikida precisely embodies some vital traits that generate an insightful artist anywhere. His social identity was ambiguous because he was of coloured/black African parentage in a community where the Xhosa tradition held sway. This may have also imbued him with a degree of critical distance that others unequivocally born into the culture might not have. Moreover, stuttering made him shy and somewhat isolated, and thus art became a medium of communication.[724] Because his work heavily relies upon allusion, it has escaped criticism as too literally presenting sacred material to a secular audience. But non-literalness creates other problems, namely being broadly incomprehensible. One critic observed, "Translating social meaning about rituals from one culture into the language of another is a difficult task, and to complicate matters he seems to want to conceal as much about his sacred material as he wants to reveal."[725]

Madikida's master's dissertation topic dealt with rituals, focusing particularly on circumcision. Fellow artist Thembinkosi Goniwe likewise wrote his master's thesis at the Michaelis School of Fine Art on Xhosa initiation and made a video of an initiate. He has also produced large-scale photos of scarification and circumcision.

Colbert Mashile, too, has explored this psychic terrain, for therapeutic reasons: traumatised by his own Northern Sotho initiation, Mashile has used art as a personal instrument of expression and healing, to substitute curative images for the pain associated with the gruesome ones he retains. His surrealistic, anthropoidal and biomorphic figures recall the work of Philip Guston. He has also been influenced by Mark Rothko,[726] although his visual vocabulary is distinctly his own, including phallic symbolism, metaphors of growth, and customary shapes such as cowry shells.

Mashile's *Tsa ka Mafuri* (2002) translates as "things discussed in secrecy, behind the house".[727] The title aptly captures the quality of something clandestine and unfathomable, and the fact that those not directly privy to the conversation must use their imaginations to piece together a plausible scenario. Reviews inevitably comment on Mashile's non-political perspective on a highly charged issue. One critic remarked there is "nothing propagandistic" about his work; it is, instead, "a poetic, emotional response".[728] Another notes it is "never prescriptive, didactic or literal".[729]

This does not mean that a broader social critique is completely absent, however. Mashile's *Third Party* shows a trio of disharmonious figures. He has explained the work as referencing media depictions of traditional activities that can sensationalise the sacred. "Mashile is concerned about the diminishing and demonising of certain customs in his tradition," writes one curator, "due to a lack of understanding by outsiders, especially the media."[730] Mashile's own cultural heritage has "entitled" him to stake claim to this cultural topography, whereas the issues of miscomprehension, misplaced motives and possible exploitation have volubly surfaced when artists who are not black African have also depicted the related practices of circumcision and initiation.

These concerns all came together, literally, in the body of Afrikaner artist Peet Pienaar. Pienaar is known for fiddling with the iconography and ephemera of his gender and clan; sports trophies and military memorabilia have been common elements in his work. He has posed as a fully-kitted Springbok rugby player in shopping malls and museums, but took performance art to the next level by proposing to have himself publicly circumcised as his contribution to an eight-man group show entitled *uBudoda: Images of Masculinity* at the Association of Visual Arts (AVA) in Cape Town in 2000. The procedure would be done by a black African female doctor. Moreover, he intended to expand the audience by providing pay-for-view internet access, and then planned to auction his foreskin live on the net. His documentation of the healing process would also be posted.

Pienaar explained his motivation as exploring disparate images of masculinity that stem from tradition or media representations. The publicity and commercial aspects of the event were also intended to highlight contemporary trends increasingly infiltrating multiple aspects of peoples' lives. But two of the other contributing artists, Thembinkosi Goniwe and Zwelethu Mthethwa, raised objections that he was trivialising sacrosanct activities and potentially offending those who honour the practice. They threatened to pull out of the show.

In the debate that followed, well-known artist and writer Sue Williamson questioned if this was an example of "cultural apartheid".[731] But Goniwe resented the fact that he was being accused of "racial censorship" by criticising Pienaar's plan, and challenged the recreation of an all-too-familiar power dynamic in Pienaar's art practice: "the white has the idea and [the] black provide[s] the labour service", he regretfully noted.[732] He explicitly made the point that Pienaar, as an Afrikaner, was a direct beneficiary of apartheid, to which Pienaar countered that black artists were reaping the lion's share of rewards in the post-apartheid era, not white ones.[733] And at a panel discussion held at the Michaelis School of Fine Art on "The politics of art, race and censorship", Goniwe charged, "When are artists going to make art about being white, and about their own identity?"[734]

For his part, Pienaar was puzzled why Goniwe fixed on his performance as addressing Xhosa rites when it could just as well suggest Jewish or Islamic traditions. Moreover, Pienaar drolly rebutted, "I don't think a black woman with a scalpel in one hand and my penis in her other hand is in a position of servitude, rather in a position of power."[735] Pienaar, too, saw this as an instance of "cultural apartheid", and like Chris Mann, the non-Xhosa playwright of *Thuthula* had asserted, Pienaar claimed "Every artist has the right to make art about whatever he or she wants".[736]

Pienaar withdrew from the AVA show and was circumcised at another locale, the Bell-Roberts Art Gallery, on the day before *uBudoda* opened. The title of his work changed from *I Want to Tell You Something …* to *For Sale/To Let*, and his circumcised foreskin was placed in a jar of formaldehyde, in which it has been displayed subsequently. A female reviewer left no doubt about which exhibition she felt was more successful. She wrote that whereas the AVA show "depicts a male consciousness that is static and lifeless", Pienaar's performance was "heartening and revelatory … and the result was the destabilising of 'masculinity' itself".[737]

Pienaar confided to an interviewer, "When people look at this exhibition 20 years from now … they're not going to see the same debate," he said. "They're going to see this as a time when white male Afrikaners were feeling oppressed by their identity. Most Afrikaners aren't circumcised … and this is a symbol of me broadening my identity."[738] In this regard, he was counterbalancing Goniwe's demand that white artists concentrate on "white" concerns. Like so many phenomena in South Africa, this topic is not one that can be precisely parsed into black and white elements.

What Colour is your Penis?

In 2004, in celebration of ten years of democracy, Iziko Museums of Cape Town assembled an encyclopaedic array of work from the collection of the South African National Gallery. Among the essays in the catalogue that accompanied this exhibition was one entitled "Rites of Passage: Refiguring Initiation", by Moleleki Frank Ledimo. Ledimo took "rites of passage" metaphorically, putting traditional practices side by side with the experiences of both black and white youths during the political struggle for freedom. For many black Africans, the passage to manhood included participation in mass demonstrations against the ruling regime and sometimes violence, forging bonds of identity and experience among age cohorts. And military service was compulsory for whites, providing a literal trial by fire that pitted them against people in black African townships or in border warfare with neighbouring states.[739]

Universalising and expanding the notion of initiation is an interesting intellectual stratagem. But on the ground, it seems like something of a hollow exercise. Some rites of passage bear the weight of the ages; others are simply ephemeral. Those that have accrued moral gravity and respect from their repetition over time are the ones that are most honoured and defended. An immensely contested set of photographs taken of North Sotho initiates, and the range of receptions they have since been accorded, are a barometer of changing attitudes toward creative depictions of traditional activities.

Documentarian and white South African Steve Hilton-Barber photographed a group of over 200 naked or near-naked initiates at a "bush school" held on his family's farm in the winter of 1990. He spent about a week there out of the six-week session, and also attended the graduation. Not only was this the place where Hilton-Barber grew up, he had an additional personal connection: the mother of the principal was the family's domestic worker, and it was through him that Hilton-Barber gained consent to photograph the boys. The go-ahead came with an uncommon precondition: Hilton-Barber had to be a circumcised man himself to gain access.[740]

The Sunday magazine section of a major newspaper published a straightforward description by Hilton-Barber of how the project evolved (the principal had asked permission to use a remote section of the farm) and what he had observed, accompanied by a selection of his images.[741] He also submitted the series to a competition sponsored by *Staffrider* (a literary and photographic journal published from 1978 to 1996, heavily influenced by the doctrine of Black Consciousness), and nabbed the R2000 prize and the opportunity to display his work in the Market Theatre Gallery, part of the famed Market Theatre where many significant anti-apartheid plays were presented.

But these images provoked a great deal of discomfort for various reasons and among a range of complainants. Black African workers at the theatre found fault with them; academic theorists did, too. Gallery visitors were blunt in the remarks they left in a comment book; audience members attending a public debate held at the theatre were as well. Opening 25 November 1990, the exhibit became the focus of a tumultuous month of activities and responses.

The objections hinged on claims of racism, voyeurism and pornography. Hilton-Barber was vilified as perpetuating some of the most egregious stereotypes from the days of colonialism, a harsh indictment of someone who considered himself to be politically progressive. His artistic rationale and his reaction were most clearly articulated in his remarks at the public debate held 12 December. He first apologised to anyone he might have offended, stating that that had not been his intention. But he also expressed dismay at the tenor of the disparaging remarks his work was evoking, which had escalated to death threats. He cited some of the outrageous entries in the comment book: "Go fuck your mother up her arse, you expose my culture"; "Show us your secrets of white women making love to dogs and forget our culture"; and "blacks are pawns in [*sic*] the white propaganda chess board".[742] He prophetically lamented "the increasingly violent and intimidatory nature of these criticisms". Hilton-Barber noted, "Some of these criticisms have been tinged with a racist chauvinism that is not only disturbing in itself but can hardly bode well for the development of a progressive and critical culture in South Africa."[743]

Some people questioned the unequal power differential inherent in his project, spanning securing permission up to the creative stance he adopted. Because Hilton-Barber had a personal connection to the site of the initiation school and its principal, his critics assumed that consent was problematic. Surely the black African in this situation could not have been on equal footing with the white man, and therefore in a position to object to his request. But Hilton-Barber shot back: "Some say that I am a white opportunist who manipulated the racist power relations in our society in order to gain access. Ironically, this assumption is itself racist and paternalistic. It supposes that the principal of the school is a weak, subordinate man who is unable to control access to the initiation ceremony in face of a powerful 'baas van die plaas' ['the boss of the farm']".[744] Hilton-Barber hoisted these protesters by their own petards: they had hastily drawn conclusions without having direct knowledge of the personalities involved or the rapport between them.

Others questioned the legitimacy of the photographer documenting such activities or publicly displaying this work. When some found fault with him exposing sacred activities to a broader public, he replied, "I have not revealed anything that was not already known … I have merely given it a visual face."[745] And still others objected to the fact that naked black bodies were being exposed to women and children,[746] whereas he would not dare to attempt to do this focusing on white bodies. Hilton-Barber found this position to be chauvinistic, and a reflection of apartheid regulations that he did not create, but which dictated what could be openly shown. He later explained, "At the time black penises were legal but white penises were banned."[747]

During the Market Theatre debate arguments were met with counter-arguments, resulting in a rhetorical impasse with neither side convincing the other of the merits of their respective positions. A scholar astutely reflected on what transpired at this session, recapping a central dynamic of the interplay of opposing forces during a culture war: "[There] were those with words and those with actions and the debate could not shift. It simply stayed in one place and the trenches were dug then and there."[748]

The controversy went beyond words, however. Black African workers at the theatre were offended by these photos and wanted them removed. But their desire ran up against the theatre's anti-censorship policy. Those workers who attended the debate on 12 December felt frustrated with the proceedings and walked out. The next day they staged a one-hour work stoppage, which they repeated on 15 December. In between these actions, someone stole all 20 of the photos. And three days later these events came full circle when the captions were vandalised. Hilton-Barber's title for his defence of this project was "In good photographic faith". These reactions angrily nullified his stated intent.

Hilton-Barber was probably guilty of one thing: naiveté. He explained, "I attempted to document a situation in a way that would allow the situation to speak for itself."[749] Yet he made obvious aesthetic choices on how to portray his subjects, which opened him up to specific criticisms, and he produced this work on the cusp between the old regime and the new, a time when many critical questions were being vociferously aired in the open. One critic derided his principal argument: "The question remains as to whether Hilton-Barber is really a man with a camera and a calling or whether this is conservatism masked as good faith. One thing is clear: art is at its most dangerous when it is disguised as truth."[750]

This particular critic's reaction to Hilton-Barber was the intellectual equivalent of the actual assault the exhibition suffered. She reiterated the history of photography's unseemly relation to surveillance and social control, and sited him squarely within it. She alleged that he rendered these boys "mute", echoing the criticism of the photos of the young gay Mozambican men. But did they in fact have a voice that was taken away? And might not Hilton-Barber's images be an important first stage in a process of them gaining visibility?

Her arguments were buoyed by citing a number of trenchant writers in the field. Her text was therefore peppered with references to silencing, power differentials and the strength of the gaze. Her invective peaked in the following passage, which also reveals her distinctive bias: "It is true that for one small moment, the *pariah triumvirate* of Hilton-Barber, the Market Theatre Gallery and *Staffrider* seemed at risk, but ... *the trinity* was restored to its exalted space."[751] An alternative or supplementary strategy for her own writing would have been to speak with some of Hilton-Barber's subjects, or the principal of the initiation school, in order to gain something of their perspectives firsthand. She could have offered them a chance to exercise their voices in a way she asserts they had been denied. She instead remained within her academic comfort zone and relied upon the remote authority of theoreticians.

Hilton-Barber may have also been "guilty" of producing work in advance of social developments and a cultural milieu that could receive it differently. In a review of the Spanish contribution to the 1995 Johannesburg Biennale, a selection of 22 Spanish and South African artists co-curated by one person from each of the contributing countries, the first individual the writer cited by name was Hilton-Barber. And the reference was a positive one, noting "the incredibly strong and highly controversial pictures of initiation rites by Steve Hilton-Barber". This reviewer obviously liked the show and saw Hilton-Barber as an integral part of it. Moreover, he remarked that the selection of work "tak[es] it beyond the abstractions of colonial thought ... the exhibition also took us beyond fashionable elements of the present multicultural debate, as well as the mute and unreflective notions of realism that were part of the colonial agenda".[752] Merely five years after its debut, Hilton-Barber's work was appreciated as part of a rejoinder to stereotypical artistic points of view, not an adherent of them.

And one of the exhibitions at the 2004 National Arts Festival at Grahamstown, *Ndiyindoda! Initiation as Rite of Passage*, included the work of several artists discussed here. A reviewer noted that Hilton-Barber's work on the subject had caused controversy in the past, but no negative responses were forthcoming over what she characterised as "a courageous and relevant exhibition".[753] And an unintended consequence of Hilton-Barber's project is that it spurred a reaction from artists like Churchill Madikida to undertake their own creative journey through this field. Madikida was angered when Hilton-Barber's photos went beyond the gallery (which he feels is "elevated" space) and were reproduced in newspapers and on postcards. "I thought no," he reacted, "this is not okay. But for me [Hilton-Barber] opened up a dialogue that I was able to participate in."[754]

While the world may have changed since the advent of democracy in South Africa in 1994, Hilton-Barber's characterisation of his own work did not. He composed two narratives about his work published a decade apart, 1991 and 2001. In the later one he recalls being accused of "ethno-voyeurism" and "cultural imperialism", and "likened to a colonial conquester [*sic*]" in 1990 when the photographs debuted.[755] During the height of the controversy he pleaded, "I would appreciate a criticism of my work that focuses on the standard of my photography and not on the colour of my skin."[756] But that was impossible at the time. In 2001 he was unrepentant about his original vision and reaffirmed his professional ethos: "They should be seen as photographs and criticised as such. I practise in good photographic faith".[757]

Guilt Tripping

A life-sized sculpture of Louis Botha, Boer War general and South Africa's first prime minister, has acted as a sentinel outside the Parliament Buildings in Cape Town since 1931. The pedestal on which he sits astride his horse reads "farmer, warrior, statesman" – the stuff of legends, a man's man. It resembles monuments in so many places around the world: gallant, yet lamentably generic. But on the morning of Heritage Day 1999, Botha appeared in a fresh guise: wrapped in a blanket ("*ingcawa*") and his face smeared with white ochre ("*ingceke*"), he had been transformed into a young initiate, fitted with a cardboard version of a hat ("*isidlokolo*", usually made from fur or hide) and with a sign draped around his neck reading "*abakwethu*" (isiXhosa for "the initiated"), concealing the general's engraved name.

This creative intervention was the handiwork of maverick Beezy Bailey, notorious for the 1991 artistic stunt where he submitted work to a competition under his own name as well as that of his fictional alter-ego, Joyce Ntobe. His pieces were rejected; "hers" became part of the collection of the South African National Gallery. The Botha work was part of the "One City, Many

Cultures" arts festival. Bailey's contribution represented a project called "PTO" (Please Turn Over) by Public Eye (a non-profit collective of artist–curators creating public art). The project dispatched artists to interact with landmarks throughout the city. Bailey deftly wove together transformation, reclamation and revisionism, putting a new face on a familiar sight.

It became a source of both pride and disgrace. Bailey reported, "A black man walked past the statue and raised his fist in the air and said 'beautiful'."[758] But other Xhosa individuals found it insulting;[759] one passed by, threatened to shoot him, and asked, "Why don't you go and do that to your own people?"[760] He also received angry phone calls from whites. Ironically, the artist's grandfather was a close friend of the general. Bailey remarked, however, "With due respect, I don't want to offend the Afrikaners, but he [Botha] is not relevant to the present set-up."[761]

This took place against the backdrop of a parliamentary debate regarding what to do with the symbols of the old regime. Bailey reflected on critics of his work, "What is going through their heads is a very strong Christian, Calvinist sense that their history is being destroyed." He felt his intentions had been misread, however. "I thought it symbolised the initiation of South Africa into a new democracy," he stated. "It is indeed painful such as the circumcision these (Xhosa) guys undergo."[762]

A sense of sacredness obviously transcends cultures. And in this case, both black and white South Africans took offence. Bailey capitulated to the condemnation and requested that a local fire brigade hose off the clay.[763] But re-examining national history and violating hallowed spaces has become a regular feature of the work of some artists.

Take Kendell Geers, who cultivated a colourful reputation during his years of working in South Africa. Fellow artist William Kentridge noted, "Kendell's métier, his subject, is offending people."[764] He was also dubbed "the *enfant terrible* of contemporary art",[765] and "the foul-mouthed shocker who made his name as art's idol-breaker".[766] Geers was denounced by many as a poseur and a fraud.

His reputation was solidified by such exhibitions as *Air De Paris* (with Joachim Schonfeldt, 1994), which a prominent reviewer trashed as "bridg[ing] the gap between trite and tripe".[767] His work included throwing a brick through the window of the Market Theatre Gallery; smearing pig's blood over the walls of another venue; and clutching a *Hustler* magazine and a towel smudged with his own semen. He resubmitted *Title Withheld (Hustler)* to the 1995 Vita Art award competition at the Johannesburg Art Gallery (JAG), complemented by *Title Withheld (Small Change)*, where he randomly scattered 14 coins throughout a gallery, insured it for R6000, and insisted that the individual pieces of change not be moved. The JAG "contained" the works by placing the *Hustler* behind a pull-up blind, and collecting the coins in a glass box, much to the displeasure of Geers.

His intended masterwork was *Guilty* (1998), reflecting Geers's claim that this was the signature emotion within the collective (white) South African psyche. He boldly asserted, "Guilt remains the single most pervasive and strongest cultural force within the New South Africa."[768]

The focal point of *Guilty* was Fort Klapperkop, a Paul Kruger-built edifice commanding a key approach to Pretoria, in the former Transvaal Republic. But Geers cast his conceptual net considerably farther than a specific place. In the run-up to the event where he planned to "occupy" the fort in the name of art and reconciliation, lower its flags and substitute an anarchist banner in their place, Geers staged an extensive poster campaign advertising the action. He timed this to coincide with an Afrikaner-led centenary celebration there featuring "a church service, *tiekiedraai* [traditional folk dances], *boeresport* [games like running in a sack], and cannon firing".[769] In Geers's vision, the participants and their activities would become part of his work, as did the publicity campaign and all the discussion, rumours and reactions it provoked.

But the Pretoria director of museums pulled the plug the day before it was to occur; pressure to do so had been applied at several key points. The director had received threats from right-wing people who were offended by the proposed interference; the sponsors, the French Institute and the Goodman Gallery, did as well. The organiser of the Afrikaner festivities declaimed, "He is playing with my integrity if he thinks I'm going to be his ball to kick around", to which Geers responded, "You know you're making confrontational art when the artworks rise up against the artist".[770] Moreover, the German ambassador had applied pressure on the French ambassador after seeing invitations featuring German police guards outfitted with shields and helmets that said "Polizei", photographed during a visit by President Mandela to Berlin. He did not feel such imagery accurately portrayed present-day Germany.

Not one to be completely outflanked, Geers (an Afrikaner by birth, but he refashioned an adult identity far removed from his birthright) hired a plane to fly over the fort and other Pretoria-area landmarks trailing a banner reading "Guilty Skuldig Molato Netyalo" (English, Afrikaans, isiZulu and isiXhosa). And as an additional component of the work he opened a bank account to fund the "restoration and development" of the site as a museum. He kicked it off with a deposit of his own funds, and suggested that the French as well as any other interested parties do so, too.[771]

An influential critic declared, "Only a four-letter word could describe the occasion – flop!" Nonetheless, she decried "The manic, hysterical need by the conservative elements in our society to censor and control is more than undesirable. Four years after our democratic elections it is inexcusable the relationship between art and other aspects of culture are still so firmly in the control of an undemocratic minority."[772] And a letter-to-the-editor writer dismissed Geers's exploits as a sadistic stunt and declared: "It is easy to be provocative, but to provoke genuine change in a non-aggressive way is difficult and requires tremendous insight … purely conceptual art is about as moving as having a joke explained to you before hearing it."[773]

Sies, Man! Vieslik

Geers intended to show up at Fort Klapperkop on the appointed day but he was prevented from doing so by police who had been posted there. An unscheduled artist appeared instead. Steven Cohen, no stranger to controversy himself, staged his own intervention on that peak – adding it to an array of sites that are as varied as a rugby stadium, voting queue, dog show, squatter camp, bridal show and the rhino enclosure at the Johannesburg Zoo – where he has imposed himself uninvited and unannounced into customary activities.

Cohen started his career working in conventional art forms infused with unconventional themes, but his own body has gradually become his practice. His appearance lurches from the grotesque to the fanciful, a drag queen crossed with an alien mutant. Count on seeing him combine such disparate elements as a gas mask, platform shoes that rise to unheard-of heights, animal parts and bodily products, sex toys, and lots of nudity.

Cohen's work would be classified as performance art within creative circles. But Cohen refuses to be pigeonholed, declaring, "I don't actually know what the fuck performance art is, yet I'm brilliant at it." He describes what he does as "Living Art", "non-contractual public interventions ... in non-art defined spaces".[774] He plunges headlong into public places so that various crowds become drawn into his appearance(s) unawares, and often unsympathetically. Cohen regularly courts danger, consternation and ridicule, a creature from another plane of existence fuelled by a raw guilelessness and honesty. He explains, "It is the power of the visual performance that lets me kick you in the stomach and grab your heart without saying a word or touching you."[775]

A high degree of unpredictability is inherent in what Cohen does. When he took the *Chandelier Project* (2002) to a squatter camp in Johannesburg's inner city, his arrival coincided with the Red Ants, municipal employees who ruthlessly evict people and demolish their illegal dwellings (in this instance to clear the way for constructing the Nelson Mandela Bridge). Cohen wore a large and elaborate chandelier, high heels and little else. Some residents embraced him – one, holding a *Hustler* magazine – literally. Others referred to him as an angel, Jesus or Mary. Still others were stunned or yelled at him to go away.[776]

In an interview he gave relatively early in his career Cohen explained, "When you grow up as *a moffie* in a country ruled by neanderthals, you soon learn there's nothing to fear but your fear."[777] Not surprisingly, victimhood of various sorts has become his signature theme. Cohen's performances have caused him to be detained by the police, beaten up by enraged observers, and removed from the premises, which is what happened at Fort Klapperkop.

Cohen arrived the day of Geers's scheduled but aborted performance wearing "a bright orange wig, black boots, a tight-fitting frock and a Star of David round his neck".[778] He called it *Patriotic Drag*. But those who were rallying there held starkly different ideas of what "patriotic" means, and forcibly escorted him off the site. One eyewitness provided this madcap description of the scene, replete with burly, tattooed men wearing leather, chains and swastikas: "[Cohen] made his way, teeteringly, towards the fort. The Village People heavy stood arms akimbo, guarding the entrance from *pollution*. Beauty approached the beast and got no further. No, he could not go in. Why didn't he go away and celebrate his own culture, the neo-Nazi and his poodle [his accomplice] suggested. The poodle gently but firmly escorted Steven back to the car. The heavy followed: they spoke in German and raised hands in Nazi salutes."[779] Cohen reportedly objected, "I was also in the army. I have a right to be here too."[780]

Cohen stated at the time, "I didn't expect such a violent reaction. I wanted to see if Afrikaans culture could make way for this kind of thing."[781] But he told a very different story just a few months later, admitting to an interviewer, "I *wanted* to hate them at Klapperkop ... And I wanted them to hate me."[782] A letter-to-the-editor writer had suspected as much, sensing that Cohen knew all along what would likely happen,[783] and a journalist concluded, "Cohen got what he wanted out of Klapperkop: a frisson of exhibitionism and an episodic purging in a series of intensely personal pain."[784]

Besides garnering a considerable amount of on-the-spot public condemnation, Cohen has been battered by critics as well. One dismissively wrote, "Cohen's work, rather than being a negotiated affirmation of public space, is more a slap in the public's face with a wet penis. He aggressively stakes his place in the public universe and continually tests the public's tolerance of his access rights to that space."[785]

Others question whether his work is genuinely political, frivolous, or perhaps even harmful. Recall the banner he carried at the 1996 annual Gay and Lesbian Pride Parade, "BRING US YOUR CHILDREN, WHAT WE CAN'T FUCK WE EAT". A reviewer of a monograph on Cohen noted that activist Zackie Achmat argued "the implicit irony contained in this conceptual performance ... would be lost on most bystanders at the parade. In a society such as South Africa, where privilege continues to protect, offensive statements made out of context have the unintended effect of placing the already vulnerable in further danger."[786] This closely parallels an aspect of the criticism of Kaolin Thompson's "ashtray". In each instance people were concerned that irony or political critique could easily be misread by those not conversant with art world conventions as confirmation of archaic stereotypes, with unanticipated and harmful social repercussions occurring long after the artist has left the scene.[787]

This critique from within one community pertinent to Cohen's identity was matched by the resistance he has sometimes received within the dance world, a place where he has commonly found an artistic home. In 1999, for example, he claimed censorship when he was not included in the line-up for the FNB Vita dance festival in Durban. At earlier events in Johannesburg and Cape Town that year his work had generated complaints from other performers (many of them ballerinas), and two of the three judges in Cape Town resigned over his performance, questioning its moral and artistic integrity.[788] Cohen and his work defy easy categorisation, but contain enormous potential to unsettle intentional and unintentional audiences alike.

Guilty Laughter

If Kendell Geers was a rather grim prankster plumbing the depths of South African guilt, Brett Murray has explored the same emotional turf with a wicked sense of humour. In 1996 he produced the exhibition *White Boy Sings the Blues*, for example, where he "Africanised" himself, alongside iconic figures such as Richie Rich and Colonel Sanders. *I Love Africa* (2000) included caricatured metal cutouts of tribesmen bearing shields with the likeness of Bart Simpson; Bart being boiled alive in a trio of metal pots that read "Guilt", "Guilty" and "Guiltiest"; and two metal cartoons, one called *Crisis of Identity* and the other *Shack as Metaphor*, featuring a classically stereotyped native (with a bone in hand, and a human skull on the ground) confronting a pith-helmeted white chap. In one image the native declares, "If another white artist brings me a portfolio of guilt, crisis of identity and memory, I'm going to throw up." In the other he pledges "If your work romanticises poverty or uses the shack as metaphor, you'll be on my next show in London." Murray's impatience with political correctness, and disgust with the constraints imposed by artistic gatekeepers, is scarcely disguised.

And his 2003 exhibition *White Like Me* spun off the Black Like Me product line (as did Laugh it Off, Chapter 5) to confront the social construction of whiteness. It featured three bronze figures with torsos like African curios but topped off by large pink balls, and a piece where three space aliens declare, "We are from the Congo – we want your women and your jobs." Employing a sort of squirm-in-your-seat jesting, this work gains added resonance in light of the xenophobic violence that erupted in South Africa in May 2008.

Murray fearlessly charges into heavily landmined symbolic territory that many artists would be scared to set foot in, skewering racial complicity and culpability, commodification, and notions of decency and propriety in both the art world and the world at large. One critic approvingly notes his "schoolboy flippancy" and floridly remarks, "Murray thumbs his nose at the tokenism that bedevils South Africa and his unregenerately impertinent creations function like an impeccably administered enema flushing all this crapulous posturing and cant out of our bowels."[789]

A notably controversial piece was *Africa*, a three-metre-high bronze statue that was installed on a hectic pedestrian mall in central Cape Town in 2000 (it provided the leitmotif for the *I Love Africa* exhibition). Murray narrates two distinct creation myths for *Africa*. One has him strolling through the city centre and spotting a trader with West African curios; across the street a stationary store was selling Bart Simpson keyrings. And voila: "I wanted to celebrate the cultural marketplace and the weird cultural hybrid which is all of us South Africans ... I wanted to celebrate that uneasy relationship."[790] A much more frequently repeated tale is that he purchased an Ivorian tourist sculpture in Abidjan, firing off his creative (and madcap) synapses.

Africa features an enigmatic but distinctively African being, with more than half a dozen brilliantly yellow Bart Simpson heads bursting out of it in various places. It is the postmodern equivalent to fetish figures that traditional people drive nails into, to release evil spirits and thereby cleanse and renew their community. It is audacious and irreverent, singular and sensational, embodying a collision of cultures, economies, value systems and iconographies. Whether this represents a positive instance of syncretism or a regrettable case of parasitic imposition of one culture onto another is left to the viewer to decide.

Africa has been well received by critics. One noted its "insouciant wit and uncanny grasp of urban geography", and observed, "It may not be a comforting vision, but it is a lot closer to the real throb of Cape Town's streets than some smug mantra of ethnic and cultural harmony."[791] And another breathed a sigh of relief that this was not one more example of the "prize-winning, post-colonial obelisks or dongles spidering our collective face like acne".[792] But *Africa* has met a mixed reception by the public, and by public officials. In fact, it was nearly unrealised.

Murray beat out over 50 other entrants in a competition sponsored by the Cape Town Urban Arts Foundation, the Association for Visual Arts, and the JK Gross Trust. But his proposal ran aground after members of the city council balked, objecting that it was culturally offensive and irreligious. The sort of cheekiness that is acceptable in a gallery made government officials queasy when they thought about it being permanently displayed in a heavily trafficked and highly visible public location.

The council was willing to go forward only after it solicited expert testimony and received positive reports from a professor of art history and a professor of Africana studies. After that, all excuses were exhausted. The deadlock had dragged on and on, however, stalling the project for well over a year, subjecting it to a scornful (and fearful) critique, and nearly dooming Murray's design. A reporter for the *Sowetan* shrewdly isolated the critical potential as well as the challenge inherent in Murray's slant on the post-apartheid world: "At a time when most people are scared to articulate themselves despite freedom of expression being enshrined in our Constitution," he wrote, "Murray's work grapples with issues that are [just] below the surface."[793]

Visual artists have been subject to continued attack on many of the same grounds as their predecessors. Andries Botha found himself in the crosshairs of disputes in both 2010 and 2011, which led to the removal of public works of art he had been commissioned to create. His multimillion-rand sculpture of King Shaka, embellishing his eponymous new airport in Durban, was removed after the Zulu royal family objected that his depiction as a herd boy debased his status as a warrior and forefather. And a trio of monumental elephants made of metal, wire mesh and stone was relocated after the ANC complained that they alluded to the logo of its rival IFP, and has been vandalised multiple times; Botha was forced to seek relief from the courts for breach of contract by the municipality. Zanele Muholi's photographs of local lesbian communities was slammed by then-Arts and Culture Minister Lulu Xingwana as "immoral" and "against nation-building" at an exhibition on Constitution Hill in 2009, whereupon she stormed out in disgust – inadvertently propelling the artist into the limelight. And when Yiull Damaso reworked Rembrandt's *The Anatomy Lesson of Dr Nicolaes Tulp* in 2010 by showing the beloved Madiba undergoing an autopsy, he was met by widespread condemnation from politicians and the public as disrespectful and practising "witchcraft", culminating in the artist receiving death threats. Partisan politics, sexuality, and respecting the traditional actively remain hot buttons.

Cold Comfort

Wordsmiths, too, have been subjected to censure. Their work sometimes sparks allegations alongside accolades, denunciation together with praise. As noted, Nadine Gordimer has been both a target and an alleged perpetrator in multiple situations of this nature.

The Publications Control Board banned *Burger's Daughter* in 1979, rebuffing such "witness literature" or "realist fiction" as an approach that it felt was revolutionary in nature and too supportive of a black consciousness perspective. It had done the same with *A World of Strangers* (1958) and *The Late Bourgeois World* (1966). In her 1991 Nobel lecture *Writing and being*, she cleverly delineated the challenges of being a novelist under a repressive regime: "[The] writer sometimes must risk both the state's indictment of treason, and the liberation forces' complaint of lack of blind commitment."[794] Because of her sympathies, the apartheid government considered her to be "too black".[795] Gordimer later delivered an address marking the dissolution of the very body that once sanctioned her.

The reception accorded her books changed with the coming of democracy. But that did not mean they were collectively embraced. On the contrary, *July's People* (1981) was banned from high school reading lists in Gauteng in 2001. The story was condemned as "deeply racist, superior and patronising. The novel seems one-sided and outdated."[796] The selection committee instead favoured books that supposedly promoted "post-apartheid values of tolerance and egalitarianism" and demonstrated an "accessibility of language".[797] Despite such fault-finding, Gordimer remains a member of the ANC, considering herself to be "a critical ally".[798]

And in 2004 Gordimer was personally condemned as a censor by a disgruntled biographer, Ronald Suresh Roberts (Chapter 5). Gordimer withdrew her authorisation of the project *No cold kitchen* after reading a draft of the book and raising objections that were not addressed to her satisfaction, a right she had contractually specified. The original South African publisher backed out as a result, as did the American one, although Roberts was subsequently picked up by another South African firm. Nonetheless, he exploded.

Roberts accused Gordimer of trying to issue a fatwa against him. Gordimer was part of the author list of the American publisher who turned him down; smelling a conspiracy against him, Roberts railed, "Haven't we had enough of New York editors scolding the natives to be rational? Is Gordimer part of that?"[799] He then argued, "As a (belatedly) published object, the book illuminates the true nature of censorship today. Private power does far more than governments these days to shape what we can or cannot read." Roberts also critiqued the literary world at large, noting "the new is still in its birthpangs [*sic*]. We have killed the snake without quite wriggling clear of the old snake skin." He concluded his attack by racialising the issue and accusing established writers of being "afraid of dusky newcomers from outside the old laager".[800]

Many people jumped to Gordimer's defence. Politician, lawyer and human rights advocate Kader Asmal and religious studies professor David Chidester dismissed Roberts's claims, declaring "[T]his is not a case of a white subject censoring a black author."[801] Prominent journalist John Matshikiza argued, "You don't come into someone's house (as he literally did), drink their tea and then tell them they're a damn racist fool when they point out that you've got some of your facts wrong. Ubuntu doesn't work like that."[802] Cultural commentator Shaun de Waal incisively noted, "Gordimer is not a government – she cannot 'ban' something; block it, yes ... (or, perhaps more precisely, she diverted it)."[803] Gordimer did not forbid Roberts from using her writings; she simply would not lend her imprimatur to the finished product. And expat author Ronald Segal argued, "Any comparison, express or implicit, between the current issue and the censorship practised by the apartheid regime is absurd and odious."[804]

Although few people openly endorsed Roberts's perspective, his new publisher – whom Roberts made a point of identifying as a "black empowerment" firm – slyly and disingenuously retaliated with the design of the book's cover. It incorporated an actual newspaper billboard of the type affixed to streetlights declaring "Gordimer bans book", flanked by a quotation from Gordimer seeming to endorse the book (it was, however, extracted from a letter she had written in response to an early draft). In an interesting twist of fate, *No cold kitchen* was nominated for the Alan Paton Award for non-fiction in 2006, whereas Gordimer's *Get a life* was overlooked by the judges of the *Sunday Times* Fiction Prize.

In 2007 a guest columnist unashamedly revealed her own predilections by announcing, "The writings of Nadine Gordimer are boring. I know this because I have never been able to stay interested beyond the first three or four pages of her books. I thought I might be a Philistine but I have heard the same comment from a few people who have actually read her." But the woman's critique cut deeper, once again raising the question of the right of artists to speak about the experiences of others. This woman elaborated, "[Gordimer] has always seemed so smug in her role as observer, interpreter and final arbiter of *our struggle*. It did not occur to her that given her privileged position she should be more humble." She accused Gordimer of inevitably holding racist attitudes, despite her impressive record of activities in the struggle. "It is clear," she wrote, "that Gordimer had a genuine dislike for the excesses of apartheid and used her standing as a writer to highlight the horrors of that system. [But] [t]o expect Gordimer to have escaped the ravages of colonial prejudice is unscientific [sic]."[805]

Nadine Gordimer's unconcealed engagement with political issues has generated attacks from conservatives and progressives, whites and blacks alike. Once hailed as a staunch crusader for human rights during an oppressive era, the more egalitarian society she could only dream of has not necessarily embraced her. But fellow Nobel Laureate for literature J.M. Coetzee, a writer known for his more allusionary style, has not been spared censure either. In fact, the careers of these distinctly different two writers display interesting overlaps and outcomes.

Thumbs Down and Nose Thumbing

J.M. Coetzee has steadfastly ignored the literary limelight. He has not lent his name to social causes. And he has likewise refused to become a member of any governmental retinue. Politicians have not ignored him, however.

Coetzee is one of only three writers to snare the Booker Prize twice, and he was awarded the Nobel Prize in 2003. But that honour became the occasion to hail one author as much as insult another. Commentator after commentator took this opportunity to compare South Africa's two most prominent literary luminaries.

One columnist wrote, "SA's second winner, J.M. Coetzee, is a far better writer than the first, Gordimer," he said. "The Nobel panel wanted to show how anti-apartheid it was and gave it to the most fashionable anti-apartheid writer, even if her books were painfully mediocre. This is not the case with Coetzee, who does not spout the politically correct message that all the wrong in the world is caused by naughty white males. His books take a deeper look at suffering."[806]

A newspaper editorial struck a similar chord: "The choice of J.M. Coetzee as Nobel Prize Laureate is refreshing because unlike some previous winners, he is not obviously politically correct … If Nadine Gordimer's 1991 triumph reflected international affirmation of the emerging democracy in this country, Coetzee's has more to do with genuine literary merit."[807]

But Coetzee's novel *Disgrace* (1999) has attracted a surfeit of critical responses. It was debated in Parliament and condemned as racist by ANC officials, who submitted it to hearings held by the Human Rights Commission on racism and the media in 2000. Moreover, Gordimer slammed the novel, saying "there is not one black person who is a real human being". Speaking more like a social scientist than a creative artist she noted, "I find it difficult to believe, indeed more than difficult, having lived here all my life and being part of everything that has happened here, that the black family protects the rapist because he's one of them." Gordimer concluded, "If that's the only truth he could find in the post-apartheid South Africa, I regretted this very much for him."[808] Others, however, have hailed the book as a masterpiece.

This novel discomfits people because it offers a view of post-apartheid South Africa that is brutally violent and struggling with heavy baggage from previous regimes; a central character who is morally bankrupt; and a future in which whites have lost both material wealth and personal dignity and must atone for the political sins of the past by being subjugated to the will of black Africans.[809] And the fact that much of the retrograde philosophical pondering of the novel comes from a professor amplifies speculation that Coetzee is directly speaking through this man. This is not the type of story that a short-lived government striving to shape a viable society could embrace. But it delighted critics such as Harvard English professor (and friend of Coetzee) Homi Bhabha, who remarked that *Disgrace* is "a work of 'open seams' rather than 'suturing' … [and] 'allows people to project onto it some of their own most heartfelt but violent feelings'."[810]

The ANC condemned *Disgrace* in 2000 because it felt the book typecast blacks as brutes, perpetuating the notion of *swart gevaar* and implying that the future held scant promise for whites in South Africa. But the party's defensiveness was tempered somewhat after the receipt of the Nobel Prize thrust Coetzee onto the world stage, bringing reflected glory to the country. An opposition political party, the Democratic Alliance, suggested that the ANC should then apologise for panning Coetzee's writing in the past.

"We highly appreciate his work as a son of the soil and believe that all of us must congratulate him," an ANC official stated in a carefully worded announcement, but "we stand by what we said and there will be no apology."[811] ANC spokesperson Smuts Ngonyama demonstrated the niggling acknowledgment of Coetzee's accomplishment by asking, "who has actually apologised for all the killings of the apartheid regime, who has explicitly apologised for that?"[812] The government's embrace of this literary luminary has been awkward and tentative at best. The editorialists quoted above concluded, "Those ANC folk who took umbrage were not too far off the mark. But *Disgrace* is more about the inner life, than an attempt to rubbish the government."[813]

Like Gordimer, Coetzee's work has been denounced as unsuitable to be taught to students. A letter-to-the-editor writer bemoaned, "Coetzee's most odious book has been jammed into the school syllabus … youths are being brainwashed with an ideological distillation of the worst of South African Anglo-Saxon culture."[814] And Coetzee's novels were scrutinised by apartheid apparatchiks but escaped the censorship that Gordimer endured. Both authors directly addressed the topic: Gordimer in the book *What happened to*

Burger's daughter or how South African censorship works (1980), and Coetzee in a collection of essays, *Giving offense* (1996).

Received wisdom has held that Coetzee's work was not judged to pose a political threat during the apartheid era because it was opaque, employed universal and not specific settings, and appealed to a select audience (similar arguments have been made about the apartheid government's relative disregard of the visual arts). Recent research has uncovered another factor that could have been in play: archival documents reveal that academics were contracted to write reports at the behest of the Publications Control Board and may have deliberately played down potentially provocative aspects of what they read to allow works to pass official muster.[815] In this respect censorship – always a cat-and-mouse game – was undermined by some creatures posing to be creatures they were not.

Coetzee has perpetrated the ultimate nose thumbing at local critics, be they South African politicians, readers, or fellow members of the literary fraternity: he joined the "chicken run" to Australia, following throngs of his fellow South Africans into self-imposed exile. Some have argued that it was payback for the harsh response *Disgrace* garnered in a society that one journalist described as a place where "the arts are expected to be a glorified version of a hamburger, instantly consumable and understandable", and a populace bearing "resentment that Coetzee's work is more challenging than watching a cricket match".[816] Others have been more munificent, contending that Coetzee may have run out of material to work with in his home country.

The feeling of betrayal lingers. One letter-to-the-editor angrily declaimed, "He should enjoy it [the Nobel Prize] where he is and hopefully not come back. His book *Disgrace* is a disgrace."[817] But the perpetually magnanimous Nelson Mandela pushed aside any bitterness or sense of insult and declared, "He might have emigrated but we shall continue to claim him as our own."[818]

Penis Gevaar

A painting exhibited by Brett Murray in 2012 brilliantly demonstrates the coalescence of the politics of race and representation, the ways in which constitutional rights such as freedom of expression and the protection of individual dignity can grate against one another, and the politics of diversion. The furore it aroused propelled *The Spear* into being the most vilified work of art ever produced in South Africa. But as extraordinary as this occasion was, the manner in which the controversy unfolded recapitulated many of the key features of art controversies from the country's past. It was a watershed moment in which the roles and definitions of culture were hotly debated and alternately venerated and reviled.

Brett Murray's exhibition *Hail to the Chief II* opened in Johannesburg on 10 May 2012. A Goodman Gallery press release issued a week prior to the opening stated, "This body of satirical work continues his acerbic attacks on abuses of power, corruption and political dumbness … a vitriolic and succinct censure of bad governance … [and] his attempts to humorously expose the paucity of morals and greed within the ruling elite." The works, which also included sculptures, etchings and silkscreens, were a mash-up of the ANC logo and insignia, iconic struggle posters, and Soviet propaganda; liberation heroes changed into tenderpreneurs (officials who use their authority to secure lucrative government contracts), idealistic freedom and resistance slogans converted into cynical materialistic mottoes. For example, *The Struggle* altered the final words that MK cadre Solomon Mahlangu uttered before he was hanged by the apartheid regime in 1979, from "Tell my people that I love them and that they must continue the struggle" to "Tell my people that I love them and that they must continue the struggle for Chivas Regal, Merc's and kick-backs". The works were both uncommonly insolent and uncomfortably insightful.

The exhibition was previewed in *City Press* on Sunday, 13 May, in what Murray characterises as "kind of a light, kind of a breezy description of me and the show".[819] Tellingly, the journalist singled out *The Spear*, based on a 1967 poster of Lenin by Soviet artist Victor Ivanov, with this prescient musing: "Of all the work on show, it's this depiction of the president that will set the tongues wagging and most likely generate some howls of disapproval."[820] Murray's version presented embattled President Jacob Zuma in a heroic pose, genitals fully exposed; a reproduction of it accompanied the article.

A cascade of angry reactions ensued over the following two weeks: the African National Congress filed an emergency court injunction to have the painting removed from display; a leader of the Shembe Church called for Murray to be stoned to death; additional threats were directed against the gallery and the gallery's staff, as well as *City Press*; SACP general secretary and the minister of higher education Blade Nzimande called for a boycott of the paper because it had posted *The Spear* on its website;[821] large protest marches took place in Durban, led by one of Zuma's four wives, and in Johannesburg; the artwork was defaced with paint in two separate incidents on the same day, after which it was taken down;[822] and in an unprecedented expansion of its powers the Film and Publications Board rated an artwork, restricting viewers to those 16 and older, even though the image was by then widely available on the internet.[823]

The Spear transfixed the country, dominated the news and public discourse, and triggered a painful dialogue around the enduring legacy of colonial and apartheid injustices in a democratic South Africa, the politics of reconciliation, the status of traditional culture and beliefs within the contemporary world, individuals' rights and responsibilities, and censorship. The country was brought to a fever pitch; at moments, a full-scale race war seemed a distinct possibility.

Spearing a Nation

The Spear controversy exemplifies a classic case of the politics of diversion. Or, as Goodman Gallery director Liza Essers characterised it, this was an instance of "manufactured rage",[824] and Brett Murray branded it "manufactured flag-waving and politicking". In the run-up to the ANC's national conference scheduled for later in the year in Mangaung, where beleaguered President Jacob Zuma hoped to be renominated to lead his party and secure a probable second term in office, attacking this irreverent depiction provided a rich opportunity for his supporters to deflect attention away from the incumbent's shortcomings. As mentioned in Chapter 1, this is an example of a proxy battle, fought *over* a work of art, but *about* much deeper matters.

Zuma's problems were manifold at this moment: he was buffeted by administrative and personal scandals, subject to fault-finding by an increasingly critical, probing press, and his credibility was at stake because of his botched efforts to meet the public's expectations of the government generating positive changes in their lives. The president was under considerable pressure and ever more vulnerable; his foibles and failures had left his arse exposed, along with his putative penis. Two newspaper headlines – one appearing before the controversy, and one as it was quieting down – capture the sense of imminent crisis: "Zuma forced to put out too many fires", and "President Zuma is under siege".[825]

The state of the economy was a key concern: when compared with 1994, unemployment was up, as was the ratio of debt to disposable income. In May, the business confidence index fell to a three-month low, along with growing concerns over the rising cost of basic necessities.[826] And education was earning a failing mark: in a memorial address delivered at the University of Johannesburg in March, renowned activist and academic Mamphela Ramphele slammed the education system as "worse than the 'gutter education' that the youth of 1976 gave their lives to overthrow". She also cited the accelerating growth of the ranks of Neets, those 18- to 24-year-olds who were neither being educated nor employed.[827]

Distressing statistics were reported with regularity within this realm: for example, out of 100 pupils who enter Grade 1, only one will graduate from university.[828] And an ongoing crisis in Limpopo, where learners enrolled in several grade levels were without textbooks well into the semester, signalled a significant breakdown in ministerial operations.

This was simply one indication of deficient service delivery, a problem that has fuelled raucous protests throughout the country. In fact, a report predicted that 2012 would tally the biggest volume of such protests since 1994.[829] A corollary was the rise in vigilante activity: communities fed up with spiralling crime rates but lacking faith in the police increasingly resort to mob justice against alleged perpetrators, including necklacing.

Moreover, scandals removed the nation's incumbent top cops from office twice in succession (Jackie Selebi and Bheki Cele), and charges of corruption, cronyism and nepotism became commonplace. The president's nephew, along with one of Nelson Mandela's grandsons, ran Aurora Mines into bankruptcy, throwing thousands out of work and prompting this barbed commentary: "Khulubuse Zuma's corpulence is the ideal metaphor for the majority of the elites within our society who live by Gordon Gekko's words in *Wall Street* – that 'greed is good' and is the driver of just about anything one's heart desires … His corpulence, in essence, is the manifestation of a lifestyle of excesses and not knowing when to stop."[830]

Zuma married for the sixth time in April in a lavish ceremony replete with silver tables and chairs and witnessed by 1500 guests. Murray quips, "Some people have an Achilles heel; he seems to have an Achilles dick." And the snickers over the president's not-so-private private life turned into a tangible backlash: there were calls for cutting back on the government's annual support of (compound) spousal benefits. Moreover, a court ruling in March determined that the National Prosecuting Authority's decision to drop corruption charges against Zuma in 2009 was reviewable.

A persistent thorn in the president's side has been Julius Malema, the rowdy former head of the ANC Youth League who was suspended for five years from the ANC for "acts of indiscipline", such as bringing the party into disrepute and sowing division within its ranks, a ruling upheld in April 2012. Once allies, Malema has subsequently attacked Zuma as a dictator and a "corrupt tribalist".[831] For example, he led supporters in song against Zuma at a rally in Limpopo in December 2011, declaring "the shower man is giving us a hard time" and tauntingly used a showerhead gesture to caricature Zuma.[832] This marked a sea change from Malema's 2008 proclamation that he would "kill for Zuma". Not surprisingly, Malema joined the critics of the ANC's campaign against *The Spear*.

Journalists were quick to pick up on the fact that Murray's painting provided a convenient target upon which the president and his followers could deflect criticism, a scapegoat for all this politician's deficiencies, an occasion for political opportunism par excellence. One editorial noted, "Zuma, 70, is not about to waste the Viagara-boost [*sic*] *The Spear* has administered to his re-election drive"[833] and a cartoon entitled "The Battle of Mangaung" depicted Zuma mounted on a horse, ready to go into combat, but instead of a jousting sword he wields a gigantic spoon, and "second helping" is crossed out to read "second transition", a reference to Zuma's vague, and discredited, proposal for prioritising economic transformation.[834]

Two adverts for advocacy groups most keenly apprehended the farcical dimension of *The Spear* attracting such an inordinate amount of public attention, to the detriment of the efforts of social interest initiatives. Childline South Africa ran a full-page newspaper announcement enumerating the resources diverted to the controversy: one painting, nine lawyers, 18 hours in court, and 187 front-page press articles, eventually culminating in 270 810 posts on Facebook and 325 987 mentions on Twitter (as of 4 June 2012). The tagline read, "For the last 7 days it's been Child Protection Week in South Africa. Unfortunately no one noticed." And the Save the Rhinos campaign cleverly conjured up an animal with an erect penis as a substitute for its horn; the catchphrase asked, "Will someone pay attention now?"

Takin' It to the Streets

Both Essers and Murray were blindsided by the uproar. Essers was on maternity leave and relaxing with her new baby when she received an urgent call from her staff: the ANC was seeking court intervention to have the painting removed, and news crews were besieging the gallery. And although an ANC stalwart had sent a complaint to Essers regarding the version of the show that appeared at the Goodman Gallery in 2011, before *The Spear* was created, Murray had dismissed any concerns that the painting might cause problems, thinking, "It's an artwork; it's in the gallery. I had no idea it was going to implode."

In fact, *The Spear* that is now familiar to a broad swath of the South African public very nearly did not exist. Murray explains, "I painted it without a dick, I thought it was interesting enough, in the context of the other work looking at Soviet memorabilia and the pseudo-Soviet kind of rabblerousing that happens here in the name of the people, but actually it's for the few, the chosen few. So it was in the context of that I thought it was interesting sans dick. And then I kind of, as is my nature, I just wanted to make something a little more provocative." Upon reflection, Murray notes, "I just decided to, rather than didn't. It's in the nature of making work, that's what happens, you make these decisions and then you stick with it."

Noted academic and commentator Jonathan Jansen keenly perceived that this was a culture war, explicitly invoking the concept and noting that "the hardline positions were cemented quickly", resulting in "the most aggressive intimidation, bullying and outright threats targeting ordinary citizens since 1994".[835] Interestingly, a writer in the proudly populist *Sunday World* became the other source that made a specific connection to this paradigm.[836]

Of course, South African artists have been scorned, and even threatened, in the past. Steve Hilton-Barber was menaced over his photographs of initiates, as was Beezy Bailey for his temporary transformation of a sculpture of Louis Botha into an *abakwethu*. Similarly, Kendall Geers and the Goodman Gallery were intimidated because of his Fort Klapperkop intervention, as was painter Yiull Damaso for his imagining of a Madiba autopsy. Even so, no South African artist has been the target of such a sustained and vicious campaign of threats as was Murray. One letter-to-the editor writer declared, "[Murray] must be prosecuted and tortured in a ferocious manner."[837] Twitter, Facebook, and radio shows were additional sites where the thirst for blood was registered, including suggestions of necklacing.

At one point Murray closed his workshop and he and his family fled Cape Town; Essers felt compelled to hire a personal bodyguard. She received calls declaring "A white person has to die for what's happened" and someone wrote "traitor" all over a car owned by one of her black staff members. Murray reflects that these comments were "screaming and vitriolic and violent and threatening". He sadly reports that his assistant of 16 years, a respected elder within his home community, also became a target of intimidation, both where he lived as well as within the presumed relative anonymity of the train: "So as is typical of South Africa, who would feel the most heat actually in the context is my assistant because he lives out in an area where lots of people are unemployed, where violence is palpable and real, and so the threats against him were going to be profoundly more focused than against me or a gallery owner or [*City Press* editor] Ferial Haffajee.[838] My first real concern prior to my own was actually his, when this whole thing blew up, is what is going to happen to Shadrack and his family?"

But nothing rivals the following pronouncement by a woman – one of thousands who marched on the Goodman Gallery on 29 May – for its bone-chillingly precise, passionate, and uncompromising assessment of the situation: "This is an old man … he [Murray] is a young boy [*sic*] … he doesn't have manners. I'll kill him."[839] Some people at that demonstration carried signs reading "Whites Hate Blacks", and another woman declared, "We're supporting Zuma because he's like our father, and the country's father. The portrait was inappropriate and [Murray] must get on a ship and go back to Europe, or wherever he's from."[840] Racism, xenophobia and blind fury were thus churned into a poisonous and explosive brew. Liza Essers was stunned by the ANC's support of such a tactic: "They haven't marched since 1994 – did you know that?"

The possibility of constructive dialogue was also somewhat truncated by numerous invocations of the legacy of Sarah Baartman, comparing Zuma's depiction by an artist to the tragic circumstances of this grossly maltreated 19th-century woman. For example, the front page of the 28 May Africa edition of *The Star* juxtaposed *The Spear* – "censored" plastered over the genitalia – with a blurred, full-length photograph of a nude indigenous women with pronounced steatopygia. Separating the two images was a quote from President Zuma set in boldfaced type: "Racism and no respect for human dignity." Such parallels have been drawn in the past: Ronald Suresh Roberts linked Health Minister Manto to the so-called Hottentot Venus when details from her medical records were published in a newspaper (Chapter 5), and an audience member put attendees of the 2003 "Sex and Secrecy" conference on the defensive when she made a similar point about exploitation of the black body in relation to nude photographs of gay black men.

But many people quickly recognised the preposterousness of such a purported analogy between a president with strong patriarchal affinities and a relatively powerless and abused woman who died in exile two centuries ago.[841] In the end, this idea did not gain much traction.

Moreover, the notion that "dignity" was compromised by an artwork surfaced as far back as 1996 in the controversy over Kaolin Thompson's *Useful Objects*, as well as with Jacob Zuma's lawsuit against Zapiro's biting depictions of him (Chapter 5).[842] With court proceedings scheduled to begin soon in his long-simmering dispute with the president, Zapiro intrepidly staked out his claim to an unencumbered realm of freedom of expression in his contribution to the 6 July issue of the *Mail & Guardian*: Zapiro drew Zuma as an upright penis on two legs and sporting the familiar shower head from its scalp. This comic figure views its reflection in a mirror hanging at the Goodman Gallery and bearing the signature of Brett Murray; it reacts with a scowl. The drawing was accompanied by a cheeky limerick: "Though sex is his publicised sport/ Zuma took the dick-painting to court/Suing Brett's free expression/Confirmed the impression/He's **as** big a dick as we thought!" Predictably, this drew both huzzahs along with hoots, but complaints by AfriForum, the ANC and the ANC Women's League failed to catch fire with a general public already fatigued by these matters.

Many commentators embraced an essentialism that could only understand *The Spear* as a racist portrayal, full stop. "To be South African … is to have a soul that *instinctively* resonates with the sound of Shosholoza", one man declared.[843] And comedian Loyiso Gola stated, "As modern as we are and we go and eat sushi and what not, this is still Africa. Black people will always interpret something like that in a different way."[844] Both these comments echo some of the arguments aired to justify the establishment of the Native Club and also underpinning the remarks of Malegapuru Makgoba, vice chancellor of the University of KwaZulu-Natal (Chapter 4), privileging an elemental (black) Africanness over other cultural viewpoints. Public Works Minister Thulas Nxesi pushed this logic further, asserting a profound inequity in the way in which different types of expression are treated: "Our culture, our freedom songs, are declared as hate speech. But their insults are declared as freedom of speech."[845]

Murray reports feeling "emasculated", "voiceless", "profoundly humiliated" by *The Spear* being called racist, and by extension his being labelled as such, in the ANC's bid to have it removed from the gallery and in much of the public dialogue that followed. Prominent poet and cultural activist Wally Serote, for example, "said the painting was 'no different to labelling people kaffirs'".[846] For Murray, as someone who had been a cultural activist in the 1980s, using his artistic skills on behalf of labour unions, the End Conscription Campaign and other progressive causes, this allegation burned. He reflected on the irony of being propelled from one extreme of the political spectrum to the other: "[In the past] the white 'brethren', including my father, would call me *kaffirboetie* because of my support for change. So I was labelled a *kaffirboetie* then and now I'm labelled as someone who would come out in public and call people '*kaffirs*'."

Both Murray and Essers reject the claim that *The Spear* was racist, but he understands that some people could interpret it in this way, and Essers admits that she's "conscious … that for some people there has been a *real* hurt and humiliation that has been brought to the surface". Both of them primarily view *The Spear* as securing Zuma's place on a roster of international leaders whose sexual exploits have also generated headlines, widespread discussion and lampooning.

While the ANC's playing of the race card and the alleged assault on Zuma's dignity may have seemed like a smart gambit at the outset, the party's court case quickly collapsed on such shaky foundations. Both sides agreed to a settlement after the ANC presented its case, a drama that was televised to the nation. The judge determined that *The Spear* was not racist; the gallery's arguments were postponed, but ultimately never aired in court; and *City Press* agreed to remove the painting from its website, to the dismay of those who felt that this set a bad precedent for journalists in the future. But Ferial Haffajee argued that her actions as a journalist had overtaken the real story.

Simply put, the ranks of proponents and detractors of the artwork cut across racial categories; there were not hidebound receptors that ensured any one person's response. "Zulu culture" is not monolithic any more than "black culture" or "white culture" is. As one man reflected, "To Murray and most other South Africans, Zuma is not Baba, to whom one submits as a child does towards a parent ... Ethnocentric culture is not a defence for a president against public critique by a citizen."[847] And a Facebook post by another black African the same day condemned Zuma as "a moron of an uneducated tribalist who hides behind culture as though blacks are that stupid".[848]

However, culture wars are not about constructive dialogue; they are about showboating and political one-upmanship. ANC Senior Administrator Gwede Mantashe's motives could not have been more transparent than when he proclaimed, "What the ANC cannot win in the courts it will win in the streets."[849] Threats of mob action such as these, issued by a major public official, are potentially much more grievous in their impact than anything an artist might produce. Jonathan Jansen lamented the power of the "semi-literate chorus" represented by the bused-in, extra-legal, rent-a-crowd nature of a boisterous public march orchestrated by a political party currently holding power, characterising it as a "slide into barbarism".[850]

Although culture wars share some basic characteristics, they are unpredictable as well. In a recent book Steven J. Tepper develops a typology of episodes of cultural conflict based on their intensity: embers, sparks, brushfires and wildfires. In order to erupt into a huge conflagration they must gain strength in numbers, visibility, and the participation of various officials. Otherwise they flame out.[851] *The Spear* emerged at a moment when the cultural and political climate was highly combustible. A match – either intentionally or inadvertently dropped under such conditions – held tremendous potential for disaster. Murray recollects, "[I]t looked like I might have produced a spark for something terrible to happen within the broader context of the country, in terms of things just being unmanaged and going out of control. I'm not sure if that was imagined, because I was right at the focus of it, but I got a sense I might be responsible for something like that. And obviously I would not want to be part and parcel responsible."

An Artistic Cold Front?

Culture wars have various consequences. On the positive side, they may propel discussions forward that might not otherwise occur. But they become very taxing to those who are directly targeted and can also exert a chilling effect on cultural production. The ramifications of a dust-up reverberate widely and deeply, often times in quite a stealth manner. One of the most serious complications, of course, is self-censorship, with artists anticipating and fearing potential consequences and thereby second guessing themselves. An editorial published just as *The Spear* controversy peaked captured this possibility: "A tone has been set. Artists beware."[852]

In the immediate aftermath, for example, a young award-winning artist about to open a major exhibition vacillated over the advisability of including a video comprised of footage shot looking out of a window in his Cape Town flat. It showed disparate images of people going about their daily lives, one of whom was a black man, at different points begging on the street or masturbating. After much emotional to-ing and fro-ing the artist decided to keep it in, and the show was well received, with no adversely critical reaction to this material.

However, a full-length print of a nude man slated to be displayed in a window at Wits University that is visible to passers-by on the street was nixed by the consensus of a hastily called meeting of faculty members. And in a similar incident, albeit within the commercial realm, an artist exhibiting her work at Johannesburg's stylish Hyde Park Corner shopping mall was forced to cover up bare-breasted women in three of her paintings after a merchants' meeting declared them "too provocative".

Moreover, Andries Botha's much-disputed elephant sculptures (Chapter 6) were defaced with red and black paint in Durban, which many people judged to be a copycat incident to what had occurred at the Goodman Gallery. And the SAB, e.tv and M-NET all refused to screen an anti-xenophobia advert by Nando's, fearing that its satire might be misinterpreted and instead spur violence against foreign nationals. The only unrepentantly defiant creative person in the public eye during this time was cartoonist Zapiro.

The evolution of a project by Andrew Putter demonstrates the artistic consequences of witnessing what had happened to a local fellow artist, but where exercising a higher degree of vigilance does not necessarily equate to being creatively corseted by current events. Putter has been working for about two years with portraits taken by Alfred Duggan-Cronin of native people throughout southern Africa, especially in the 1920s and 1930s. He has been interested in the possibilities of restaging some of them, while being aware of the potential pitfalls of being a privileged white photographer working with black subjects and determining how they are represented.

He explains, "When *The Spear* happened one of the things that it did was it suddenly made me much more conscious of the effects my work might have on its audiences. Now these are things that I think about, but suddenly there seemed to be much more at stake because of what had happened to Brett. He'd been terrorised. And it made me realise that I needed to be *really* careful about what I was doing."[853]

But rather than compel Putter to abandon or fundamentally alter his venture, this led him to generate a fresh approach: "The upshot was that I started to become ethically more sensitive to my sitters and I began to start putting myself in *their* shoes in a way that I hadn't done to the degree that I was doing after what had happened to Brett. The project began to develop in such a way that I wanted to include far more of how they saw themselves." He made sure, for example, that none of his participants was uncomfortable with their portrait being included with his recreation of an *umkhwetha*, or male initiate.

Eventually Putter prepared a double set of portraits: one in which 18 contemporary Xhosa individuals decided what clothes to pose in for colour shots of themselves, along with black-and-white images in which they have donned hired beadwork and other types of traditional fashion and have been posed to reflect what their grandparents or great-grandparents might have looked like and how an early 20th-century photographer might have depicted them. These transformations bridge a gap between generations and lifestyles, and the arresting results, in Putter's words, "affirm but also destabilise certain colonial representations of amaXhosa 'traditions'".

In the end, Putter did make one artistic concession: he decided not to feature any of the women bare-breasted. As he describes it, "I can't guarantee that I can shield my sitters from any potential shitstorm that might emerge around that. And my first responsibility is to my sitters. That's the ethical upshot of the whole project. And so I decided to leave it out."

Interviewed less than two months after the flare-up over his painting, Brett Murray was alternately chastened, funny, angry, frustrated, fearful and wounded. Reflecting on what had occurred, he stated, "100% I wouldn't do it again, and 100% I would. Because I think I have a right to do what I do, say what I say, think what I think, and I think every poet, playwright, thinking person, non-thinking person has a right to air their views as they see fit." Murray concluded, "If I say that I wouldn't do it then the bullies have won, basically they have silenced dissent, they have silenced criticism."

But Murray has been left with an acute dilemma. Should he decide to branch out into new artistic territory, he runs the risk of being accused of "copping out", capitulating to the powers-that-be. But if he continues to work in the same vein he runs the risk of further denunciation. In a humorous moment, Murray teases that he "should have painted daffodils and portraits of my friends' pets". Ironically, influenced by the fact that he has two young children, Murray had been imagining his next body of work to be innocent and fun-filled, reflecting his kids' perspective on the world.

As he states, "Political expression's been the monkey on my back since the 1980s, it's been something I've fed and it's been fed by the twists and turns of this place." But such a potential creative U-turn has been brought to a standstill: "And now unfortunately my cards have been dealt, I've been given a hiding and my fear's sort of slowed and anger is slowly returning, and I can't not respond. Well, I can, but I just, I can't do that playful stuff any more. And I'm quite angry about that in and of itself because it feels like it's an unnatural progression of where I really wanted to take my work. It's more than likely I'll carry on doing what I do, carry on taking potshots."

Murray concludes, "I can't help myself. They just present my subject matter to me on a plate. So I suppose I have to use it. Well, I don't have to, but it's my default setting. This is what I do."

And in the End

The explosion over *The Spear* dissipated as quickly as it was detonated. But the episode has secured as important a place in South Africa's democratic history as other notable events that have brought citizens together or pushed them apart in dramatic fashion. Some people, including Murray, are disappointed that the court case did not continue: it could have resulted in a clearer sense of vindication for him, although he acknowledges that if the case had progressed to the Constitutional Court, he probably would have been forced to leave the country because of the sustained public pressure that might generate.

A legal decision also could have provided clarification of the respective limits of the constitutional rights to individual dignity and freedom of expression. Those precedents await future clashes of interests, thereby stranding creative people in a murky no man's land where they must tread carefully. Some complained that with the exhibition of *The Spear*, "Democracy has gone too far this time."[854] Until there is a legal interpretation of the limits of artistic expression, such emotion-based judgements will likely continue to be aired.

The Spear meteorically attained the type of iconic status that generates multitudes of spoofs. One painting, *The Shield*, created by a group of offended black artists, recalls the Ernest Cole photograph of African mineworkers submitting to a full body inspection. But in this instance a row of five naked whites is being examined by a black doctor, "to check whether or not these people were suitable to stay in the new South Africa".[855] Liza Essers, General Koos de la Rey, Helen Zille, Eugene Terre'Blanche, and Zapiro make up this miscellany of racial miscreants, with questionable status in what seems to be a steadily dissolving rainbow nation.

That is one type of response – a race-based tit-for-tat that may provide a fleeting sense of pleasurable payback, but little else. As Murray projects the future, he envisions going forward "not less cautiously but more informed, possibly, and hopefully it won't be fearful, and hopefully it won't be with some idea that you have someone looking over your shoulder. If the lesson is that I must be cautious, that I must be fearful," he says, "then I think it's a problem."

As to the future of creative expression in South Africa, Murray hopes that "I've maybe blown down the walls a bit".

Liza Essers describes herself as "shell-shocked" and "completely post-traumatic stressed and in a washing machine of turmoil", yet determined to safeguard her gallery as a neutral space where a broad variety of ideas and viewpoints is supported.

And *The Spear* has taken its place in history. Did it hit its mark and bring the president to book for his failures and misdeeds, or did it unintentionally confirm Zuma's status as a target of disgruntled constituents and a victim of political intrigue, thereby boosting his popularity in the minds of some? Like so much contemporary art, which is capable of spawning multiple inter-pretations, both consequences are likely true.

* * *

Employing his impish yet razor-sharp wit, Brett Murray's *Mantra* features a naughty Bart Simpson standing before a blackboard, chalk in hand, having repeatedly written "I must learn to speak Xhosa". This represents penance for the bungling cartoon figure, a stark reminder that he has failed to master essential life skills. The image tidily compresses white guilt with contemporary compulsion, a not-so-subtle reminder that life in South Africa has irrevocably changed and whites must accommodate to the new status quo.

CHAPTER 7

Searching for a Hero:
Reviving the Vanquished

... the battle in 1976 was for human rights, now it is for self-expression.

André Miller, 2004

A white boy grows up in South Africa, adoring Tintin. His story is quite an ordinary one. Craft markets throughout the country are chock-a-block with wooden figurines of the characters from these stories, confirming their continued appeal. But for two such youngsters, now grown into men, Tintin has become a channel through which they bawdily vent contemporary frustrations and anxieties, and onto whom they project their darkest desires. If critics in Europe have been offended by the semiotics of the original Tintin books by Hergé, they could very likely become apoplectic if they were to view the ways that artistic collaborators Conrad Botes and Anton Kannemeyer have made over this naïf.

Kannemeyer has parodied the cover of *Tintin in the Congo*, the same illustration that editorial cartoonist Zapiro redrew to skewer the antics of its politically correct detractors (Chapter 6). Renamed *Pappa in Afrika* on the front of an issue of Botes and Kannemeyer's celebrated *Bitterkomix*, Kannemeyer's version foregrounds the familiar jalopy conveying Tintin and his party of stalwarts through Africa. But in this rendition it rattles through a post-apocalyptic landscape rather than a pristine one: smoke billows up in the distance, skulls and bones litter the ground, an amputee hobbles around, blood seeps out of a prone body, and a sinister-looking soldier wielding an automatic weapon threatens to walk right out of the frame to assault the viewer. The facial features of all these black Africans are, for the record, hideously stereotyped. Moreover, Kannemeyer's postcard *Groete uit Suid-Afrika* ("Greetings from South Africa") shows our hapless hero fleeing for his life from enraged natives – not exactly an appealing come-on for tourists.

Botes has also reinterpreted Tintin: his version of *Tintin in Africa* presents a muscle-teed hipster who saunters easily through an urban crowd while merrily shouldering an outsized boombox. He is jet black, and bears an uncanny resemblance to General Electric's Reddy Kilowatt mascot from years past; his head looks like an offbeat Christmas ornament. Botes has also plopped Tintin into loads and loads of shit (but more on that later). One critic has declared that Tintin is Botes's "Everyman".[856]

This chapter centres upon creative depictions and representations of a particular group, the Afrikaner. And it will bring us full circle back to the opening event of this book: the indaba addressing Mbongeni Ngema's controversial song "AmaNdiya". The focal point will be on another song that likewise dominated the headlines, aroused popular fears, and elicited impassioned commentary from wary public officials. In this instance "De la Rey", celebrating a Boer general who has been dead for nearly a century, captivated Afrikaners who embraced it as a modern anthem and propelled its singer/songwriter Bok van Blerk into stardom in 2007. At the same time, it raised fears of a resurgent Afrikaner nationalism.

An uncommonly tender episode in *Bitterkomix* 10 (2000) shows the budding friendship between Themba and Daniël: they hang out, play, draw, and even pee together ("Cross swords, Dude," the two mutually exclaim in intersecting dialogue balloons). These are scenes of casual interaction between boys from different racial groups that are still woefully unusual but would have been unimaginable even a few years ago.

At the end of the day Themba asks to borrow some of Daniël's comics and trots off bearing a stack with *The Blue Lotus* from *The Adventures of Tintin* series on the top. But Themba returns moments later and hands them back; his parents won't allow him to read racist material. A bewildered Daniël asks his father in Afrikaans, "As Themba dit nie mag lees nie, hoe sal hy ooit weet wat fout is daarmee. ['If Themba isn't allowed to read them, how will he ever know what's wrong with them?']" Such small gestures of generosity and sincere stabs at communication and mutual understanding – and the factors that trip them up – reveal how immense the social distance remains between diverse people in South Africa, and how mystifying it is for them to know how to adapt to continually changing circumstances.

Unfulfilled Promises

Certain depictions of Afrikaners have raised as much ire as have images of black Africans. The year before Steve Hilton-Barber's images rocked the Market Theatre Gallery, for example, another photographer had caused a furore there.[857] Their subject matter may have been markedly different from one another, and the groups that objected were somewhat differently constituted, but the issue of ambiguous creative intent dogged them both.

In 1989 the Afrikaans newspaper *Vrye Weekblad* ("Free Weekly", which supported a more critical stance towards the National Party government than other such publications) sponsored an exhibition featuring sculptures by Brett Murray and the photographs of Gideon Mendel.[858] Murray's satirical, unflattering authority figures were silently taken in by visitors. But Mendel's colour images of the 150th commemoration held in 1988 of the Great Trek, the Afrikaner foundation myth, spurred outrage.[859]

The Great Trek was endlessly hyped in textbooks during the apartheid era and remains a central trope in Afrikaner identity. According to this tale

Afrikaners disgruntled with British rule in the Western Cape set out to build an independent society where their language and culture could flourish in freedom. Under God's watchful eye these Voortrekkers pushed into the country's interior, purportedly a nearly virgin, unpopulated land.[860] On the 100th anniversary in 1938, a reenactment of the trek generated immense excitement across the country, culminating in a massive gathering of people on a site outside Pretoria on 16 December.[861] There the cornerstone was laid for what would become the highly emblematic Voortrekker Monument.

Whereas the 1938 trek united Afrikaners through a heightened sense of group identity and common cause, the 1988 reenactment unravelled into cross-factional rivalries. Three different marches strained to reach Pretoria. And when the participants arrived they were dispirited and contemptuous of one another. The years of political struggle by black Africans during the intervening years had brought the Afrikaner-dominated government to its knees; it was the eve of a major new political dispensation. This commemoration became a bust, a pathetic final gasp of ethnic pride.

Gideon Mendel documented trekkers slouching towards this local Bethlehem, the sacred Voortrekker Monument. It was an ideal example of staged authenticity: early on, travelling on tar proved so difficult that the wagons were loaded onto trucks and only set down in certain places. At times men were forced to pull them. Mendel captured them straining like beasts, braaiing, or holding contests for the longest beard.

In one memorable shot Mendel showed a preacher on a barren stage, his arms earnestly extended, and standing in front of an immobile wagon, but with no congregants in sight. In another, notorious right-wing leader Eugene Terre'Blanche was depicted as a model *paterfamilias* surrounded by his family. Mendel called his series of 56 photos *Beloofde Land* ("Promised Land").

The photographs elicit various readings. The people Mendel captured may seem like sincere pilgrims or laughable throwbacks to an outmoded era. They can appear to be ordinary or misguided or demagogues, fools or outlaws. But was Mendel humanising, caricaturing or satirising them?

One reviewer gushed with praise, calling Mendel's work "magnificent", a "profound, moving and beautiful exhibition" displaying "moral force". He favourably compared the shot of a cheerless young man on a horse to works done by Albrecht Dürer and Francisco Goya, observing, "This is a Quixote without windmills, a horseman who missed the apocalypse." He concluded, "What Mendel has done so brilliantly is to show the self-imposed LACK of freedom, the joylessness, the absence of vision, and the FEAR that characterised the 1988 commemoration of the Great Trek."[862]

But others interpreted the series differently. And they felt outraged. Some black Africans were upset that these images seemed to salute rather than condemn Afrikaner nationalists, that they were propaganda rather than critique. Playing on stage at the Market Theatre at the time was *Goree* by Matsemela Manaka (a two-woman performance with song and dance, and featuring a young Sibongile Khumalo); some patrons complained to the playwright that they were offended by these images being shown in the same building. And in an action that presaged what would happen to Steve Hilton-Barber's work, cast members removed five of the photos on Human Rights Day, commemorating the 1960 event in which police opened fire on black Africans protesting the pass laws in Sharpeville, a township outside Vereeniging in what was then the Transvaal, killing 69 and injuring many more. In response to the outcry over the photos the *Vrye Weekblad* hosted a public debate at its offices that attracted 80 people.[863]

A major point of contention was the ambiguity of the images: Mendel had provided no text that would have illuminated his intent. Fellow photographer Paul Weinberg demanded, "The photographer has a responsibility to ideologically frame these pictures ... [it was] art which has not clarified its ideological position."[864] One critic accused Mendel of being a "closet fascist".[865] At a time when politics was literally black and white, the question was raised whether it was possible to have subtlety in art without running the danger of misinterpretation. But at the end one attendee lamented that the discussion became "bogged down in semiotics, media theory, and what is documentary and what is art and so on",[866] without assuaging the public's feelings of outrage.

The fury that individuals felt towards Mendel's work transcended race as well as political proclivities. As was to be the case with Kaolin Thompson's "ashtray", some people feared that artistic interrogations of subjects such as authoritarianism or sexism might be misconstrued as support for those dogmas instead.

Snap Judgements

David Goldblatt has a firm lock on a place in the pantheon of South African photographers. The common chord that reviewers have struck for years when assessing his work has been the way Goldblatt sensitively captures the mundane, the quotidian, the ordinary moments and gestures, which become deeply revelatory of larger social realities. During the period of intense political struggle in his country, Goldblatt was sometimes put at odds with his fellow practitioners who felt they were obliged to become "cultural workers".[867]

Some of Goldblatt's early work did indeed reflect the role of artist as social activist. But when Goldblatt assessed his long career in 2007 he stated, "I realised that I was neither a missionary with a camera nor a political activist ... I realised that what I really wanted to engage with through the camera was people's values and how they were expressed. Headline events were the culmination of underlying conditions ... I wanted to probe those conditions by going to their roots in people's lives".[868] Goldblatt consequently considers himself to be "a lone figure" in South African photography.[869]

Today Goldblatt's work tends to push critics to lyrical heights. One eloquently remarked that his "photographic corpus grows from residuals, interstices, intimations in the sun". He continued, "It is also a daunting exposition in the South African register of what Michel Foucault theorised as the 'microphysics of power': the unremarkable, when ordered just so, glints with raw systematic power ... Goldblatt's topic is less 'apartheid' *per se* than the spectrum of three centuries of white settler rule."[870] And André Brink lauds Goldblatt for "rescuing the insignificant individual from oblivion, by defying death, by taking note, by lending human value to a life that otherwise might have remained forever unnoticed". Brink equates black-and-white photography with poetry: images and words are reduced to their essentials. Colour, he likens to prose. To Brink, Goldblatt is "the true poet of black and white".[871]

Despite his impulse to fly beneath the radar, Goldblatt's first book became a cause célèbre. But its odyssey from conception to publication was onerous and protracted. The critical reception it was accorded was dismissive and harsh. The response of the book-buying public was unenthusiastic, nearly undetectable. And the ordeal nearly derailed his career.

Goldblatt published *Some Afrikaners photographed* in 1975. It was the culmination of seven years of probing the lives of primarily rural, working-class Afrikaners. Today most viewers are moved by the obvious compassion he displays for these people, the intimacies he reveals. And the political and cultural climate is much different now than it was when the book debuted. Unlike the earlier incarnation, it became an instant classic after it was reissued as *Some Afrikaners revisited* in 2007.

The first suggestion that Goldblatt was treading in sensitive territory was when, in 1969, a chilling headline appeared in the Afrikaans newspaper *Dagbreek en Sondagnuus* (*Daybreak and Sunday News*) that blasted "Bloed Sal Kook Oor die Foto's" ["Blood Will Boil Over These Photos"]. This was after Goldblatt published a small selection of his work in the Swiss periodical *Camera*. This critic damned the images in prose equally as harsh as the title of the article. He accused Goldblatt of manipulating the light to portray his subjects in an unflattering way, for example. He singled out an image that showed a woman standing in a spot just below the Voortrekker Monument, watching her child peer into a replica Zulu hut, "bum in the air". The juxtaposition of these disparate iconic structures was unsettling; the critic assumed it had to have been intentionally constructed, a photomontage. The English language press was hardly more sympathetic: when the book was published in 1975, the editor of the *Sunday Times* withheld the review copy from his staff.

But a fresh reconsideration dismisses this initial assessment as "political dissembling under the guise of art criticism".[872] According to a well-known local media and cultural commentator, Goldblatt's work was considered "subversive" at the time; "Simply buying this book became a politicised action."[873]

Few did and it was remaindered, much to the chagrin of collectors who today will pay premium prices to secure a copy. What is now seen as a compassionate portrait of a people was condemned at the time as an attack on them. What, exactly, was the problem?

In a fundamental respect, *Some Afrikaners* represented the "return of the repressed". The images provided irrefutable evidence of what contemporary Afrikaners who wished to appear urbane and sustain their political power preferred to cover over, namely their not-so-distant agrarian roots. These photos were like poor relations who unexpectedly show up at a posh event and demand to be accepted. Goldblatt's Afrikaner subjects were "then"; his Afrikaner critics were "now".

Moreover, in his introduction Goldblatt dared to air a dirty ethnic secret: not only did he reference the commonly known Dutch, Huguenot and German roots of the group, but also mentioned the blood of Hottentots, Malays and black Africans that became part of the mix as well.[874] This was more than an embarrassment; it undermined the doctrine of racial purity that was at the heart of apartheid and supported its elaborate apparatus of control. "He produced unflinching portraits of a self-contained community living on the fringe of modernity," one journalist wrote, "at a time when Afrikaners and their history were 'a thorny subject'."[875]

Some Photographers Contrasted

Looking through *Some Afrikaners*, similarities to photographs taken in America during the Great Depression era of the 1930s are immediately apparent: the quiet dignity of the individuals, the obvious meagreness of their lives. A significant proportion of these American images were produced under direct sponsorship of the government; they were hailed as sensitive documents when they first appeared and continue to be treasured. The resemblance of Goldblatt's work to the photographs of Walker Evans seems obvious.

South African academic Sally Gaule offered a comparison of these two men in 1996. Unfortunately, she oversimplified the American experience, and overlooked the most appropriate bodies of their work to compare. Gaule proposes that Goldblatt and Evans were "looking through different prisms" (her choice of title), when in fact their depth of field was strikingly analogous.

She argues, for example, that the social documentary movement in 1930s America "held to a national purpose", whereas South African photographers aimed "to expose the injustices of the apartheid system".[876] But the American images blend both compassion and criticism. They could have an ironic edge, expose racism, or indict the failure of capitalism. Gaule focuses on Walker Evans as an employee of the Farm Security Administration (FSA), but fully half of the images she reproduces by him are actually from another project altogether, the book he co-published with James Agee, *Let us now praise famous men* (1941).

Gaule also asserts that Evans worked for the government (one segment only out of a lengthy career) whereas Goldblatt "always worked independently of political organisations, maintaining personal control over the production and dissemination of his images".[877] But the images and text that comprised

Let us now praise famous men were originally commissioned by *Fortune* magazine, which ultimately rejected the work; a book publisher subsequently cancelled a contract with Evans and Agee as well. And Goldblatt's first photo essay on platteland Afrikaners appeared in the society magazine *Tatler*, as "The people of the plots" (1964).[878] Moreover, Evans and Agee's book initially registered yearly sales only in the double and triple digits before it was ultimately embraced as a timeless American volume; Goldblatt's book would have never been published had it not been for the subvention of a friend.

The most significant misstep Gaule committed is that she opted to compare Evans's *American photographs* with Goldblatt's *In Boksburg*; the obvious pairing would be *Let us now praise famous men* with *Some Afrikaners photographed*. Oddly, she mentions neither book. She characterises Goldblatt's vision as "deeply critical and acerbic",[879] yet that was certainly not the case with *Some Afrikaners*. She notes that Evans's subjects distinctively stare directly into the camera, but some of Goldblatt's Afrikaners do, too. Moreover, she artificially constructed side-by-side comparisons, for example, placing a Walker Evans church next to a David Goldblatt house, taken 50 years later. She could have rather juxtaposed it to one the churches that David Goldblatt shot, of which there were many.

What remains to be explained is that for all the similarities between their subject matter, why did American documentary photographs of the rural poor not elicit the intensely hostile response that Goldblatt's *Some Afrikaners* did? The catalogue accompanying a retrospective of over 50 years of his photography claims, "The Afrikaners themselves … could not accept the mirror that he held up to them."[880] Afrikaners were locked into a rearguard struggle to confirm their group's inherent superiority, whereas the Great Depression was a great equaliser.

The Depression humbled a majority of the population, spoiling what many Americans thought of themselves. When they saw the images of the victims of economic hard times, they either recognised themselves, or empathically understood the economic predicaments of the people being depicted. The Depression created a brotherhood of suffering that magical thinking could not wish away. To be poor was not an embarrassment, it was stark reality.

But for Afrikaners in the 1970s, to be poor invalidated a key benchmark they used to set themselves apart from non-whites.[881] Such images were intolerable. The hostile response was fuelled by both race- and class-based anxiety and hatreds.

Not to be overlooked either is that fact that David Goldblatt may have been "white", but he was not a member of the Afrikaner tribe. One journalist noted that he was very aware of his appearance as a "hirsute outsider looking much like a communist Jew".[882] And another wrote, "[A]ccording to Goldblatt, it was never spelt out, [but] it was suggested that he, as an outsider, had no right to depict Afrikaners."[883] Not only does this raise once again the problem of who may legitimately represent whom, but the anti-Semitic sentiments within the Afrikaner community are well documented. The rejection of *Some Afrikaners photographed* was, therefore, overdetermined.[884]

In 2004 Goldblatt returned to Gamkaskloof, one of the isolated locales he had photographed decades before. Its nickname was Die Hel (The Hell) because of its exposure to the intense sun of the Karoo. But the site had become a ghost town in the 1980s as its residents either died off or gradually scattered to other more viable places.

Goldblatt's images at first captured, and now elegise, an existence that is long outmoded. The modest former homes of the people have been refurbished to provide shelter to ecotourists in a recently established nature reserve in the New South Africa.[885]

And depictions of Afrikaners continue to be provocative. An attention-grabbing headline on the cover of a *Sunday Times Lifestyle* section in June 2012 blared "Shooting the boer", with the explanatory subhead "Turning the lens on the new Afrikaner". Highlighting bare head-and-shoulder portraits of hip Afrikaners in their 30s and 40s such as Yo-landi Vi$$er of rave-rap duo Die Antwoord, Roelof Petrus van Wyk's *Jong Afrikaner* exhibition was generating outraged Facebook posts from right-wing brethren even before it opened at a gallery in Cape Town.

What Colour is your Penis (2)?

In the run-up to David Goldblatt releasing *Some Afrikaners revisited*, a selection of the photographs was exhibited at the Michael Stevenson Gallery in Cape Town in 2006. They were paired with a radically different creation, in what was either a stroke of curatorial genius or madness. In one room visitors saw Goldblatt's evocative black-and-white pictures; in another, bold colour illustrations from the raucous and irreverent *Bitterkomix*, magazines drawing heavily upon Afrikaner language, culture and history. One reviewer remarked, "The juxtaposition is a mind-boggling presentation of Afrikaner cultural extremes. Some viewers will be enraged, some will be thrilled."[886]

These two bodies of work represent fundamentally contradictory outlooks. "'It is almost a matter of principle with me,' Goldblatt noted, 'to make open-ended photographs, so viewers can form their own opinion.' Unlike *Bitterkomix*. They vigorously show and tell all the bits that generations concealed."[887]

Bitterkomix was launched in 1992 by Botes and Kannemeyer while they were students at Stellenbosch University. Their attendance predated the controversial Mark Coetzee at the same school (Chapter 6). Sharing a common spirit of creative questioning and defiance, artists such as these have keenly vented the uncertainties confronting white South Africans in general, men more particularly, and Afrikaner men most specifically in the transition from apartheid to democracy and multiracialism. For these are the people whose sense of entitlement and wellbeing has been under the greatest threat. Botes readily admits, "A lot of my work is about the loss of power."[888] And one critic observed, "*Bitterkomix* is an artistic milestone in a society attempting to unclench its fists from the battles of the past."[889]

Kannemeyer and Botes each have distinctive styles, and they have spun individually successful artistic careers off of their work on *Bitterkomix*.[890] But their publications are instantly recognisable: gaudy colours, bold lines, and highly charged subject matter. These artists brashly raid the cultural archive for inspiration; critics have perceived the influences of Francisco Goya, Hieronymus Bosch, George Grosz, Giorgio de Chirico, William Blake, Edvard Munch and contemporary pop culture (Richie Rich and Mickey Mouse, for example) coursing through their work. In one man's estimation, *Bitterkomix* is "Sweet and sour candy for the eye and the mind".[891]

Botes calls his approach "forensic theatre", which a journalist has described as "rich in satire, aiming to create new meaning from objects with pre-established significance. These objects exploit religious iconography and sexual references – sensitive subjects in Calvinism."[892] Botes and Kannemeyer subscribe to a no-holds-barred approach: nothing is sacred, nothing is beyond the pale. Their Afrikaner upbringings during the final stages of apartheid provide their creative ground. Botes has remarked, "People may call me sick and twisted but the space I grew up in [Bellville, a middle-class Afrikaner enclave outside Cape Town], and still live in, is sick and twisted."[893] And Mark Kannemeyer (Anton's brother, and also a contributor to *Bitterkomix*) observed, "Church in Stellenbosch then was like in the American South, where they used to burn [rock music] records. It was insane."[894] In their work these men have turned the weight of the Afrikaner tradition, with its emphasis on obedience to authority, conformity to traditional gender roles, and commitment to an abstemious, righteous, respectable and prudent lifestyle, against itself.

Scatology, eschatology and sex, lots and lots of sex, are fused into a bawdy mix. Where once there had been silence, now comes chatter; to address the extreme restrictions of the past, licence reigns in its place. To cite simply one example of their distinctively transgressive style: the Voortrekker Monument is, yes, monumentally defiled in a drawing by Mark Kannemeyer that appeared in *Bitterkomix* 5 (1995), showing the behemoth King Lizard perching atop the building, having just shat and sporting a large erection, and shouting "Haha! Fokof laaities! ['Fuck off, youngsters"]. A journalist remarked upon "the artists' answer to society's impulse to conceal and suppress an impulse they derisively label 'effie-logic' – condom logic. Implicitly, there is nothing 'safe' about *Bitterkomix*."[895] Professor Gregory Kerr, who became embroiled in the attempts to censor Mark Coetzee's work, and who supervised both Kannemeyer and Botes during their university studies, has dubbed them "outrage artists".[896]

Sex in *Bitterkomix* is polymorphous perverse and racially catholic. *Boerenooientjies hou van pielsuig* ("Afrikaner maidens like blowjobs") presents a panoply of anonymous penises and a corresponding number of Afrikaner women eagerly fellating them. Colossal black penises penetrate white ladies in numerous drawings, the nightmare of the *swart gevaar*, the fabled black menace, unleashed.[897] And in *Boetie*, a father strokes his young son's penis while the two lie in bed, a domestic horror that is never broached in public.

This has driven a wedge between Anton Kannemeyer and his father, a renowned professor of Afrikaans language and literature; they have not spoken for years. Reactions to *Bitterkomix* by the public have frequently been negative as well. *Gif: Afrikaner Sexcomix* was the first book to be banned by the post-apartheid government, in 1994. And an exhibition of drawings that same year at Stellenbosch University elicited many angry rejoinders in the response book.

Moreover, during the *Sex and Sensibility* exhibition at the NSA gallery in Durban, an irate viewer spraypainted over the series *Boerenooieentjies hou van pielsuig* in his disgust at the explicit images of fellatio. The vandal proudly signed the visitor's book, providing his contact information and his rationale: such "immoral art" should not be seen by children. But the curator rebuked his act, stating, "South Africans are ready for this kind of exposure. It's time we stopped mollycoddling them. It's not up to us at the gallery to uphold moral standards."[898]

Furthermore, a show by Botes at the Johannesburg Art Gallery (JAG) in 2004 prompted a security guard to write him a note complaining, "'God has given you a great talent but you have wasted it by blaspheming it.' The letter went on to put Botes in the same category as Hitler, Stalin, Pol Pot, Idi Amin and Nero – all enemies of Christianity."[899] One of the images that upset the man was *Holy Shit* (reverse glass painting, 2003), which shows a black Tintin trapped in a quagmire of shit that has spewed down from the heavens, out of the mouths of God, Jesus and the Holy (Casper the Friendly) Ghost. Kannemeyer's drawing of a black angel fellating the artist reportedly disturbed workers at Spier Contemporary,[900] and the first publisher they solicited for their book *The big bad* Bitterkomix *handbook* balked at the material that Kannemeyer and Botes had done for the *Hustler*-style magazine *Loslyf* as being "obscene". The artists were forced to look elsewhere.

A Stellenbosch University lecturer has noted, "The root of Botes's anxiety or tension – a tension that gives his work its force – could be summarised in J.M. Coetzee's formulation: 'No longer European/Not yet African'." In this man's estimation Botes's work reflects "the pain of the white male body; a body estranged, untenanted, at war with its psychic, cultural and historical inheritance".[901] And that sense of betwixt and between, previously entitled and now deposed, securely moored in the past but now cut adrift, is reflected in the distinctive way these artists use pastiche. Much of the subject matter of the *Bitterkomix* artists is predictably controversial, to be sure, but their collapsing of cultural categories and blending of disparate elements is what truly unsettles many viewers. It is the "impurities"[902] they create that must be eradicated.

Significantly, two different commentators on Kannemeyer and Botes have invoked terms that reflect the changing nature of the despised epithet "*kaffir*". Their former professor alludes to *kaffirboetie*, a term used to label white deviants and reinforce the racial hierarchy (think of Daniël, above, and his friendship with Themba). But another cites the 1989 pronouncement by singer/songwriter André Letoit (a.k.a., Koos Kombuis), "We are Afrikaffirs. We live in grey areas."[903] This was the proud and defiant pronouncement of an alternative Afrikaner culture, of which Kannemeyer and Botes are both progeny and progenitors.

Anton Kannemeyer's *Alphabet of Democracy* (2008) audaciously confronts the racist history of South Africa as well as the contemporary fears that infect everyday life for whites living in the country. His "j is for Jack Russell" features a family pet lying against a blanket spotted with red. A human hand sticks out from beneath. It is his master, a farmer, dead. The past exploits of the Afrikaner, "No longer European/Not yet African", are very much subject to reassessment and their future in this place very much a question mark.[904]

Consider the Alternative

Koos Kombuis's invocation of "Afrikaffirs" was a declaration of insubordination. The Afrikaner hierarchy had been besieged by thousands of toyi-toying black African schoolchildren in the townships. The last thing they needed was for their own kids to become cheeky and defiant in the 1980s as well. Nevertheless, a new front of resistance was opening up, literally in their own living rooms.

Kombuis was one of the central figures in a 1989 musical tour that was short-lived but much mythologised. One of his songs, "Boer in Beton" ("concrete"), included the following lyrics:

I am an Afrikaner in the city

* * *

And I know I don't belong here
I sit in bars late at night
But I no longer know the smell of the land

* * *

I beg to be consoled where I can
In this land of tin and glass
I am in sackcloth and ash.

This easily could have been the lament of one of David Goldblatt's subjects in *Some Afrikaners photographed*, a poor rural person displaced by economic, social and political factors as the 20th century sped along. But for the most part, Kombuis and his cohorts on the Voëlvry circuit sang about themes that weighed heavily on the minds of youthful urban Afrikaners, especially young men: compulsory military service, the sterility and smug security of the middle-class existence of their parents, the moral bankruptcy of their leaders, and the elaborate, restrictive apparatus of apartheid those men had constructed. Sometimes the lyrics even explored forbidden territory such as abandoning duty or love across the colour bar. Satire was plaited with sorrow, exasperation with adventure.

This music echoed the earlier revolts of students and other young people in the West, compressing the creative output and attitudes of the beats, hippies and punks into an eddy of outrage, hedonism and self-assertion. Notably, three of the Voëlvryers were the sons of ministers, giving their rebellion both personal and social dimensions.[905] Their songs became a knife through the paternal heart wielded with a danceable, pulsating beat. A book on underground urban cultures observes, "At least black activists could vent their anger by throwing stones and Molotov cocktails at the cops. But young progressive Afrikaners were at a loss." It goes on to reflect, "It was a painful paradox. Because of our skin-colour you were automatically part of a repressive regime. Koos [an alternative band performing in Johannesburg at the time] were a metaphor for the deep revulsion for that system."[906]

All the fervour, pleasure and excesses of the Voëlvry tour – variously described as Boere Beatlemania or a South African Woodstock[907] – was documented by photographer Steve Hilton-Barber. Organisers saw it as another version of the Great Trek, although they fantasised about travelling in a radically modified type of *ossewa*. And this all occurred just after the furore that had broken out over Gideon Mendel's documentation of the earnest commemoration of the trek that had become so bungled the year before.

The name Voëlvry itself carried a dual set of expressive meanings. On one hand it conveyed "feel free; free as a bird; ... free penis; free love". On the other, it signified "'outlawed,' wanted dead or alive".[908] And with members of one the bands calling themselves Die Swart Gevaar, their intentions and sympathies were unmistakably announced. These musicians wished to stir up rebelliousness at the same time that they intended to send chills down the spines of all manner of authority figures.

Voëlvry ran into numerous obstacles: bannings by SABC radio,[909] the cancellation of concerts on several Afrikaans-medium college campuses, and denunciations by politicians and religious leaders (one of whom unpersuasively raised the spectre of blasphemous messages being subliminally inserted into the music, which supposedly could only be consciously recognised by playing records backwards). It spawned a culture war pitting orthodoxy against progressivism at the same moment that that term was initially being defined in America. Yet rather predictably, every hurdle that was raised to subvert Voëlvry's success generated more interest and enthusiasm for the bands' circuit instead.

Afrikaners with a liberal bent were quick to recognise Voëlvry's appeal. After watching a performance in inner-city Johannesburg, Max du Preez recalls, "I knew right there that this was a sort of turning point, that Afrikanerdom would never be quite the same after this."[910] His *Vrye Weekblad* co-sponsored the tour, along with Shifty Records. And a young Antjie Krog, writing in that paper about the impact of the concert held in the small city of Kroonstad in the former Orange Free State, declared she "felt liberated and impassioned ... because in a town and country where the cry has always been: take, take, take, there is now a song: give, give, give".[911] But Voëlvry's participants dispersed after only two months due to a clash of outsized egos and the cumulative impact of too much jolling. How significant, then, was it?

Looking back, Shaun de Waal notes, "It was like all the pent-up resentment against a heavy-handed, militarised Calvinist patriarchy burst forth – a boil lanced by the Voëlvryers.[912] And musician Valiant Swart reminisces that Voëlvry was "a musical mass-action campaign." He argues, "The old people had had their time and now it was our turn."[913] Yet Hermann Giliomee makes no mention of the tour in his magisterial book *The Afrikaners: Biography of a people* (2003).

A common strategy for examining Voëlvry has been to simply quote and then deconstruct the lyrics, many of which are razor sharp. One academic researcher carried this approach a step further, however, and asserts that many in the audience did not understand the irony of the lyrics. In fact, they misinterpreted them as an *endorsement* of consumerism or racially discriminatory practices, and not as a critique.[914] Moreover, "Apart from those who were evidently tone-deaf in picking up a different ideological beat, for another section of the audience it was a matter of preaching to the converted."[915] At best, therefore, Voëlvry had a limited reach.

Whatever political impact Voëlvry had was unintentional at best. Koos Kombuis openly admits, "We never thought about liberation. But we had black friends and we knew what was being done to them and we knew it was wrong and we said so." He recalls, "If that helped with liberation, then great. But we never went out to be political revolutionaries; we went out to get laid."[916]

Moreover, the struggle against apartheid that had steadily escalated over the preceding years was already on the verge on success: Mandela's release would occur in February 1990, and negotiations would soon commence over constructing a new, more egalitarian South Africa. These imminent changes were the fruit of a sustained political offensive to which Voëlvry was simply a minor addendum.

Nonetheless, the Voëlvry musicians did succeed in uncoupling the Afrikaans language from its oppressive associations. They borrowed from within the Afrikaner establishment and opened up the possibility of imaging new social spaces and arrangements; possibly, even, a new order of interracial cooperation and creative cross-fertilisation. And they further troubled a relatively small and beleaguered ruling elite that could no longer maintain its hegemony.

Afrikaner resistance had broken out in other forms as well. The writers known as the Sestigers (from the Afrikaans for "sixty") – such as Breyten Breytenbach, Etienne le Roux, and André Brink – were critical of Afrikaner nationalism beginning in the 1960s, and searched for their voices as individuals, and not as mouthpieces of the *volk*. The Tagtigers followed in the 1980s, and *die Grens Roman* ("the border novel") chronicled the disenchantment of soldiers deployed to fight in South West Africa and Angola. Afrikaner intellectuals withdrew their support from the apartheid regime little by little.[917] But these literary expressions did not have the mass appeal that popular music did, and their audiences weren't necessarily the broad base of young people from which future leaders of the country could potentially be drawn, either.

Campus Unrest

The Voëlvry musicians arrived and swiftly decamped at each venue. But sometimes their impact lingered. Sizeable student demonstrations took place at Stellenbosch University, for example, decrying the decision by the administration to cancel the on-campus performance of the bands there. Bolstered by their collective show of strength, students continued to register their discontent with the status quo, including initiation of the demand that university residences be racially desegregated.[918]

The students' eagerness to formulate their own mini "rainbow society" in 1989 reflects a sense of utopianism that has rapidly deflated. Less than two decades later, the desegregation of university residences had become a hotly contested redoubt against racial integration, cultural assimilation and the perception that racial politics is a zero-sum game within which white South Africans are perpetually the losers.

In traditionally Afrikaans-medium universities in Stellenbosch, Pretoria and Bloemfontein, students have been particularly alarmed over two issues: the perceived "anglicisation" of campuses through increasing amounts of instruction being given in English, and the desegregation of their living quarters. In some instances white Afrikaner students have sought judicial relief to stave off change. In others, they have harassed non-white students and staff or have directed violence against them. Students have been physically attacked, verbally assaulted, and have had their rooms trashed. In one instance, the son of the national defence minister was assailed with abusive language and threatened with a gun after a minor traffic incident with a white student at the University of the Free State (UFS) in Bloemfontein. In the aftermath of that episode a student affairs official bemoaned, "student heads at the various residences told her they were 'not interested in a human rights workshop because they don't want their traditions to be affected'".[919]

According to Jonathan Jansen, former dean of the education faculty at the University of Pretoria and currently rector and vice chancellor at UFS, "It is difficult to overstate the importance of residence ['*koshuis*'] culture in the historically Afrikaans universities." Traditionally, seniors must be addressed as "'oom' (uncle), 'admiral' (admiral) or 'generaal' (general)," reflecting "quasi-military styles of command and control over new students". But black African students refuse to play this game.[920] White students feel something is being taken from them; blacks feel alienated and fearful.

The most publicised of recent racially charged campus incidents occurred in 2008 at the University of the Free State. Four male students from the Reitz hostel videotaped a mock initiation ritual in which they duped four elderly black African cleaners into eating food that the young men had urinated upon. The scene of these women's humiliation shocked and outraged viewers throughout the country, generating comparisons to the scenes of cruelty committed by American soldiers that was uncovered at Iraq's Abu Ghraib prison. The UFS experience conclusively demonstrated that bigotry, dehumanisation, and the abuse of power and racial privilege are not anachronisms. They, sorrowfully, persist in the younger generation. A black African columnist noted, "[T]he [David] Bullard piece is to print what the University of the Free State video is to digital media. They are both crude, base and pathological."[921]

UFS has closed the residence and intends to transform it into an Institute for Diversity, possibly offering a degree in "diversity management".[922] Nevertheless, according to one journalist, "Dogged tussles for the racial souls of former Afrikaans universities are springing up on campuses across the country."[923] The white-based political party Freedom Front Plus (FF+) has egged on students to resist change, a trend that one columnist bluntly condemned: "How the FF+ [affiliated] students arrive at the conclusion that living in an integrated hostel will force them to give up their membership of the Dutch Reformed Church, stop them from speaking Afrikaans and force them to eat pap with every braaied boerewors ['grilled sausage'], is a leap beyond my imagination." She continued, "But if your own history has taught you the extent to which people will brutalise others in defence of a 'culture', then I suppose it is understandable that paranoia exists in some Afrikaner circles."[924]

The tumult surrounding the conversion of formerly Afrikaans-speaking campuses into dual-medium institutions, in accordance with a 2002 Department of Education mandate, has been no less acute. It became particularly pronounced at Stellenbosch University where current students, graduates and Afrikaner intellectuals engaged in a prolonged and acrimonious debate over the policy, eventually leading to the resignation of the vice chancellor. The extreme polarisation of positions that occur during culture wars was very much in evidence: the group endorsing English was accused of denying the heritage of Afrikaans and capitulating to historical guilt, while the Afrikaans enthusiasts were labelled as reactionaries, desiring to retreat into a "volkstaat of the mind". References to "the 'suicide' of Afrikaans", and the characterisation of English as the "'killer language' ... putting Afrikaans on a 'slippery slope to anglicisation and extinction'", signified the excessiveness of the ramped-up rhetoric.[925]

Schools are a site where racial tensions explode in many places: they are one of the most visible places where social policy is initiated and social issues are played out face to face. They become a laboratory where young people are expected to resolve conflicts for which their parents are responsible yet have not themselves addressed satisfactorily. Race-based social networking groups are another place where long-brewing racial tensions surface: young people from a broad range of racial and tribal affiliations in South Africa have created exclusive sites where ethnic and cultural pride reigns. The question is, at what point do they evolve from expressions of principle and honour to become locations for reinforcing racism?[926]

In a No Man's Land?

In 2004 Julian Roup published *Boerejood*, a book exploring his dual heritage of being the offspring of an Afrikaner and a Jew. He extolled many shared features of bonhomie and the priority placed on family and community life, and also noted that Afrikaners and Jews commonly feel that they are discriminated-against minorities. In a brash statement that one could easily imagine emanating from a Jewish patriarch with a long beard and a deeply rooted middle-European accent, Roup declares: "History is trouble. When there is no trouble there is no history."[927]

Roup travels the country to interrogate a variety of knowledgeable people about the present situation of the Afrikaner, accounting for approximately 60% of the whites in a country where approximately 91% of the overall population is non-white. A theme that regularly emerges is the lack of robust guidance or a sense of direction, despite relative economic wellbeing. A professor of Afrikaans and Dutch literature tells him, "I may not have liked the apartheid leaders, but they were powerful. There are no strong leaders any more. In that sense the Afrikaner is like the African: an African wants a strong leader." He concludes, "It's weird in a way that we saw Mandela as a leader and Mandela is black."[928] And when he asks a professor of history at Stellenbosch University (who has written on the Voëlvry movement) about Afrikaner leadership, Roup reflects about what he is told, "There is no one with any charismatic appeal … 'They will not easily forsake the comfort of middle-class existence for the uncertainty of politics under the dominant and autocratic ANC rule'."[929]

Remarks such as these go a long way towards explaining why when Afrikaners as a group are portrayed these days it is with a surfeit of negative descriptors. Scan the news and editorial pages of South African publications and you'll see certain terms recurring: "alienated", "marginalised", "traumatised", "in the middle", "vacuum", "*gatvol*", "identity crisis", "leaderless", "restless", or "rudderless".

One writer speaks of Afrikaners experiencing "power loss syndrome"; another counters that with "spoiled brat syndrome: they are unable to see anyone's suffering but their own".[930] Antjie Krog notes that Afrikaners have been "sidelined"; John Matshikiza said they've been "disempowered", existing in a perceived "desert of isolation".[931] Max du Preez believes his fellow Afrikaners feel "unloved and unwanted" and are suffering feelings of "skaam-kwaad (literally translated, 'ashamed-angry')".[932] Hermann Giliomee calls Afrikaners "emasculated", a perception ratified by journalist Christi van der Westhuizen who perceives "a crisis in Afrikaner masculinity".[933] And Dan Roodt laments that Afrikaners are "a conquered people" who are being "air-brushed from history".[934] These are all riffs, of course, on Malegapuru Makgoba's notion of the "dethroned male", which led him to draw the analogy between South Africa's whites and baboons (Chapter 4). As a result, newspaper editor Tim du Plessis believes many Afrikaners have "emigrated inwardly".[935]

The feeling of *gatvol* stems from many issues discussed previously, such as the sense of siege because of high rates of crime, especially farm murders; the loss of historic touchstones such as place names and the diminishing position of Afrikaans in public discourse; and official employment policies that privilege non-whites over whites.[936] Dan Roodt goes as far as speaking about a present-day "second ethnic cleansing of the Afrikaner from South Africa", the first being at the hands of the British during the Anglo-Boer War. He floridly asserts that "the ANC regime is far closer to the tradition of 20th-century totalitarianism as exemplified by Hitler or Stalin than they [Afrikaners] ever were".[937]

One journalist characterised the current racial situation as a standoff, in the following terms: "the Rainbow Nation versus the De la Rey factor". "This," she explained, "is how young South African students are currently squared off in racial trenches on the former exclusively Afrikaans university campuses."[938] The Rainbow Nation, of course, is the vision of a multiracial yet non-racist society endorsed by architects of South African democracy such as Nelson Mandela and the Reverend Desmond Tutu. But as these men have aged their public influence has steadily declined. Different groups are more likely nowadays to focus on their own relative welfare than on the interests of the polity as a whole.

The "De la Rey factor" refers to the rock ballad released in 2007 by Bok van Blerk (Louis Pepler, a former construction manager, born in 1978). His CD quickly set sales records, the song electrified audiences at concerts, cultural festivals and sporting events, but it also aroused criticism and suspicion on the part of non-Afrikaners who supposed it could mobilise a political surge against the current government. Afrikaner youth in the post-apartheid era, it seemed, had at last found a heroic source of inspiration.

"De la Rey" became an anthem of ethnic pride and solidarity, as well as an allegedly anti-democratic mouthpiece. It called forth avid support along with scornful alarm. It also generated a volume of news coverage and commentary that equalled, or even surpassed, any of the foremost cultural debates that have engaged South Africans over the past decade.

Sound and Fury

How can we understand the enigmatic and wildly popular Vernon Koekemoer, who became the improbable spokesperson for such commonly recognised South African enterprises as cellphone giant Vodacom and Nando's? Grotesquely musclebound, sporting an unfashionable mullet haircut, and absurdly decked out in tight shorts, moon boots, and a shirt with cut-off sleeves that he's knotted at his midriff, Koekemoer delights people across colour lines. He represents the World Wrestling Federation colliding with Dogpatch, and a bit of gender exaggeration and confusion thrown in. Koekemoer looks like a mutant waitron on steroids who might as likely tip over from his outsized bulk as punch you out for gawking.

When journalist Mary Corrigall braved an interpretation of this pop phenomenon she invoked the phrase "dethroned" more than once. She also remarked, "He is as South African as Mrs Ball's and Ouma Rusks. He is a caricature of the Afrikaans 'oke'." When Corrigall digs for an explanation of Koekemoer's allure, she notes: "Advertisers need to generate sales, which means they need to appeal to their target audience: young black men who probably will go buy a product that pokes fun at white men." And quoting an academic, she observes he "also presents an escape from the bleak realities facing the country".[939]

Vernon Koekemoer may provide welcome comic relief. But he hardly offers a contemporary role model for young Afrikaners. For that they were forced to refer back to General Koos de la Rey, a Boer War hero who had been dead for nearly a century, thereby confirming many of the characterisations of collective anomie cited above.

The song's lyrics capture the perspective of a young Afrikaner who watches his farm being burned by British soldiers (Khakis); the women and the children of the community have been removed to concentration camps. In the video, Van Blerk is featured as the downcast, bloody-faced fighter clutching a rifle. But a steady military drumbeat in the background suggests his resolve to continue in battle:

> On a mountain in the night
> I lie in the darkness and wait
> In the mud and blood I lie cold,
> as rain clings to my pack
>
> And my house and my farm
> Burned down to coals
> So that they can catch us
> But those flames and fire
> Now burn deep, deep inside me

De la Rey, De la Rey
Will you come and lead the Boers?
De la Rey, De la Rey

General, General, as one man
We'll fall in around you
General De la Rey

Hear the Khakis laugh,
A handful of us against their whole great might,
With the cliffs lie here against our backs,
They think it's all over

But the heart of a Boer lies
Deeper and wider
That they'll still discover
He approaches on a horse,
the lion of the West Transvaal

De la Rey, De la Rey, etc.
[chorus]

Because my wife and child
Waste away and perish in a concentration camp
And the Khakis are walking
Over a nation that will rise up again

De la Rey, De la Rey, etc.
[chorus]
General, General, can you come and lead the Boers?
We are ready.[940]

This song is simply one example of a recent profusion of Afrikaans pop music that has helped mould the self-image of a generation of young people who wish to shed the historical baggage of responsibility for the injustices their forebears committed, and seek to carve out an identity that reflects their own contemporary circumstances. Van Blerk's lyrics have revived the reputation of a heroic commander who was something of a maverick, at turns a pacifist, a *bittereinder* (bitter-ender), and a proponent of reconciliation, and reshaped him into a modern iconic figure. Van Blerk has made history seem cool to a generation that generally feels detached from it (Van Blerk is cool, too: he sports a soul patch, after all, but has not strayed far from rockstar macho; he withdrew his name as a nominee in the 2007 Sexiest Man survey sponsored by a gay website).

Van Blerk, in fact, demonstrates an uncharacteristically keen sense of history. Speaking with a journalist the singer cited Steve Biko's idea that it's important for youth to know their culture: "[A]t the moment, in South African schools," Van Blerk noted, "there's four lines in the history books that children get taught at school about the Anglo-Boer War, and I think that's crazy. It's like it never happened, like they want to wipe it away."[941] In this regard "De la Rey" can be seen as a backlash against revisionism. "We are the *currently* disadvantaged," Van Blerk boldly declared, "not the *previously* disadvantaged."[942]

And in a couple of notable instances the song's revitalisation of the general emboldened unknown protestors to counter the "Africanisation" of place names, a trend that many Afrikaners feel is unwarranted and spiteful. What was once Jan Smuts Airport was changed to the neutral Johannesburg International in 1994, but then altered again to OR Tambo International in 2006 to honour the prominent struggle figure and one-time ANC president, Oliver Tambo. But someone spraypainted one of the new markers with "De la Rey International". Moreover, a photograph included in the exhibition *Jive Soweto* at the Hector Pieterson Museum in 2007 showed a street sign for "NELSON MANDELA-RYLAAN" in Potchefstroom (the site of Afrikaans cultural festival Aardklop and Potchefstroom University, an Afrikaans branch of the North-West University); it had been spraypainted in such a way that only "DELA-RYLAAN" remained.[943]

All this reminds us that the type of dissent called out at any specific moment is crucially shaped by the nature of what's conventional; the establishment gets the dissidents it deserves, in other words. As historian and political analyst Giliomee notes, "Above all it ['De la Rey'] is prized because it satisfies the Afrikaner youth's desire for political incorrectness. How better to show up the Afrikaners in their middle age, who tend to live on their knees politically, by singing a song about a fearless leader in the past who was driven by his convictions and prepared to pay the price for unpopularity?"[944]

Many commentators connect the dots between the Voëlvry musicians during the apartheid era and today's performers. However, contrast the South Africa where Afrikaner leaders prohibited television from entering the country until 1976, to the present, when there is an MTV-format Afrikaans pop station featuring music videos. Some observers now speak of DNA: *Die Nuwe Afrikaner* (The New Afrikaner). One states, "DNAs play rock because they feel like it, they don't want to talk about the sins of their fathers, they don't want to be thanked for rescuing their language. They just want to speak Afrikaans and have a jol." The general ethos can be summed up as, "I am Afrikaans, but not like my pa."[945]

A regular on the scene is Karen Zoid, who performs in both English and Afrikaans, and mixes maskanda, rock and country on the same album. Should there be any doubt that she is thumbing her nose at conventional Calvinist morality, she includes drag queens as part of her act. In fact, Afrikaans bands are considered to be more experimental than English-language ones: they have a niche market in South Africa and are not competing with international musicians.[946]

The most controversial of the contemporary Afrikaans bands has been the one with the most provocative name: Fokofpolisiekar ("Fuck Off Police Car"). The group formed in 2003, attracted a high-testosterone crowd, but voluntarily went on hiatus in 2007.[947] The biographies of its members overlap in key ways with other artistic rebels.

The musicians hail from Bellville, the same place where Mark Coetzee confronted censorious reactions to his artwork (Chapter 6), as does Conrad Botes. The musicians met in a charismatic church there; the father of one of them was a *dominee* of a Dutch Reformed Church, like some of the Voëlvry musicians. The lyricist and guitarist Hunter Kennedy states he was 12 when apartheid ended. Like Justin Nurse, he lived South Africa's contemporary history as it unfolded, but had to fill in what had come before on his own (Rian Malan's *My Traitor's Heart* was his primary sourcebook). Fokofpolisiekar's "Brand Suid-Afrika" (Burn South Africa) includes the following lyrics, rejecting complacency:

Landmines of guilty feelings in a one-man concentration camp
you moan about the situation of our country
well fucking do something about it
burn South Africa.

"People don't realise that their children can think for themselves," argues bassist Wynand Myburgh – exactly the threat that Mark Coetzee's Stellenbosch University exhibition raised. Drummer Snakehead Venter discloses, "We're seen as this force who's out to steal people's children," fears raised as well by the activities of Steven Cohen and Mark Hipper. And Hunter Kennedy reveals how a sense of marginality became a fount of creativity for them: "[The] outsider thing was significant … Whether it was skate culture, metal music, a charismatic church, f**k, whatever. We've never felt part of the mainstream. To top it off, we were Afrikaans as well."

Moreover, Kennedy explains, "When I was in high school it felt *kak* to be Afrikaans. I didn't want to be part of that culture. Perhaps, in a way, we've helped make it possible for people to be proud of who they are."[948] This sense of reclamation and self-assertion is central to the success of many Afrikaans bands. The book about the 1980s alternative band Koos includes this remark about seeing that group perform at the University of the Witwatersrand, an English-medium university: "At Wits, Afrikaans was like farting."[949] Today's performers have helped neutralise and refresh the lingering stench of the language. One highly enthusiastic journalist effusively declared, "It's cool to be Afrikaans again," predicting that the language is "the phoenix destined to rise from the ashes," whereas photographer Roelof Petrus van Wyk argues, "It's a good thing it's [Afrikaans] been suppressed because it makes people a little bit angry about it, gives it a bit of energy."[950]

Fokofpolisiekar generated the most headlines over an incident where Wynand Myburgh capriciously signed an autograph on a fan's wallet at 5 a.m. that read "Fuck God". Fuelled by a night of drinking, it was intended as a joke, yet it spawned accusations of blasphemy, Satanism and religious hate speech. An email campaign culminated in a full-page ad in *Beeld* sponsored by the Christian media action group Jesus Project. A gospel group called Prophet that defended Fokofpolisiekar was banned from Radio Tygerberg in Cape Town. And the furore deepened after a large group of churches in Oudtshoorn, site of the annual Afrikaans cultural festival Klein Karoo Nasionale Kunstefees (KKNK, the Little Karoo Arts Festival), threatened to withdraw the use of their venues unless Fokofpolisiekar was dropped from the 2006 line-up. Many prospective attendees threatened to boycott as well. These were significant risks because the festival pumps millions into the local economy.

The band's manager complained, "This reaction echoes old National Party tactics. They will not compromise." Nevertheless, Fokofpolisiekar apologised, and a deal was worked out whereby the band could perform at KKNK as long as it did not use anti-religious phrases in its songs.[951]

An Accidental Anthem

One chronicler of the scene delineates three modes of contemporary Afrikaner music. Andries Bezuidenhout states that nostalgics sing traditional songs, longing for a past uncomplicated by crime and affirmative action; romantics are apolitical, focusing on good-time rock; and cynics complain about the contemporary state of things, are ironic, and reject feeling guilty about apartheid. These themes merge in actuality, or appeal to different groups at different times.[952]

Some representative examples of lyrics include this critique of the ANC's priorities, by Klopjag ("Raid") in "Nie Langer" ("No longer"): "Stop wasting money on name changes/there are people without homes and children without food/who is to blame now?" This song acknowledges the reversal of fortune for the Afrikaner community, yet defiantly declares, "I will stand at the back of the queue/and wear my rainbow on my sleeve/but I won't say sorry any more." And Die Melktert Kommissie's (literally, "The Milk Tart Commission") "Proudly South African" offers a similar appraisal of government policies: "Toyi-toyi-toyi toys are us/we are being played with/by people from above/classrooms are overcrowded/but lunchboxes are empty/everyone eating politics/instead of moving on." However, Bezuidenhout critiques both the Voëlvry musicians and present-day artists for failing to "transcend ... the narrow politics of the 'self'".[953]

His point is well taken. Yet even creations that would appear to be escapist or solipsistic can trigger broader social responses. A good idea of the range of reactions to "De la Rey" was evident at a "critical thinking forum" sponsored by the *Mail & Guardian*. The lively public event included a panel of well-known speakers, moderated by former SAfm presenter John Perlman. Journalist John Matshikiza called the song "threatening". Rocker Karen Zoid said she was "ashamed" of it, condemning "De la Rey" as "scary", "Nazi shit". Dan Roodt, on the other hand, noted that "It reflects the pessimism of a nation that is dying" and playwright Mike van Graan characterised the song as "a plea for help from the ancestors". An audience member who was also an Afrikaans singer sought to diffuse anxieties that "De la Rey" was intended as a battle cry for a political movement. She made her point by damning Van Blerk and his two collaborators with faint praise by declaring, "Believe me those … boys are not the biggest intellectuals. I shared a house with one of them. They chose De la Rey as a legend because it rhymed. That is all". The song, she concluded, "was written as a hit, not an anthem".[954] (Van Blerk candidly admits that "De la Rey" was selected because it rhymes with the word *lei* ("lead").)

"De la Rey" was first performed in August 2006 at the Aardklop Festival in Potchefstroom. Its popularity was quickly reflected in the sale of over 100 000 CDs, a tally that continued to grow. The CD eventually achieved platinum status multiple times. Crowds of young people at concerts and sporting events were clearly stirred by the lyrics, which they roared while linking their arms and rhythmically swaying, or with their hands held respectfully over their hearts. In a few instances people displayed the old South African flag at such gatherings or sang the Afrikaner hymn "Die Stem [van Suid-Afrika: The Call of South Africa]" (which makes up part of the current South African national anthem). And Tim du Plessis, editor of *Rapport*, described a remarkable incident where people on holiday reenacted a tactic the Voortrekkers used for mutual defence and instilling solidarity by pulling their cars into a laager-like circle, opening the doors, and synchronised playing the CD.[955]

It was an inspired recovery and update of a highly emblematic Afrikaner custom. Playwright and television producer Deon Opperman reacted to "De la Rey" by saying, "Fuck, we're disappearing. It's a call to identity, to selfhood. It's saying, I'm still here. It's not: 'We need a general to take us to war'."[956] But that's precisely the interpretation that others embraced.

Foremost among a number of public officials who expressed anxiety over "De la Rey" was Arts and Culture Minister Pallo Jordan. Speaking in Parliament, he supported Van Blerk's right to sing the song, but raised concern about it at the same time: "Sadly," he said, "the popular song is in danger of being hijacked by a minority of right-wingers who not only regard De la Rey as a war hero, but also want to mislead sections of Afrikaans-speaking society into thinking that this is a 'struggle song' that sends out a 'call to arms'." So while championing freedom of expression, Jordan's principles were tempered by a caveat: "As the accused in the current 'boeremag' trial are discovering, those who incite treason, whatever methods they employ, might well find themselves in difficulties with the law."

Echoing many other commentators, Jordan elided the differences between ethnic pride and ethnic extremism, sanctioning the song on the one hand, but warning devotees to tread carefully on the other. "Even if he [Van Blerk] is composing a song to organise against the incumbent government," Jordan argued, "he has the right to do that – provided that whatever opposition he is organising is within the restraints of our constitution."[957]

Jordan concluded, "Unless the composer, performer and his audiences regard themselves as in a state of war with the rest of the population of South Africa, the song is merely a historical curiosity."[958] He even wished Van Blerk international commercial success on the order of Solomon Linda's "Mbube (The Lion Sleeps Tonight)". But Jordan's remarks made it clear that even though "De la Rey" might fall within the limits of the law, it came perilously close to exceeding them. He implied that fans should curb their enthusiasm. Enjoyment and diversion meant one thing; a ground swell of ethnic mobilisation was entirely different. And unwelcome.

For his part, Van Blerk sent out mixed messages regarding how he felt about his song possibly being commandeered for narrow political purposes. While he insisted that the old state flags be taken down during his performances and refused to accept one that a fan tried to force on him at a concert, he appeared in the exclusive Afrikaner enclave of Orania and also met with one of the Boeremag trialists. And whereas no restrictive measures were undertaken on an official level, the management at Loftus Versfeld in Pretoria first proposed a ban of the song at rugby matches, supposedly in deference to its racially mixed spectators, and then reversed itself after an outcry from many diehard fans. But "De la Rey" was banned from two commercial radio stations in Namibia. A boss there was more skittish than people in neighbouring South Africa and expressed an exaggerated degree of sensitivity: "It's a historical song," he acknowledged, "but there are too many loose ends who want to make political gain out of it … we will not play it because we have many cultural group [sic] listening to our station."[959]

Moreover, two spin-offs of the song ran into difficulties. A parody played on Highveld Stereo generated a complaint to the BCCSA. The refrain asked, "De la Rey, De la Rey, do you want to flirt with the Boers?/Because you're gay, De la Rey?" And when the general was asked if he wants to lead the Boers, the phrase "No, I don't want to" was repeated in the background. The presenter subsequently apologised, realising it was "disrespectful".[960] And a precocious nine-year-old Afrikaans singer named Son-Isha came up with a version entitled "De la Rey Needs a Girlfriend". She had previously been a darling at Radio Pretoria, an Afrikaans-language radio station. And the broadcaster had slotted a two-part interview with her about the song. But the second part was cancelled after employees saw a photo on her website showing her performing in a Zulu outfit at the Voortrekker Monument.

The rationale that was offered was "the fact that she word [sic] a traditional Zulu outfit and performed near the cenotaph went against station policy".[961] But what policy could possibly be so specific? The incident calls to mind the David Goldblatt photo of a woman and her child at the same site years earlier that caused an uproar because it depicted both the monument and a Zulu hut in the same frame. It also raised the question of how much rainbow – or mixing of hues – is tolerable in the Rainbow Nation.

Genre Confusion

A website called www.english.ohmynews.com inadvertently revealed the danger that critics believed was inherent in the torrent of support for "De la Rey". It argued, "This resurgence of pride is not intended to come at the expense of black people, it is … the rebranding – if you will – of a once powerful group within a multicultural nation."[962] But when does branding become important? Precisely at the point that some venture is operating in a competitive environment and wishes to gain a comparative advantage. And because of the lingering, unresolved legacies of apartheid, any whiff of Afrikaners mustering together can be unsettling.

Sunday Times editor Mondli Makhanya was one of the many journalists, political commentators, intellectuals and other opinion leaders who spoke out about "De la Rey" and the response it evoked in young Afrikaners. He asserted, "[I]n the past two years, there has suddenly been a surge in tribal thinking among Afrikaners … and a sense that it is time to fight back against something." He went on to note, "I have read the lyrics of the song and they are quite … well … 'struggle' oriented."[963]

Rapport editor Tim du Plessis rendered a similar judgement, stating: "I do get the sense of a gear shift taking place [among Afrikaners]. People are feeling more assertive than before." But where Makhanya perceived an impending threat, Du Plessis simply saw a new stage in Afrikaners adapting to their radically changed circumstances. "Does all this mean an Afrikaner rebellion is brewing?" Du Plessis asked. "I don't think so. Rise and resist to achieve what? End up in C-Max [Prison] like the Boeremag trialists?"[964] And a blog posting bristled at the ominous potentiality and power some people were ascribing to the song, complaining that "whenever Afrikaners get together in groups of more than 3, it must be the boeremag plotting to overthrow the government".[965] Van Blerk likewise downplayed the potential influence of his lyrics by setting them apart from other notorious South African chants: "I am not singing 'bring your machine-gun' or 'Kill the Boer'!"[966]

A significant voice that entered the public discussion came from a woman who holds what is surely one of the most interesting jobs in South Africa: Zelda la Grange, Nelson Mandela's executive personal assistant. The fact that she is an Afrikaner adds a dimension of wonder regarding how these two people from vastly different backgrounds and generations work with such obvious ease and mutual respect for one another. Reflecting Mandela's humanistic style, La Grange universalised the contemporary struggle of Afrikaners, remarking: "We are all groping in the dark for something that we all desire." La Grange saw this as an opportunity for young Afrikaners to channel their anger and frustration into action by becoming involved in mainstream politics, to transform their passivity into engagement. She asked, "Are our own insecurities … not also a result of our own complacency? We love to make a noise but we don't really make a substantial effort". La Grange concluded, "the Afrikaner is, like other groups in our country, merely trying to identify with something that protects the group's interests. We are, therefore, no different from the black people in this country."[967] From this perspective, therefore, the support for "De la Rey" represented a healthy expression of ethnic allegiance without necessarily signalling a desire to increase group tensions or to renew ethnic dominance.

"De la Rey" was psychoanalysed, historicised and vilified. Antjie Krog argued that the song represents a psychological coming-to-terms with the monstrous deeds committed by fellow members of one's own heritage. She declared the Boer general to be "an honourable ancestor" who "becomes the surrogate father, not to lead to uprising, but to assist children to deal with their guilt in such a way that they can successfully integrate their past into a new society".[968]

Others interpreted the song as a not-so-veiled indictment of Afrikaner leaders who "capitulated" to the demands of the anti-apartheid movement, "handed over" the reins of government to majority rule, and had failed to proactively advocate for their people under the new political dispensation. One writer argued, "This song indirectly is a condemnation of the likes of FW de Klerk, Pik Botha and Marthinus van Schalkwyk, considered sellouts and despised for 'cosying up' to the ruling elite instead of promoting the rights of an Afrikaner minority feeling increasingly socially excluded by black domination."[969] An article posted on a website that focuses on crime throughout southern Africa concurred, but argued with much more passion: "there is a search for new leaders – no De Klerk's [sic] – but leaders who will FIGHT for the Afrikaners. These people are not longing for NEGOTIATORS … they're longing for WARRIORS!!"[970] Van Blerk himself joined this chorus stating, "It's being proud of who you are and knowing where you come from. To have a backbone and know where you're going."[971]

The main problem that some others perceived to be inherent within Van Blerk's work was its musical shortcomings, not any political implications. And these detractors were wickedly critical. Postings to one website trashed his artistic abilities. "Musically … I think the song is irrelevant to 2007, lame anthemic [sic] soft whiteboy rock," one person wrote. And another concluded, "I guess he's playing the same card that tons of garbage christian [sic] rock bands play in order to sell … Just switch De La rey [sic] with Jesus (or Ala [sic] and so on …) same thing … poor dude's spent all this time learning how to play guitar, it's time to pay the bills somehow …"[972] Others noted that Van Blerk was better known for such party songs as "Vodka en OJ" than rabble rousing.

Critic Chris Roper trashed the singer more fiercely than anyone. "People of South Africa, you can sleep easy in your beds," Roper announced with mock reassurance. "There will be no rebellion of the Afrikaner rightwing, no revolution of the De la Rey generation. We have listened to their soundtrack, and if the songs on this CD are anything to go by, they'll all be too pissed to stand up, never mind rise up." He gave Van Blerk a backhanded compliment by noting "De la Rey" was the standout track on the CD. "The rest," he cautioned, "are the usual blend of boring beats, plangent guitar chords, and choruses that are as catchy as syphilis during an intervarsity rugby tournament." Dismissing Van Blerk as "the Britney of Boerepop," Roper delivered this final punch: "If hip-hop thrives on fat guys inexplicably being worshipped by chicks with big tits, Afrikaans music of the Bok van Blerk variety lives and dies on an increasingly rose-coloured nostalgia."[973]

Max du Preez concurred with Andries Bezuidenhout's assessment of the relatively narrow impact of the Voëlvry musicians, after he observed the behaviour of members of the generation that has embraced "De la Rey". Du Preez noted, "The kids standing in the pubs in Pretoria with their hand on their heart, and their wild eyes, go outside and they get into their BMW convertibles. They're not suffering. It's an imagined suffering."[974]

This broad variety of sentiments recapitulates the way the "AmaNdiya" episode brought opposing notions of cultural production into focus: the belief that culture is either a passive object or an active creator of reality. Those who subscribe to the first perspective felt that "De la Rey" was an authentic reflection of the post-apartheid sentiments of young Afrikaners, and should therefore be freely promoted and used as a springboard for further reflection. According to Van der Westhuizen, "Freed from the dual straitjacket of apartheid and Afrikaner nationalism, many Afrikaners are exploring what it means to be white; what the historical legacies mean."[975] But for those who heard the song as a veiled expression of Afrikaners chafing over their lives under a black majority government, who believe there is little difference between expression and action, and fear culture as possessing a power and agency of its own, "De la Rey" held a dangerous potentiality. They believed this song should be denounced and possibly regulated lest it galvanise subversive exploits.

The Democratic Alliance addressed this latter point but put it in a broader perspective. It issued a statement noting that "Bok van Blerk's song 'De la Rey' is not nearly as 'potentially subversive' as ANC deputy president Jacob Zuma's song 'Umshini Wami'".[976] Nevertheless, about a year and a half after "De la Rey" was first publicly performed, a malicious incident at a school demonstrated that it had taken on a life of its own. Corresponding to the type of episode where black Africans alluded to Mbongeni Ngemi's "AmaNdiya" while justifying their maltreatment of East Asian merchants (Chapter 2), students at a formerly Afrikaans-medium high school greeted a new principal with an Indian surname with boos, and spontaneously sang "De la Rey". They then stormed out of an assembly and sang Christian hymns and "De la Rey" outside the principal's door.

Bok van Blerk's composition did not trigger this behaviour: the episode capped off two years of turmoil at the school regarding religious tolerance. Some white parents had feared that recognition of other religions like Islam would turn the school away from Christianity. A significant racial split had opened up because black parents supported the rejection of a Christian-only oriented school. This was, therefore, a complex and multilayered situation.[977] But like "AmaNdiya", "De la Rey" became a convenient way to articulate festering feelings of discontent. While it did not generate those thoughts, to be sure, the song allowed them to be publicly expressed in a rousing, collective form.

The Colour of Pain

Dr Wally Serote was a prominent figure in the anti-apartheid struggle and is a well-regarded writer, poet and cultural activist. He was also the CEO of Freedom Park until he retired in 2011, a mammoth human rights project whose aim is to commemorate those who have been victims of oppression or fought against it, from slavery to the Anglo-Boer War and through apartheid. It features a museum, library and amphitheatre, as well as a Garden of Remembrance and a Wall of Names at the memorial site called Sikhumbuto, which is intended to personalise the suffering of South Africans across many generations by posting the names of people who died in the name of freedom. Seventy-five thousand have been recorded; up to 135 000 will be, eventually.

Freedom Park's hilltop location is highly significant: it faces the Voortrekker Monument across the valley, a counterweight to the Afrikaner experience that revered shrine reflects. Freedom Park is a "legacy project", the beneficiary of an initiative by Nelson Mandela to redress the imbalances and deficiencies in official sites of remembrance such as monuments, memorials and museums. These are typically new ventures that bring previously unacknowledged aspects of history to light. Freedom Park is also an offshoot of the Truth and Reconciliation Commission, and is intended to be a place where mutual understanding and healing can be facilitated.

Serote was one of the countless public figures who spoke about Bok van Blerk's "De la Rey". "I was so excited about the new Afrikaner leader," he remarked. But then Serote realised this had been a musical resurrection, not a celebration of a contemporary person. "I was very disappointed to hear that De la Rey was a dead general," Serote said.[978] This is but one example of those unexpected moments revealing the depth of the chasm of unawareness and misunderstanding that exists between different groups in South Africa, caused by systematic racial oppression.

The African National Congress has prioritised Freedom Park and Thabo Mbeki banked on it to become a key part of his legacy as president. Early on, however, critics of Freedom Park expressed concern that the narrative inscribed there would favour the ANC's perspective of itself as the party of national liberation, while discounting the contributions of other groups such as the Pan Africanist Congress or the United Democratic Front. More recently, whites have complained about the exclusion of South African Defence Force (SADF) conscripts from the Wall of Names.

Arts and Culture Minister Pallo Jordan, who endorsed Van Blerk's right to sing "De la Rey" but tempered his remarks with a cautionary note, compared

SADF soldiers to the Germans serving under Hitler. This allusion was taken up by others as well, such as a former political prisoner on Robben Island who declared that incorporating the names of SADF soldiers would be "like Nazi victims and fascist troops having the same wall of remembrance". He counselled, "you can't put all those eggs in one basket".[979] Jordan argued that in both those historical moments young men were forced to make a choice. And by opting to answer the call of the apartheid government instead of resisting it, Jordan felt that members of the SADF did not have a legitimate claim for their names being inscribed onto the wall.

But popular Afrikaans singer Steve Hofmeyr, a highly visible spokesperson on social issues affecting his community, such as farm murders, offered a vigorous counterclaim. He recalled, "I was a youngster when I was in the army. I had been taught to hate Cubans [fighting in Angola] and communism and that we were fighting to protect South Africa from communism, and then it struck me. If you can include Cubans and communists [on the wall] then you can include youngsters who fought with me." He has since become an active campaigner for the inclusion of white conscripts. "When we achieve that," Hofmeyr argues, "Freedom Park will be the most powerful symbol of reconciliation anywhere in the world. We'll be pioneers."[980]

All white men were subject to compulsory service in South Africa from 1967 to 1993, with the length of required service successively increasing over that period. But the issue of their addition to the Wall of Names has been championed primarily by Afrikaners, who perceive the omission of these men to be an additional example of being marginalised or effaced from history. Passions have been intense on both sides of the issue.

Proponents of the addition of SADF conscripts argue that they were youthful victims of intense indoctrination.[981] It would have been difficult for them to resist induction, they object (although many men with the financial means went into exile; others went to jail for their beliefs; and groups such as the End Conscription Campaign opposed South Africa's military engagement in neighbouring countries, as well as the use of the SADF in black African townships). One letter-to-the-editor writer saw this as a further example of what some people have labelled "Boer-bashing"; this former SADF officer, sounding like he's lost none of his fervour as a true believer, claimed "I never served apartheid – I fought naked communist terror … I fought honourably, never against civilians, but against communists from the other side of the world – Cuba. I fought for liberty from the greatest crime against humanity: communism."

He claimed, "reconciliation means the submission of whites to everything the ANC believes in," and wrapped up by saying, "I appeal to all South Africans not to dirty themselves by ever visiting this place of shame."[982]

But men such as these who were once championed as fighting "terrorists" are now reviled as oppressors. Therefore, opponents to their inclusion at Freedom Park claim it would dishonour the memory of those who died in the freedom struggle to have men who fought against them venerated in the same place.

Jody Kollapen, head of the South African Human Rights Commission, pondered, "[W]hat is this memorial about? Is it a list of names of people who died in war or is it to commemorate those who died for freedom? And if it is for freedom, then it is by definition a limited monument."[983] Serote argued that 2800 Cubans who died in the border war between Angola and Namibia have been recorded because they were "liberation forces". "The other people," as he refers to members of SADF, "were fighting for my oppression."[984] A woman who lost her husband and brother to SADF attacks concurred, stating with an acute sense of anguish, "It will be an insult for them to be teamed up with the people who wanted to kill us."[985] And another woman proclaimed, "it doesn't make sense that people who killed us should now be seen as heroes. When I think about it, it makes me feel sick."[986]

At the end of the day, the people in control of who shall be remembered and who is snubbed at Freedom Park must balance lofty universalistic goals such as reconciliation and nation-building against specifically honouring those whom history has now judged to be righteous. And with the attenuation of Cold War boogiemen, it's difficult to reconstruct the zeitgeist that led young South African white men – regardless of the degree to which they served of their own free will, or understood the repercussions of their mission – to take up arms against forces they believed were threatening their freedom, an objective that has now been discredited.

Serote has stated, "There is no white pain or black pain or Indian pain or coloured pain. If we can see that, maybe we can resolve all of this."[987]

Regrettably, this is an elusive, utopian vision. It is subverted by group-based claims to a hierarchy of suffering whereby different racial factions and vested interests jockey for the official recognition and endorsement of their grief, to the diminution of the experiences of others. So whenever there is a move by one group to modify its position in these relative rankings, others then rally to destabilise those claims and to fortify their own hard-won positions.

Rainbow's End?
Yellow is the New Black

*... memory is the cement we use to build the future as
much as the emulsion in which we contain the past.*

Ivor Powell, 2007

*As the people say, at the moon's change of phases
The new moon for one night
Holds the old moon in its arms.*

Bertolt Brecht, 1987

Consider these vignettes from the New South Africa:
- A black African real estate developer brings suburban-style clusterhouses
  to a township outside Johannesburg; key to her marketing strategy is the
  freedom residents will have to perform ceremonies such as ritual slaughter
  in their backyards, within a community of culturally like-minded
  neighbours;
- "Party apartheid" or "colour-coded clubbing" stalls uninhibited racial
  mixing in urban bars and nightspots; if too many jollers from any group
  patronise a place, it creates an atmosphere that becomes uncomfortable
  for others and deters them from coming;
- A Xhosa *imbongi* is persona non grata at many tribal events because she is
  a woman; she repositions herself, performing instead for multinational
  corporations and collecting sizeable fees by teaching top executives about
  corporate social responsibility through revered forms of praise poetry;
- Street hawkers and taxi drivers commit a series of assaults on women
  wearing miniskirts in central Johannesburg because they disapprove of
  contemporary forms of dress that they feel are immodest and "belittle"
  their culture; hundreds of women later defiantly don the offending
  clothing in a protest march condemning sexual harassment and challenging
  the male dominance of public space;
- At the venerable Rand Club in downtown Johannesburg a grand portrait
  of Nelson Mandela deposes a portrait of Queen Elizabeth II from the

prime vantage point over the main staircase; but new policies such as a modified fee scale, relaxed dresscode and other stabs at being hip cannot offset the aura of this place being saturated with time-honoured racial and class privilege;

- A black African man working at the fashionable Sandton City shopping centre complains that the site does not cater to his tastes: the shopping centre features Western music and fare, forcing him outside to a taxi rank to procure his own variety of comfort food;

- A young Afrikaner leads a group of his fellow students to the Union Buildings in Pretoria to publicise their conviction that they are victims of racial discrimination; they darken their faces to claim eligibility for some of the perks of Black Economic Empowerment.

Taken together, these anecdotes reveal a society cross-cut by significant divisions and spawning a multiplicity of responses.[988] They present people who are disgruntled yet dynamic; thwarted yet enterprising; dented yet defiant; clannish yet contemporary; alienated yet engaged; and conservative yet conflicted. These accounts expose the manifold ways in which cultural beliefs shape peoples' understandings and actions. They also illustrate how culture and tradition can be experienced as either being written in stone or something much more malleable; as a source of restrictions or innovation; as obstacles or opportunities. Such tales provide insight, therefore, into South Africa in the 21st century, a nation continuously redefining what it represents and one being created through ongoing clashes over values, symbols and ideas. Collectively they characterise episodes in an ongoing culture war.

As the World Turns

South Africa was the world's darling in 1994. A human-rights-based society supplanted one rooted in life-numbing, systematic oppression. A notorious pariah state was welcomed back into the world community. Hope prevailed, the nation was blessed, and the future seemed limitless. It was an exhilarating time.

And just as the Voortrekkers felt that they had received a sign of divine selection when they triumphed over their Zulu opponents at the Battle of Blood River in 1838, a different moment of salvation united people across racial, religious, class and cultural lines in 1995 after the underdog Springboks won the Rugby World Cup. When then-President Nelson Mandela donned a Springbok jersey it marked the apogee of harmony and a fresh national identity; it confirmed that the gods of sport were giving this fledgling nation a celestial thumbs-up.

The next year, then-Deputy President Thabo Mbeki delivered a rousing speech to inaugurate his concept of an African Renaissance. In his "I am an African" address, Mbeki hailed all those people whose worldly experiences and accrued wisdom had shaped him. He first honoured the Khoi and the

San, ancient inhabitants of Southern Africa who were decimated by the waves of various new arrivals to the region. And then he hailed Westerners: "I am formed of the migrants who left Europe to find a new home on our native land," he said. "Whatever their own actions, they remain still, part of me." This extended an offer of absolution and a generous invitation to whites to embrace the new political dispensation.

Mbeki's list of existential debt continued with Malay slaves, and only then did he cite his own black African forbears. He next identified with the Afrikaner victims of the Anglo-Boer War, and acknowledged those South Africans who had come from India and China as indentured labourers, "who taught me that we could both be at home and be foreign".

His speech was inclusive in scope and humanistic in tenor. Mbeki asserted, "[W]e refuse to accept that our Africanness shall be defined by our race, colour, gender or historical origins." South Africa, he declared, "belongs to all who live in it, black or white".

A huge public celebration erupted once again after the Springboks recaptured the World Cup in 2007. President Mbeki joined the festivities, as his predecessor had done. But this time victory also provided the occasion for national introspection. Commentator after commentator noted the "untransformed" nature of the sport over the intervening dozen years: the winning squad contained two coloured players, while the rest were white.

One editorial stated, "Many of SA's European opponents have more black players than SA. It's quite bizarre."[989] A newspaper article posited, "Imagine, for a moment, that you knew nothing about SA while watching the World Cup; you would be forgiven for thinking SA is a white country with the peculiarity of a black president. SA is, in essence, a white country populated by an impotent and invisible black majority."[990] And a final observer noted "a team that looks nothing like the nation. Yet, in a way, it looks exactly like the nation. SA remains a divided place, even between English and Afrikaans speaking South Africans. Rugby in SA is first and foremost an Afrikaner homeland."[991]

If the promise of the 1995 World Cup victory and the "I am an African" speech had been sustained, and the potentiality of the progressive constitution adopted in 1996 been realised, there would be scant social space in which to nourish cultural wars within South Africa. But to the disappointment of people across the racial and economic spectrums, the unfolding reality has not matched those dreams.

An especially dismaying headline appeared in the *Sunday Times* in 2007, declaring "'I wish they had hanged me'". The speaker was an aging survivor of the Sharpeville Six, a group of people who narrowly escaped execution for a killing that had occurred during a rent strike. They were angry that more than R100 000 was being used to host a luncheon for them by the local mayor on New Year's Day; meanwhile, they were all struggling to subsist. "I blame the people who fought for us to be spared from Death Row," their spokesperson declared. "If we were hanged we wouldn't be facing this problem [of unemployment and poverty]. We have lost our dignity. We can't even tell our children about our past. Poverty has reduced us to nothing."[992] Something similar had happened in 2006, when survivors of the Boipatong massacre protested that R2 million was being committed to erect a monument to honour those victims. As important as the official fostering of memory has become in this country, people derive scant solace from the acknowledgment of their past heroism if their lives have not been materially altered.

The preceding chapters have repeatedly examined cultural clashes involving different racial groups and opposing world views, battles in which various constituencies challenge the rights, behaviours or beliefs of one another. The dismantling of apartheid brought tremendous freedom, to be sure. But it also unleashed social forces that had been held in check by that repressive system, or which could only flourish in a fresh climate of equality and independence.

In 1994 Kendell Geers produced *Untitled (ANC, AVF, AWF, CP, DP, IFP, NP, PAC, SACP)*. The artwork consisted of membership cards he had collected by personally joining nine political parties spanning the ideological gamut. His face peering out from these credentials concretised both the promise and the muddle of the transition from tyranny to democracy. The various culture wars that have erupted during the initial years of an egalitarian South Africa reflect those same contradictory properties.

Chinatown Showdown

New York Times columnist David Brooks has argued that multiculturalism and identity politics have become passé in America. From his perspective, 9/11 generated the longing for a national identity that trumped tribalism. He stated: "After years of individualism ... people are ready for an appeal to citizenship ... [T]he decline of multiculturalism and the rebirth of liberal American nationalism is a significant event."[993] Veteran South African journalist Max du Preez has argued similarly, declaring, "Thirteen years after we became a democracy, tribalism is the one potential fault line in our society about which we don't have to worry about too much."[994]

Despite the typical astuteness of these two writers, culture wars continue. And varieties of tribalism are typically their source. With its characteristic racism, sense of superiority, and intense group competition, tribalism has surfaced in South Africa in ways that are bittersweet and bewildering, frightening and fraught.

Before Mbongeni Ngema's "AmaNdiya" questioned the allegiance of Indian South Africans and condemned their exploitation of black South Africans, "Fong Kong" by Hunger Boyz Senyaka, with lyrics in English and isiZulu, proclaimed, "Chinese came to South Africa to rip us off, selling their fakes to us." Chinese goods, which are increasingly saturating the African market, thereafter started to be called Fong Kong.[995] And predating David Bullard's allegedly racist column, John Matshikiza produced a series of articles in the *Mail & Guardian* about Johannesburg's burgeoning Chinatown that raised many eyebrows because it seemed to contradict his typically forthright yet humanistic perspective.

The story began with Matshikiza's ire at being refused admission to a Chinese-run massage parlour. He had made a phone appointment but explained to his readers that when he showed up, the women who were employed there scurried away in horror. He claimed the female proprietor said, "Prease, prease", "Can I herp you?" and then informed him that they only serve a Chinese clientele. But her assertion was undercut after Matshikiza saw a white man stroll in. He concluded, "I guess it's a reversal of the old days, and whites are now honorary Chinese or something."

Matshikiza was referring to the widespread but mistaken idea that the Chinese were declared to be "honorary whites" during apartheid, and therefore not subject to its restrictions. But that designation was actually limited to Japanese and Taiwanese, important trading partners with South Africa at that time. A photo accompanying the article showed the journalist standing in front of a Chinese business and wearing a T-shirt that featured a large caricatured "native"; it also bore the logo "Welcome to Africa/now go home".[996]

After Matshikiza endured some criticism from readers he tried to minimise what he had written by attributing the incident to a simple cultural misunderstanding, but with the implication that the Chinese must adapt to their new surroundings: "I need cabbage. I want to be able to explain what cabbage is," he argued. "Otherwise both parties lose out … That is all that language is about, surely? So why all the excitement?"[997]

But the incident would not go away and Matshikiza eventually offered a meagre apology. The *Mail & Guardian*'s ombudsman determined he was "invoking latent, racist fears", but that the column fell short of being hate speech. Matshikiza admitted he'd been "gobsmacked" at the negative response to what he had written, and confessed, "On reflection, I must have been losing it. I was guilty of becoming complacent, and writing as if regular readers were fully aware of my irreverent style. Bad mistake." He concluded by cautioning against the "Thought Police", and an editor's note explained, "John Matshikiza is pissed off and on sabbatical at his own request."[998] And in this way a notable journalistic partnership ended, with a progressive writer subscribing to hoary stereotypes and misconceptions.

Coconuts, Bananas and Black Diamonds

The way in which new empowerments commonly trigger resentment, resistance, racism and unreason was dramatically demonstrated by a situation that evoked South Africa's past at the same time that it illuminated the here and now.

In 2008 the Chinese Association of South Africa (Casa) won a victory in the Pretoria High Court for a cause it had championed since 2000. The ruling classified Chinese South Africans as black, thus making them eligible to become beneficiaries of affirmative action and Black Economic Empowerment (BEE). But because this quest began before BEE came into being, its proponents denied that theirs was a case of economic opportunism; for them it signified formal recognition of injustices endured by community members in the past.

During apartheid, for example, the Chinese had had their land expropriated and were moved to locations; they could not use white beaches or sit on trains (they were forced to stand). Moreover, they were not allowed to vote, were excluded from white schools, and were required to secure permission in advance from prospective neighbours before being permitted to move into white districts. South African Chinese were once labelled coloured; in 1994, they had been reclassified as white.

Chinese were elated over the court's decision. A mantra of sorts was repeated that Chinese represented the yellow in the South African flag.[999] One person proudly signed a letter-to-the-editor, "P. Woon (new black South African)".[1000] And a Chinese woman named Queenie Kingston, interviewed after the successful verdict, personified a cultural hybridity that demonstrates the far-from-unusual blending of customs and behaviours springing from the interaction of different sorts of South Africans: "[When] I came out of court," she proclaimed, "I was ululating. And toyi-toying."[1001]

Counterbalancing this jubilation was a torrent of incredulity and criticism expressed by (other) black South Africans. "[A] practical joke" declared one; "a false classification" and "immoral", claimed others.[1002] Another asserted this was "a slap in the face for the black public", whereas an additional person called this "pork barrel politics at it best".[1003] John Matshikiza dismissed the Chinese as "blacks of convenience" and raged "the whole world wants to join the tribe" while a letter-to-the-editor writer cautioned, "Africans, please wake up and smell the invasion".[1004] Anger became jumbled with exaggeration, fear and paranoia.

The most stunning public condemnation of the court decision came from Labour Minister Membathisi Mdladlana. He accused the Chinese of mistreating their black African workers and of pretending to not be able to speak English during inspections of their businesses. Mdladlana engaged in egregious typecasting: "Chinese pretend to be dumb, when they are not. We know they are not. Chinese are very clever people." He sarcastically concluded, "I suppose if I stand up now and say I want to be classified as pink, so maybe a court will agree that you are pink, even if you are not pink."[1005] But one journalist condemned Mdladlana's "offensive and bullying insinuations worthy of an apartheid-era minister", and pointed out that the "yellow peril" was the "first cousin to swart gevaar".[1006]

The minister's outrage, however, was echoed by National African Federated Chamber of Commerce (Nafcoc) president Buhle Mthethwa. "Where does it end?" she asked. She argued that the Chinese were a relatively insignificant, ancillary concern; BEE needed more time to bear fruit for the majority of black South Africans and the economy required more time to develop, before the claims of others could be considered. Nafcoc stated, the "BEE cake [is] 'too small to share'".[1007]

Nafoc was supported by groups such as the National African Federated Chambers of Commerce, the Black Management Forum, and the Black Lawyers' Association. These groups and more issued a joint statement accusing the government of not consulting with them and charging that backroom deals must have been struck: "It appears that our government entered into a secret pact with the Chinese applicants to ensure that they prevailed in a climate of complete secrecy."[1008]

The legal ruling provided John Matshikiza the opportunity to continue the rant he had launched the year before by detailing the ways that Chinese shopkeepers had supposedly exploited their black customers during apartheid. He explained, "Corner shops, fast-food takeaways and fahfee gambling scams [an illegal betting game based on a catalogue of numbers matched to dream symbols] were all in the hands of Chinese operators, who lived in pretty much closed communities, and largely stayed away from blacks. They made their bucks from the black community more than anyone else … it was the immigrant poor feeding off the local poor, and sometimes getting rich out of the unequal relationship."[1009]

But a letter-to-the-editor writer challenged people who took this sort of position. He maintained that corner shops run by "ma-Charlie" or "Mr King" defied Calvinist custom by opening on Saturday afternoons and on Sunday for the convenience of their customers. These spots also sold the ingredients for traditional beer.[1010] Nevertheless, Matshikiza let his imagination run wild, proposing "The main question is: now that we've finally found our rights as blacks, what is the potential for a billion Chinese also to climb on the bandwagon?"[1011] It was a prospect that Matshikiza absurdly feared might overwhelm the locals by sheer numbers.

This also provided the occasion for many others to vent their frustration over possibly being shoved into an economically disadvantageous position. A Freedom Front Plus youth leader declared, "A rich person immigrating [sic] from China will enjoy more privileges than a poor Afrikaner whose forefathers have lived here for over 300 years."[1012] This was a misconception, however: only Chinese living in the country before 1994 would be reclassified as black, an unintentionally postmodernist riff on race that privileged personal experience – date of arrival – over phenotype.

In actuality, there are three communities of Chinese in South Africa, each with a distinctively different history. The first came as colonial labour as early as 1655, and many others arrived in the 1860s as indentured workers destined for the goldmines (but most were sent back after completing their jobs). The Taiwanese were welcomed in the 1970s and 1980s for economic reasons, and the newest immigrants have come since 1994, numbering perhaps two to three hundred thousand. These are the people that John Matshikiza encountered in Johannesburg's Chinatown, and that the labour minister assailed for their treatment of factory workers.[1013]

Critics raised certain criteria time and again regarding whether or not the Chinese "deserved" recompense: had they really suffered? And had the Chinese actually resisted apartheid? Lack of solid or accurate evidence did not deter people from weighing in. A man who listed his affiliation as the University of Zululand wrote, "I do not have sufficient historical facts about our brothers and sisters of Chinese origin but with the little information I do have, it is clear that there were almost no squatter camps for them. There were no pass laws for them; there was no Bantu education for them."[1014] He was, of course, minimising their travails. And a fruit and vegetable shop owner asked, "Where were they when we fought the whites and apartheid? They were there with the whites having a nice time, but today they are black like us."[1015]

To counteract such claims, others proffered such derogatory apartheid-era references as "Ching Chong" (a name Chinese considered as offensive as "*kaffir*", and used by both blacks and whites), and a man recalled a headline during a parliamentary debate on the status of Chinese that once read, "Two Wongs don't make a white."[1016] Casa chairperson Patrick Chong also noted that the earlier Chinese are subject to being called "bananas" by more recent arrivals: yellow on the outside, but white (Westernised) on the inside (he further noted that the more established Chinese, if they are fluent in their native tongue at all, speak an outmoded dialect, distancing them from the newcomers).[1017]

Moreover, racial entitlement for black South Africans, Indians and coloureds is not contingent upon *any individual's* actual involvement in the liberation struggle; proof of participation is not required. This debate occasioned an inevitable trumpeting by Chinese of their group's contributions to the cause of democracy: the Chinese linking up with Gandhi to challenge unjust "Asiatic" laws; exile for some and deaths in detention for others; and the refusal of the Chinese to participate in the Tricameral Parliament. But Chinese actions and sentiments were generally not publicly detectable during apartheid. As one man noted, they mostly suffered in silence, "following the adage to 'taste bitter and tolerate hardship'".[1018]

In the zero-sum game of interethnic struggle for recognition and relative privilege in South Africa, where the so-called black diamonds (the new black African high-rollers) have been the most obvious beneficiaries of BEE, the apartheid experience supplies a handy archive of references and practices with which to describe contemporary phenomena. During this controversy more than one commentator invoked the infamous "pencil test" that racial classification boards once used to categorise people (see Chapter 4). One columnist who made such a citation condemned the persistent official cataloging of individuals, arguing, "The disgusting Employment Equity Act (EEA), which enforces racial classification, is essentially apartheid II, perpetuating the legacy of apartheid. It makes it illegal for an employer to classify a worker as a human being. He must classify him as a racial specimen."[1019]

For all the denials by commentators such as Max du Preez, new empowerments spark off negative responses by groups that feel they are becoming correspondingly disadvantaged. Tribalism remains a root source of culture wars.

Colonial Conundrums

Several years before the controversy over David Bullard's 2008 *Sunday Times* column about precolonial Africa, the *Mail & Guardian* had featured an excerpt from a book by conservative pundit Dinesh D'Souza, *What's so great about America*. The newspaper ran its selection under the banner "Two cheers for colonialism". D'Souza sang the praises of the matchless synergy between science, democracy and capitalism that enabled the West to triumph. And while D'Souza recognised that colonialism damaged its subjects, in the final analysis he judged it to be a positive force. "[M]y life would have been much worse had the British never ruled India," he affirmed.[1020]

But the *Mail & Guardian* guaranteed that this outlook would not go unchallenged: at the top of the D'Souza article it promised its readers, "Next week John Matshikiza retaliates". He countered by accentuating the excessive costs of colonialism borne in human terms, citing the extreme brutality meted out on Belgian-run rubber plantations, for example. Matshikiza also argued that scientific knowledge predated what the colonials brought forth, and noted that these intruders consolidated what had previously been independently functioning kingdoms.[1021] These therefore represented two "native" positions, very much at odds with one another: where D'Souza perceived advancement, Matshikiza mostly saw pain.

Gayatri Chakravorty Spivak speaks to this sort of tension, comparing the colonial encounter to "a rape that produces a healthy child". But, she writes, "Imperialism cannot be justified by the fact that India has railways and I speak English well. Many of the functionaries of the civilizing mission were well-meaning." Spivak notes, "but alas, you can do good with contempt or paternal-maternal-sororal benevolence in your heart."[1022] This intrinsic contradiction of colonialism – destructive, to be sure, yet generating benefits for its subjects as well – lay beneath a controversy that broke out over an amalgamation of charitable efforts bearing the names of two of the most legendary men in Southern Africa: the Nelson Mandela Foundation and the Rhodes Trust.

The Mandela Rhodes Foundation was established in 2003 to promote the development of leadership capacity throughout Africa by awarding scholarships to students and fellowships to working professionals. The worthiness of its goal was not disputed; rather, the collective banner under which it was being pursued came under fire. Critics of the venture argued that Mandela's name was both sullied by association with Cecil Rhodes at the same time that it legitimised a man whose exploits many people condemn. In the heat of the debate Rhodes was labelled a racist and a thief, an inhuman warlord who oppressed black Africans, destroyed their families, forced them from their land, and laid the groundwork for apartheid.

One man protested, "[M]oney is being used to purify sinners ... and thus buy out people from hell to heaven." But, he argued, "History must not be re-engineered to cleanse those who amassed wealth through brutal oppression of black people. And Mandela should not be used as an ointment that performs this ritual."[1023] Dr Adekeye Adebajo, himself the recipient of a Rhodes scholarship, argued similarly. He questioned, "Has Mandela perhaps not taken reconciliation too far in rehabilitating a figure that Africans should have condemned to the pit-latrine of history?"[1024] The writer was executive director of the Centre for Conflict Resolution in Cape Town; for a man in this position to take an extreme stance like this demonstrates the anguished emotions the enterprise brought forth.

Others balked at the notion that reconciliation can be taken "too far". Reconciliation, after all, has been the hallmark of Nelson Mandela's personal philosophy and his political policies. Playing the blame game never gained much traction during his administration; the larger objective of building an egalitarian and harmonious society, one where public servants would be avatars of honesty and scrupulousness, prevailed over everything else. As time has passed, however, Mandela's vision finds fewer advocates or embodiments of these ideals. The steady stream of criminal indictments against government officials bears mute testimony to what many feel is a significant lowering of the bar of ethical behaviour and accountability in the country.

One commentator suggested, "Siyazi mos ukuthi wonke umuntu uneNdiya lakhe," [We all know that everyone has their Indian], meaning success depends upon having a facilitator, a benefactor, a "fixer". In Jacob Zuma's case it was wealthy businessman Schabir Shaik, who was convicted of funnelling bribes to the politician. This journalist further elaborated, "all the senior politicians ... have their Indians... [except] some Indians are not always real Indians. They are sometimes politically connected white businessmen. And sometimes they are black economic empowerment tycoons. The common denominator was that they 'look after' senior political figures and in turn 'get looked after' in kind."[1025] Given this taken-for-granted assumption about the nitty-gritty mechanics of politics, Jacob Zuma's supporters have felt that in recent years their champion has been unfairly held responsible for behaviour that is routinely expected, as well as tolerated.

What made Nelson Mandela so noteworthy was that he led a "bloodless revolution", in stark contrast to events that unfolded in other African countries from the mid-20th century onwards. In conjunction with the creation of an infrastructure of human rights, that distinction made South Africans feel exceptional, and rightly so. South Africa has been christened "a winning nation", "glorious global champions", and "the world's greatest fairy tale".[1026] But beliefs such as these have been more difficult for many people to sustain in light of more recent problems.

Writer Rian Malan noted the erosion of this idea of exceptionalism with regards to the exposé by the *Sunday Times* of Health Minister Manto

Tshabalala-Msimang's unprincipled conduct. And filmmaker Ben Cashdan, director of the Thabo Mbeki documentary that the SABC balked at airing, reflected on what he had seen evolve under the man's presidency. "We've all lost our virginity, we've all lost our innocence," Cashdan ruminated. "Mandela made us all feel like we were virgins. Even Mbeki, in the early days, you know, before he fell on his face over AIDS and Zimbabwe, made us feel that we were something special in the world ... [But] from being an idealistic little spot on the planet," he noted, "where somehow we were all part of a project to create good in this country, we are now ripping apart our democratic institutions."

Cashdan pointedly concluded, "We're all in 'Zumania' now."

Prague Spring or Winter of Discontent?

Jane Duncan, formerly of the Freedom of Expression Institute, highlighted the bifurcation of the South African public: one segment valuing the media and regularly consuming its various expressions, but the majority of people existing beyond the reach of where the media generally cast their news nets. The lives of these people are largely ignored by reporters, while they in turn barely pay attention to what journalists have to say. The extent of this gulf was revealed by two highly significant events in South Africa's newly democratic history.

The first played out in December 2007 at the ANC's congress in the city of Polokwane in Limpopo. The main objective of the gathering was to elect a party president, the usual springboard to the presidency of the country as well. In the normal scenario incumbent President Thabo Mbeki would be replaced by a new leader since his own constitutionally mandated two terms as South Africa's president were winding down. But Mbeki decided to put himself forward for an additional term as ANC president, as a prelude to possibly changing the Constitution and serving beyond the legal limit of ten years. And that put him head to head with Jacob Zuma, the former deputy president whom Mbeki had discharged because of the politician's legal troubles.[1027]

Zuma, of course, had been battered incessantly in the press and had struck back at the media as well. Going in to the congress, Zuma's reputation appeared to be heavily damaged. But mainstream journalists were largely out of touch with the feelings of the general population; the tabloid *Daily Sun* had its finger much more firmly on that pulse. So when Zuma emerged the victor, it was a counterintuitive revelation for anyone who believes the media play a pivotal role in a nation's politics. The conventional media did not reach into the rank-and-file of the ANC, nor had it taken an accurate measure of the extent of disenchantment felt by people on the whole. Zuma shrewdly noted, "I have been convicted by those who have a right to write."[1028]

In addition, dissatisfaction with their post-apartheid lives has, as noted, erupted in large and frequent public protests over service delivery, as well as in cultural conflict. People have taken to the streets as a means to express their discontent to a much greater extent than they have turned to the mainstream media as a mouthpiece for their concerns. Their wide-ranging frustration culminated in the explosion of xenophobic violence, which broke out six months after the Polokwane conference, severely undercutting the country's collective identity as a harmonious, multiracial society. Report after report indicated that many people were targeted because they failed a "language test" administered by marauding mobs: individuals were asked to name certain body parts in isiZulu. If they could not, if their accent was suspect, or if they did not recognise archaic usages that "natives" could reasonably be expected to know, they would be attacked.

It was an imprecise gauge at best: a third of those murdered were actually South African citizens. It became, in effect, a "21st-century pencil test",[1029] with life-and-death consequences. As cited in Chapter 3, one observer chillingly noted, "Jacob Zuma's signature tune, 'Umshini Wam', has become the soundtrack for the xenophobic upsurge".[1030] The perpetrators of the violence apparently believed that the ascent of Zuma to the presidency would inaugurate a splendid new era, one in which power would flow away from the "Xhosa Nostra" to the Zulus, and would ensure that "authentic" South Africans would prevail over alien others. Shortly afterwards a Zuma supporter declared, "He [Zuma] will tell people to start [putting money] with guys in my language. White is a language. Indian is a language and they have all the money. The Xhosas have had all the money opened up for them, now it is the Zulus' turn."[1031]

Jacob Zuma's victory within the ANC ruptured politics-as-usual and opened up political possibilities. It was accompanied by talk of a "second transition". The first one references the political struggle that successfully liberated South Africa; the second would be the development of a more equitable distribution of resources. In reality two economies exist in the country: the formal one, still disproportionately benefitting whites, and the informal one, providing subsistence for non-whites. The neoliberal policies and market fundamentalism endorsed by the South African government since 1994 have left the bulk of the previously disadvantaged population as continuing-to-be-disadvantaged.

Mark Gevisser, award-winning biographer of Thabo Mbeki, soberly noted the heightened sense of uncertainty among South Africans in mid-2008 and drew a comparison between that situation and the mood of the country in 1994, when it was first reconstituting itself. He remarked, "[W]e are not 'the rainbow children of God' with a pot of gold waiting for us on the other side. We are merely ordinary – a messy, unpredictable, developing nation, with a history of violence and deep inequalities, led by flawed and grubby (and even corrupt) human beings, rather than liberating gods." That suggested heightened challenges as well as opportunities. "We have entered a transitional era again," Gevisser predicted.[1032] And University of Cape Town law professor Richard Calland observed that the ANC "is introducing a level of institutional uncertainty that could yet create democratic vulnerability and even a constitutional crisis".[1033]

That sense of shifting balances of power and fresh social arrangements, the anticipation of either imminent collapse or triumphal restructuring, provide the ideal conditions for propagating culture wars.

Talkin' 'bout a Revolution

Journalist Maureen Isaacson openly posed a question that was on the minds of a lot of people in 2008: "Is the revolution over," she asked, "or is it just beginning?"[1034]

The specific provocation for her remark was an explosion of war talk that was saturating the proclamations of a number of highly placed public figures, threatening violence if established political processes did not produce the results they desired. At a Youth Day rally commemorating the 16 June uprising of students in Soweto, African National Congress Youth League (ANCYL) President Julius Malema boldly declared, "We are prepared to die for Zuma. We are prepared to take up arms and kill for Zuma."[1035] The direct referent was to what could happen should anything prevent Jacob Zuma from ascending to the presidency of the country, either due to his being entangled in the courts at the time of the 2009 general election, or should he be convicted of any wrongdoing.

Following on the heels of the outbreak of xenophobic violence just a few weeks before, it seemed like a particularly incendiary remark. Opposition party leaders blasted Malema and filed complaints with the South African Human Rights Commission (SAHRC); that body gave him 14 days to retract the statement and apologise.

But Malema, characterised by one observer as a "misguided missile",[1036] stood his ground. He allowed the SAHRC's deadline to pass. His proponents meanwhile generated a spate of minimalisations and rationalisations. Malema, they argued, was misunderstood, quoted out of context, or his remarks were taken too literally or blown out of proportion.

As ANCYL president, Malema was heir to a position once held by the controversial Peter Mokaba, a man Malema referred to as a mentor. The editorial cartoonist Wilson Mgobhozi linked Mokaba's invocation of "Kill the farmer, kill the Boer" to Malema's own blunt statement, tagging them as "ANC young lunatics". Zapiro zeroed in on this, too: he offered a drawing of a huge monument to Zuma with a cluster of acolytes paying homage through chants of "lie", "cheat", "steal" and "kill" (the last declaration coming from Malema). Zuma's likeness sits Buddha-style, with the ubiquitous shower spigot sprouting from his head and with him clutching a machine gun emitting flames, while a soundspeaker embedded in his mouth repeats "mshini Wam".[1037]

While this debate was raging, Cosatu's general secretary Zwelinzima Vavi likewise called on supporters at a funeral of an ANC stalwart to be "prepared to shoot to kill" for Zuma. The Young Communist League also supported Malema, saying it was a general statement, not aimed at anyone in particular.

Both men refused to apologise. In the end Malema quelled the uproar to some extent by pledging not to use the word "kill" again in public, but agreeing to substitute "eliminate" instead. For his part, Vavi said he regretted the hard-hitting sentiment he had expressed, yet by and large he was unrepentant. Vavi pleaded, "Why should we be asked to apologise for the love we have for fellow revolutionaries? There will be no apology from me … We cannot apologise for what we are."[1038] His words strongly paralleled those of Mbongeni Ngema when he was rebuked for "AmaNdiya" and similarly resisted admitting to any wrongdoing. The defence offered by all these men relied upon appeals to history, tradition, and the sovereignty of their culture. Malema insisted, "Don't impose liberal language (on us). We are using this (word) 'kill' to determine our passion and love in defence of the revolution." And Vavi declared, "all those who have been distressed by our commitment to lay down our own lives for our revolution … do not come from this tradition".[1039]

Jacob Zuma was present at the 16 June event when Julius Malema uttered his credo. But Zuma made no public comment about it then, or afterwards. Statements like those from Malema and Vavi confirm the worst fears of many South Africans, especially members of racial minorities, and stoke the paranoia of those who have prophesied a "Night of Long Knives" after Nelson Mandela's death.

Compromise(d)

Julius Malema's agreement to diminish the pitch of his rhetoric ever-so-slightly was the main outcome of a compromise brokered by the SAHRC. That took a bit of the heat off Malema, but turned it up for the SAHRC.

The commission's decision to accept his anaemic gesture and not push the matter reinforced a widespread perception that the SAHRC is ineffectual, lacks authority, and can be swayed by public opinion or public figures (Winnie Mandela accompanied Malema to his hearing, for example). The most common descriptor of the SAHRC in the aftermath was "toothless", although some observers were less forgiving. One wrote that the SAHRC was "caricatured as an ANC lackey and a servant of the bourgeoisie" and another predicted that "the impression will be cemented in the minds of many that it is easier [for the SAHRC] to deal with little white salon owners and employers of domestic workers than to confront black mob leaders".[1040] The episode provided yet another test of the limits of acceptable speech, expressive terrain that is among the most contested in South Africa.

More than a decade and a half into the democratic dispensation, the evolving definition of those boundaries has been indistinct at best. When the Cape High Court decided against the culture jamming group Laugh it Off in the South African Breweries trademark case, the judge ruled that the slogan

Black Labour/White Guilt exceeded the boundaries of protected expression and bordered on hate speech. This was an instance where harm was not proven, however; rather remarkably, an editorial viewpoint on racism was conflated with racism itself.

The noteworthy resilience and refashioning of catchphrases such as "One settler, one bullet" and "Kill the Boer, kill the farmer" demonstrate the vigor of apartheid-era tropes and their resonance in contemporary South African culture; the outrage their many variations generate is answered by denials that these mottos in fact connote what they appear to. Groups that regularly feel threatened nowadays, such as Afrikaner farmers or Indians, interpret such slogans as obvious incitements to violence. To them, crime continually targets members of their communities and attests to their vulnerability; speech and action cannot be uncoupled.

But comrades from the liberation struggle or free-speech advocates write off such linkages; they see the phrases as inconsequential cultural artifacts or broad-spectrum statements that should not be taken literally or personally. The SAHRC designated "Kill the Boer, kill the farmer" as hate speech after an appeal of its initial judgement. That was a welcome but belated decision for people who feel besieged by such talk, but judged by others as an instance where the misplaced anxiety of thin-skinned complainants displaced reason.

South Africa boasts a number of regulatory bodies and legal venues where such matters can be adjudicated. The BCCSA, the Broadcasting Complaints Commission of South Africa, ruled that a radio talk-show host was guilty of hate speech after he referred to Afrikaans-speaking rugby players as "thick Dutchmen". But the Equality Court ruled that "boesman" was not, when referring to Khoisan people.

As stated previously, the three exceptions to the constitutional guarantee of freedom of expression are propaganda for war, imminent incitement of violence, and advocacy of hatred toward groups based upon race, ethnicity, religion, or gender. The latter provision allows for the imprecise concept of group psychological harm to feature into deliberations about the acceptability of discourse. With South Africa's violence-riddled past, giving weight to such a factor is understandable. But it also complicates rendering judgements that are consistent, or detached from such factors as the lingering effects of historical injustice or the differential ability of groups to successfully press a case on their own behalf in the here and now. The conflicting goals of guaranteeing the expression of a broad range of ideas and yet assuring a multitude of groups that their well-being is also protected generate the sort of claims and counterclaims that characterise culture wars.

The slim threshold between speech and action was dramatised by Zuma's supporters when the politician was brought to court again in August 2008 because of the ongoing investigation of various charges of graft against him. As with earlier hearings, thousands of his supporters staged an open-air spectacle that represented street theatre cum military manoeuvers, tradition amalgamated with a contemporary sense of spin, and comedy mixed with threat. One observer characterised it as "the miscegenation of pop music and politics".[1041]

Some in the crowd burned *impepho*, an age-old way of summoning the ancestors. A man planned to sprinkle a potion made from ground crocodile heart on the courthouse steps; after the judge walked over it, he would assuredly rule in Zuma's favour. A seven-year-old *imbongi* charmingly sang out JZ's praises.[1042] And King Goodwill Zwelithini led a ceremony that linked the modern-day politician to the proud Zulu past. An expert on Zulu history explained, "the ceremony had great significance in traditional Zulu culture because when 'a nation's hero was *going to war* he would be blessed by the king and be advised on how to conduct himself during war'".[1043]

Such rituals were complemented by military posing: some wore camouflage jackets and flaunted cardboard machine guns. Cadres from the Military Veterans Association of Umkhonto we Sizwe (MK, "Spear of the Nation", the armed wing of the ANC during apartheid) appeared in combat outfits, mobilised in battle formations, and provided an honour guard for Zuma to and from court. They claimed they had been "deployed … to ensure the judge does not make an arrogant decision". According to one report, "the willingness to fight [was] palatable". Some people shouted in isiZulu, "We will bring this building down if they find Zuma guilty" while others chanted "No Zuma, no country".[1044] And there were, as would be expected, enthusiastic choruses of "Umshini Wam".[1045] Parsing speech and sloganeering from intimidation and imminent danger requires wisdom of a Solomonic scope and depth in such situations.

Mandating Commitment

How can a government respond to such deep and pervasive divisiveness? In 2008 the minister of education, at the urging of President Thabo Mbeki, proposed a pledge of allegiance that would be recited daily by schoolchildren. The goal of such practices from a communal point of view is to inculcate pride and loyalty – vital collective goals. But sceptics typically view such practices as hollow exercises at best, indoctrination at worst. In fact, a similar proposal was put forward in 2000 but nixed because it resonated too deeply with the autocratic tenor of apartheid. It is not difficult to fathom why contemporary South African politicians would float such a scheme, however: theirs is a fledgling democracy, lacking the symbolic weight of time-tested, nationally shared secular rituals, and struggling against the centrifugal forces of anomie and disillusionment, racism and tribalism (tellingly, this proposal was put forward just before the outbreak of xenophobic violence that year).

Critics voiced particular concern over a phrase in the opening of the oath: "We the youth of South Africa, recognising the injustices of our past, honour those who suffered and sacrificed for justice and freedom." It brought out a familiar chorus of complaints that questioned the usefulness of such drills for nation building. To some ears, this was a step backwards rather than forward, picking at old wounds instead of allowing new connective tissue to grow. From this perspective, it seemed like finger pointing at white South Africans; they need not have been explicitly named as villains to understand the implication of this reference. Another possible naysaying interpretation of the pledge was that the wording implied that injustice was part of the past rather than flourishing, albeit in some fresh iterations.

Prominent academic Jonathan Jansen labelled it "policy posturing", the tendency of politicians to rely upon figurative silver bullets to address multifaceted issues in order to demonstrate their ostensible performance of official duties.[1046] And the recurring promotion of an essentialist image of "Africanness" surfaced in the letter-to-the-editor columns. One man wrote, "Our education is suffering from imitation sickness." The pledge, he noted, had been modelled on the United States. "We think, act, talk and behave like Westerners," he argued. "African education," he decried, "is modelled on Western education."[1047]

Initiatives such as these are apt to spark off culture wars because they highlight values that are promoted as being germane to the entire body politic, and advocate certain instruments for implementing and promoting them. But in any contemporary, democratic, multicultural society, reaching agreement on such ideas and symbols may be a chimera.

The Art of War

To return to the opening chapter, James Hunter defined culture wars as public conflict arising from the clash between "*the impulse toward orthodoxy*" and "*the impulse toward progressivism*".[1048] In particular, this refers to people being polarised over hot-button issues such as race and ethnicity; the body, sexuality and sexual orientation; identity politics; religion; and patriotism and national identity.

In the United States these struggles have largely been the result of social change generated by the impact of various civil rights movements, initiated by African-Americans, women, gays and lesbians, and others. Groups that were formerly overlooked or invisible are now in-your-face. People who were relatively impotent have captured a greater measure of social power. A broader range of values currently vie for validation. And increasingly, these internal debates have been shaped by events and trends happening within the international arena.

Americans have been differentially affected by the past half century of social change, depending upon their own distinctive circumstances. But South Africans *as a whole* have been impacted by living through the ongoing, fundamental transformation of their society, once resting upon a system of acute racial privilege and exclusion to now being based upon democratic entitlement. They have been propelled into an utterly new world, in crucial ways being shaped through their own efforts, but partially moulded by global events as well. The objective of "nation-building" is a frequently invoked and familiar phrase to South Africans, yet would be meaningless to countless Americans.

Past social arrangements are all open to intense scrutiny in contemporary South Africa. Groups are flexing their political muscle in ways that were formerly unimaginable. And cultural tensions, once diminished or suppressed through the deliberate segregation of racial and ethnic groups, now emerge with greater likelihood as different constituencies recover, create anew and promote distinctive values and beliefs, rituals and symbols. This liberated and expanded semiotic marketplace has become a crucible for generating cultural conflict as different segments of people confront one another, each rallying under the banner of their own special sense of identity. For example, Bok van Blerk cited his perception that Afrikaner history has nearly been written out of school textbooks as his inspiration for composing "De la Rey"; his song was a particularistic protest against the sort of revisionism that is occurring within his country with regularity.

Certain culture wars have flared up in both America and South Africa: the battle over same-sex marriage, for example. But in South Africa the debate has been contoured in ways that distinctly reflect the country's history, such as the invocation of an essential "Africanness" that rejects gay activity as supposedly being a colonial import. Overlays of tradition – "invented" or "authentic", retrofitted or revived – distinguish these battles from those occurring elsewhere, even when the basic issue is the same. The orthodoxy and fundamentalism that James Hunter highlighted is not simply reducible to religious sources in South Africa; all manner of traditions and belief systems must be considered.

In every instance, however, culture wars are contests for relative position, struggles over status and power. And the ways in which they unfold demonstrate remarkably similar characteristics: the rhetorical impasse that occurred during one of the debates over controversial photographs shown at Johannesburg's Market Theatre revealed a central dynamic of the interplay of opposing forces. As one observer noted then, "there were those with words and those with actions and the debate could not shift. It simply stayed in one place and the trenches were dug then and there."[1049] This extremely polarised, dig-in-the-heels mentality reduces the discursive space within which moderate opinions and conciliatory gestures can be expressed, thus sustaining these battles.

The appeal to tradition has openly pitted proponents of certain orthodoxies against those endorsing more contemporary perspectives. Or, to put this tension in more general terms, it references the conflict between tribalism and universalism. The brouhaha over the exhibitions *Purity and Danger* and *Gay Rights Rites Rewrites*, the play *Thuthula – Heart of the Labyrinth*, or the display of photographs of gay black African men or people with AIDS revealed such conflicts between world views, thereby highlighting the politics of representation. The reluctance by gender traditionalists to align constitutional guarantees of equality with a broadening of the conferral of traditional honours, such as allowing women to assume tribal leadership, is another manifestation of this broad issue, underscoring the contradiction between subject and citizen, collectivity and individual, custom and constitution. It is a tension that has long been noted: during the height of apartheid, for example, political scientist Gwendolen Carter differentiated between South Africanism (promoting the goal of common citizenship) and what she called an Africanist position (emphasising particularistic black South African goals).[1050]

Moreover, in the debate over Kaolin Thompson's "ashtray" or Mark Hipper's allegedly pornographic depictions of children, black African government representatives were unusually candid in their expression of alarm over the values that these young white artists exemplified. In the first instance an official lamented, "It's most frustrating to act within the framework of the law."[1051] In the second, another acknowledged her "conservative African background" that made her opposed to pornography.[1052] Accordingly, as several other examples have shown, interrogations of topics such as authoritarianism or sexism might be misconstrued as support for those dogmas instead. Furthermore, Jacob Zuma's many allusions to the dictates of tradition – "compelling" him to have sex with a woman who instead called the incident rape, for instance, or "obliging" him to physically strike someone he perceived to be homosexual – echo the extra-legal sources and imperatives of the positions that those other two public servants embraced years earlier.

Black Africans have enlisted the appeal to traditional culture much like social conservatives in America have used the Bible to certify their beliefs and actions. In many instances this has been a cynical, exculpatory exercise. It reflects a view of culture as static, culture as the last word, culture as a bludgeon, culture as a way to stifle dialogue. When someone adopts this sort of essentialist position, it puts others on the defensive; any criticism of traditional beliefs or their adherents is destined to sound disrespectful or racist.

The synergy between a cluster of factors accounts for the profusion of culture wars within contemporary South Africa:

- the country bears a tumultuous history of oppression under colonialism and apartheid;
- more recently, it has experienced fundamental social change;
- former victims and their oppressors live in the same society, assuring an ongoing discussion about injury and reparation;
- it is home to a multiplicity of groups with social identities that are becoming reinvested with significance;
- there is an enduring, deeply experienced sense of group inequality;
- a growing crisis of confidence in leadership is apparent;
- appeals to traditional authority and an elemental "Africanness" coexist with a human-rights-based political structure;
- and South Africa has been drawn into a globalised economy of goods, people and ideas.

The interplay between these elements releases a profusion of energy. This imbues public life in South Africa with a tremendous sense of vibrancy and potential. At the same time, however, it can appear to imperil social cohesion and jeopardise the vision and attainment of a just and non-racial democracy.

* * *

Albie Sachs embodies the immense transformation that has swept South Africa: as an ANC activist living in exile he was severely injured by a car bomb planted by South African security agents. Then he became a Constitutional Court judge.

In 1989 he argued that all types of artists were about to become the beneficiaries of an enormous gift: the freedom to engage with the entirety of the human condition in their creative work.[1053] It is a theme that many others have since taken up. Njabulo Ndebele speaks of "the rediscovery of the ordinary",[1054] and Zakes Mda has wrestled with what it means to have the liberty to explore the nuances of peoples' lives and not feel responsible to focus solely upon politics and social issues. Writers like themselves now have the opportunity to push beyond stock characters and narrative formulas.

But that prospect carries a cost. "We have become normal," Mda observes. "It's very painful to become normal."[1055]

Sachs addressed an audience at the National Arts Festival in Grahamstown in 1991, referring once again to the need to liberate artists from aesthetic constraints. He talked then about the difficulties of formulating a new society that would embrace all its citizens and encourage free expression. He understood, however, that given South Africa's anguished past it could be a challenge to tolerate certain types of speech that might seem hurtful, hateful or dangerous to particular groups and to the common weal.

Sachs called for forbearance and mutual understanding, in a statement that sounds remarkably fresh more than two decades later. It also epitomises the predicament upon which culture wars flare up. He declared, "I am one of millions of South Africans for whom everything we hold dear is about to open up, while I fear that for many of you everything you most cherish seems about to close down."

Sachs then implored, "Can we speak to one another?"[1056]

Endnotes

Chapter 1

1. See Dubin, 1995b for an account of the varied responses to this book.
2. Dubin, 1992: 15, 17.
3. An impressive amount has been written about South Africa; the general outlines of its history and politics are fairly well known. A book written by journalist Allister Sparks during the apartheid era remains one of the best chronicles of major historical events that have shaped the character of the major population groups, and the relations between them (see 1990); his follow-up volume is a valuable record of the country's transition to democracy (see 1994). For an excellent account of contemporary events, see Gevisser (2009).
4. See Hunter, 1996a: 246.
5. Hunter, 1991: 42–43, emphasis in the original.
6. Goodstein, 2004.
7. Dubin, 2006b.
8. See Gans, 1974.
9. See, e.g., Davis and Robinson, 1996, DiMaggio et al., 1996, Fiorina et al., 2005, Williams, 1997, Wolfe, 1998.
10. Brint, 1992: 439.
11. Hunter, 1996b: 246–247.
12. Ongoing skirmishes more than a decade and a half later make Richard Goldstein's purported last words – "The culture war is over! We won! (For Now)" – seem overly optimistic, while also recognising the incessant nature of the phenomenon; Goldstein, 1996.
13. Scott, 1997. Appomattox Court House in Virginia was where General Robert E. Lee of the Confederate forces surrendered to General Ulysses S. Grant in 1965, signalling the end of the Civil War.
14. Lyman, 2001.
15. Weber, 2004, Kirkpatrick, 2004.
16. Brooks, 2007.
17. Spivak, 1998: 332, 334.
18. See Durkheim, 1956.
19. Foucault, 1980: 128; emphasis in the original.
20. See Bakhtin, 2008.
21. See Ben-Yehuda and Goode, 1994, and Stewart and Harding, 1999: 299–301.
22. See, e.g., Turner, 1969, 1974.
23. See, e.g., Habermas, 1989 (1962), and Calhoun, 1992. For a critique of the utility of employing "public sphere" in analysing museums, a frequent site of culture wars, see Bennett, 2006.
    The editors of a collection of what they characterise as a "second wave" of South African writing (reflecting experiences of the post-apartheid period)

announce, "In putting this book together, we chose stories that would fill a gap in the public arena. South Africa is still a country in which public discourse is thin"; Nuttall and McGregor, 2007: 13. Notably, all the contributors were affiliated with Wiser, a research institute at the University of the Witwatersrand in Johannesburg, the same institution where Carolyn Hamilton ran the Constitution of Public Intellectual Life Project, a collaborative research initiative examining contemporary South African themes and using Habermas as its theoretical foundation.

See the comments of Jane Duncan in Chapter 5 of this volume regarding what she assesses as a noticeably bifurcated South African public: the discursive practices of one group are evident in such realms as the mass media, publishing and academia; another segment, marginalised from these domains, uses public protest as its forum.

24 Hoad, 2004. The competition was held at the Sun City resort in 2001. During the apartheid years, this playground of forbidden pleasures such as gambling and racy entertainment operated in the "native homeland" or "Bantustan" of Bophuthatswana, one of the artificially created political entities that granted citizenship to black Africans while excluding them from the rights and privileges accorded white South Africans. Evita Bezuidenhout, the stage persona of comic Pieter-Dirk Uys, quipped that they existed "so that people can cross borders to go and pinch black bottoms"; quoted in Trillin, 2004: 72.

25 If this had been the kingdom of Swaziland, in southern Africa, it would not be idle speculation: King Mswati III routinely plucks a new bride from participants in the yearly Reed Dance.

26 An Islamic religious opinion, in this case, a death warrant. The term became best known to a non-Muslim audience when a death sentence was issued by Iran's Ayatollah Khomeini against Salman Rushdie, author of *The Satanic Verses* (1988), which this leader deemed blasphemous.

27 Miles, 2003: 54. Sunna is the body of traditional Islamic social and legal custom.

28 *Ibid.*: 58.

29 Back, 2004.

30 *Vanguard* [Nigeria], 2002a.

31 *Vanguard* [Nigeria], 2002b.

32 *The Guardian*, 2002.

33 Hoad, *op. cit.*: 79. In a local twist, underscoring the passions that such events can arouse, the winner of a regional pageant in the Miss Teen India SA competition was a Xhosa girl. The choice so outraged the audience that the judges were forced to flee the venue in order to escape the fury of the incensed audience, and the girl's mother was also concerned for her daughter's safety; see Sokana, 2007a.

34 Moreton, 2002.

35 Cartoons and comics have frequently come under attack for alleged moral or cultural transgressions, which does not necessarily diminish the sense of shock when this occurs. Examples include congressional investigations into alleged links between comic books and delinquency in the US in the 1950s; an attack by the religious right on cartoon character Spongebob Squarepants for spreading suspected "pro-gay propaganda" in 2005; and

numerous instances of censuring – and censoring – episodes of the animated television series *South Park* due to perceived blasphemy, racism, and other irreverent scenes (but in 2006, the programme was blasted by some people for refusing to show an image of Muhammad, yet regularly ridiculing Jesus and Christians, and for lampooning Tom Cruise and Scientology). Mention must also be made to the knack of the creators of *The Simpsons* to provide what is essentially a running log of culture war issues. Significantly, a Comic Book Legal Defense Fund exists in the United States to support creators and distributors who may run afoul of the law (as did a Georgia retailer in 2007 after being charged with distributing obscene matter to a minor; the publication in this instance was a graphic novel that, incidentally, pictured Picasso in the nude).

36 José Bové, a French sheep farmer, achieved near-heroic status after he severely vandalised a McDonald's restaurant in 2000. Dubbing himself a French Gandhi, this campaigner against "McDomination" similarly viewed this multinational corporation as the devilish face of globalisation, and an enemy of traditional production methods and local commodities. But his countrymen barely reacted after McDonald's announced plans to open an outlet in a shopping arcade beneath the Louvre in 2009; in the interim, "McDo" had become a French favourite.

On a more serious note, concern over protecting local cultural production and sustaining cultural diversity was the rationale for Unesco's Convention on the Protection and Promotion of the Diversity of Cultural Expressions, adopted in 2005 (the United States was one of two countries opposed). In some instances countries stipulate that local quotas of movies, television shows and books be met to counter the hegemony of large producers of material such as the United States.

37 Venezia, 2006.

38 Simpson, 2006, emphasis in the original.

39 A personal reminiscence by the prominent cultural commentator Richard Goldstein is worth quoting at length: "I offer this memory of a cartoon that delighted me as a child. It was an animated trip to Africa, replete with nurturing lions, chatty monkeys and bouncing pickaninnies. It ended with a map of Africa, drawn in black. 'And so we bid farewell to the dark continent,' the narrator intoned. Then a pair of huge white lips burst forth from the map, crooning 'Bah-bye!' This image enchanted me then and embarrasses me now, but the fact that it remains embedded in my imagination says something about the enduring power of cartoons"; Goldstein, 2005: 7.

40 *New York Post*, 2006. This practice was not exclusive to South Africa: novelist Chimamanda Ngozi Adichie includes such a scene in her 2007 novel about the Biafran War in Nigeria in the 1960s, *Half of a Yellow Sun* (New York: Knopf/Anchor, p. 377).

41 Polgreen, 2006.

42 *South African Yearbook*, 2007/2008: 6. These figures are based upon the 2001 census; more recent estimates peg the number at 47.5 million. The Muslim population is concentrated in the Western Cape and KwaZulu-Natal provinces.

43 De Villiers, 2006.

44 *Mail & Guardian*, 2006b.
45 *Mail & Guardian*, 2006a.
46 Mahomed, 2006.
47 Reported in Naidoo, 2006.
48 Wright, 2006, Kimmelman, 2006.
49 The prohibition of depictions of Muhammad can have ironic, and unintentional, consequences. When a project was launched in 1955 to restore the statues of ten notable historical lawgivers embellishing the façade of a courthouse on New York's Madison Square, ambassadors from several predominately Muslim countries requested that Muhammad be removed from the collection. Officials complied, thereby obscuring the Prophet's contributions to intellectual world culture; see Kifner, 2006.
It is also worth noting that a 2006 production of Mozart's *Idomeneo* by Berlin's Deutsche Oper was cancelled, and then rescheduled, over concerns that the inclusion of the severed head of Muhammad (along with those of Poseidon, Jesus and Buddha) would generate security problems. The same production had gone forward without notice in 2003 – *before* the cartoon incident erupted.
And finally, an installation by German artist Gregor Schneider was rejected from the 2005 Venice Biennale because it might offend Muslims; the work consisted of a large scaffolding draped with black fabric, echoing the Kaaba, the shrine in Mecca's Grand Mosque. A version was displayed outside Hamburger Kunsthalle in 2007, however, as *Cube Hamburg 2007*; see Magill, 2007.
In 2012 four men were convicted of planning to attack the Danish newspaper that published the cartoons.
50 Spiegelman, 2006. This echoes Americans renaming French fries "freedom fries" to protest France's lack of support for the US invasion of Iraq in 2003. Moreover, in the anti-German furore that swept America during World War I, sauerkraut became "liberty cabbage".
51 Fattah, 2006.
52 Siegel, 2006; Spiegelman, *op. cit.*: 46.
53 Taheri, 2006.
54 Vincour and Bilefsky, 2006.
55 Taheri, *op. cit.*
56 *Ibid.*, and Vincour and Bilefsky, *op. cit.*
57 Masood, 2006.
58 Peters, 2006, emphasis in the original.
59 Friedman, 2006.
60 Honey, 2006, italics added. This buzzword attained popularity in the late 1960s/early 1970s, especially in connection with Professor Wimpie de Klerk, a politician and brother of FW de Klerk, a former president of South Africa.
61 Spiegelman, *op. cit.*: 43.
62 This distinction was notably elaborated by Mamdani, 1996.
63 Hunter, 1996a: 244.
64 For a rare exception, see Comaroff and Comaroff, 2003: 448.
65 See, e.g., Comaroff and Comaroff, 1999: 283, and Comaroff and Comaroff, 2001: 631, 649, 650.

66 Comaroff and Comaroff, 1999: 284.

67 *Ibid.*: 295. See, also, Ashforth, 2000, 2005.

68 Meaning "fine brush" in Afrikaans, a wide range of distinctive scrub varieties seen on the Cape coast such as rooibos and honey bush, aloes and protea. In many cases, their seeds germinate only after being exposed to fires.

69 Comaroff and Comaroff, 2001: 630, 650.

70 Comaroff and Comaroff, 2003: 454

71 I first identified this phenomenon in Dubin, 1992. Its continued applicability, relevance, and explanatory power has been backed up by a continuous array of new situations.

72 Rothstein, 2006. Such imagined sightings are not unusual during times of heightened emotion. In the 1993 exhibition *Back of the big house: The cultural landscape of the plantation* (Washington, DC: Library of Congress), some employees railed against a photograph of a white overseer on horseback brandishing a gun. No such photo was displayed, however. And during the furore raised by the exhibition *Miscast: Negotiating Khoisan history and material culture* (Cape Town: South African National Gallery, 1996), some visitors alleged that the genitals of Bushmen were on display (they were not), and others claimed that they saw a photograph of Sarah Baartman (the "Hottentot Venus"), even though her death in 1815 predated the invention of the medium; see Dubin, 1999, 2006a.

73 See Dubin, 2000. The painting that was controversial in London was a portrait by Marcus Harvey of Myra Hindley, a child murderer. Moreover, the artist executed the work by using the handprints of small children as "pixels" to compose her face. Hindley is notorious in Britain, but relatively unknown to Americans.

74 This information comes from an interview conducted by the author with Marisa Cardinale in New York City, 24 January 2006. For additional information on this exhibition, see Dubin, 2006c.

75 See Dubin, 1992: 97.

76 *Ibid.*: 181.

77 Quoted in Attwood, 1997.

78 *The Age*, 1997.

79 Douglas, 1970. According to Douglas, every society organises experiences and phenomena in binary oppositions such as masculine and feminine, sacred and profane, or public and private. Whereas the line may be drawn differently across societies, it will be drawn; events and behaviours that violate these boundaries can generate anxiety, fear, anger and derision, and will possibly merit punishment.

80 For a more extensive discussion of transgressive art, see Dubin, 2001.

81 *ChinaDaily.com*, 2007.

82 Quoted in Fortescue, 2007. That power, inherent in certain images, is what I concentrated on in my book *Arresting Images* (1992). See, also, Freedberg, 1989.

83 Quoted in *ABC [Australian Broadcasting Corporation] Premium News*, 2007.

84 Bolt, 2007. See the further discussion (see note 90) regarding the controversy over the Danish cartoons the previous year.

85 Another article argued, "It has once more confirmed that the Christian

community can deal with controversy without resorting to intemperate language or erratic behaviour ... Bearded Orientals may be juvenile but it again demonstrates that the Christian faith is mature enough to see it for what it is"; *The Australian*, 2007. The writer conveniently omits instances where artwork that offended Christian sensibilities has been attacked, even in Australasia (see below).

86 Courtney and Kovate, 1998. The photograph by Sam Taylor-Wood was also included in the aforementioned controversial exhibition *Sensation*.

87 Quoted in *The Dominion*, 1998.

88 *The Evening Post*, 1998. In an interesting parallel, the man who was convicted for criminal mischief after smearing Chris Ofili's work *The Holy Virgin Mary* with white paint when it was shown in Brooklyn in 1999 also had a previous conviction for protesting outside an abortion clinic. This demonstrates both the interconnectedness between various sites of contestation, and the fact that people who embrace a fervently anti-abortion position bear a cluster of values and beliefs that comprise a distinct world view, not simply a one-issue stance; for details, see the classic work by Luker, 1985.

89 *BBC Worldwide Monitoring*, 2007.

90 Charter, 2007. Calls were issued for the beheading of the artists in the episode involving the Danish cartoons as well. In 2008, three men were arrested for plotting to murder the cartoonist who drew the image of Muhammad's turban as a bomb. Seventeen Danish newspapers reprinted it as a show of support for freedom of expression, which then set off another series of demonstrations around the world. As a consequence, Denmark closed its embassies in Algeria and Afghanistan. Osama bin Laden also released a message warning Europeans of unspecified action against them because of the re-publication of the cartoons. Mention should also be made to the murder of director Theo van Gogh by a Dutch-born Islamist in Amsterdam in 2004 because of his film *Submission*, about the mistreatment of women under Islam.

91 Ibison, 2007.

92 Slackman, 2006: 1.

93 Gettleman, 2007.

94 Polgreen, 2007. This echoes an earlier situation in Chicago, where members of the City Council who attracted considerable attention by marching to the School of the Art Institute of Chicago and removing an unflattering painting of the deceased Mayor Harold Washington in 1988 later found themselves the focus of investigations and indictments for malfeasance. See Dubin, 1992.

95 Polgreen, *op. cit.* This theme was reflected in a satirical play *The Phantom Crescent*, which focused on the differential application of shari'a law to the poor and the wealthy. It was banned in either its written or performed versions in Nigeria, but as is often the case with proscribed works, became widely circulated through unofficial channels; see Pelser, 2007.

96 For a good example of the problems Scandinavian countries have experienced by absorbing increasing numbers of immigrants over the past few decades, see Caldwell, 2006.

97 Quoted in Miller, 2005.

98 *School Library Journal*, 2007. After the book was published, the real-life penguin couple, Silo and Roy, who in fact hatched and raised a chick named Tango, split after a six-year relationship, a development not overlooked by some moralists. Homosexual or same-sex bonding behaviour is common among animals; see Bagemihl, 1999. Gay-rights advocates cite this as evidence of homosexuality being "natural"; to opponents, this confirms it is "animalistic".

99 The policy was changed by the new Obama administration: news photos of returning American casualties are now allowed, with the approval of the families.
Photographer Paul Fusco created a project called *Bitter Fruit*, where he documented the funerals of American soldiers killed in the Iraq conflict. He reports that in every instance military personnel harassed him and any other journalists attempting to cover the events, although he met no such resistance from family members or other locals; see Roychoudhuri, 2004.

100 The cancellation of the play generated a great deal of publicity, and it was subsequently championed by several Off-Broadway New York theatres, which turned over their stages to the students; it was thereby exposed to an audience that was much larger than they could have ever envisioned.

101 Kristof, 2006.

102 Jardin, 2006.

103 Gustin, 2006. Blogging and text messaging have become an important way of exchanging otherwise restricted information in Robert Mugabe's censorious regime in Zimbabwe, however; see *Star*, 2008.

104 Kristof, *op. cit.*

105 A set of requirements drawn up by an African-American board member of General Motors in 1977 (amended in 1984), an American corporation that also operated significant production facilities in South Africa, which mandated that employees receive equal treatment, regardless of race, both within and outside the workplace. The apartheid system was in obvious contradiction of these principles.

106 Nocera, 2006.

107 See Hunter, 2006.

Chapter 2

108 Turning history into a tourist attraction is rampant in post-apartheid South Africa. uShaka Marine World, an oceanarium/theme park/shopping centre that opened on the Durban ("playground of the Zulu kingdom") waterfront in 2004 peddles curios from Zulu huts, and payphones are mounted upon metal backdrops shaped like war shields.

109 This antipathy can be pushed to comically absurd lengths: after a gay activist died in 1993 his father spoke the following words at a memorial service in his honour: "There was just one thing that bothered me about my son's life that bothered me [*sic*] … So let me tell you, if you're a man, wear men's clothes. If you're coloured, act coloured. Above all, if you're black, don't wear Indian clothes. If you do this, how will our ancestors recognise [and protect] you?" According to the author of the article, the son "had been something of a drag queen, with a particular penchant for Indian saris" (Donham, 1998: 3). The family thought of him as a girl – he

wore a girl's uniform to church, and performed typical women's tasks in the household – so the issue was not crossdressing, but "What the father was most upset about was dressing 'across' race, and the implications that had for ancestral blessings" (*Ibid.*: 8–9).

110 To cite some of the obvious parallels, both Jews and Indians are likely to appear to be the proximate "face" of power and privilege, in their roles as shopkeepers, landlords, civil servants and professionals.

111 A common pattern of whites and non-whites being mutually fluent in African languages occurs among whites who have been raised in rural settings, where both their early caretakers and principal playmates are non-white. This spawns a degree of intimacy among people at the lower end of the socioeconomic scale that can somewhat mediate the cross-racial rivalry and prejudice commonly assumed to exist among people in the working class.

Significantly, Indians who run businesses serving predominantly non-white clientele frequently become fluent in African languages as well.

One scholar has argued that after a century of black Africans and Indians living and working in close proximity to one another in KwaZulu-Natal, certain beliefs and practices have merged, resulting in polyculturalism. She focuses on traditional medicine, where practitioners and their patients come from both groups, and the medicines (muti) they dispense reveal a blending of mutual influences; see Flint, 2006. She also cites Fanagalo, a linguistic amalgamation of isiZulu, English and Afrikaans that allowed workers and bosses from different backgrounds to communicate with one another (p. 372). As compelling as her evidence is, she fails to discuss other social spaces where such cultural fusions may have occurred, however.

112 This version was distributed during the KwaZulu-Natal Dialogue Initiative Symposium held 26–27 July 2002 in Durban. It was prepared at a workshop held before the indaba organised by the Diakonia Council of Churches. No one raised objections to this translation at the indaba. The song "AmaNdiya" was featured on the CD *Jive Madlokovu*.

113 *Woza Albert!* reimagined the second coming of Christ in South Africa; *Asinamali!* explored the lives of five prisoners and their struggles under an oppressive legal system; *Township Fever* was based on a strike by South African railway workers; and *The Zulu* was drawn from the 1879 Battle of Isandlwana, where the British suffered a decisive defeat by their Zulu opponents.

114 FNB, the First National Bank of South Africa, supports the arts in a variety of ways; the Naledis are theatre awards initiated in 2003.

115 Bauer, 2002.

116 Heard on SAfm radio, 17 July 2003. This amount translated to about $4 million at the time.

117 Van Graan, 2004. Ngema continues to generate controversy: in 2008 he was tapped to develop a play called *Lion of the East: Gert Sibande and the Potato Boycott* to celebrate the life of an ANC activist who publicised the harsh working conditions of farm labourers. A provincial government allocated R22 million for it, along with R9 million for a statue in the man's honour. Put into perspective, the National Arts Festival in Grahamstown has an annual budget of R18 million, and the Market Theatre in

Johannesburg mounts approximately 20 productions per year, spending between R10 and R12 million; see Mbanjwa, 2008, Tolsi, 2008b.

118 Zulu, 2003.

119 Molema, 2003. In 2011, Ngema threw an engagement ceremony for one of the four women he was currently betrothed to marry.

120 Bauer, *op. cit.*

121 From an interview conducted by the author with Mbongeni Ngema in Johannesburg, 10 September 2003. This and all subsequent unattributed quotes derive from that interview.

122 *Press Trust of India Limited*, 2002a.

123 South African Press Association, 2002a.

124 Ngema was referring to a 2001 incident where a black African board member made dismissive, racist remarks about the woman at the helm of Durban's Playhouse Company, who was Indian. Mandela publicly condemned the remark as divisive and threatening to the Indian minority. When the battle over "AmaNdiya" was peaking, an Indian reporter and photographer were harassed and forced to leave a meeting they were covering at the Playhouse in support of Ngema and black empowerment, convened by a group called Concerned Africans; this is also a place with which Ngema has been associated (see Laganparsad, 2002). A week later, something similar happened outside the Durban High Court, where a large group of Ngema's supporters sang "AmaNdiya" and attacked an Indian journalist and photographer; the mob also threatened to slit the photographer's throat if his work were to be published (see Govender, S., 2002).

125 Author's fieldnotes, 26–27 July 2002. All subsequent unattributed quotes derive from my notes, as did my description of the events at the indaba in the introduction.

126 From an interview conducted by the author with Sue Brittion in Durban, 19 August 2003. All subsequent unattributed quotes derive from that interview.

127 From an interview conducted by the author with Father S'Thembiso Tshongase in Phoenix, Durban, 18 August 2003. All subsequent unattributed quotes derive from that interview.

128 From an interview conducted by the author with Joy Ellappen in Phoenix, Durban, 18 August 2003. All subsequent unattributed quotes derive from that interview.

129 Bridgraj, 2002: 8, 9.

130 BCCSA is a self-regulatory body of broadcasters, an arm of the National Association of Broadcasters. Membership is voluntary, but includes the lion's share of major media sources; affiliates sign a code of conduct.
Ngema countered that his was "love speech" because of the frankness of his words.

131 See Clegg and Drewett (2006) for an interesting overview of the censorship of music during the apartheid era, where a central board reviewed lyrics before songs were allowed to be broadcast on the government-controlled media; the mixture of languages ("bastardisation") was forbidden; and white performers who wished to perform before non-white audiences were forced to obtain government permission.
Perhaps the most well-known instance of the government's banning of

music during the apartheid era was Pink Floyd's *The Wall* because it was adopted by protesting students.

132 From an interview conducted by the author with Console Tleane in Johannesburg, 13 January 2004. All subsequent unattributed quotes derive from that interview.

133 Sue Brittion sees the issue of mistranslation as spurious. It is worth quoting from my interview with her at length: "I think he [Ngema] knew very well that there would be problems with translation. Zulu is a very poetic language and people constantly struggle with it. [When working on in-house publications if] any four of our Zulu-speaking members of staff are asked to translate the same paragraph, they come up with four different versions, and we'll hotly contest which one is the correct version. Zulu is a wonderful language, you know, it's been claimed by one of our bishops as a heavenly language. There is no such thing as literalness; everything is in some way poetical, a metaphor. So of course it was going to be mistranslated. It's mischief-making."

134 The Independent Electoral Commission is a publicly funded but independent body that oversees South Africa's elections.

135 This man was not mentioned by name, but it was Emeritus Professor of Law Kobus van Rooyen, who previously sat on the Publications Appeal Board, beginning in 1975, and served as its chair from 1980 to 1990.

136 In times past, Indians were prevented from settling in, or even travelling through other parts of the country, particularly the Boer republics of the Transvaal and the Orange Free State, as a result of the Immigration Act of 1870. The law remained in effect for over a century. Natal was a British colony, and as subjects of the Commonwealth, Indians were accorded more rights in this province than elsewhere.

137 Multigenerational family sagas have become a familiar fictional way to capture the history of Indians in South Africa; two such examples are Hassim, 2002 and Govender, 2006.

138 An article published in 1950 reported that "As far back as 1936, eight out of every ten Indians had been born in the Union [of South Africa]"; Alexander, 1950: 232.

139 Naidoo, 2003. In this article, the author casts a dubious eye at a sanitised reenactment of the arrival of the first boatload of indentured Indians at Durban Harbour in 1860.

140 "The Coolies Here", *Natal Mercury*, 22 November 1860, reprinted in Naidoo and Chetty, 1981: 52.

141 Naidoo and Chetty, *op. cit.*: 173, 189.

142 A novel published by an Indian lawyer and politician revealed an additional dimension of exploitation, detailing how white bosses sexually abused indentured Indian women; see Poovalingam, 2003.

143 Zulus would gravitate back to their kraals to attend to their lives there, and were thus considered undependable; Naidoo and Chetty, *op. cit.*: 34. The submissive demeanour of the Indians later changed as they became politicised and resisted many of the governmental restrictions placed upon them.

144 Meer, 1969: 61.

145 *Ibid.*, and Ebr.-Vally, 2001: 275–277.

146 *Ibid.*: 280.
147 Meer, *op. cit.*: 85–86.
148 Desai, 1996: 124. A news article in 1994 reported that 80% of the Indians in Natal were working class (Maier). And a 2007 survey cited a "poverty index" whereby 100 is absolute poverty (people "have nothing"), whereas 1 means they "have it all". The major racial groups scored as follows: Blacks, 46; coloureds, 25; Indians, 12; whites, 7. So while there may still be a significant Indian working-class population, Indians overall have experienced greater economic success than black Africans; Boyle, 2007c.
149 Meer, *op. cit.*: 113.
150 The violence in Rwanda broke out on 6 April; the elections in South Africa were on 27 April. According to a poll taken a year later, 71% of Indians voted for FW de Klerk's National Party, the same political party responsible for implementing apartheid, under which they had been maltreated. The violence underway in Rwanda at the time was simply an additional factor that caused Indians to fear for their safety under black rule, and to reject the triumphant African National Congress; see Raghavan, 1995.
151 Lacey, 2002. The bureaucratic categories of Tutsi and Hutu were established by Belgian colonisers; the Europeans favoured the Tutsi minority during their administration of the country, generating envy and antagonism. The Hutu majority systematically attacked Tutsis and moderate Hutus even though they share many cultural similarities, and extensive intermarriage had obliterated many supposed biological differences.
152 Temple-Raston, 2002: 18, and *Sunday Times*, 2003.
153 *Ibid.* They were all convicted on all charges; two received life sentences (the harshest that could be meted out), while the third received a prison sentence of 35 years.
154 See McNeil, 2002. Besides his songs, Bikindi was accused of specific actions: e.g., driving a vehicle that broadcast anti-Tutsi messages; see Craig and Mkhize, 2006: 42. In December 2008 he was convicted of incitement to commit genocide for making the pronouncements from the car, but not specifically for his music.
155 The title is a thinly coded reference to the Hutus (traditionally farmers) versus the Tutsis (traditionally herders). A second song by Bikindi, "Nanga Abahutu" ("I Hate Hutus") singled out Hutus who seemingly break ethnic ranks with their brethren.
156 Kanuma, 2002. Veteran South African journalist Max du Preez, 2002, also made the connection to the Rwandan tragedy.
157 Quoted in Hansen, 2005: 308.
158 From an interview conducted by the author with Ela Gandhi in Durban, 21 August 2003. All subsequent unattributed quotes derive from that interview.
159 See Madlala, 2002, De Haas, 2002.
160 *Press Trust of India Limited*, 2002c.
161 *The Hindu*, 2002.
162 From an interview conducted by the author with Vivian Reddy in Durban, 22 August, 2003. All subsequent unattributed quotations derive from that interview.

163 Hlongwa, 2002.

164 *The Times of India*, 2002a.

165 *Natal Witness*, 2002. Indians occupy 70% of Durban Unicity (government) jobs, a very visible fact that provokes anger and envy; *Echo*, 2002.

166 Jung, 2000: 9.

167 Nowbath, 1949a: 211.

168 Webster, 1977: 35.

169 Popke, 2000: 240.

170 Webster, *op. cit.*: 30. The government maintained a monopoly on the manufacture of beer offered for sale to black Africans, and operated the only legal drinking establishments for them. Widespread bootlegging occurred, however, dominated by Zulu women. Desai notes that Thursday was the traditional day off for black African domestic workers, which would have meant the beer halls were likely jammed with patrons; *op. cit.*: 10.

171 Local History Museums, 2001. The rumour about the decapitated head is also mentioned in Meer, 2002: 116.

172 "Many of the African fatalities and injuries were the result of police and military action"; Local History Museums, *op. cit.*

173 Nowbath, *op. cit.*: 209.

174 Webster, *op. cit.*: 25. Webster reports, based on a government commission's findings, that while the first day of rioting was spontaneous, the subsequent violence was planned, and word of it widely disseminated (pp. 30–31).

175 Meer, 2002: 118, Nowbath, 1949b: 211–212.

176 *Ibid.*: 211

177 Webster states that the official inquiry established this as a fact; *op. cit.*: 29.

178 From an interview conducted by the author with Ravi Govender at the Durban Cultural and Documentation Centre, 20 August 2003. Meer, 1969, also talks about whites urging black Africans to violence in 1949; see p. 36. And Meer, 2002, refers to the rumour about the police transporting rioters to the scene; see p. 117.

179 Govender, 2006: 271, and Meer, 2002: 117, 118. Meer further argues that the Nationalist government wished to repatriate Indians to India, and that ruining them financially would be a strong incentive for them to leave; see p. 119. Such proposals had been suggested long before this time; see Jhaveri, 1933.

180 The so-called Doctors' Pact, which united the Natal and Transvaal congresses with the African National Congress. At various times the two racial groups either collectively joined political efforts or resolutely kept their interests separate, depending upon specific issues as well as the broader contours of the political landscape, and the predilections of the respective leadership.

181 Alexander, *op. cit.*: 231. Father Tshongase cites an isiZulu term, *gobongwane*, which means "empty box" and is a dismissive, derogatory term for Indians. He explains that an empty box, like a box of matches, is something that is light and can easily be pushed around. He states further that the word continues to be used, but as the meaning has become more generally known, black Africans are less likely to invoke it. In fact, doing so could provoke retaliation from Indians.

182 Popke, *op. cit.*: 243.

183 Meer, 1969: 89.

184 Naidoo and Chetty, *op. cit.*: 189.

185 For more information on the violence, see Hughes, 1987. Situations of racial or ethnic violence typically suppress individual characteristics and magnify group identities. But this is never absolute. In the violence that broke out after Kenya's contested presidential elections in 2008, for example, middle-class status significantly mediated tribal identities, a person's profession and other achieved attributes being more important determinants of their beliefs and actions than ancestry; see Gettleman, 2008.

186 Cato Manor remained a place of volatility. In 1959, in reaction to police raids that smashed home-brew operations there, as well as some police killings, enraged Zulu women marched into a municipal beer hall armed with sticks where they attacked men and wrecked the place.

187 Meer, *op. cit.*: 116, emphasis in the original.

188 Arkin et al., 1989: 290.

189 Noble, 1994. Edwards, 1994, describes the machinations of political patronage on the part of the House of Delegates (see below) that led to this favouritism.

190 Maier, *op. cit.* A book on South African "urban legends" recounts the same story (Goldstuck, 1994: 55–56), and a similar one where a maid asks to borrow a tape measure from her madam: she wishes to change the curtains when she takes over title to the house (p. 51). See, also, Noble, *op. cit.*

191 Maier, *op. cit.*, Raghavan, *op. cit.*, Noble, *op. cit.*

192 Gibson, 2004: 40, 42–43, 49–50.

193 Leggett, 2004.

194 Forrest, 2003. Most recent surveys underscore these trends: in 2007, Indians were the only group whose members felt they had less control over their lives than in 1990, during the apartheid era; see Govender, S., 2007a.

195 *New York Times*, 2002.

196 One newspaper account remarked upon the "huge turnout from the South African Indian community", a perception greatly at odds with my own firsthand observation. Another report claimed that most of the Indians in attendance were drawn from religious groups: Christian, Hindu and Muslim; if true, that would have limited the potential of striking cross-racial business deals there; see *The Times of India*, 2002b, and Naidoo, 2002.

197 This practice was commonplace; see Desai, *op. cit.*: 37. The Afrikaans terms for the tin mug and plate used for this purpose are *blikbeker* and *blikbord*. In 2009 popular maskanda performer Phuzekhemisi released a new song, also entitled "AmaNdiya". He claimed that it was partially inspired because "there are some Indians that look down on us and some treat our people (who work for them) like slaves"; Mahlangu, 2009.

198 Bauer, C., 2002.

199 Jubasi and Mkhize, 2002. This forum presaged the Native Club, to be discussed in Chapter 4.

200 Quoted in Govender and Mkhize, 2002.

201 Khumalo, 2003. In 1984 South Africa established a Tricameral Parliament, with each of three racial groups allotted their own subdivision: whites,

coloureds, and Asians (predominantly Indian). The House of Delegates was the Asian body, but it received lukewarm support from its constituents, many of whom felt it was relatively impotent and symbolised collaboration with the apartheid regime. Black Africans were stripped of any political rights in South Africa, but granted citizenship in a cluster of ethnic homelands or Bantustans.

202 From an interview conducted by the author with Mpendulo Nyembe in Durban, 19 August 2002.

203 *The Star*, 2003.

204 Specifically, between the years of 1960 and 1994, which only partially covered the apartheid era.

205 Bose, 2003.

206 Naidoo, S., 2008.

207 *Sunday Times*, 2006a.

208 Smith, 2006.

209 *The Star*, 2006. This song translates from the isiZulu as "My machine, my machine, please bring my machine." The overt reference is to a machine gun; the subtext is sexual. This song will be discussed in detail in Chapter 3.

210 Govender, S., 2007b. A film released the same year and screened in South Africa, *Gandhi My Father* (Feroz Abbas Khan, dir., 2007), explored the troubled relationship between Gandhi and his son Harilal (who even converted to Islam at one stage in order to defy his father). It exposed a dimension of Gandhi's private life, and while critical, the movie reveals the complexity of the man, rather than seeking to condemn his basic moral character.

211 Clark, 2005. This was one of many proposed changes that met public opposition. Some people decried being burdened with the government's choices of heroes to be commemorated; others resented the loss of their particular honorees. In 2008, 10 000 protestors carrying traditional weapons marched against the change of a highway in Durban that had previously borne the name of the Zulu-based Inkatha Freedom Party leader Mangosuthu Buthelezi to Griffiths Mxenge Highway, reflecting the ongoing struggle between these two political parties (Mxenge was Xhosa and an ANC member); some demonstrators even threatened to blow up the highway.

212 Naipaul, 1980: 109.

213 Naidu, 2002.

214 Sewchurran, 2003. Community activist Joy Ellappen agrees that new immigrants – and she specifically cited Pakistanis and those from "Arab countries" – have treated black Africans badly and "have caused major upheavals".

215 Rademeyer, 2005.

216 *Ibid.*

217 *Ibid.*

218 *Weekend Argus*, 2006.

219 Khumalo, 2005.

220 Such was the case, for example, during protests in Kliptown, outside Johannesburg, in 2007; see Bangerezako, 2007.

221 Kockott, 2004. Webster reports that the commission of inquiry into the 1949 Cato Manor riots described tensions arising from Indian men using their financial clout to seduce black African women, but then abandoning them and offspring they may have sired (*op. cit.*: 40–41). And during an ethnographic study of public housing projects in Chicago in the early 1990s conducted by an American of Indian heritage, the investigator discovered that local African-Americans conflated people of Indian and Middle Eastern heritage, using "Ay-rab" as a generic term (see Venkatesh, 2008: 228). Furthermore, the author describes an incident in which enraged community members stormed a local shop threatening to kill a Middle Eastern employee they claimed had raped a 16-year-old African-American girl, and given her a venereal disease. As it turned out the charges were apparently mistaken; even so, the store owner turned over cases of beer and soda to appease the crowd's anger. The investigator himself was mistakenly suspected of sexually exploiting local young women after he convened a writing workshop with them (*ibid.*: 90–93, 217–218).

222 As mentioned, one important source of tension – and a point that Ngema highlighted in "AmaNdiya" – is that Indians have failed to support the ANC in the general elections held since 1994. A leader of the Minority Front Party, a group allied with the ANC, stated, "I've heard it on many occasions that Indians should get a thrashing like in 1949 because they're siding with Whites during elections"; quoted in Naidu, *op. cit.*

Chapter 3

223 As noted, the apartheid regime banned expression that it felt was dangerous, e.g., *The Wall* by Pink Floyd. On the other hand, the same song was played repeatedly by anarchists during riots in Athens in 2008 to rally support against their government. And British gay activist Peter Tatchell launched the Stop Murder Music campaign in 2005 against homophobic lyrics in reggae music that he believed generated violence against gays and lesbians. The operation succeeded in cutting into the success of concerts and record sales, and major artists signed a pledge against such expression. The artist Sizzla, however, initially reacted to attempts to control his discourse in much the same way that Ngema had: "They can't ask me to apologise," he said. "They've got to apologise to God because they break God's law"; quoted in Petridis, 2004.

224 The American spiritual is shown in the movie *A Truly Wonderful Adventure* (Lederie Bosch, dir., 2007), which shows mourners singing it at the funeral of an 11-year-old coloured boy killed by police in a Cape Town township in 1980 during a period of widespread school boycotts and street demonstrations. *Amandla! A Revolution in Four Part Harmony* (Lee Hirsch, dir., 2002) highlights the great breadth of anti-apartheid songs, using period film clips as well as contemporary interviews with key performers of the time.

225 Godwin, 2007: 6, 7.

226 Steinberg, 2008: 203.

227 Venter, 2003c.

228 Maluleke, 2003.

229 Venter, 2003a.

230 Venter and Mothibi, 2003, Venter 2003b.
231 The issue of the public music broadcasts was settled after a judge ordered the Department of Correctional Services to disconnect speakers in the section where the Boeremag prisoners were being held, but the men were required to supply four of the non-Boeremag prisoners with radios and batteries so they might listen to whatever music they wished to, because they couldn't afford such equipment themselves; *ibid*. The trial dragged into 2012; by 2009 its costs were estimated at R30 million.
232 *CNN.com*, 1994.
233 www.wikipedia.org, 2007.
234 Govender and Rondganger, 2004.
235 *News24.com*, 2007c.
236 Boloka, 1999.
237 *News24.com*, 2007d. The phrase comes from the national lottery slogan, "Tata ma'chance, Tata ma'millions".
238 Evans, 2002.
239 South African Press Association, 2002b.
240 Press Trust of India, 2002b.
241 South African Press Association, *op. cit.*
242 www.stormfront.org, 2006.
243 www.rhodesian.net, 2003.
244 See Terreblanche, 2003.
245 www.stormfront.org, *op. cit.*
246 This is derived from an interview conducted by the author with Jane Duncan in Johannesburg, 8 August 2008.
247 South African Press Association, 2004.
248 Viljoen, B., 2003
249 In the midst of this controversy, notorious white racist Eugene Terre'Blanche was murdered by two of his farmworkers, purportedly in anger over unpaid wages. This high-profile incident during a time of intensified racial tension validated the fears of those who believe in the linkage between hate speech and crime.
250 Rapitso, 2006.
251 *Ibid*. An article with the striking headline "Mercenary motives mug lobolo, taking its dignity", detailed how a group carrying lobola to the prospective bride's house was mugged, the thieves having been tipped off by the prospective bridegroom, and also reported how another man tried to trick his would-be in-laws by paying in fake bills; see Khumalo, 2008. The article was accompanied by a picture of Jacob Zuma's new fourth wife, her plump face beaming from a thick collar of money placed around her neck and attached to her hat during her wedding to the politician.
252 An interesting accommodation was made between these two approaches to the practice of medicine in 2007 when the Traditional Health Practitioners Act was passed, allowing traditional healers to register as businesses and be eligible for reimbursements from medical-aid claims; see Khanyile, 2007. Implementation, however, has been slow.
253 Quoted in Mabuza, 2003. Despite the accommodating regulation in Johannesburg proper, the council in the adjacent township of Alexandra tried to close down a man's business of selling live goats and sheep for

slaughter. It wrote him a letter that it is "inconsistent with the vision of Johannesburg as a 'world-class African city'"; see Silverman and Charlton, 2004.

254 Ntshangase, 2006.

255 Becker, 2006.

256 Von Bonde, 2003.

257 Ntshingila, 2006.

258 Khumalo, 2006.

259 See Dubin, 2006a, Ch. 3.

260 Jung, 2003: 436, 445.

261 Khumalo, *op. cit.*

262 LaFraniere, 2005.

263 Moya, 2005.

264 Mthethwa, 2007. Another source credits Andile Gumede with reviving virginity testing in 1993; see Reuters, Johannesburg, 2001.

265 Mthethwa, *op. cit.*

266 Leclerc-Madlala, 2001: 538. The Reed Dance in Swaziland is shown in the documentary film *Without the King* (Michael Skolnick, dir., 2008). An ethnomusicologist and cultural researcher argues that the Reed Dance was phased out during Shaka's rule and, like mass virginity testing, is an "invented tradition". He calls the latter "living proof of how desperate people can abuse culture and heritage to satisfy personal desires"; Xulu, 2007.

267 Parashar, 2004.

268 Leclerc-Madlala, *op. cit.*: 540. Another report indicates that even virgins resort to doing such things as inserting animal fat or Panado tablets into their vaginas to "highlight" their hymens. A shout by the tester of *Intombi nto* indicates that the girl is a virgin; *Khona ogudlayo* ("someone has paved the way") declares she is not; Ndlovu, 2007.

269 Moya, *op. cit.*

270 Leclerc-Madlala, *op. cit.*: 539–540. A girl may receive a "B" grade, having had one or two experiences of intercourse, and still be certified a "virgin".

271 The status of virgin also brings financial returns: according to Leclerc-Madlala, "The standard ten head of cattle could be supplemented by an additional head, the 'eleventh cow', if the girl was found to be a virgin. This cow was known as *inkomo kamama*, mother's cow, and was given to the girl's mother as a sign of thanks from the in-laws for providing them with a 'pure' daughter-in-law" (p. 544).

272 Govender and Mkhize, 2003.

273 Oliphant, 2006.

274 Tolsi, 2007b.

275 Mthethwa, 2005.

276 Zondi, 2007. The Children's Rights Act does not ban male circumcision, but allows a young man the right to refuse to participate in it.

277 One writer notes, "For the majority of women who live in rural areas, customary law basically consigns them to be minors all of their lives, under their fathers, their husbands, their brothers, or who[m]ever"; LaFraniere, *op. cit.*: A14.
The Zulus discontinued the practice of circumcision under Shaka. But in

April 2010, President Jacob Zuma announced that he had recently undergone the procedure, and King Goodwill Zwelithini called for its restoration as an AIDS prevention measure.

278 Leclerc-Madlala, *op. cit.*: 546.

279 That same year a minor flare-up occurred over the ritual slaughter of a goat at a Xhosa village that had been erected for the festival.

280 Randall, 2003, Mjekula, 2003, Philp, 2003. The incursion of contemporary culture into traditional realms is wonderfully captured in Zakes Mda's *The Heart of Redness* (2000) where a tribal chief names children after cellphones and satellite dishes.

281 Jack, 2003.

282 *Ibid.*, and Philp, *op. cit.* As is typical in such cases, none of the people who criticised the play had actually viewed it.
A sad footnote was another controversy that beset the production: two of the lead male actors were accused of raping two women while the play was in rehearsal in Grahamstown. There were some calls for them to be dropped from the roster, but ultimately the play went forward as cast; see Adkins, 2003.

283 Jack, *op. cit.*

284 Mann, 2003.

285 Randall, *op. cit.*; emphasis added.

286 Mantshantsha, 2006. Eleven kings are supported through public coffers; their salaries alone amounted to R10 million in 2009. The allotment to the Zulu royal house increased to R40 million in 2009, and an additional R60 million was earmarked for renovation of his palaces; Piliso, 2009.

287 For example, in 2003 the Cape High Court invalidated customary law whereby women were denied inheritance because of being female as unconstitutional, and the Constitutional Court has supported a woman's right to assume positions as local chiefs. In several instances this has resulted in fierce battles where women have stepped forward to take up power. In one case a five-year struggle has resulted in ten people being killed and extensive property damage, with the woman wishing to take charge being forced into hiding; Sokana, 2007b. The Congress of Traditional Leaders of SA does not endorse the Constitutional Court decision, and in a case in North West Province some villagers support a women's attempt to wrest control from an uncle and younger brother, but others reject her bid. One man announced, "This whole thing of women chiefs is unheard of in our village. It would be like cursing our future generation [*sic*] if we were to allow the principles of our tradition to be bent because we want to be like other nations." The woman herself cites the constitutional guarantee of gender equality and has stated, "There's no custom that is static … it is dynamic and changes all the time… To be a chief is a birthright … We don't only belong in the kitchen"; see Thakali and Gerardy, 2008.
For a study of the current status of traditional leaders in South Africa, see Ntsebeza, 2005.

288 Hiney, 2006: 2.

289 Because his body was never found, his followers clutched onto the hope that Makana would return to them, for a long time. President Mandela

suggested that Robben Island be renamed in Makana's honour, and a ferry that transports visitors from the mainland to the island is named after him.

290 Sesanti, 2003.

291 *Ibid.*

292 Kennedy, 2005. For a feminist discussion of this issue, see Alcoff, 1991/1992.

293 Brink, 1996. This issue comes up repeatedly; see, e.g., the discussion in Chapter 6 of several controversies over white artists depicting the custom of black African male initiation.

294 Yengeni was ordered to remain under the supervision of correctional services for two years, and expected to perform 16 hours of community service per week; Mafela et al., 2007a, and Dawes, 2007. His critics felt Yengeni's situation involved a heavy dose of special treatment, including the fact he was granted permission to leave the Cape Town area to buy the bull, even though this was outside the perimeter he was supposed to stay within; Peters and Keating, 2007.

295 See *Saturday Star*, 2007.

296 Oliphant, 2007. According to this article "to have been in jail is considered *ihlazo* [a blemish]". Cleansing is necessary to remove bad luck.

297 *Ibid.*

298 Mafela et al., *op. cit.*

299 The commission is an 18-member government body; the Icamagu Institute is a private information and resource centre that advocates on behalf of traditional religion and culture.

300 The Animals Protection Act prohibits unnecessary suffering; the investigation was terminated once the SPCA determined it did not have adequate evidence to lay criminal charges in this case, however.

301 Johnson, 2007.

302 Osshar, 2007. All sides to the controversy raised ridiculous comparisons. The CEO of the National Heritage Council called the criticism of Yengeni "selective treatment", and asserted "The SPCA doesn't complain about fishermen hooking animals in their mouths. We have not heard their complaints about game hunting. We have not heard their complaints about motorists and airlines ... for knocking insects which are in the way"; see Burbidge, 2007.

303 Jacobson, 2007.

304 Quoted in Oliphant, *op. cit.*

305 *Ibid.*

306 Dawes, *op. cit.* After the ANC's December 2007 Polokwane meeting, Yengeni was elected to its national executive committee.

307 Boyle, 2007b.

308 *Op. cit.*

309 www.eProp.co.za, 2006.
The lyrics of "Umshini Wam" are rather simple, and repetitive:
My machine my machine
Please bring my machine
My machine my machine
Please bring my machine
My machine my machine

Please bring my machine
Please bring my machine
You're pulling me back
My machine, please bring my machine.

In 2009 Reddy found himself in the middle of a new controversy: he was implicated in the bribery of the Free State premier in order to gain approval for another casino.

310 Wines, 2007.

311 Gordin, 2006b.

312 Blair, 2006.

313 Her father was a freedom fighter who died in exile in Zimbabwe. She herself went into exile in the Netherlands after the trial.
Gunner (2008) writes an extensive history of "Umshini Wam", but strangely, does not directly address the sexism implied in it.

314 Ansell, 2007.

315 See Maughan, 2006, and Gordin, 2006a.

316 Ansell, *op. cit.*

317 Motsei, 2007: 96, 31.

318 Quoted in *ibid.*: 143.

319 *Ibid.*: 193. Motsei weaves together many strands of traditional beliefs and contemporary theory. She also compares Khwezi to Sarah Baartman (the so-called "Hottentot Venus") because both women were scrutinised by Western science (a doctor testified that Khwezi was mentally ill because of the trauma she had suffered during her life); see p. 186. Baartman's tragic fate has made her a common point of reference, even where the equivalence of torment may be significantly disproportionate. For example, when the record-smashing runner Caster Semenya was subjected to medical sex classification testing by the International Association of Athletics Federations, some observers derided the decision as treating her like a "freak" in a public "spectacle"; see Dineo-Gqola, 2009.

320 Something similar happened in 2008 when women in miniskirts defiantly protested at a Johannesburg taxi rank after a woman was assaulted there for dressing that way; see Chapter 8.

321 Motsei notes that the court did not call in "expert testimony" by Zulu elders to confirm or deny Zuma's pronouncements about Zulu culture; *op. cit.*: 185. Another writer condemned Xhosa politician Mbulelo Goniwe for also using "culture" as a way to cajole a young woman to have sex with him, and thereby excuse irresponsible behaviour; see Sokupa, 2007.
In 2009 ANC Youth League President Julius Malema reopened the debate over whether or not a rape had occurred by alleging that a woman who had not enjoyed sex would not wait until the morning to leave the house, nor would she have requested breakfast and taxi fare. His comments triggered a firestorm of criticism, and he was accused of hate speech and gender discrimination in a hearing conducted by the Equality Court. After being found guilty, he apologised 16 months later.

322 Robertson, 2006. Motsei, *op. cit.* notes some similarities between African customs and the Bible regarding paying bride price. Moreover, since Khwezi's father was dead, there would be no one to negotiate lobola for her:

"The one man who could have acted as her father-figure was the one in the dock defending himself against having raped her"; pp. 108–109.

323 Well-known commentator Rian Malan noted that the accuser "was acquainted with Ronnie Kasrils, a KGB-trained master of the dark arts of espionage, presumably including honey pots"; see Malan, 2006. Malan also speculated that there was anger over Zuma being held accountable for purportedly taking a "relatively small" amount of bribe money, when many other prominent ANC members have profited hugely from their political connections.

324 Khumalo, S., 2006.

325 Mangcu, 2007.

326 Rossouw, M., 2008.

Chapter 4

327 *The Star*, 2003.

328 *Sowetan*, 2003. Perhaps not surprisingly, Moyo called former US Secretary of State Colin Powell an Uncle Tom for saying that the Zimbabwean government was "tyrannical"; see Moyo, 2003.

329 A history and complete glossary of Gayle is provided in Cage, 2003. The repressiveness of the 1950s was exemplified by the Immorality Act of 1957, which prescribed a six-year prison term for two men kissing (see the pioneering volume by Gevisser and Cameron, 1995, for a thorough history of gay life in South Africa and Hoad et al., 2005, for a more recent examination of the topic). Gayle gradually permeated the sexual underground throughout the country, and it continues to be used today.

330 Epprecht, 2004. Gays and lesbians have been persecuted in many African countries, e.g. Uganda, where a radio station was fined over a talk show featuring men discussing homosexuality because it supposedly "breached media standards" (*The Star*, 2004), and gays and lesbians have been publicly "outed" in a place where sodomy is punishable by life imprisonment (see Zvomuya, 2006).

331 Wieringa and Morgan, 2005.

332 South African Press Association, 2001. Swapo led the fight for Namibia's independence, and is the current ruling party.

333 *Outright SA*, 2001.

334 *Exit* [South Africa], 2001b.

335 *Mail & Guardian*, 2001.

336 *Exit* [South Africa], 2001a.

337 Cornish, 2003.

338 *The Namibian*, 1997.

339 Günzel, 1997.

340 BBC News radio broadcast, 1998.

341 *Ibid.*

342 Bath, 2000.

343 *Ibid.* Tatchell attempted to arrest Mugabe in 1999 in London, then in Brussels in 2001, where the activist was beaten unconscious by bodyguards. In 2004 Tatchell attempted to lay charges against Mugabe for brutality, homophobia and repression of civil rights (Zimbabwe is part of the Commonwealth), but a judge ruled that Mugabe had immunity because of

his position. As noted, Tatchell has also campaigned against homophobia in music, especially targeting reggae singers.

344 *365Gay.com*, 2006. In one of those juicy scandals that turn up in the high ranks of politics and religion all too frequently and worldwide, Canaan Banana, the first president of Zimbabwe, was convicted of sodomy and indecent assault in 1998 after a series of revelations about him coercing men into having sex with him. A Methodist minister, he served a brief bit of jail time and later died in exile.

345 Bellis, 2002; see Fig. 14, p. 351. Interestingly, Froud was one of the self-identified straight contributors to this exhibition.

346 Carew, 2002.

347 www.worldonline.co.za, 2001.

348 As I wrote this manuscript, I regularly raised this number as new and higher reports came in. A 12 December 2008 article in the *International Herald Tribune* reported the (hyper)inflation rate at 8 quintillion per cent (that means 18 zeroes). At the beginning of 2009, the old Zimbabwe dollar was phased out, and in 2012 the economy was regaining some degree of normalcy.

349 Events in Zimbabwe since 2000 have gone relatively unremarked by other African leaders, including South Africa's former President Thabo Mbeki, who insisted that "quiet diplomacy" was the way to proceed, although his efforts were so quiet that they seemed nonexistent. Whether or not to comment upon the deteriorating living conditions that the bulk of Zimbabweans have experienced has been a dilemma for South African intellectuals, who risk appearing to be "race traitors" for protesting Mugabe's rule. One man asked, "Should black intellectuals, for example, speak out against a white regime's repression of its citizens, but keep quiet when the repression is by a black government, as is happening in Zimbabwe?" (Monageng, 2006). See the discussion of the Native Club, below.

350 Indians living in Zimbabwe experienced what has become a familiar African scenario for those of their ethnicity when police and officials from various agencies raided their homes and businesses and confiscated records, valuables and foreign exchange (such as dollars) in 2003. Because white Zimbabweans had essentially been stripped of their power and resources, Indians feared they were next to be exploited. The government cited Indians for "economic sabotage", blaming them for the country's fiscal train smash; Indians instead saw this as a desperate attempt by the government to grab much-needed cash; see Ismail, 2003.

351 A comprehensive study of life for political prisoners on Robben Island reports that their self-initiated code of conduct forbade homosexuality, and masturbation was defined as "queer" (Buntman, 2003: 241, 246). Another source offers this transgressive joke about two beloved leaders of the struggle for freedom: "Mandela lies in bed on the evening after his release and Winnie enters the bedroom. The old man is already half asleep when she starts making advances. Softly she strokes his hair and then puts her hand under the blankets. Whereupon Mandela wakes up and mumbles: 'Not tonight, [Walter] Sisulu'." (Luirink, 2000: 11).

352 Palmer, 2004. In 2007, however, the SABC admitted that it had eliminated some gay sex scenes from its miniseries *After Nine* and planned to conduct

"postmortems" on talk shows in order to "re-contextualise" those scenes; Sosibo, 2007.

353 See Sowaga, 2004, and Mofokeng, 2006.

354 James, 2002.

355 Ntuli, 2003.

356 De la Harpe et al., 1998: 70.

357 Mthembu, 2005.

358 Tolsi, 2006. The global gay and human rights communities – the latter playing a significant role in the anti-apartheid movement – brought an awareness of gay identity that opened different possibilities for such men in South Africa (Donham, 1998: 12–13). Some gay men in Soweto cited the importance of a gay character appearing on *Dynasty* for the founding of the local gay movement (*ibid.*: 15). Dennis Altman has written extensively about the globalisation of the gay rights movement and its impact within many national contexts, and ties it to related phenomena such as increased urbanisation, consumerism and individualism; see 1996, 2004.

359 Ngcakani, 2007.

360 Khunou, 2004b. This local man identifies himself as a Bishop of the Berachah Bible Church in North West Province. Akinola has been outspoken against same-sex marriage or the ordination of homosexual priests who are not celibate.

361 Ndungane, 2004.

362 Tolsi, *op. cit.* Cape Town has garnered a reputation as an international gay tourist destination, and has profited considerably from this type of branding. Local tourism offices feature a Pink Map to area attractions.

363 Sokupa and Majova, 2006.

364 Lamola, 2006.

365 Tolsi, *op. cit.*

366 Duguid, 2002.

367 De Vos, 2006.

368 Meiring, 2006.

369 Barker, 2005.

370 Sama Yende, 2005.

371 Musgrave and Hartley, 2006.

372 Khunou, 2004a.

373 The indictment was eventually dropped by the women involved. On the issue of political correctness at universities, and campus speech codes, see Kors and Silvergate, 1998.

374 Makgoba, 2005. The position of chancellor at South African universities is a largely symbolic title; in practice, the vice chancellor runs the institution.

375 *Ibid.* Mathosa died in a car accident in 2006 at the age of 29.

376 Makgoba has overseen a tumultuous time on the UKZN campus, which has included strife between Indian, black African and white members of the campus community, as well as controversial administrative decisions regarding hirings and firings, and support for the Centre for Civil Society, which provides outreach to low-income communities and researches urgent social issues. Faculty members and advocates of free expression have voiced concern over what they feel has become an increasingly restricted atmosphere for open inquiry there.

377 *Business Day*, 2006.
378 Morrell, 2005.
379 Muller, 2005.
380 Sparks, 2005.
381 In an example from 2003, a radio presenter declared that 80% of the Springbok rugby team consisted of "thick Dutchmen", referring to the squad's under-par performance and implying that racial transformation of the team was necessary. In that instance, the BCCSA ruled that it was not hate speech and did not incite harm.
382 Matshikiza, 2004b.
383 McLeod, 2005. The awareness of such cultural preferences, forged under oppression, has a parallel with the African-American experience and so-called "chitlin [chitterling]" or "ghetto" tests of knowledge designed to highlight the built-in cultural biases of intelligence measures.
384 Morris, 2005. With the generations-long history of people and ideas regularly going back and forth between rural and urban settings in South Africa, it's extremely difficult to label anything authentic or not.
385 Hofmeyr, 2005, and Roodt, 2005. Headline writers playfully went wild with this story; the titles of these two cited references were "Going ape" and "You can't have your banana and eat it".
386 Amato, 2005b.
387 Donaldson, 2007d. The same article reported that a prayer service for the minister held in Pretoria was stocked with 20 homeless people bused in from a shelter in the central Johannesburg precinct of Hillbrow. One of them told the interviewer he had no idea what the event was or why he was there, beyond the promise of free food.
388 George and Cohen, 2007. This report confirmed the "imported" material detailed in the preceding quote.
389 After Thabo Mbeki resigned the presidency in late September 2008, Manto Tshabalala-Msimang was ousted from the Health Department.
390 In the book *A child called freedom* (London: Century, 2006), British journalist Carol Lee argues that the students who revolted against Bantu education in 1976 found inspiration in classics such as Tennyson's poem "Charge of the Light Brigade" and *Oliver Twist*, by Charles Dickens. Students saw past differences of nationality, race and class and took inspiration from the scrappy nine-year-old's quest for a better life.
391 Mbeki, 2007.
392 Deputy Health Minister Madlala-Routledge advocated the use of antiretrovirals to combat HIV/AIDS, whereas Minister Tshabalala-Msimang and Mbeki were labelled AIDS denialists, and as a result were continuously ridiculed for promoting a dietary regime including the African potato, olive oil, lemon and garlic. Satirist Pieter-Dirk Uys joked that this regimen would prevent HIV "if a woman puts olive oil on the African potato and then inserts it into her k'waaa [sic], like a boulder in the mouth of a cave"; Trillin, 2004: 79.
393 Mbeki, *op. cit.*
394 One of the places the announcement ran was in the *Mail & Guardian*; see March 10: 28.
395 Majavu, 2006.

396 Molewa, 2006.

397 Adebajo, 2006b.

398 Ngobeni, 2006.

399 Quoted in Carroll, 2006.

400 Since 1994 the group has renamed itself the Afrikaner Bond (AB), and claims to be open to women and non-whites, but has a low profile and contributes little to public debate in the country.

To cite just one article that made the connection between the Native Club and the Broederbond, a headline blared "ANC wants 'black broederbond'", which it described as similar to the Afrikaner Broederbond "that promoted poor Afrikaners and advanced their financial causes ... this movement had spearheaded the establishment of life assurance firm Sanlam, banks Volkskas and Volksbank – all Afrikaner institutions – and various other economic giants, some of which still exist today"; Pressly, 2007.

401 Potgieter, 2006. See, also, Rapetsoa, 2006, and Greig, 2006. Comparisons were also made to the all-white settlement of Orania.

402 Memela, 2006a.

403 *Ibid.* This man championed the current government and named names, providing lists of those intellectuals who were approved, and those who were disapproved.

404 Kadalie, 2006. At a certain point President Mbeki announced that the Native Club would not be racially exclusionary – even Afrikaners might participate – but that hardly seemed a credible possibility given its origins, the exclusion of particular black Africans, and the subsequent defence of the necessity for a racially exclusive "think tank".

405 The pencil test was cited again in 2008 when xenophobic violence claimed the lives of scores of foreigners in the country ("the 21st century pencil test"). Roving mobs asked potential victims to correctly provide the isiZulu names for various body parts, or checked their pronunciation of certain words. If satisfactory responses were not forthcoming, people could be subject to aggression. But this "test", like its apartheid-era analogue, was flawed: South African citizens of non-Zulu backgrounds could answer "incorrectly" as well; see Ndlovu, 2008, and the discussion in Chapter 8.

406 Kadalie, *op. cit.*

407 *Ibid.*

408 Bezuidenhout, 2006. In 2007 Evita announced her candidacy for president, holding a machine gun that she hoped to give to her rival, Jacob Zuma (see Chapter 3). She pledged that she would exclude millionaires who had amassed their fortunes through BEE (in this case, Broederbond Economic Empowerment) deals from her cabinet; see Breytenbach, 2007.

409 Greig, *op. cit.*

410 Du Preez, 2006a.

411 Makoe, 2006.

412 Bunsee, 2006.

413 See, for example, Gigaba, 2006b, and Adebajo, *op. cit.*

414 Bunsee, *op. cit.*, and Kadalie, *op. cit.*

415 Mtimkulu, 2006.

416 Govender, 2007.

417 *Ibid.*

Chapter 5

418 Bunsee, 2006.

419 Burbidge, 2006.

420 At the time when LIO was thrust into the public's awareness in 2002, the company consisted only of Nurse, his business partner and a designer.

421 Nurse and Verridjt, 2003: 35.

422 Author's notes from a lecture entitled "Words & Corporates", delivered 28 June 2003 by Justin Nurse at Wordfest, part of the National Arts Festival in Grahamstown. Nurse was quoted elsewhere stating, "In the same way that junk food pollutes your body, so too can junk advertising pollute your mind"; Ellis, 2003b.

423 *Noseweek*, 2002.

424 Merten, 2004.

425 Garner, 2002.

426 Klein, 2004b. In 2007, Carling Black Label deposed Castle as the most popular beer in South Africa.

427 Kemp, 2003.

428 This bit of history figured into Mbongeni Ngema's *Sarafina!*: a teacher asks her students when the first man arrived in South Africa, but draws blank faces. When she amends the question to the first *white* man, they reply in a chorus, Jan van Riebeeck.

429 Hooper-Box, 2002b.

430 *Ibid.*

431 From an interview conducted by the author with Justin Nurse in Cape Town, 30 October 2003. This and all subsequent unattributed quotes derive from that interview.

432 This is not to imply that he is a member of the elite. Employing domestic help remains commonplace and affordable among large segments of the white population in South Africa, and for most black and Indian middle-class families, too.

433 Author's notes, 28 June 2003. Rumours also circulated at the time that SABMiller had made threats against members of the media who might air such a story.

434 See Dubin, 1995a: 22; see also 1995c, 1996.

435 Nurse and Verridjt, *op. cit.*: 33.

436 Featured in Williamson, 1989: 90. Parodies often run the danger of touching sensitive nerves: in 2011 three young people reenacted the Sam Nzima photograph of the fatally wounded Hector Pieterson being carried by another boy away from the chaotic demonstrations on 16 June 1976, with his grief-stricken sister running alongside. The parody photo went "viral" on the internet, to the dismay of many: the sister seems joyous; the boy subbing as Hector is holding two quarts of beer; and a cigarette dangles from his guardian's mouth.

437 Quoted in Kemp, 2003.

438 Trademark law is predicated on protecting a brand from being confused with another product, or from uses that are harmful to it (dilutes its viability). Dilution can take the form of either blurring or tarnishing; see Berg, 2003.

439 Hemson, 2003.

440 Ellis, 2003a, emphasis added. A key ruling in the US that helped establish the legitimacy of parody was a 1988 case argued before the Supreme Court that pitted the Rev. Jerry Falwell against *Hustler* magazine and publisher Larry Flynt. *Hustler* ran a parody of an advertisement for Campari liqueur that claimed Falwell's first sexual experience was with his own mother, in an outhouse, while he was drunk. The court decided in favour of Flynt, arguing that public figures cannot sue for emotional distress they supposedly experience because of parodies.

441 *Noseweek, op. cit.*: 40.

442 Kirby, 2003b.

443 Kirby, 2003a.

444 *Ibid*. In exchange for its casino gaming licence at Gold Reef City, situated between Johannesburg and Soweto, Abe and Solly Krok were required to provide some type of community amenity, so they built the Apartheid Museum across from the amusement complex; see Dubin, 2006a: 193–194.

445 Legal expenses were covered through pro bono work by lawyers as well as the generosity of supporters. For example, billionaire South African jetsetter Mark Shuttleworth contributed R150 000; Chikanga, 2005.

446 In the next judicial hearing, the lawyer representing SAB bewailed the possibility that if the court sided with LIO, a profusion of additional objects bearing objectionable slogans would be issued, such as mugs and trinkets – a classic case of fearing the initiation of a "slippery slope".

447 *Mail & Guardian*, 2004.

448 Laugh it Off Promotions generates an annual publication on South African youth culture and the Chronicles Calendar.

449 Quoted in Merten, *op. cit.*

450 Amato, 2005a.

451 *Cape Argus*, 2002. The grievance was later dismissed.

452 Klein, 2004a.

453 Krouse, 2005. Moodie (1994) explains that during much of the 20th century alcohol use by miners facilitated a sense of camaraderie among "home fellows" hailing from the same area, but its consumption later changed from promoting solidarity to becoming a means of psychological escape. Rebellious youth condemned excessive drinking as undercutting the liberation movement (see Chapter 5, espec. 177–178).

454 Du Plessis, 2003, and Schroeder and Ellis, 2003. This assertion was habitually repeated but without specifying what body was conferring that honour. An article that appeared in *Sawubona*, the in-flight magazine of South African Airways, after the legalities were over lavished praise on SAB's employment equity and empowerment efforts from the executive level to farmers and other suppliers, and dating from the 1970s and 1980s. It reads like an infomercial, and since no author is listed, may well have been something of the sort; see *Sawubona*, 2006.

455 Chikanga, *op. cit.* The Constitutional Court first convened in 1995.

456 Van Graan, 2005.

457 Author's interview, 2003.

458 This and all subsequent unattributed quotes derive from an interview conducted by the author with Jane Duncan in Johannesburg, 8 August 2008.

Three important legal decisions provide a bit of a counterpoint to this general trend. In the 2002 case of *Islamic Unity Broadcasting Authority vs the Independent Broadcasting Authority, the Jewish Board of Deputies and others,* the Constitutional Court struck down a portion of the Broadcasting Code of Conduct that had prohibited material that "prejudices relations between sections of the population" as too vague, with the likelihood of closing down debate. In 2006 the *Mail & Guardian* successfully argued its case that an exposé of wrongdoing by a former top public official was protected speech; Judge Mohamed Jajbhay had barred publication at a lower judicial level. And the 2007 ruling in the e.tv/Baby Jordan case prohibited prepublication censorship of material; in this instance, prosecutors had worried that the airing of a television documentary on a notorious murder would undermine the possibility of having an impartial presentation of the facts of the case in court.

459 Maughan, 2003.

460 Laugh it Off made headlines again in 2009 after it marketed a shower gel called Zuma, spinning off the story of the politician's alleged rape of an HIV-positive woman. The company was threatened once again with a lawsuit, this time by the ANC.

461 Mpofu, 2006.

462 This and all subsequent unattributed quotes derive from an interview conducted by the author with Ben Cashdan in Johannesburg, 14 August 2008.

A respected South African who criticised the SABC's decision to drop the Mbeki documentary from its schedule nevertheless characterised an earlier film by Cashdan by saying, "As a piece of propaganda it was superb. As a piece of journalism it sucked"; see Green, 2006.

463 Quoted in De Waal, S., 2007. The documentary was eventually screened by the SABC on 3 October 2007.

464 Quoted in Wolmarans, 2007.

465 A much shrewder analysis of the controversy over the film than most was offered by *Mail & Guardian* editor Ferial Haffajee. She contrasted Hani (the radical) to Mbeki (the realist) and noted, "Its subtext appears to be this: what might our country have been like if the radical had not been killed?" Like others, she claims the SABC generally reported on Mbeki in a straightforward style, with no analysis, and that the film was different in this regard; see Haffajee, 2007.

466 Quoted in Ncube, 2006. According to Mark Gevisser, that part of Mandela's speech has been deleted from the ANC website (2009: 359, note 2).

467 Quoted in Nare, 2006.

468 Mpofu, 2007b. This was the most publicised but not the only example of the SABC refusing to air certain stories. It also cancelled an interview with Jacob Zuma, and did not show film of a story on the booing of Deputy President Phumzile Mlambo-Ngcuka at a rally (reports stated that the SABC either denied it had footage of the incident, or its photographer wasn't there when the incident occurred, although he apparently was). See Molele, 2007.

469 *Weekender,* 2006.

470 Quoted in De Waal, S., *op. cit.*

471 I attended a screening at MuseuMAfricA in Johannesburg, 20 July 2007.

472 Donaldson, 2007c. The film was cut down from an original 45 minutes.

473 Zapasnik, 2006.

474 De Waal, S., *op. cit.*

475 Mpofu, 2006.

476 See *Ibid.*, and Rondganger, 2006. In 2009 the SABC refused to air the pilot for *Z News*, a satirical news show modelled on the British series *Spitting Image*, using caricatured puppets. It had commissioned cartoonist Zapiro to produce it, but a spokesperson for the broadcaster likewise labelled Zapiro "right wing". The programme subsequently garnered a great deal of support on Facebook and YouTube, and the SABC was poorer by R1 million.

477 Matshikiza, 2007e.

478 Barron, 2004.

479 Quoted in Yeld, 2007.

480 Moya, 2007.

481 Donaldson, 2007b.

482 Laurence, 2007. Moreover, in 2007 Anthony Brink accused his former friend Roberts of plagiarising significant parts of his own yet-to-published manuscript in the Mbeki biography, throwing the authenticity of Roberts's work into doubt and causing his publisher to postpone a second printing of the book.

483 Jones, 2007.

484 Davids, 2006.

485 See Ismail, 2007a.

486 *News24.com*, 2007b.

487 *Citizen*, 2007.

488 *News24.com*, 2007b.

489 Ismail, *op. cit.*

490 Eaton, 2007.

491 *Sunday Times*, 2007b.

492 Groenewald and Mgibisa, 2007.

493 Naidu et al., 2007.

494 Eaton, *op. cit.*

495 Quoted in Da Costa and Webb, 2006.

496 *Citizen*, 2006c. In 2009 a scandal broke over the falsification of crime statistics in the provinces where South Africa's three major cities are located. The charges included widespread, wilful destruction of dockets, non-registration of some crimes, and reducing charges to less serious offences – all in an effort to diminish the perceived severity of law-breaking and enhance the supposed efficacy of law-enforcement efforts.

497 *Ibid.* A newspaper article calculated that 83 tourists attending the soccer tournament would likely be murdered while in South Africa and stated, "Statistically hundreds more will be raped, assaulted and robbed". It went on to argue, "The maimed, the raped and the injured will go home carrying one clear message ... 'Never visit South Africa again'." It was an astonishing indictment of the government's feeble crime-fighting efforts; Kirk, 2006a.

498 Adams, 2006a.

499 *Ibid.*
500 Bamford, 2006a.
501 Adams, *op. cit.*
502 Bamford, 2006b.
503 Adams, 2006d.
504 Adams, 2006a.
505 Adams, 2006c. A new variation on the phrase entered the realm of global popular culture via the 2009 science fiction film *District 9* (Neill Blomkamp, dir.), set in a futuristic Johannesburg where residents feel under siege by the prolonged visit of alien creatures, the "prawns". In the midst of the struggle to relocate the aliens to a new camp, one of the testosterone-charged soldiers screams, "One prawn, one bullet". (The movie's title alludes, of course, to the apartheid government's destruction of District 6 in Cape Town, and the relocation of its non-white residents to much less desirable outlying sites; the "prawn" epithet echoes the targeting of "cockroaches" (Tutsis) during the 1994 genocide in Rwanda.)
506 Bullard, 2008f.
507 Gerardy, 2008b.
508 *Ibid.*
509 Bullard, 2008e.
510 Bullard, 2007e, b. Bullard claimed that his firing might not have been about racism at all, but due to his criticism of the *Sunday Times* and the corporation that owned it. Bullard wrote in *Empire* in February 2008 about "'creeping mediocrity' in the newsroom" but refused to apologise (Bullard, 2008: 23). In an article published in June in *Empire*, but written before his dismissal, he foretold his own firing and wrote, "I understand the need for a newspaper, particularly one in a transforming society, to reach new markets. That is why we carry so many articles about black celebs and what they drive and how they spend their money. In fact, we have now written about so many of them that there is a very real danger that we are running out of 'write-uppable' darkies" (Bullard, 2008b: 20).
511 Bullard, 2007d.
512 Bullard, 2007a.
513 Bullard, 2008e.
514 Bullard, 2008d.
515 Bullard, 2007a. These remarks were amazingly prescient: in 2009 Jacob Zuma declared that the ANC was invincible, and would rule until the second coming of Jesus – a comment that elicited a great deal of backlash.
516 Bullard, 2007c.
517 Bullard, 2007e.
518 Bullard, 2008c.
519 Mculu, 2008.
520 Berman, 2008.
521 Landman, 2008.
522 Du Preez, 2008.
523 Bullard, 2008a.
524 Gerardy, 2008b.
525 See Bullard, 2008a.
526 Gerardy, 2008a.

527 Leithead, 2005.

528 Bloom and De Wet, 2008: 37.

529 *Ibid.*: 35.

530 Bullard, 2008a.

531 Malala, 2008a.

532 Quoted in Ngalwa, 2008.

533 *Ibid.*

534 Roberts, 2008.

535 Malala, *op. cit.* Some of the commentary implied that black Africans could have only one response to Bullard's column, and that would be repulsion; otherwise they were pathetic victims displaying false consciousness. Monare (2008) wrote, "The only black person who can find this satirically funny is a sorry human misfit whose mental faculties and brain were really damaged by apartheid or colonialism. If Bullard thought this was amusing, he has underestimated the emotional sense of black people or does not believe we have such senses at all."

536 *Ibid.*

537 Jazbhay, 2008.

538 Dlamini, V., 2008.

539 Bloom and De Wet, *op. cit.*: 37.

540 Quoted in *Business Day*, 2007b.

541 *Business Day*, 2007a.

542 Quoted in Ajam et al., 2008.

543 Southey, 1999.

544 Brouard, 2008.

545 Ajam et al., *op. cit.*

546 Serrao, 2008.

547 Isaacson, 2007b.

548 *Mail & Guardian*, 2007d, emphasis added.

549 Malan, 2006.

550 Roberts, 2007.

551 Kupe, 2007a, and Donaldson, 2007d.

552 Kupe, *op. cit.*

553 Barron, 2007. Krüger, 2007 states, "Of late, some newspapers have quite systematically deployed the most ridiculous images available of [the] Health Minister ... in a clear attempt to cement a view of her as simply crazy."

554 See the excerpts and summary of the case in Jajbhay, 2007.

555 Rademeyer, 2007b.

556 *Sunday Times*, 2007a.

557 Malan dubbed Pahad "the Big Man's Rottweiler" and pegged the value of the government's advertisements as R150 million (*op. cit.*: 54). David Bullard referred to Pahad's perspective on things as "Essop's Fables" (2007c).

The *Sunday Times* editor believed he was being monitored by the National Intelligence Agency and that the tax records of him and his reporters were being scrutinised; Malan, *op. cit.*: 46.

This is not the only instance wherein the government has used boycotting of advertising in reprisal for media coverage of which officials disapproved.

In Grahamstown, angry over a story regarding missing funds in the municipality, bureaucrats withdrew ads from the local *Grocott's Mail*; they acted similarly in Port Alfred and Pietermaritzburg over other matters. A university professor of journalism condemned "public resources [being] used to skew media houses towards avoiding critical coverage", and declared such economic shunning to be an "arbitrary use of power" that "contradicts constitutional rights to freedom of expression, as well as the rights to democratic and accountable government"; see Berger, 2008. Another source reports, "ANC members want to centralise government advertising through a single government advertising unit which they say will assist in the economic use of government adspend. But fears are that government spending could be used to punish media organisations critical of it by not placing ads with them"; Kgosana, 2007. In 2012 the ANC called for advertisers to boycott *City Press* after it published Brett Murray's controversial painting *The Spear* (Chapter 6).

558 Momberg, 2007.

559 *Ibid.*

560 Isaacson, 2007a.

561 *Mail & Guardian*, 2007a.

562 Cahill, 2007.

563 Malan, *op. cit.*: 55.

564 Molusi, 1991: 25.

565 See Mazwai, 1991, and Konigkramer, 1991.

566 South African Institute of Race Relations, 1991: vi.

567 *Ibid.*: 52.

568 Reported in *ibid.*: 49, 50.

569 Printed in the *The Star*, 6 July 2006: 14.

570 Maughan and Gifford, 2006. This case was finally scheduled to be heard in October, while this book was in production.

571 Thorpe, 2006.

572 *Ibid.* Zapiro's work continues to spark controversy: as mentioned in note 476, Chapter 5, in 2009 the SABC pulled a film that featured his material, just before it was to be broadcast on an investigative news show. The *Mail & Guardian*'s ombudsman called the SABC "a national embarrassment", and accused it of *broadcastus interruptus*; Krüger, 2009. The timing was significant: this occurred just before the national election that swept Zuma into the presidency.

573 Kirk, 2006b.

574 Quoted in Pannick, 2005.

575 Zuma's fervour for suing continued after Polokwane: he had just won damages from *Rapport* for defamation when he filed a new complaint over a headline he considered degrading and defamatory. Zuma charged "layout foul play"; *News24.com*, 2008. In 2009 Zuma won R1.3 million in damages from the British newspaper *The Guardian* because it labelled him a criminal and rapist. In 2011 he revived his lawsuit against Zapiro's "rape of justice" cartoon on the basis of the Constitution's guarantee of his right to dignity. Zapiro's showerhead cartoons, which have become iconic, have also led some critics to call for him to drop the gimmick, arguing that his point has been made.

576 Derby and Ensor, 2006.

577 *Sunday Times*, 2006b.

578 Moya, 2006.

579 Gigaba, 2006a.

580 Adams, 2006b.

581 Terreblanche and Stephen, 2007. The board's decisions about what to ban can be controversial, e.g. an entry in the 2007 Durban International Film Festival was pulled from the programme after the board objected to the depiction of child sexual abuse, even though supporters of the Brazilian film argued that it carried a strong anti-abuse message; see Tolsi, 2007a.

582 Minnie, 2008 and Kupe, 2007b. This heavy dependence upon income from advertising left the SABC with a tremendous shortfall due to the global financial crisis that began in 2008, and therefore seeking a substantial bailout from the government.
The SABC is critiqued in every way imaginable, including the charge that because 70% of its broadcast time is in English, it is dominated by "a small stratum of 'Afro-Saxons'"; Giliomee, 2003b, citing Ali Mazrui.

583 Naidu, 2008c. It is important to note that in some rural areas, "SABC radio services are the only source of regular information and entertainment". Therefore, one prominent academic argues, it is important that it be "independent and not unduly influenced by political and commercial imperatives"; see Kupe, 2007b: 38.

584 Basson, 2007.

585 Naidu, 2008a.

586 Naidu, 2008c.

587 Minnie, *op. cit.*

588 Haffajee, 2008.

589 Naidu, 2008f.

590 Fisher, 2007.

591 Quintal and Carter, 2007.

592 Mafela et al., 2007b.

593 Carter, 2008.

594 Naidu, 2008b.

595 Habedi, 2006.

596 The drama over Dali Mpofu's multiple suspensions dragged out for a year and a half. He was finally awarded a significant "golden handshake" consisting of bonuses, damages, and legal fees. Factoring in all of its own legal fees as well, the SABC spent R22 million on this case, reaching a settlement at a time when it was already facing a mammoth financial crisis; see Naidu, 2009. As mentioned in an earlier note, the broadcaster sought a R2 billion government bailout in 2009; its unpaid debts to writers, actors, musicians, independent producers and others in the television production industry were generating a major ripple effect throughout the creative community, jeopardising individual livelihoods and threatening to bankrupt companies.

597 Quintal, 2006b.

598 Quintal, 2006a.

599 Broom, 2006.

600 Quintal, 2006b.

601 Memela, 2006b.

602 *Citizen*, 2006b.

603 Swart, 2006: 2.

604 Wade, 2006.

605 Quoted in Naidu and Isaacson, 2006.

606 Krüger, 2007, *op. cit.*

607 Mpofu, 2007a.

608 *Ibid.*

609 Rademeyer, 2007a.

610 *Ibid.*, and *Mail & Guardian*, 2007b.

611 Naidu, 2008d.

612 Leshilo, 2007.

613 Donaldson, 2007a.

614 *Ibid.*

615 Pelser, 2008.

616 Msomi, 2004.

617 Addison, 2008.

618 *Ibid.*

619 Gordin, 2008b.

620 Quoted in Isaacson, 2008a.

621 Isaacson, 2007a.

622 *Mail & Guardian*, 2008.

623 Quoted in Boyle, 2007a.

624 Krüger, 2007. Banda (2008) pointed out that similar measures in Zimbabwe and Zambia have been used to control the media.

625 Quoted in Isaacson, 2008a.

626 The debate over both the proposed media tribunal and the Protection of Information Bill heated up from mid-2010 and throughout 2011 when ANC leaders strongly argued for the necessity of both. Critics believed this was in response to numerous exposés of official misconduct, and likened the schemes to returning to the "bad old days" of apartheid-era censorship. The threat of the implementation of these measures also triggered a negative outcry internationally. As of this writing, the National Council of Provinces was still debating the measure, now known as the Protection of State Information Bill.

627 Malala, 2008b: 20. The passing of the baton of power in December 2007 within Swapo, the ruling party of Namibia (just before the ANC's historic gathering in Polokwane), was quite different – meticulously orchestrated by former party leader and president Sam Nujoma. The party's youth wing euphemistically called it "guided democracy"; see Grobler, 2007.

628 Naidu, 2008e.

629 Quoted by Laurence, 2008; Chuenyane, 2009.

630 Duncan's position is validated by journalist Anton Harber in his book *Diepsloot* (Jonathan Ball, 2011), about the Johannesburg-area township. He discovered that lack of access to the media was central to frustrations erupting as public protests in the streets.

631 Groenewald, 2007c, and Groenewald and Joubert, 2007. An alternative information source circulating in 2008 was a DVD that alleged that after seven days of mourning Mandela's death, black South Africans would commence the slaughter.

632 Van Gass, 2006.

633 South African Press Association, 2007.

Chapter 6

634 Quoted in Joseph and Jacobson, 2007.

635 Mtshali, M., 2007.

636 Yaqoob, 2003.

637 See Friedman, 1996b.

638 Friedman, 1996a. Schmahmann, 1999, claims that Friedman's interpretation of *Useful Objects* as a vagina eclipsed alternative readings, although it is clear from this quote that Friedman offered more than one possibility in her second article about the artwork. Schmahmann writes, based upon a telephone conversation with the artist, "Thompson did not intend for the work to convey this meaning ... this does not mean that it is an illegitimate interpretation; it need hardly be emphasised that the intentions of an artist cannot be used to circumscribe the limits of meaning in an artwork" (note 7, p. 235). However, Schmahmann neither reports what the artist's intentions were, nor does she offer alternative interpretations of the piece.

639 Kgositsile, 1996. File under "be careful what you wish for": a male artist constructed a sculpture out of a silicone penis and a cigar, named it *After the Revolution*, and presented it to a representative of the female speaker of Parliament, Frene Ginwala. He stated, "The artwork serves as a reminder that the previous apartheid state jailed artists, censored sculptures and sought to control the thoughts of individuals"; see Bowyer, 1996.

640 The proposed expansion of the scope of this legislation was debated in 2007/2008; see Chapter 5.

641 Kgositsile, *op. cit.* Kgositsile reportedly admitted later that she might have reacted differently had she known that the artist responsible for making *Useful Objects* was a woman and a feminist; Friedman, 1996b. In other words, viewers often base their evaluation of an artwork on what they see, which may be validated or even altered by knowing the artist's biography and demographic characteristics.

642 Gasa, 1996.

643 *Ibid.*

644 The "failure" of audiences to perceive irony and misconstrue artistic/curatorial intentions was famously demonstrated in two other situations: *Miscast: Negotiating Khoisan History and Material Culture* (South African National Gallery, 1996), and *Into the Heart of Africa* (Royal Ontario Museum, Toronto, 1989); see Dubin, 2006a for details. For an example of an article that demonstrated defensiveness and a lack of empathy for those not conversant with the art world, see Schmahmann, 1996.

645 Clark, 1996.

646 Shown in Bedford, 2004: 103.

647 Friedman, *op. cit.*, 1996a.

648 Shapshank, 1997.

649 Sey, 1996.

650 Hunter, 1996.

651 Atkinson, 1997a. Schmahmann, *op. cit.*, 1999, makes the important point that because Kgositsile was interested in the popular dissemination of

images, it made her resemble 19th-century censors who made a distinction between nude images in high art (which suited their elevated sensibilities) and lower-class pornography (which was mass produced and potentially dangerous by stimulating their animalistic urges). This leads her to "question whether legislation which supports this type of hierarchical distinction between different kinds of audiences has any place in the new South Africa" (p. 231). For a discussion of the Victorian nude, see Beisel, 1993.

652 Douglas, 1966. See, also, Dubin, 1992: 5–6.

653 Taylor, 1997: 43.

654 Atkinson, 1997c, 1997e. Kurgan followed this up with *Home Truths*, where she presented drawings of the same photographic images. One critic slammed this as potentially more risky and abusive because visitors were able to take reproductions away with them, which they could use in whatever context and in whatever manner they wished to. This raised the issue of fine versus mass art once again; see Geers, 1997. And another critic wrote, "Although the second medium provides a distance between viewer and child, the psychic bonds and processes at play are no less fetishised"; Atkinson, 1997d.

655 Atkinson, 1997b: 47. Although Mapplethorpe is predominately known for his homoerotic images, two of the photos in question in the 1990 Cincinnati case were of small children: a naked boy standing on a chair, and a girl whose genitals were partially exposed from under her dress.
Geers, *op. cit.* charged that the images "are essentially paedophilic in nature despite the mother's intentions … Kurgan has introduced us to her private world disguised as art".

656 Atkinson, 1997e, 1997c.

657 Kurgan, 1998: 3.

658 Personal communication, 28 July 2008.

659 Teale, 1996.

660 Knox, 1998.

661 Moolman, 1998.

662 Teale, *op. cit.*

663 Quoted in Dodd, 1998.

664 A criminal charge was laid against Hipper for lewd depictions of a minor, but the decision of the Film and Publications Board exonerating him prevailed; see *Business Day*, 1998. And although a few officials and agencies claimed to be acting on behalf of the welfare of others, attendance at a forum held in Grahamstown to discuss the exhibition and the issue of child pornography was poorly attended; Rademeyer, 1998.

665 Sulcas, 1998.

666 Knox, *op. cit.*

667 Quoted in Sulcas, *op. cit.*

668 Moolman, *op. cit.*

669 Greig, 1998a.

670 Moolman *op. cit.* Hipper's work proved to be controversial again at the National Arts Festival in 2009: his sculpture *Body Mask*, a torso that featured both breasts and male genitalia, was removed from display at the Albany Museum.

671 Spencer-Smith, 1982.

672 Korber, 1982.

673 *Ibid.*

674 De Waal, S., 1996.

675 Braude, 1996.

676 Bauer, C., 1996.

677 Bellis, 2002: 331.

678 Dunn, 1996. As is typical in such instances, the notoriety brought record crowds to the museum.

679 Braude, *op. cit.*, and Douglas, 1996. This sampling included pieces by Steven Cohen, Andrew Verster and Andrew Putter.

680 Bellis, *op. cit.*, 329. This group of works was later relocated upstairs. Bellis's account of curating this exhibition, and retrospectively analysing what happened, is unusually candid and insightful. Her co-curator was Wessel van Huyssteen.

681 Bauer, *op. cit.*

682 Bellis, *op. cit.*, 332, 333.

683 It is presented in Bellis as Fig. 12, p. 349.

684 *Ibid.*: 329.

685 *Ibid.*: 343.

686 Friedman, 1996c. Stellenbosch University is the current name of an institution that was referred to in the past as the University of Stellenbosch. For consistency's sake, I refer to it throughout as Stellenbosch University.

687 Malan, 1996.

688 Friedman, *op. cit.*

689 Malan, 1997.

690 Friedman, 1997.

691 *Ibid.*

692 De Villiers, 1997. Mark Coetzee continued to explore the male body and gay identity: a show in Cape Town in 2001, for example, included photodocumentation of his placing a wreath of flowers spelling out MOFFIE on the grave of Oscar Wilde in Paris, and photos of his own outstretched arm with derogatory terms such as "faggot" seemingly carved into it (the impression was from scratching the negative, not his actual flesh).

693 *Ibid.*

694 Malan, *op. cit.*

695 Malan, 1998.

696 *Ibid.*

697 Roper, 1998b.

698 Kerr, 1998.

699 Malan, *op. cit.*

700 *Pretoria News*, 1995.

701 Wa ka Ngobeni, 2000.

702 Dubin, *op. cit*: 225.

703 Quoted in *ibid.*

704 Von Stauss, 2004: 46.

705 *Ibid.*: 50.

706 *Ibid.*: 52.

707 *Ibid.*: 58–59.
708 Mametse, 2003.
709 *Ibid.*
710 Mothibi, 2003.
711 Reid and Walker, 2003.
712 *Mail & Guardian*, 2003.
713 Reid and Walker, 2004: 98.
714 *Ibid.*: 99.
715 Miller, 2004.
716 *Ibid.* In an instance of life imitating art, a 21-year-old Xhosa man sued his father and ten other men in Equality Court for abducting him, circumcising him without his consent, and then forcing him to eat his own foreskin. The young man argued that what happened to him was both unconstitutional and violated his Christian principles; see Huisman, 2009. The judge ruled that circumcision is illegal unless consented to by the young man being initiated.
717 Sichel, 2002.
718 Sichel, 2006.
719 *Ibid.*
720 Sichel, 2005.
721 Quoted in Richards, 2004: 56.
722 Brodie interview, 2003: 3. Another person working with this subject matter deserves mention: in Mgcineni Sobopha's *Mix Media Blanket Series* the artist brands the type of blankets used in initiation with explicit images of circumcision.
     Moreover, an obvious artist to discuss in relation to his mixture of traditional ritual and contemporary reality is Samson Mudzunga, who has been embraced by a globalised art world but much criticised for his work, and even arrested for his performances, in his home community. Mudzunga has been written about extensively, and is omitted here simply due to space considerations.
723 Richards, *op. cit.*: 52
724 O'Toole, 2004.
725 Johnson, 2003.
726 Ledimo, 2004b: 238.
727 *Ibid.*
728 Johnson, 2002.
729 Gresié, 2006: 81.
730 Van den Ende, 2004: 103.
731 Williamson, 2000.
732 Goniwe, 2000. Similar issues surfaced in a video by Steven Cohen, *Maid in South Africa* (see below for details).
733 Pienaar's language was much blunter: "it's actually black artists who are putting the zeroes behind their artworks in this country, and black artists who are taken on world tours, and they who can afford new BMWs"; Pienaar, 2000.
734 Quoted in Van Bosch, 2000.
735 Pienaar, *op. cit.*
736 *Ibid.*

737 Twiggs, 2000.

738 Matthews, 2000. Performance artists Peter van Heerden and André Laubscher have also staked out male Afrikaner identity and history as their creative terrain. In 2006, for example, they reenacted mock executions at Boer War and apartheid-era sites. And in 2008 Van Heerden was whipped and hung on a cross during a performance art piece at the Klein Karoo National Arts Festival in Oudtshoorn. People threw beer bottles and insults at him, including the epithet *kaffirboeties*. There were even calls to the police to stop the performance; see Huisman, 2008. The struggle of Afrikaners to cultivate a meaningful identity in the post-apartheid era is the subject of the next chapter.

739 Ledimo, 2004a.

740 White photojournalist Brent Stirton self-censored his work on Xhosa circumcision by agreeing to the king's terms of not showing penises; Pollock, 2003.

741 Hilton-Barber, 1990.

742 Quoted in Hilton-Barber, 1991: 36, and 2001: 40. The 1991 publication was his December 1990 remarks at the Market Theatre.

743 Hilton-Barber, 1991, *op. cit.*: 36.

744 *Ibid.*: 38.

745 *Ibid.*

746 A similar criticism was raised by Khoisan people over the exhibition *Miscast: Negotiating Khoisan History and Material Culture* (1996); see Dubin, 2006a: 66–69.

747 Hilton-Barber, 2001: 42.

748 Rosen, 1992: 11.

749 Hilton-Barber, 1991: 38.

750 Rosen, *op. cit.*: 7. A letter-to-the-editor with the provocative title "Those circumcision photos: arrogance or ignorance?" responded to Hilton-Barber's defence of his work (O'Neill, 1991). The writer claimed that a black photographer likely would have never carried out such a project, but if he had, "the black community would have had at least the power ... the exhibits would have been withdrawn". He demonstrates his own arrogance, presuming to know what would happen in such a hypothetical situation.

751 Rosen, *op. cit.*: 11, emphasis added.

752 Michelsen, 1995.

753 Gresié, 2004: 63.

754 Murinik, 2004: 81.

755 Hilton-Barber, 2001: 42, 45.

756 Hilton-Barber, 1991: 39.

757 Hilton-Barber, 2001: 41.

758 Agence France-Presse, 1999.

759 Minty, 2006: 432.

760 Mbita, 1999.

761 *Ibid.*

762 Agence France-Presse, *op. cit.*

763 Kennedy, 1999.

764 Quoted in Jacobson, 2005.

765 Donaldson, 1999.

766 Willoughby, 2005.

767 Friedman, 1994.

768 Geers, 1998.

769 Ferguson, 1998.

770 Blignaut, 1998. Ferguson reports that the Pretoria City Council also banned the intervention.

771 Geers, *op. cit.*

772 Ferguson, *op. cit.*

773 Hammond, 1998.

774 Cohen, 1999: 55.

775 *Ibid.*

776 Cohen, 2002.

777 Shaw, 1993.

778 Hopkins, 2001: 41

779 Greig, 1998b, emphasis added. Another critic wrote, "The assembled right-wingers were confused. But mostly, they were pissed off. Believing that Geers was a German artist who painted with his own shit, they stood proudly to announce, *'Ons is nie kuns nie'*" (We are not art); Atkinson, 1998.

780 Seeger and Bristowe, 1998. Beezy Bailey also ran afoul of those in charge of a military installation: in 1996 a work of his was banned from display at the Cape Town Castle, headquarters of the South African Defence Force. The piece, *Stag Party*, featured 13 clay penises surrounding two clay breasts.

781 *Ibid.*

782 Levin, 1998: 27.

783 "Belinda", 1998.

784 Levin, *op. cit.*: 27.

785 Roper, 2002.

786 Reid, 2004: 63.

787 Cohen's controversial video *Maid in South Africa* (2005) featured his octogenarian ex-nanny and housekeeper Nomsa Dhlamini clothed in lingerie, high heels and nipple caps. A soundtrack repeated in the background, "If you don't want to fuck me, then fuck off." She, meanwhile, dusted and cleaned. Many people were offended by the piece, and it raised questions about the exploitation of black labour and the perpetuation of stereotypes in a way similar to Piet Pienaar's use of a black female doctor in his performance piece about circumcision. Dhlamini also appeared with Cohen in *Cradle of Humankind* at the Grahamstown festival in 2012, and although some critics again raised the question of exploitation, the response was mostly laudatory.

788 Blignaut, 1999. In 2008 the Education Department removed Cohen from its visual arts curriculum list of materials as "not suitable for school learners", as if acknowledging the potency of the "threat" in his infamous statement about children; see *South African Art Times*, 2008.

789 Pollak, 2000.

790 Quoted in Underhill, 2000.

791 Wierzycka, 1998.

792 Wilhelm, 1999.

793 Mokoena, 2002.

794 Quoted in Asmal and Chidester, 2004. The bans on *A World of Strangers* and *The Late Bourgeois World* were lengthy: 12 years and a decade, respectively. The ban on *Burger's Daughter* was lifted after six months, leading some to argue that Gordimer was being held up as a token example of the broadmindedness of the apartheid government.

795 *Ibid.*

796 McGreal, 2001. *Hamlet* was also excluded because William Shakespeare was alleged to be "too Eurocentric".

797 Swarns, 2001.

798 Carroll, 2003.

799 Schoonakker, 2004. Farrar, Straus and Giroux reportedly rejected the manuscript because of its "meandering quality", and the fact that Roberts inserted himself into the narrative.

800 Jacobson, 2006.

801 Asmal and Chidester, *op. cit.*

802 Matshikiza, 2004a.

803 De Waal, S., 2004b.

804 Schoonakker, *op. cit.*

805 Qunta, 2007. A remarkably similar statement was made about J.M. Coetzee: "The man must be a literary genius – everybody says so. So maybe I'm a Philistine, but I believe that most people read for enjoyment. I did not enjoy *Elizabeth Costello*. In fact, I skipped pages – the boring bits"; Els, 2003.

806 Kenny, 2003.

807 *Citizen*, 2003.

808 Quoted in Donadio, 2007.

809 A key scene in *Disgrace* is when Lucy, the professor's daughter, is gang-raped by three black intruders, an event about which one critic writes, "Her womanly flesh is the notepad on which the debt of colonists is written and payment extracted"; Horrell, 2002: 29. A reviewer of Gordimer's *Loot* (2003) suggests she alludes to *Disgrace* in her own writing when a woman is presented with the opportunity to join a polygamous marriage, just as Lucy was offered marriage as future "protection" (De Kock, 2003).

810 Donadio, *op. cit.*

811 Quoted in Momberg, 2003.

812 *Ibid.*

813 *Citizen*, *op. cit.*

814 Blatchford, 2003.

815 See De Kock, *op. cit.*

816 De Waal, S., 2003. To add insult to injury, Coetzee was featured in an ad campaign sponsored by the Australian government targeting immigrants who have not taken out citizenship. He moved to Adelaide in 2002, and later became an Australian citizen; *Citizen*, 2006a.

817 Mpanza, 2003.

818 Momberg, *op. cit.*

819 From an interview conducted by the author with Brett Murray in Woodstock, Cape Town, 6 July 2012. All subsequent unattributed quotes derive from that interview.

820 Blignaut, 2012: 12.

821 This is another robust example of the politics of diversion: Nzimande was

called out by the *Mail & Guardian* for leading the march against the Goodman Gallery on the same day he was expected to attend a critical meeting to straighten out a mess at the Central University of Technology in Bloemfontein, in his capacity as minister of higher education and technology; see Macfarlane, 2012.

822 Recall that a clergyman spraypainted Steven Cohen's *Pope Art* and Christians stole a Bible from a Mark Coetzee work that also included a penis (Chapter 6); moreover, a man spraypainted a *Bitterkomix* image of fellatio exhibited in Durban, to be detailed in Chapter 7.

823 Following an appeal by the Goodman Gallery, this ruling was overturned in mid-October 2012, after the furore had largely died down.

824 From an interview conducted by the author with Liza Essers in Johannesburg, 4 June 2012. All subsequent unattributed quotes derive from that interview. Moreover, the contingent nature of controversies is revealed by the relatively "non-event" status accorded a painting displayed at the AVA Gallery in Cape Town in August 2012. Ayanda Mabulu's "Umshini Wam" *(Weapon of Mass Destruction)* also depicted Zuma with his genitals exposed, but some combination of the artist's race (he is black), and the communal fatigue resulting from the battle that had unfolded merely months earlier, let this work pass with minimal commentary and no social disruption.

825 Prince, 2012, Mkhabela, 2012.

826 Vollgraaff, 2012.

827 Mtshali, N., 2012a.

828 Mtshali, N., 2012b.

829 Sama Yende, 2012.

830 Oppelt, 2012.

831 Moloto and Mofokeng, 2012.

832 Ngalwa, 2011.

833 *Citizen*, 2012.

834 In *Sunday Independent*, 24 June 2012: 16.

835 Jansen, 2012.

836 Thepa, 2012.

837 Lento, 2012.

838 Recall that Haffajee has been embroiled in controversies before, such as when she published one of the Danish cartoons of Muhammad while she was editor of the *Mail & Guardian* (Chapter 2), and when she was condemned as a "black snake in the grass" for *City Press*'s investigation into the financial dealings of Julius Malema (Chapter 5). In fact, one journalist argued that the attack on *City Press* was partly motivated by an ANC vendetta against the paper because of its penetrating investigative reporting: "It is ironic that *The Spear* exposes Zuma's most painfully private parts at the same time that the press has succeeded in exposing his inner core" (De Waal, M., 2012).

839 Quoted in Smith, J., 2012.

840 Chauke et al., 2012.

841 See, e.g., Gevisser, 2012.

842 One of the most widely circulated commentaries on this controversy was by Achille Mbembe, who argued that "the black body is still a profane body", thereby suggesting a link with other controversial artworks such as

Robert Mapplethorpe's contested photograph *Man in Polyester Suit* (1980); see Mbembe, 2012.

843 Lamola, J., 2012, emphasis added.

844 Bauer, N., 2012.

845 Quoted in Merten, 2012.

846 Quoted in Bauer, N., *op. cit.*

847 Ndletyana, 2012.

848 Reported in Nxopo, 2012.

849 Quoted in *Sunday Times*, 2012.

850 Jansen, *op. cit.*

851 Tepper, 2011: 49–50.

852 *Citizen, op. cit.*

853 From an interview conducted by the author with Andrew Putter in Cape Town, 9 July 2012. All subsequent unattributed quotes derive from that interview.

854 Quoted in Naik, 2012.

855 Shown in Ngcobo, 2012.

Chapter 7

856 De Waal, S., 2004a.

857 Oliphant mentions another, even earlier disputed exhibition at the Market Theatre Gallery in 1987, when Kim Gray presented photos of black prostitutes. The criticism at that time was the "implication" that all black women were prostitutes (1991/1992: 9).

858 Years later, Mendel's images of people with AIDS were included in the 2000 International AIDS conference in Durban, whereas the work of another photographer was excluded; see Chapter 6.
Editor Max du Preez characterised the *Vrye Weekblad* as anti-establishment, explaining, "We had no respect for authority, and we saw it as our duty to make fun of the Fathers of the Volk"; see Du Preez, 2006b: 6.

859 Witthaus argues that Murray's work was broadly drawn satire and allegorical, and not as specific as Mendel's, thereby sparing it the same type of criticism; see Witthaus, 1989.

860 A contemporary critic writes off the Great Trek as "a largely unstructured migration of the malcontent and the marginalised ... which was reinterpreted by proto-Nationalist ideologues as an heroic exodus"; Powell, I., 2007: 23

861 The Day of the Vow or the Day of the Covenant venerates the date in 1838 when, with God's blessing, a vastly outnumbered contingent of Voortrekkers defeated a huge force of Zulus at the Battle of Blood River.

862 Van Zyl,1989.

863 Perlman, 1989.

864 *Ibid.*

865 Godby, 2000: 73.

866 *Ibid.*

867 In 1989, with the dawning of a new South Africa in sight, Albie Sachs wrote of the expanded possibilities for artists to focus on love, ambiguity, and the broadest range of human emotions and experiences. He rejected the necessary "impoverishment of art" that had existed during the

resistance struggle – which he caricatured as "The more fists and spears and guns the better" – and called for new flights of imagination; see Sachs, 1990: 20.

868 Goldblatt, 2007: 12–13. Goldblatt voiced the same sentiments in his introduction to *South Africa: The structure of things then* (1998): "I don't regard myself as a missionary. I am not in the business of beating a drum … Over the years I have been asked by various people if they can use my photographs for a directly political concern, in other words for advocacy, and I have nearly always refused, because, on the whole, I didn't want other people attaching their messages to what I had done"; quoted by O'Toole, 2008: 32.

869 Powell, A., 2006: 5.

870 Bleach, 1998: 53, 57.

871 Brink, 2007.

872 Powell, I., *op. cit.*: 19.

873 Ronge, 2007.

874 Powell, I., *op. cit.*: 20.

875 Powell, A., *op. cit.*: 4.

876 Gaule, 1996: 19. Interestingly, early in his career Goldblatt took photographs of squatter camps, a phenomenon that American photographers of the 1930s would certainly endorse documenting.

877 *Ibid.*: 23.

878 Godby, 2005: 34. Goldblatt was an assistant editor at *Tatler*; this and another published essay, plus some additional images, ultimately made up *Some Afrikaners photographed*.

879 Gaule, *op. cit.*

880 Goldblatt, 2001: 6. Goldblatt also created a body of work on Afrikaners of a professional standing, but opted to exclude these images from this book; see Goldblatt, *op. cit.*: 17.

881 The apartheid system provided job guarantees for whites in government and industries such as the railroads, which sustained white affluence relative to the non-white population.

882 Powell, A., *op. cit.*: 4.

883 Oliphant, *op. cit.*: 9.

884 Many Afrikaners criticised South Africa's decision to enter World War Two supporting the Allied side, and some expressed openly pro-Nazi sentiments. Godby (2005: 34, 36) argues that *Some Afrikaners photographed* represents Goldblatt working out his feelings about the Nationalists taking power in the postwar period, and his ambivalent feelings about Afrikaners based upon having been a small-statured Jew living among them in his youth.

885 See de Vries, 2007b, and Powell, A., *op. cit.* According to Powell, on that trip Goldblatt met the last surviving member of a family he'd photographed, but the woman had not been a subject of his.

886 Ashton, 2006. Much of the text of *Bitterkomix* is in Afrikaans, but English is mixed in as well.

887 *Ibid.*

888 Quoted in Gurney, 2004.

889 Karac, 2007.

890 For example, Botes won the prestigious ABSA (Bank) Atelier Award in 2004, and both men have exhibited widely, in South Africa and abroad.

891 *Ibid.*

892 Sassen, 2004. Another writer noted, "Botes is a cultural embalmer. He conducts a forensic examination of things past bringing together the fractured elements and recontextualising them with a heavy dose of ambiguity"; Gurney, *op. cit.*

893 Carew, 2004.

894 De Vries, 2007a.

895 Morris, 2006: 51.

896 Kerr, 2002: 135–136. Mason writes that Kerr "risked his own career in defending them [Kannemeyer and Botes] against the university establishment" (2004: 14).

897 An image by Kannemeyer called *White Nightmare, Black Dicks* pictures two frightened white men frantically trying to control penises that look like giant snakes or water hoses that are swaying wildly through the air. One guy says to the other, "Oh my God!! These black dicks are outa control!" The images were drawn over pages from an article published in *Der Spiegel* about South African whites fleeing the country.

898 Ismail, 1995a. According to one report, the same work was rejected for an exhibition at Stellenbosch University, where Anton Kannemeyer was then lecturing, because of its explicitness; see Ismail, 1995b.

899 Quoted in De Waal, S., 2004a.

900 De Vries, 2007a. Spier Contemporary is a biennial exhibition of contemporary South African art held in Stellenbosch.

901 Jamal, 2004: 44, 45.

902 See Barnard, 2006: 147–148. She shrewdly cites the apartheid mindset that obsessively desired that different "races" and their distinctive cultures not mix, as well as its distrust of the "polluting" influence of popular culture (the government banned television until 1976, for example). Her analysis is obviously indebted to Mary Douglas, a name that is conspicuously absent from her bibliography, however.

903 See Kerr, *op. cit.*: 137, and cited in Barnard, *op. cit.*: 148. Grey areas referred to places such as the high-density Hillbrow neighbourhood in Johannesburg that were officially declared to be exclusively for white residents, but eventually become racially integrated, before 1994.

904 Other entries in Kannemeyer's alphabet include "b is for black" and "w is for white": in each case, adjectives borrowed directly from dictionaries demonstrate the negative associations with one colour ("dirty", "sullen", "malignant") and the positive ones linked to the other ("pure", "honorable", "free from guilt"). An additional example is "n is for nightmare", which pictures four bald white men, their eyes downcast, carrying a black man with caricatured facial features who's relaxing on a platform suspended from their shoulders. The team wears what look like Egyptian wrapped skirts or East African kikois, and the entire image is superimposed in front of the Voortrekker Monument; what was formerly a tribute to Afrikaner greatness has become the site of their degradation.

905 Grundlingh, 2004: 487.

906 Excerpted in De Vries, 2006. The book is *Club Risiko: de jaren tachtig, toen*

en nu. (Amsterdam: Nijgh & Van Ditmar, 2006.)

907 Hopkins, 2006: 201, 19.

908 *Ibid.*: 14, and Kombuis, 2006: 236.

909 According to Hopkins, "Before a song could receive airplay on the SABC, the record and lyric sheet had to be submitted for consideration to a committee, which studied it in terms of five criteria: politics, religion, sex, drugs and poor taste. Those not considered satisfactory had deep gouges cut in them with a carpet knife to prevent accidental airplay" (*op. cit.*: 51–52).

910 Du Preez, 2006b: 6.

911 Quoted in Hopkins, *op. cit.*: 173.

912 De Waal, S., 2006.

913 Quoted in Owen, 2008: 6. Swart would have likely been a participant in the tour, but he had been called to military service.

914 See Schuler, 1990, for another example of an audience misinterpreting an artist's message, in this case American performance artist Karen Finley.

915 Grundlingh, *op. cit.*: 504.

916 Hopkins, *op. cit.*: 143. The likelihood of any musical group or event directly affecting political events is slight, but the importance of the Czech band Plastic People of the Universe – and the government's prosecution of its members – in fuelling an underground movement of cultural resistance is frequently cited (most recently in Tom Stoppard's play *Rock 'n' Roll*, 2006).

917 See Roup, 2004: 145, 169–170, and Hopkins, *op. cit.*: 69.

918 *Ibid.*: 183–185. In Stellenbosch and elsewhere where their campus performances were thwarted, Voëlvry relocated to nearby sites.

919 Joubert, 2008.

920 Waldner, 2007a. Jansen has written a study of contemporary white youth entitled *Knowledge in the Blood: Confronting race and the apartheid past* (Palo Alto: Stanford University Press, 2009) in which he states that even though they did not directly experience apartheid they narrowly stereotype black Africans, question the competence of black Africans to run the country, and are not optimistic about their own futures due to a number of government policies that they feel disadvantage them vis-á-vis their black age mates. As of 2009, he is the rector of the University of the Free State.

921 Dlamini, J., 2008.

922 Gower, 2008. In a gesture of reconciliation, Rector Jonathan Jansen also withdrew the university's complaint against the students in 2009 and invited them to re-enroll. The case went to trial in 2010, the students pleaded guilty to *crimen injuria*, and were fined R20 000 each; the university also offered the cleaners R1 million each for the humiliation they had suffered. In 2010 the university launched a programme to send selected first-year students to universities worldwide to gain a more global perspective on issues such as leadership and diversity; in 2011 Archbishop Desmond Tutu opened the Institute of Studies in Race, Reconciliation and Social Justice across from the Reitz residence; and Oprah hailed the "miraculous transformation" of the university when she was awarded an honorary degree there in 2011.

923 Waldner, 2007c.

924 Rossouw, R., 2008. Not surprisingly, some white students at the university

were shocked after a black candidate was elected to be president of the student body in 2009.

925 See Visser, 2007: 12–14.

926 Rank, 2008, reports that there are 150 sites linked to Afrikaners, as well as groups for Indians, coloureds, Zulus, Xhosas, etc. As was the case with the anti-crime sites discussed in Chapter 5, some of them regulate offensive speech, such as the use of *"kaffir"*.

927 Roup, 2004: 40, 46. A major theme of the book on the Afrikaners by Giliomee is protest and revolt, pitting the Afrikaners against the Dutch and the English, as well as black Africans.

928 *Ibid.*: 100.

929 *Ibid.*: 131, quoting Albert Grundlingh.

930 Groenewald, 2007b, quoting Theo Venter, a political analyst, and Anderson, 2007.

931 Krog, 2007, Matshikiza, 2007a.

932 Du Preez, 2003, 2007.

933 Giliomee, 2003b, Van der Westhuizen, 2007.

934 Quoted in Groenewald, 2007a.

935 Roodt, 2007, Du Plessis, 2007 (borrowing an idea from Nick Binedell). Du Plessis makes the important point that Afrikaners lost their relative privilege and not their basic rights. Moreover, according to Visser (2007), more Afrikaans-speaking whites are currently emigrating from the country than English-speaking whites. He refers to the *bly of gly debat* (stay-or-go debate) among Afrikaners; pp. 4–5.

936 As cited in Chapter 4, in 2003 the BCCSA ruled that a radio talk show host was guilty of hate speech (and fined the station he worked for) when he referred to Afrikaans-speaking rugby players as "thick Dutchmen" and had implied the portrayal referred to all Afrikaners.

937 Roodt, *op. cit.* Roodt defends apartheid by stating that Dr Hendrik Verwoerd, a former minister of native affairs and prime minister, built schools and houses for black Africans, "he did not gas them, send them to camps in Siberia, or have them massacred and buried in mass graves" – cold comfort, indeed, to the multitude of victims of the National Party regime; *Ibid.* Roodt has himself been compared to Hitler.

Although he was a critic of apartheid when he was younger, he now refers to "the apartheid myth" and argues that it was "not the crime against humanity it has been made out to be", notwithstanding a "few abuses". With an argument that parallels David Bullard to a degree, Roodt maintains that Afrikaners "selflessly administered the state and created a myriad of institutions for the benefit of others", more so than other white groups did for non-whites in Africa; see 2003b. Roodt accuses "white English leftists" of distorting the general perception of apartheid as being comparable to racial genocide, when it was the English who were guilty of such a campaign in their treatment of Afrikaner women and children during the Anglo-Boer Wars; see 2003a.

938 Waldner, 2007a.

939 Corrigall, 2008.

940 I put this together from a number of translations, all of which demonstrated slight variations. Van Blerk wrote the song along with two friends. Max du

Preez noted, "After the Anglo-Boer War there is nobody in Afrikaner history that you can glorify except maybe rugby players"; quoted in McGreal, 2007.

941 McDowall, 2007. Other Afrikaner heroes are receiving a contemporary "makeover" as well: Andries Pretorius, the 19th-century hero of the Battle of Blood River, was dubbed "charismatic ... the Obama of his day"; Salafranca, 2009.

942 Quoted in Salzwedel, 2007: 48, emphases in the original. A latter-day namesake of the general – in this case a 20th-century member of the Conservative Party – was active in a movement to urge the United Nations to recognise Afrikaners as a "subjugated", "indigenous community"; Jung, 2000: 141.

943 See the photograph with the altered street sign reproduced in Vallie, 2007b. Moreover, 60% of the signage bearing new names in the town were stolen and dumped in a local river (*Mail & Guardian*, 2007c).

De la Rey's name has long been stamped upon streets and institutions: columnist Barry Ronge noted that the suburb he grew up in was called Delarey and he attended Laërskool Generaal De La Rey, both in the Johannesburg area. But like so many historical references, these were largely unremarked aspects of the built environment until recently; see Ronge, *op. cit.*

Working on similar symbolic terrain, six white men replaced street signs for Nelson Mandela Drive with those bearing the name of Clive Derby-Lewis, convicted of the murder of SACP leader Chris Hani.

944 Giliomee, 2007.

945 Peters, 2004.

946 See Owen, 2007, and Gedye, 2007.

947 The group continued to perform gigs, however, and in 2008 released a new recording. The 2009 film *Fokofpolisiekar – Forgive Them for They Know Not What They Do* (Bryan Little, dir.) documented its development and gradual dissolution.

948 All quotes from Wiechers, 2006.

949 Excerpted in De Vries, 2006.

950 Vallie, 2007a, and Roberts, 2012.

951 See Wiechers, *op. cit.*, De Olim, 2006, Breytenbach, 2006. Koos Kombuis also ran afoul of some religious folk when he published a book in 2003 entitled *The Secret Diary of God*. These days Afrikaans cultural festivals may feature black (and brown) as well as white performers, and can attract a racially mixed crowd.

952 Bezuidenhout, 2007: 9–10. A CD by the group Kobus! is entitled *Skuldgevoelvry* (100% guilt-free).

953 *Ibid.*: 13. These lyrics are taken from this source.

954 All quotes from Groenewald, 2007a.

955 Du Plessis, *op. cit.* Gunner reports a similar incident when taxi drivers outside Johannesburg's Supreme Court blared the banned song "Msholozi" (Zuma's clan name) in chorus during the man's rape trial (*op. cit.*: 45–46).

956 Ritchie, 2007b.

957 See Groenewald, 2007b; *News24.com*, 2007a; Ritchie, *op. cit.*

958 *News24.com*, *op. cit.*

959 Hamata, 2007.

960 Pretorius, 2007. It also became the impetus for a one-man play about the general scripted by Rian Malan and staged at the 2008 Klein Karoo National Arts Festival.

961 Ottermann, 2007.

962 www.english.ohmynews.com, 2007.

963 Makhanya, 2007.

964 Du Plessis, *op. cit.*

965 blogmark.mg.co.za, 2007.

966 Quoted in Salzwedel, *op. cit.*

967 La Grange, 2007.

968 Krog, *op. cit.*

969 Kadalie, 2007. These men are, respectively, the last president before the advent of democracy; a former foreign minister; and a leader of the National Party who defected to the ANC.

970 www.africancrisis.org, 2007.

971 Quoted in McDowall, *op. cit.*

972 www.themuso.co.za, 2007.

973 Roper, 2007.

974 Quoted in McGreal, *op. cit.*

975 Van der Westhuizen, *op. cit.*

976 *The Star*, 2007b. Giving credence to the idea that multiple readings are possible for any creative work, "De la Rey" was reportedly a big hit with American soldiers in Baghdad; McDowall, *op. cit.*
An article on the Afrikaans-language long-running hit television music show *Noot vir Noot* cheekily suggested that it would be fun to see a celebrity politician episode featuring a sing-off between Freedom Front Plus leader Pieter Mulder and former ANCYL President Julius Malema performing "De la Rey" and "Shoot the Boer"; Roberts, 2011: 15.

977 Mthethwa, 2008. Recall as well in Chapter 2 that two Indian teachers were threatened with being burned alive in 2005 by people who objected to their way of speaking and their food, and their possible "contaminative" effects on the local culture; in that instance, the protestors were black Africans.

978 Claasen, 2007.

979 Ismail, 2007c.

980 Ritchie, 2007a.

981 This perspective is captured in fictional form at the opening of the novel *Moffie*: "I had been thrown into hell; herded into the Defence Force, into the abattoir of its border war like an animal to slaughter, with no say over my own destiny. Forced to kill people I don't know, for a cause I don't believe in"; Van der Merwe, 2006: 11.

982 Edwards, 2007. For the idea of "Boer-bashing", see Van Oostrum, 2003.

983 Ismail, *op. cit.*

984 Barron, 2006.

985 Ismail, *op. cit.*

986 *Ibid.*

987 Ismail, 2007b.

Conclusion

988 This stratagem also echoes James Hunter's "stories from the front", which he used to introduce the concept of "culture wars" (1991).

989 *Weekender*, 2007.

990 Mngxitama, 2007.

991 Cohen, 2007.

992 Khupiso, 2007.

993 Brooks, 2006.

994 Du Preez, 2007.

995 Hooper-Box, 2002a.

996 Matshikiza, 2007d.

997 Matshikiza, 2007c.

998 Matshikiza, 2007b.

999 See Ho, 2008, and Gerardy, 2008b.

1000 Woon, 2008.

1001 Gerardy, *op. cit.*

1002 See Seme, 2008; Pheko, 2008; Napo, 2008.

1003 Quoted in Dibetle, 2008b, and Sikhakhane, 2008.

1004 Matshikiza, 2008, Awa, 2008.

1005 Rondganger, 2008. At the same time, the *Sowetan* newspaper described the Chinese in South Africa as "insular" and "among the most racist people" in the country; see Gerardy, *op. cit.*

1006 Rostron, 2008.

1007 Khuzwayo, 2008.

1008 Dibetle, 2008b; see, also, Mthethwa, 2008 and Sikhakhane, *op. cit.*

1009 Matshikiza, 2008.

1010 Ford, 2008.

1011 Matshikiza, 2008.

1012 Mabuza, 2008.

1013 See, for example, Accone, 2008; *Citizen*, 2008; Molefe, 2008.

1014 Seme, *op. cit.*

1015 Dibetle, 2008b.

1016 Dibetle, 2008a, and Gerardy, 2008b.

1017 Rondganger, *op. cit.*

1018 Wu, 2008, and Dibetle, 2008a.

1019 Kenny, 2008. In an incident cited in Chapter 1, a young Xhosa girl won a regional pageant for Miss Teen India in 2007, a controversial decision that sent the judges fleeing in the face of an enraged audience. A text message reprinted in the *Sunday Times* by someone identified only as "Sheldon" commented, "I thought being Indian was exclusive. I didn't know it was negotiable under Black Economic Empowerment" (August 5: 17).

1020 D'Souza, 2002: 31. The anger over the West's treatment of indigenous peoples is enduring: when England's Prince Harry was 18 he produced a series of paintings emulating the Australian Aboriginal dot technique. A spokesman for the group asked, "How much more can England take off aboriginal people? ... This is more than just about copyright. It is cultural theft"; see *New York Daily News*, 2003.

1021 See Matshikiza, 2002.

1022 Spivak, 1998: 332–333.

1023 Mamaila, 2003.

1024 Adebajo, 2006a.

1025 Makhanya, 2008.

1026 Harding 2008, and Gevisser, 2007, 2008.

1027 Some rightwing Afrikaners interpreted the clash between Mbeki and Zuma in light of the prophecies of Boer War-era prophet Siener van Rensburg. The Boeremag had previously thought that the death of Nelson Mandela would trigger the mass murder of South African whites, but in some versions also fantasised about the reestablishment of white minority rule in its wake. With the Boeremag's failed attempt to assassinate Mandela in 2002, and the false rumours of Madiba's death in 2007 (Chapters 3 and 5), one of the Boeremag defendants claimed that a vision by Van Rensburg of two bulls fighting was actually the "correct" signifier of cataclysmic change and the mass slaughter of whites; see Waldner, 2007b.

1028 Sefara and Mapiloko, 2008.

1029 Ndlovu, 2008.

1030 Rossouw, M., 2008.

1031 Tolsi, 2008a. Vendors at Polokwane did a brisk business selling T-shirts bearing the logo "100% Zulu-boy" to Zuma supporters, as well as T-shirts and kangas displaying his name. This heightened sense of tribalism was reflected by the slogans of other groups as well, such as "100% Pedi". Delegates were only permitted to wear clothing displaying Mbeki's name and image, however, and some of them condemned the ANC for duplicating the conduct of the apartheid government; see Terreblanche and De Lange et al., 2008, and *The Star*, 2007a. As president, Zuma was accused of implementing a "Zulufication" of the cabinet as a symbolic rebuke of the influence of Xhosas under the incumbencies of Mandela and Mbeki.

1032 Gevisser, 2008.

1033 Calland, 2008. Survey results reported in 2008 confirmed a shift in the public mood: "40% of adult South Africans are no longer committed to the country and some 29% are actively seeking to emigrate or have thought about doing so". A significant negative change was detected between April 2007 and July 2007; see Donnelly, 2008. Some corroborating evidence was provided by statistics gathered in Israel: immigration to that country by South African Jews increased by 90% during 2008; see Liphshiz, 2008.

1034 Isaacson, 2008b.

1035 Quoted in Webb, 2008. Malema "flipped the script" in 2011 when he was challenging Zuma's authority as the country's leader; at that time he lauded former President Mbeki's leadership skills.

1036 Mamaila, 2008.

1037 The cartoons appeared, respectively, in *The Star*, June 19, 2008: 18, and in the *Sunday Times*, June 22, 2008: 20.

1038 Sokana, 2008.

1039 Mkhwanazi, 2008.

1040 Isaacson, *op. cit.*, and Sefara, 2008. The latter quote likely refers to two incidents in 2003 when a barber in the Pretoria area refused to cut the hair of the SAHRC's Jody Kollapen because it had a whites-only policy (he launched a complaint with the Equality Court), and a young coloured woman who had just graduated from a course in beauty therapy was denied a job by a salon owner who told her that white clients would not want someone like her touching them.

1041 Tolsi, 2008a. The charges against Zuma at this point included the allegation he had received R4 million that he had not reported to the revenue service or Parliament.

1042 Da Costa, 2008.

1043 Hlongwa, 2007, emphasis added.

1044 See Gordin, 2008a, De Lange et al., 2008, and Sefara and Mapiloko, *op. cit.* Interestingly, inside the courtroom disgraced ANC official Tony Yengeni took a front-row seat in the public gallery.

The charges against Zuma were dismissed on procedural grounds, but prosecutors continued to pursue the case. Finally, in April 2009, all charges against him were dropped, shortly before the national elections, which swept Zuma into power as president of the country.

1045 In spite of his history, Zuma still attracts a significant amount of support from women. Some of them in these crowds wore T-shirts with Zuma's face and the pledge "I Love You Daddy", and others sported tops saying "Marry Me Zuma"; see Tolsi, 2008a.

1046 Bloch, 2008.

1047 Tshabalala, 2008.

1048 Hunter, 1991: 42–43, emphasis in the original.

1049 Rosen, *op. cit.*: 11.

1050 Carter, 1965.

1051 Moolman *op. cit.*

1052 Moolman, *op. cit.*

1053 Sachs, *op. cit.*

1054 De Waal, S., 2008.

1055 Swarns, 2002.

1056 Sachs, 1991: 49.

Glossary

askari	during apartheid, guerillas who were captured and then worked for the government
braai	cookout, grilling meat
dominee	a clergyman
gatvol	"fed up"
imbongi	praise singer
impimpi	a spy/informer
indaba	meeting, summit
jol	a good time
kaffir	a racial epithet for black Africans
koeksisters	sweet, doughy treats
kwaito	a contemporary urban pop musical style related to house music
kak	"shit", "rubbish"
laager	a circular, self-protective wagon formation used by the Voortrekkers; also refers to a self-imposed, narrow mentality
lekgotla	while this traditionally meant community justice publicly determined, originally under a tree, these days the meaning is much wider and includes any organised meeting
maskanda	a modernised type of Zulu folk music
mealie pap	a traditional porridge made from ground maize
muti	traditional medicine
ossewa	a wagon, used for overland travel by the Voortrekkers (Afrikaner pioneers)
platteland dorp	a remote town, synonymous with being narrow-minded or unsophisticated
sies, man	an expression of disgust

siestog	"shame"
smiley and walkies	chicken head and feet
swart gevaar	perception of a black threat
tokoloshe	a mythical creature, sometimes mischievous, sometimes dangerous
tsotsi	a petty thief, gangster; a corruption of "zoot suit"
ubuntu	group solidarity and interdependence
vieslik	"disgusting"

Bibliography

Accone, Darryl, 2008. "'Yellow peril' slurs stain the rainbow nation", *Mail & Guardian*, 18 May: 25.

Adams, Sheena, 2006a. "Dancing in front of the courts won't help", *Saturday Star*, 29 July: 5.

————, 2006b. "'There won't be censorship'", *Independent on Saturday*, 19 August: 2.

————, 2006c. "War of the websites as opponents vie to defend and attack SA crime", *Weekend Argus*, 29 July: 15.

————, 2006d. "When fighting crime is betraying your country", *Saturday Star*, 29 July: 4.

Addison, Graeme, 2008. "Sticks and stones and inflammatory headlines", *Weekender*, 28 June: 1.

Adebajo, Adekeye, 2006a. "A most unsavoury rehabilitation", *Mail & Guardian*, 21 July: 27.

————, 2006b. "Natives boobed – on strategy alone", *Sunday Times*, 23 July: 37.

Adkins, Brett, 2003. "Actors facing rape charges appear in popular festival play", *Weekend Post* [Eastern Cape], 5 July: 2.

Agence France-Presse, 1999. "'Artistic liberty' enrages Afrikaners", 25 September.

Ajam, Kashiefa, Fiona Gounden, and Nwabis Msutwana-Stemela, 2008. "Readers in a flap over anti-gay article", *Saturday Star*, 26 July: 8.

Alcoff, Linda, 1991/1992. "The problem of speaking for others", *Cultural critique*, 20: 5–32.

Alexander, Fred, 1950. "South Africa's Indian problem", *Far Eastern survey*, 19 (21): 230–232.

Altman, Dennis, 1996. "Rupture or continuity? The internationalization of gay identities", *Social text*, 14 (3): 77–94.

————, 2004. "Sexuality and globalization", *Sexuality research & social policy*, 1 (1): 63–68.

Amato, Rob, 2005a. "Formerly condemned inmates living in limbo", *Sunday Independent*, 13 March: 6.

————, 2005b. "Liberal baboons must keep quiet now", *Sunday Independent*, 27 March: 2.

Anderson, Mark, 2007. "Afrikaners *not* victims", *Mail & Guardian*, 20 April: 26.

Ansell, Gwen, 2007. "The lady's not for burning", *Mail & Guardian*, 18 May: 4.

Arkin, A.J., K.P. Magyar, and G.J. Pillay, eds, 1989. *The Indian South*

Africans. Durban: Owen Burgess Publishers.

ABC [*Australian Broadcasting Corporation*] *Premium News*, 2007. "Jesus-Osama piece not meant to offend: artist", 30 August.

The Age [Australia], 1997. "Viewing the art of offence", 10 October: 18.

Ashforth, Adam, 2000. *Madumo: A man bewitched*. Chicago: University of Chicago Press.

————, 2005. *Witchcraft, violence, and democracy in twentieth-century South Africa*. Chicago: University of Chicago Press.

Ashton, Len, 2006. "Goldblatt and *Bitterkomix* make strange bedfellows", *Sunday Independent*, 29 October.

Asmal, Kader, and David Chidester, 2004. "In defence of Nadine Gordimer", *ThisDay*, 31 August: 11.

Atkinson, Brenda, 1997a. "Borrowed images", *Mail & Guardian*, 31 October: 5.

————, 1997b. "Critical response", *de arte*, 56 (September): 44–48.

————, 1997c. "The display of taboos", *Mail & Guardian*, 16 May: 28.

————, 1997d. "Of loss, love and longing", *Mail & Guardian*, 31 July: 39.

————, 1997e. "Taboo or not taboo", *Mail & Guardian*, 23 May: 32.

————, 1998. "Guilty of over-hype", *Mail & Guardian*, 23 January.

————, and Candice Breitz, eds, 1999. *Grey areas: Representation, identity and politics in contemporary South Africa*. Johannesburg: Chalkhorn Hill.

Attwood, Alan, 1997. "Shock of the not quite new", *Sydney Morning Herald*, 10 October.

The Australian, 2007. "Bearded controversy", 31 August: 17.

Awa, Ngozi, 2008. "Any special treatment for SA citizens in China?" letter-to-the-editor, *City Press*, 29 June: 28.

Back, Irit, 2004. "Muslims and Christians in Nigeria: Attitudes towards the United States from a post-September 11th perspective", *Comparative studies of South Asia, Africa and the Middle East*, 24 (1): 211–218.

Bagemihl, Bruce, 1999. *Biological exuberance: Animal homosexuality and natural diversity*. New York: St Martin's Press.

Bakhtin, Mikhail, 2008. *Rabelais and his world*. Translated by Hélène Iswolsky. Bloomington: Indiana University Press.

Bamford, Helen, 2006a. "Anti-crime website in race hate battle", *Saturday Star*, 19 August: 1.

————, 2006b. "Websites at war", *Independent on Saturday*, 19 August: 3.

Banda, Fackson, 2008. "Beware the guardians", *Mail & Guardian*, 1 February: 22.

Bangerezako, Haydée, 2007. "Making government listen", *Mail & Guardian*, 27 July: 14.

Barker, Jean, 2005. "Rites vs rights", *Mail & Guardian*, 26 August: 31.

Barnard, Rita, 2006. "*Bitterkomix*: Notes from the post-apartheid underground", pp. 142–154 in Kannemeyer and Botes, eds.

Barron, Chris, 2004. "The unlikeable Mr Roberts", *Sunday Times*, 3 October: 7.

————, 2006. "So many questions (interview with Mongane Wally Serote)", *Sunday Times*, 31 December: 25.

————, 2007. "So many questions (interview with Mukoni Ratshitanga)", *Sunday Times*, 19 August: 25.

Basson, Adriaan, 2007. "SABC: simply incredible", *Mail & Guardian*, 7 September: 4.

Bath, Emma, 2000. "Britain's troubles with Mugabe", *BBC News Online*, 3 April. Downloaded 2 April 2008.

Bauer, Charlotte, 1996. "The art of being gay", *The Star*, 17 March: 13.

————, 2002. "Don't cry for me, Sarafina!" *Sunday Times Lifestyle*, 16 June: 8.

Bauer, Nickolaus, 2012. "Freedom vs dignity in art debate", *Mail & Guardian*, 15 May: 6.

BBC News radio broadcast, 1998. "Homosexuality and hatred in Zimbabwe", 12 August. news.bbc.co.uk. Downloaded 31 March 2008.

BBC Worldwide Monitoring, 2007. "Muslim reaction to publication of prophet cartoon in Swedish newspaper", 3 September.

Becker, R., 2006. "A load of bull about culture", *Sunday Times*, 17 December.

Bedford, Emma, ed., 2004. *A decade of democracy: South African art 1994–2004*. Cape Town: Iziko Museums of Cape Town.

Beisel, Nicola, 1993. "Morals versus art: Censorship, the politics of interpretation, and the Victorian nude", *American sociological review*, 58 (2): 145–162.

"Belinda", 1998. "Art needs wisdom and playfulness, not intelligence and cleverness", letter-to-the-editor, *Sunday Times*, 25 January.

Bellis, Joan, 2002. "Colonizing the queer: Some problems in curating South Africa's first national gay and lesbian art exhibition", pp. 327–351 in Woodward et al. eds.

Bennett, Tony, 2006. "Exhibition, difference, and the logic of culture", pp. 46–69 in Karp et al., eds.

Ben-Yehuda, Nachman, and Erich Goode, 1994. "Moral panics: Culture, politics, and social construction", *Annual review of sociology*, 20: 149–171.

Berg, H., Attorneys, 2003. "Lawyers 1 *Noseweek* 2", *The Law of the Brand* (newsletter), April: 1–3.

Berger, Guy, 2008. "Advertising is not a weapon", *Mail & Guardian*, 27 June: 32.

Berman, Laurence, 2008. "Bleating at Bullard just meets him on home turf", letter-to-the-editor, *Sunday Independent*, 20 April: 6.

Bezuidenhout, Andries, 2007. "From Voëlvry to De la Rey: Popular music, Afrikaner nationalism and lost irony", 2 February. litnet.co.za. Downloaded 22 May 2007.

Bezuidenhout, Evita, 2006. "Exclusive! Evita joins Native Club", *Mail & Guardian*, 23 June: 23.

Bhana, Surendra, and Bridglal Pachai, eds, 1984. *Documentary history of Indian South Africans*. Stanford, CA: Hoover Institution Press.

Blair, David, 2006. "Zulus dance for joy as Zuma corruption case is thrown out", *The Telegraph*, 21 September: 22.

Blatchford, Mathew, 2003. "A good book – burn it", letter-to-the-editor, *Mail & Guardian*, 24 October: 38.

Bleach, Gordon, 1998. "Between the fine print and a hard place", *Nka: Journal of contemporary African art*, Fall/Winter: 52–57.

Blignaut, Charl, 1998. "The siege of Fort Klapperkop", *Mail & Guardian*, 16 January: 11.

———, 1999. "'Filthy' artist Cohen cries censorship", *Mail & Guardian*, 29 October.

———, 2012. "White noise", *City Press 7*, 13 May: 12–13.

Bloch, Graeme, 2008. "Reciting an oath is not a solution", *Sunday Times*, 24 February: 22.

blogmark.mg.co.za, 2007. 2 December. Downloaded 27 February 2007.

Bloom, Kevin, and Phillip de Wet, 2008. "Bullard, in hindsight", *Empire* 1(6), 16 June: 35–37.

Boloka, Gibson, 1999. "African renaissance: A quest for (un)attainable past", *Critical arts*, 13(2): 92–103.

Bolt, Andrew, 2007. "Osama, where art thou hanging?" *Herald Sun*, 31 August: 30.

Bonner, Philip, ed., 1977. *Working papers in Southern African studies: Papers presented at the ASI African Studies Seminar*. Johannesburg: African Studies Institute, University of the Witwatersrand.

Bose, Soumitra, 2003. "Gandhi is still a target of disrespect", *The Times of India*, 24 February.

Bowyer, James, 1996. "Ashtray goes to the heart of censorship", *Sunday Times*, 8 September.

Boyle, Brendan, 2007a. "ANC wants media to be controlled", *Sunday Times*, 2 September: 15.

———, 2007b. "Morality: above the law, beyond black and white", *Sunday Times*, 4 February: 21.

———, 2007c. "War on poverty being won", *Sunday Times*, 4 February: 11.

Braude, Claudia, 1996. "Judge makes homophobia and race link at rights exhibition", *Sunday Independent*, 17 March: 21.

Brecht, Bertolt, 1987. *Bertolt Brecht poems, 1913–1956*, edited by Willett, John, Ralph Manheim, and Erich Fried. London and New York: Methuen.

Breytenbach, Karen, 2006. "Controversial band can play at KKNK", *Pretoria News*, 24 March: 2.

———, 2007. "Evita in race – with Zuma's weapon", *The Star*, 18 January: 7.

Bridgraj, Ajith, 2002. "Ngema, the 'greedy racist'", *Drum*, 27 June: 8–9.

Brink, André, 1996. "Speaking in voices", pp. 12–19 in *Reinventing a continent: Writing and politics in South Africa, 1982–1995*. London: Secker

& Warburg.

———, 2007. "Goldblatt renders the mundane extraordinary", *Sunday Independent*, 1 July: 14.

Brint, Steven, 1992. "What if they gave a war …?" *Contemporary sociology*, 21(4), July: 438–440.

Brodie, David, 2003. Email interview with Churchill Madikida, unpublished manuscript, Johannesburg Art Gallery.

Brooks, David, 2006. "The death of multiculturalism", *New York Times*, 27 April: A27.

———, 2007. "The next culture war", *New York Times*, 12 June: A 23.

Broom, Bob, 2006. "Why should continued deceit and silver-tongued denials be forgiven?" letter-to-the-editor, *The Star*, 26 June: 24.

Brouard, Pierre, 2008. "Tough to tolerate intolerance", letter-to-the-editor, *Weekender*, 9 August: 8.

Bullard, David, 2007a. "Are those killed by crime seen by Mbeki as dispensable?" *Sunday Times Business Times/Careers*, 14 October: 1.

———, 2007b. "Chateau Plascon, drink of champions and real Zulu men", *Sunday Times Business Times/Careers*, 16 December: 1.

———, 2007c. "Come on, Mr Pahad, you can still take up my generous offer", *Sunday Times Business Times/Careers*, 18 November: 1.

———, 2007d. "Look out for me in a drunken three-in-a-bed orgy", *Sunday Times Business Times/Careers*, 28 October: 1.

———, 2007e. "What comes after freedom of speech? The urge to censor people", *Sunday Times Business Times/Careers*, 30 September: 1.

———, 2008a. "Burnt at the stake", *Empire* 1(6), 16 June: 27.

———, 2008b. "Fears of a bitter retirement", *Empire* 1(6), 16 June: 20–21.

———, 2008c. "The tribe has spoken, but Thabo's still on the island", *Sunday Times Business Times/Careers*, 17 February: 1.

———, 2008d. "You will find a really low road at the end of this rainbow", *Sunday Times Business Times/Careers*, 30 March: 1.

———, 2008e. "Uncolonised Africa wouldn't know what it was missing", *Sunday Times Business Times/Careers*, 6 April: 1.

Bunsee, Bennie, 2006. "When it comes to media struggle is still on", *The Star*, 13 July: 14.

Buntman, Fran, 2003. *Robben Island and prisoner resistance to apartheid*. New York: Cambridge University Press.

Burbidge, Matthew, 2006. "Zuma's revenge", *Mail & Guardian*, 4 July.

———, 2007. "The big beef", *Mail & Guardian*, 26 January: 10.

Business Day, 1998. "Charges laid over child art exhibition", 13 July.

———, 2006. "Those quotas are academic, really", 10 June.

———, 2007a. "Between the devil and", 21 November.

———, 2007b. "Devil's advocate cast out", 19 November.

Cage, Ken, 2003. *Gayle: The language of kinks and queens*. Johannesburg: Jacana.

Cahill, Lee, 2007. "Firing robs Mbeki of all credibility", letter-to-the-editor,

Sunday Times, 19 August: 18.

Caldwell, Christopher, 2006. "Islam on the outskirts of the welfare state", *New York Times Magazine*, 5 February: 54–59.

Calhoun, Craig, ed., 1992. *Habermas and the public sphere*. Cambridge, MA: Harvard University Press.

Calland, Richard, 2008. "The dark side of the Second Transition", *Mail & Guardian*, 15 February: 29.

Cape Argus, 2002. "Beer-drinking cricket lovers 'have nothing against milk'", 4 March.

Carew, Douglas, 2002. "Complaints body rejects Zimbabwe request to ban video as SABC apologises", *Sunday Independent*, 22 September: 4.

————, 2004. "Conrad's hopeful heart of darkness", *Weekend Argus*, 3 July: 15.

Carr, David, 2007. "Oprah puts her brand on the line", *New York Times*, 24 December: C1, 8.

Carroll, Rory, 2003. "Gordimer's people", *Mail & Guardian*, 30 May: 10.

————, 2006. "South African club tries to reclaim word 'native'", *The Guardian* [London], 16 June: 19.

Carter, Chiara, 2008. "Khumalo sparks fresh SABC board spat", *The Star*, 7 April: 5.

Carter, Gwendolen M., 1965. *African concepts of nationalism in South Africa*. Edinburgh: Centre of African Studies.

Charter, David, 2007. "Cartoonist shrugs at Islamic death threat: 'It's good to know how much one is worth'", *The Times* [London]: 17 September: 39.

Chauke, Amukelani, Andile Ndlovu, and Roshan Nebhrajani, 2012. "Blade: destroy 'Spear' painting", *The Times*, 30 May: 5.

Cheah, Pheng, and Bruce Robbins, eds, 1998. *Cosmopolitics: Thinking and feeling beyond the nation*. Minneapolis: University of Minnesota Press.

Chikanga, Kenneth, 2005. "Laugh it Off can now guffaw after ruling", *Sunday Independent Business Report*, 29 May: 1.

ChinaDaily.com, 2007. "Christ-like bin Laden image stirs debate", 31 August.

Chuenyane, Gershwin, 2009. "Burn, the beloved country", *City Press*, 26 July: 6.

Citizen, 2003. "JM Coetzee's eloquent move", 4 October: 8.

————, 2006a. "Ad campaign features JM Coetzee praising Australia", 3 August: 11.

————, 2006b. "SABC must come clean", 22 June: 12.

————, 2006c. "SA crime website goes live", 7 July: 10.

————, 2007. "FNB anti-crime campaign will go forward", 5 February.

————, 2008. "Let Chinese BEE", 4 July: 12.

————, 2012. "Pity Zuma won't heed this advice", 1 June: 12.

Clark, Craig, 1996. "Protect citizens from artworks with a sense of irony", *Sunday Independent*, 1 September.

Clark, Grant, 2005. "SA outcry at 'insult' to Gandhi", *BBC News*,
    17 March.

Claasen, Cobus, 2007. "'A pity De la Rey is dead", *Beeld*, 23 March.

Clegg, Johnny, and Michael Drewett, 2006. "Why don't you sing about the
    leaves and the dreams? Reflecting on music censorship in apartheid
    South Africa", pp. 127–136 in Drewett and Cloonan.

CNN.com, 1994. "From murder comes reconciliation, hope", 9 December.
    Downloaded, 6 6 June 2005.

Cohen, Steven, 1999. "Thoughts on performance", *de arte*, 59 (April): 55,
    57.

———, 2002. "Amid darkness, lights shine on heaven and hell",
    Sunday Independent, 17 February: 10.

Comaroff, Jean, and John L. Comaroff, 1999. "Occult economies and
    violent abstractions: Notes from the South African post colony",
    American ethnologist, 26 (2): 279–303.

———, 2001. "Naturing the nation: Aliens, apocalypse and the
    postcultural state", *Journal of Southern African studies*, 27 (3): 627–651.

———, 2003. "Reflections on liberalism, policulturalism, and ID-ology:
    Citizenship and difference in South Africa", *Social identities* 9 (4):
    445–473.

Cornish, Jean-Jacques, 2003. "Nujoma gets into Mugabe mode", *Mail &
    Guardian*, 5 September: 12.

Corrigall, Mary, 2008. "Why Koek is kwaai", *Sunday Independent*, 6 July: 25.

Courtney, Bernadette, and Tania Kovate, 1998. "An artist shrouded in
    mystery", *The Dominion* [New Zealand], 4 April: 21.

Craig, Dylan, and Nomalanga Mkhize, 2006. "Vocal killers, silent killers:
    Popular media, genocide, and the call for benevolent censorship in
    Rwanda", pp. 39–52 in Drewett and Cloonan.

Da Costa, Wendy Jasson, 2008. "Crocodile concoctions and a young
    imbongi", *The Star*, 5 August: 1.

———, and Boyd Webb, 2006. "Minister snaps over 'crime whinges'",
    The Star, 2 June: 5.

Davids, Nashira, 2006. "Now for the best sideshow in town", *Sunday Times*,
    3 December: 6.

Davis, Nancy J., and Robert V. Robinson, 1996, "Religious orthodoxy in
    American society: The myth of a monolithic camp", *Journal for the
    scientific study of religion*, 35 (3), September: 229–246.

Dawes, Nic, 2007. "Back with Zuma", *Mail & Guardian*, 19 January: 3.

De Haas, Mary, 2002. "Apartheid still singing in SA", *The Independent*
    [Durban], 27 July: 7.

De Kock, Leon, 2003. "Waiting for the censors", *Sunday Times Lifestyle*,
    16 February: 12.

De Kok, Ingrid, and Karen Press, eds, 1990. *Spring is rebellious: Arguments
    about cultural freedom*. Cape Town: Buchu Books.

De la Harpe, Roger and Pat, Barry Leitch, and Sue Derwent, 1998. *Zulu*.

Cape Town: Struik Publishers.

De Lange, Deon, Sibusiso Mboto, Sipho Khumalo, Karen Maughan, and Alex Eliseev, 2008. "Chilling warning over Zuma trial", *Mercury*, 8 August: 1.

De Olim, Charles, 2006. "Controversial Afrikaans band suffers Christians' wrath", *Saturday Star*, 11 March: 2.

Derby, Ron, and Linda Ensor, 2006. "Free press in danger", *Weekender*, 12 August: 2.

Desai, Ashwin, 1996. *Arise ye coolies*. Johannesburg: Impact Africa Publishing.

De Villiers, Charl, 1997. "All hell breaks loose over art", *Sunday Times*, 27 July: 5.

De Villiers, Johannes, 2006. "Cape protest: not the last", *News24.com*, 9 February. Downloaded 2 October 2006.

De Vos, Pierre, 2006. "Gays and lesbians now 'separate but equal'", *Mail & Guardian*, 15 September: 35.

De Vries, Fred, 2006. "Outcasts of the eighties", *Mail & Guardian*, 28 July: 4.

———, 2007a. "Exposing the stereotypes", *Weekender*, 9 September: 10.

———, 2007b. "On the road from hell to Die Hel", *Weekender*, 17 November: 1–2.

De Waal, Mandy, 2012. "Battle goes far beyond controversial painting", *The Star*, 31 May: 19.

De Waal, Shaun, 1996. "Written on the body", *Mail & Guardian*, 19 January.

———, 2003. "Screening Coetzee", *Mail & Guardian Friday*, 17 October: 4.

———, 2004a. "Hellish humour", *Mail & Guardian Friday*, 14 May: 2.

———, 2004b. "The authorised version", *Mail & Guardian*, 13 August: 3

———, 2005. "Writing white", *Mail & Guardian*, 3 June: 14.

———, 2006. "Having a national party", *Mail & Guardian Festive Reading*, 24 November: 12–13.

———, 2007. "SABC's bid to stop Mbeki doccie screening fails", *Mail & Guardian*, 20 July: 8.

Dibetle, Monako, 2008a. "'Ching Chong' like the K-word", *Mail & Guardian*, 4 July: 14.

———, 2008b. "'No BEE for those who didn't fight'", *Mail & Guardian*, 4 July: 14.

DiMaggio, Paul, John Evans and Bethany Bryson, 1996. "Have Americans' social attitudes become more polarized?" *American journal of sociology*, 102 (4): November: 690–755.

Dineo-Gqola, Pumla, 2009. "A 21st-century Baartman", *City Press*, 23 August: 5.

Dlamini, Jacob, 2008. "White South Africans' pride is misplaced", *Weekender*, 19 April: 7.

Dlamini, Victor, 2008. "The offence of ethnic stereotypes", *Empire* 1(6), 16 June: 31.

Dodd, Alex, 1998. "Censorship row over child nudes", *Mail & Guardian*, 10 July.

The Dominion [New Zealand], 1998. "Accused believed kicking statue was a lawful act", 25 August.

Donadio, Rachel, 2007. "Out of South Africa", *New York Times Book Review*, 16 December: 35.

Donaldson, Andrew, 1999. "On the small screen", *Sunday Times*, 31 January: 21.

———, 2007a. "Close your eyes and think of Iceland", *Sunday Times*, 28 October: 2.

———, 2007b. "It's the 'native' that causes all the trouble", *Sunday Times*, 4 February: 2

———, 2007c. "A short film about a short politician", *Sunday Times*, 22 July: 2.

———, 2007d. "Wafer-thin piety hides host of sins", *Sunday Times*, 30 September: 2.

Donham, Donald L., 1998. "Freeing South Africa: The 'modernization' of male–male sexuality in Soweto", *Cultural anthropology*, 13 (1): 3–21.

Donnelly, Lynley, 2008. "South Africa's mood sours", *Mail & Guardian*, 11 July: 2.

Douglas, Mary, 1966. *Purity and danger: An analysis of the concepts of pollution and taboo*. London: Routledge & Kegan Paul.

———, 1970. *Natural symbols: Explorations in cosmology*. New York: Vintage Books.

Douglas, Rod, 1996. "Art of discretion", letter-to-the-editor, *Sunday Times*, 7 April: 17.

Drewett, Michael, and Martin Cloonan, 2006. *Popular music censorship in Africa*. Hampshire, England: Ashgate Publishing Ltd.

D'Souza, Dinesh, 2002. "Two cheers for colonialism", *Mail & Guardian*, 10 May: 30–31.

Dubin, Steven, 1992. *Arresting images: Impolitic art and uncivil actions*. New York: Routledge.

———, 1995a. "How I got screwed by Barbie: A cautionary tale", *New art examiner*, November: 20–23.

———, 1995b. "Poisoned pens and rattled sabers: Two years of defending a book about controversial art", *New art examiner*, February: 26–29.

———, 1995c. "*That* girl!: The saga continues", *New art examiner*, January: 6.

———, 1996. "The Barbie exhibition: Show but don't tell", *Curator* magazine, 39 (1) March, 1996: 15–18.

———, 1999. *Displays of power: Memory and amnesia in the American museum*. New York: New York University Press.

———, 2000. "How 'Sensation' became a scandal", *Art in America*, 88 (1),

January: 53–59.

———, 2001. "Censorship and transgressive art", pp. 1588–1592 in Smelser and Baltes, eds.

———, 2006a. *Transforming museums: Mounting Queen Victoria in a democratic South Africa*. New York: Palgrave Macmillan.

———, 2006b. "Uncivilized wars in civil(-zed) places: 'Culture wars' in comparative perspective", pp. 477–493 in Macdonald, ed.

———, 2006c. "Our Man in Havana: Robert Mapplethorpe", *Art in America*, June/July, 2006: 127–131.

Duguid, Sarah, 2002. "Love and law in a small town", *Mail & Guardian*, 5 July: 10.

Dunn, Ricardo, 1996. "Controversy out of the closet", *Mail & Guardian*, 9 February.

Du Plessis, Carien, 2003. "SABMiller castles Laugh it Off", *ThisDay*, 11 November: 15.

Du Plessis, Tim, 2007. "De la Rey rides again", *Financial Mail*, 9 February: 64.

Du Preez, Max, 2002. "Why is ANC silent on Ngema's racist song?" *The Star*, 18 June: 18.

———, 2003. "Afrikaners' sense of loss and identity and insecurity clearly visible", *The Star*, 18 September: 14.

———, 2006a. "A club of pompous, self-important fat cats", *The Star*, 25 May.

———, 2006b. "Introduction", pp. 6–8 in Hopkins.

———, 2007. "Only one SA tribe left that won't play nice", *The Star*, 22 February: 18.

———, 2008. "Free speech should have its limitations, too", *The Star*, 24 April.

Durand, Johann, 2003. "'Hate speech' cannot be allowed to divide South Africa," letter-to-the-editor, *Citizen*, 19 September: 23. (Came right after Du Preez)

Durkheim, Emile, 1956. *The division of labor in society*. New York: Free Press.

Dyantyi, Aurelia, 2003. "Now it's wives and mistresses", *The Star*, 16 July: 13.

Eaton, Tom, 2007. "A fine white whine", *Mail & Guardian*, 9 February: 26.

Ebr.-Vally, Rehana, 2001. "Diversity in the imagined *Umma*: The example of Indian Muslims in South Africa", pp. 269–300 in Zegeye.

Echo, 2002. "It's not hate speech: Ngema", 6 June.

Edwards, Iain, 1994. "Cato Manor: Cruel past, pivotal future", *Review of African political economy*, 61: 415–427.

Edwards, P., 2007. "Let's honour all our fallen fighters", letter-to-the-editor, *Sunday Times*, 7 January: 18.

Eggers, Dave, 2006. *What is the what: The autobiography of Valentino Achak Deng*. San Francisco: McSweeney's.

Ellis, Estelle, 2003a. "Judge's ruling wipes the smile off the face of Laugh it

Off", *The Star*, 17 April: 3.

———, 2003b. "Laugh-it-Off spoof adds fuel to Diesel's displeasure", *The Star*, 24 June: 6.

Els, Henriette, 2003. "Coetzee's latest isn't much fun", *Citizen Weekend*, 1 November: 17.

Enwezor, Okwui, Tracy Murinik, and Liese van der Watt, 2004. *Personal affects: Power and poetics in contemporary South African art*. New York and Cape Town: Museum for African Art and Spier.

Epprecht, Marc, 2004. *Hungochani: The history of a dissident sexuality in Southern Africa*. Montreal: McGill-Queens University Press.

Evans, Gavin, 2002. "Two faces of Mokaba", *Mail & Guardian*, 14 June: 4.

The Evening Post [New Zealand], 1998. "Statue kicker plans to leave NZ", 29 September.

Exit [South Africa], 2001a. "Gays under threat in Africa", 136 (June): 1.

———, 2001b. "Nujoma raves against gays but faces protests for human rights", 136 (June): 5.

Fattah, Hassan M., 2006. "At Mecca meeting, cartoon outrage crystallized", *New York Times*, 9 February: A1, 14.

Ferguson, Lorna, 1998. "It turned out to be a right-hand turn", *The Seer*, 30 January: 12.

Fiorina, Morris, Samuel J. Abrams, and Jeremy C. Pope, 2005. *Culture war? The myth of a polarized America*. New York: Pearson Longman.

Fisher, Ryland, 2007. "ANC bias tarnishes a national treasure", *Sunday Times*, 28 : 23.

Flint, Karen, 2006. "Indian-African encounters: Polyculturalism and African therapeutics in Natal, South Africa, 1886–1950s", *Journal of Southern African studies*, 32 (2): 367–385.

Ford, Sam, 2008. "Minister clueless about SA Chinese", letter-to-the-editor, *The Star*, 3 July: 17.

Forrest, Drew, 2003. "SA's Indians the most gloomy", *Mail & Guardian*, 3 January: 6.

Fortescue, Elizabeth, 2007. "Osama bin Christ insulting to Jesus and Mary", *Daily Telegraph*, 31 August.

Foucault, Michel, 1980. *The history of sexuality*, vol. 1: *An introduction*. New York: Vintage Books.

Freedberg, David, 1989. *The power of images: Studies in the history and theory of response*. Chicago: University of Chicago Press.

Friedman, Hazel, 1994. "Two artists who are legends in their own minds …", *The Star*, 22 August.

———, 1996a. "Is this an insult to black women?" *Mail & Guardian*, 16 August.

———, 1996b. "On the verge of optimism", *Mail & Guardian*, 2 August.

———, 1996c. "Storm in a loincloth", *Mail & Guardian*, 29 November.

———, 1997. "Bible-punchers pinch Bible art", *Mail & Guardian*, 31 July: 36.

Friedman, Thomas L., 2006. "Empty pockets, angry minds", *New York Times*, 22 February: A19.

Gans, Herbert J., 1974. *Popular culture and high culture*. New York: Basic Books.

Garner, James, 2002. "Law of the brand", *Big Issue*, February/March: 22–24.

Gasa, Nomboniso, 1996. "'Shock people in an empowering way'", *Mail & Guardian*, 23 August.

Gaule, Sally, 1996. "Photographs of Walker Evans and David Goldblatt: Seeing through different prisms", *de arte*, 54: 19–31.

Gedye, Lloyd, 2007. "Afrikaans music gets interesting", *Mail & Guardian*, 4 May: 1, 3.

Geers, Kendell, 1997. "Taking a risk with her children's bodies", *The Star*, 12 August.

———, 1998. "A conscience-stricken nation", *Star Tonight*, 21 January: 13.

George, Zine, and Lauren Cohen, 2007. "Quick! A broom! Manto's coming!" *Sunday Times*, 12 August: 5.

Gerardy, Justine, 2008a. "Fired for his opinion, Bullard bites back", *Saturday Star*, 12 April: 3.

———, 2008b. "Wrongs of past made right", *Saturday Star*, 21 June: 8.

Gettleman, Jeffrey, 2007. "Hundreds of Sudanese demand execution of British teacher", *New York Times*, 1 December: A6.

———, 2008. "Kenya's middle class feeling sting of violence", *New York Times*, 11 February: A1, 10.

Gevisser, Mark, 2007. "For a manic-depressive nation it's euphoric victory or hellish despair", *Sunday Times*, 28 October: 25.

———, 2008. "No fairy-tale ending for us", *Sunday Times*, 29 June: 3.

———, 2009. *A legacy of liberation: Thabo Mbeki and the future of the South African dream*. New York: Palgrave Macmillan.

———, 2012. "Zuma is no Saartjie Baartman", *City Press*, 10 June: 30.

———, and Edwin Cameron, eds, 1995. *Defiant desire: Gay and lesbian lives in South Africa*. New York: Routledge.

Gibson, 2004. *Overcoming apartheid: Can truth reconcile a divided nation?* New York: Russell Sage Foundation.

Gigaba, Malusi, 2006a. "Freedom of expression is not absolute", *Sunday Times*, 15 October: 36.

———, 2006b. "Native Club not for apologists", *The Star*, 7 June: 14.

Giliomee, Hermann, 2003a. *The Afrikaners: Biography of a people*. Charlottesville: University of Virginia Press.

———, 2003b. "Whites have been left emasculated", *Sunday Times*, 28 September: 20.

———, 2007. "On FNB, De la Rey, and our guardians against unwelcome news", 2 March. www.ever-fasternews.com. Downloaded 27 May 2007.

Godby, Michael, 2000. "Gideon Mendel's 'Beloofde Land'", *Nka: Journal of contemporary African art*, 11/12: 72–79.

———, 2005. "From shouting to talking", *Art South Africa* 4 (1): 32–36.

Godwin, Peter, 2007. *When a crocodile eats the sun*. London: Picador.

Goldblatt, David, 2001. *Fifty-one years, David Goldblatt*. Barcelona: Museu d'Art Contemporani de Barcelona.

————, 2007. "Some Afrikaners photographed and some Afrikaners revisited: Notes on how they came to be", pp. 11–17 in Goldblatt, *Some Afrikaners revisited*, Cape Town: Umuzi.

Goldstein, Richard, 1996. "The culture war is over! We won! (For now)", *Village voice*, 19 November: 51–52, 54–55.

————, 2005. "Cartoon wars", *The Nation*, 21 February: 6–7.

Goldstuck, Arthur, 1994. *Ink in the porridge: Urban legends of the South African elections*. London: Penguin.

Goniwe, Thembinkosi, 2000. "Is it cultural apartheid or what one makes? Question on representation", 11 July, www.artthrob.com. Downloaded 21 April 2008.

Goodstein, Laurie, 2004. "How the evangelicals and Catholics joined forces", *New York Times*, 30 May: WK4.

Gordimer, Nadine, 2001. "Twenty-one years later", *Critical arts*, 15(1/2): 21–23.

Gordin, Jeremy, 2006a. "A country of living dangerously", *Sunday Independent*, 24 December: 13.

————, 2006b. "Courtroom dramas have had the nation enthralled", *Sunday Independent*, 7 May: 9.

————, 2008a. "Zuma's trial exposes two separate realities", *Sunday Independent*, 10 August: 8.

————, 2008b. "Ombud ruling slammed by media watchdog", *Sunday Independent*, 10 August: 3.

Govender, Peroshni, and Lee Rondganger, 2004. "'Kill the Boer' row in lion case", *The Star*, 18 February: 1.

Govender, Prega, 2007. "Universities told to cut back on arts", *Sunday Times*, 29 July: 8.

Govender, Ronnie, 2002. "Protect us from Ngema's poison", *Sunday Times*, 16 June: 19.

————, 2006. *Song of the Atman*. Johannesburg: Jacana.

Govender, Suthentira, 2002. "Ngema claims 'victory'", *Sunday Times*, 30 June.

————, 2007a. "At least we're semi-proudly South African", *Sunday Times*, 9 September: 7.

————, 2007b. "Gandhi smeared as 'Indian Hitler'", *Sunday Times Extra*, 7 January: 1.

————, and Thabo Mkhize, 2002. "Indo-African summits 'waste of time'", *Sunday Times*, 21 July: 3.

————, 2003. "Zulu virgin marking outlawed after rapes", *Sunday Times*, 22 June: 6.

Gower, Primarashni, 2008. "R4m to live in perfect harmony at UFS", *Mail & Guardian*, 6 June: 14.

Green, Philippa, 2006. "Fear and favour at SABC", *Sunday Times*, 25 June: 39.

Greig, Robert, 1998a. "Honest artist mistaken for child pornographer", *Sunday Independent*, 12 July.

———, 1998b. "Pretoria's camp cowboys give a girl a nazi turn", *Sunday Independent*, 25 January.

Gresié, Yvette, 2004. Review of *Ndiyindoda! Initiation as rite of passage*, *Art South Africa*, 3 (1): 62–63.

———, 2006. Review of *Colbert Mashile*, *Art South Africa*, 4 (4): 80–81.

Grobler, John, 2007. "Swapo's inevitable change", *Mail & Guardian*, 30 November: 18.

Groenewald, Yolandi, 2007a. "De la Rey – is it just a song?" *Mail & Guardian*, 18 May: 17.

———, 2007b. "The De la Rey uprising", *Mail & Guardian*, 16 February: 12.

———, 2007c. "Mandela is 'alive and well'", *Mail & Guardian*, 23 February: 10.

———, and Pearlie Joubert, 2007. "Not yet uhuru", *Mail & Guardian*, 2 March: 8.

———, and Mbuyisi Mgibisa, 2007. "Crime left to fend for itself", *Mail & Guardian*, 16 March: 8.

Grundlingh, Albert, 2004. "'Rocking the Boat' in South Africa? Voëlvry music and Afrikaans anti-apartheid social protest in the 1980s", *International journal of African historical studies*, 37 (3): 483–514.

The Guardian [Nigeria], 2002. "Nigeria: Kaduna Christians oppose trial of riot suspects in Shari'ah courts", 30 November.

Gunner, Liz, 2008. "Jacob Zuma, the social body and the unruly power of song", *African affairs*, 108: 27–48.

Günzel, Erhard, 1997. "Outrage over gay-bashing", *Windhoek Advertiser*, 31 January.

Gurney, Kim, 2004. "And now for a good slap in the face …", *Business Day*, 4 June: 17.

Gustin, Sam, 2006. "Good-time Tiananmen on Google", *New York Post*, 3 February: 9.

Habedi, Dan, 2006. "Broadcaster must be apolitical", letter-to-the-editor, *The Star*, 27 June: 15.

Habermas, Jürgen, 1989 (1962). *The structural transformation of the public sphere: An inquiry into a category of bourgeois society*. Cambridge, MA: MIT Press.

Haffajee, Ferial, 2007. "What's in the canned Mbeki doccie", *Mail & Guardian*, 16 June: 24.

———, 2008. "The SABC go-round", *Mail & Guardian*, 6 June: 4.

Hamata, Max, 2007. "De la Rey hit song hijacked by right wingers", 23 February. www.informante.web.na. Downloaded 22 May 2007.

Hammond, Brad, 1998. "Art needs wisdom and playfulness, not intelligence and cleverness", letter-to-the-editor, *Sunday Times*, 25 January.

Hansen, Thomas Blom, 2005. "Melancholia of freedom: Humour and nostalgia among Indians in South Africa", *Modern drama*, 48 (2): 297–315.

Harding, Tony, 2008. "We cannot now ask South Africa to judge itself by a lower standard", letter-to-the-editor, *Sunday Times*, 24 February: 20.

Hassim, Aziz, 2002. *The lotus people*. Durban: Madiba Publishers.

Hemson, Crispin, 2003. "Beer must stand test of truth", *Sunday Times*, 27 April: 18.

Hilton-Barber, Steve, 1990. "The affairs of men", *Sunday Star Magazine*, 25 November.

———, 1991. "In good photographic faith", *Staffrider*, 9 (3): 35–39.

———, 2001. Untitled artist's statement, pp. 40–45 in Tilkin, 2002.

The Hindu, 2002. "Racial overtones in Indian's murder", 31 May.

Hiney, Tom, 2006. "Is royalty still relevant?" *Sunday Independent Life*, 16 July: 2–3.

Hlongwa, Wonder, 2002. "Sporadic Indian-African attacks", *City Press*, 8 June.

———, 2007. "African gods asked to bless JZ's cause", *City Press*, 16 December: 5.

Ho, Ufrieda, 2008. "Chinese locals are black", *Business Day*, 19 June: 1.

Hofmeyr, Steve, 2005. "Going ape", letter-to-the-editor, *Mail & Guardian*, 1 April: 20.

Honey, Peter, 2006. "Jihad and the war of values", *Financial Mail*, 24 February.

Hoad, Neville, 2004. "World piece: What the Miss World Pageant can teach about globalization", *Cultural critique*, 58 (Fall): 56–81.

———, Karen Martin, and Graeme Reid, eds, 2005. *Sex & politics in South Africa*. Cape Town: Double Storey Books.

Hooper-Box, Caroline, 2002a. "Controversial AmaNdiya to face 'hate speech' test", *Sunday Independent*, 9 June: 3.

———, 2002b. "SAB seeks gag on anti-brand artist", *Sunday Independent*, 15 September: 5.

Hopkins, Pat, 2001. "Princess Menorah", pp. 38–42 in *Eccentric South Africa*. Cape Town: Zebra Press.

———, 2006. *Voëlvry: The movement that rocked South Africa*. Cape Town: Zebra Press.

Horrell, Georgina, 2002. "JM Coetzee's *Disgrace*: One settler, one bullet and the 'new South Africa'", *Issues in English studies in South Africa*, 7 (1): 25–32.

Hughes, Heather, 1987. "Violence in Inanda, August 1985", *Journal of Southern African studies*, 13 (3): 331–354.

Huisman, Biénne, 2008. "Festival delivers the good, bad and ugly", *Sunday Times*, 30 March: 5.

———, 2009. "Son takes parents to court over circumcision", *Sunday*

Times, 9 August: 6.

Hunter, Cheryl, 1996. "Vagina-shaped ashtray leads to complaint", *The Star*, 10 September.

Hunter, James D., 1991. *Culture wars: The struggle to define America*. New York: Basic Books.

———, 1994. *Before the shooting begins: Searching for democracy in America's culture war*. New York: Free Press.

———, 1996a, "Reflections on the culture wars hypothesis", pp. 243–256 in Nolan, ed.

———, 1996b, "Response to Davis and Robinson: Remembering Durkheim", *Journal for the scientific study of religion*, 35 (3): 246–248.

———, 2006. "The enduring culture war", pp. 10–40 in Hunter and Wolfe.

———, and Alan Wolfe, 2006. *Is there a culture war? A dialogue on values and American public life*. Washington, DC: Brookings Institution Press.

Ibison, David, 2007. "Sweden risks crisis over Prophet picture", *Financial Times* [London], 30 August.

Isaacson, Maureen, 2007a. "No free lunches or beetroot people for the embattled media", *Sunday Independent*, 29 October: 8.

———, 2007b. "Weeding out Mandela's old brand, cable theft and white women", *Sunday Independent*, 22 July: 8.

———, 2008a. "'Our media has no memory'", *Sunday Independent*, 6 July: 8.

———, 2008b. "'The struggle is far from over'", *Sunday Independent*, 20 July: 4.

Ismail, Farhana, 1995a. "Anti-porn protester sprays sex painting", *Sunday Tribune*, 22 October.

———, 1995b. "Artist shocks viewers", *Cape Argus*, 29 October: 7.

———, 2003. "Harassed Indians are on the verge of quitting Zimbabwe", *Sunday Independent*, 9 February: 4.

Ismail, Sumayya, 2007a. "FNB to go ahead with anti-crime campaign, *Mail & Guardian*, 5 February, www.mg.co.za. Downloaded 3 June 2008.

———, 2007b. "Freedom Park: own up to 'our' pain", *Mail & Guardian*, 23 March.

———, 2007c. "One man's terrorist … ", *Mail & Guardian*, 16 March: 10.

Jack, Mawande, 2003. "Xhosa monarchy up in arms over play", *City Press*, 8 June: 8.

Jacobson, Celean, 2005. "SA art 'lacks passion, pride'", *Sunday Times*, 8 May: 8.

———, 2006. "Interview with Ronald Suresh Roberts", *Sunday Times Lifestyle*, 4 June: 16.

———, 2007. "Ritual slaughter of bull by former South African lawmaker causes outcry", 25 January. Associated Press Worldstream. Downloaded 26 March 08.

Jajbhay, Mahomed, 2007. "A duty to tell South Africa the truth about its health minister", *Sunday Times*, 2 September: 29.

Jamal, Ashraf, 2004. "Through glass darkly", *Art South Africa*, 2 (3): 41–47.

James, Cheri-Ann, 2002. "A conservative bunch", *Mail & Guardian*, 12 November: 6.

Jansen, Jonathan, 2012. "When doubt is good", *The Times*, 7 June: 15.

Jardin, Xeni, 2006. "Exporting censorship", *New York Times*, 9 March: 23.

Jazbhay, Saber Ahmed, 2008. "The wounds of the past have yet to heal", letter-to-the-editor, *Saturday Star*, 19 April: 14.

Jhaveri, Omar H.A., 1933. "Presidential address", Johannesburg, 19–20 August, pp. 170–174 in Bhana and Pachai, eds, 1984.

Johnson, Ashley, 2003. "A rare poetic response to rituals", *Business Day*, 23 April, www.lexisnexis.com. Downloaded 1 May 2008.

————, 2003. "Art", *Business Day*, 22 April: 9.

Johnson, Brent, 2007. "A whole lot of bull", letter-to-the-editor, *Mail & Guardian*, 8 February: 24.

Jones, Nomfundo, 2007. "A childish vendetta", *Mail & Guardian*, 19 January: 23.

Joseph, Natasha, and Celean Jacobson, 2007. "Don't ban Tintin, says Zapiro", *The Star*, 30 July: 1.

Joubert, Peralie, 2008. "Lekota's son on race war", *Mail & Guardian*, 14 March: 8.

Jubasi, Mawande, and Thabo Mkhize, 2002. "Now Ngema starts African lobby group", *Sunday Times*, 20 June.

Jung, Courtney, 2000. *Then I was black: South African political identities in transition*. New Haven: Yale University Press.

————, 2003. "The politics of indigenous identity: Neoliberalism, cultural rights, and the Mexican Zapatistas", *Social research*, 70 (2): 433–462.

Kadalie, Rhoda, 2006. "A coconut knocks on the door of the Native Club", *Business Day*, 1 June.

————, 2007. "On the Cape Flats, Madam sings its own De la Rey", *Business Day*, 22 February.

Kannemeyer, Anton, and Conrad Botes, eds, 2006. *The big bad* Bitterkomix *handbook*. Johannesburg: Jacana.

Kanuma, Shyaka, 2002. "Songs of hate", *Mail & Guardian*, 28 June.

Karac, Jaroslav, 2007. "Tintin in Hell marks artist's profound emotional progression", *Sunday Independent*, 20 May: 11.

Karp, Ivan, Corinne A. Kratz, Lynn Szwara, and Tomas Ybarra-Frasuto, eds, 2006. *Museum frictions: Public cultures/global transformations*. Durham, NC: Duke University Press.

Kemp, Yunus, 2003. "Chill, SA Breweries told over satirical T-shirts", *Cape Argus*, 21 February: 8.

Kennedy, Dawn, 2005. "TRC films stimulate debate and catharsis", *Sunday Independent*, 23 January: 11.

Kennedy, Ray, 1999. "Boer War hero goes native", *The Times* [London], 24 September.

Kenny, Andrew, 2003. "Nobel Prize for boredom", *Citizen*, 7 October: 13.
————, 2008. "Chinese and apartheid", *Citizen*, 24 June: 13.
Kerr, Gregory, 1998. "Art report a triumph of armchair journalism", *Mail & Guardian*, 15 May: 2.
————, 2002. "Die kind lig sy hand teen sy moeder: young Afrikaners and the art of outrage", pp. 132–139 in Kannemeyer and Botes, eds, 2006.
Kgosana, Calphus, 2007. "Media freedom on agenda of ANC battle of ideas", *City Press*, 16 December: 27.
Kgositsile, Baleka, 1996. "Poor taste must not pose as art", *The Star*, 13 August.
Khanyile, Slindile, 2007. "Medical aids prepare to take on healers", *Star Business Report*, 11 December: 1.
Khumalo, Fred, 2006. "Killing a bull with bare hands to show bravery is … a lot of bull", *The Star*, 17 December: 25.
————, 2008. "Mercenary motives mug lobolo, taking its dignity", *Sunday Times*, 3 August: 25.
Khumalo, Sibongile, 2005. "Leave, 'or we'll burn you alive'", *Sunday Times*, 13 September.
Khumalo, Sipho, 2003. "It's the Reddy connection", *The Star*, 27 August: 15.
————, 2006. "JZ trust to cash in on Zuma ringtone", *Mercury*, 26 October, www.Iol.co.za. Downloaded 1 March 2007.
Khunou, Bishop Moagi, 2004a. "Morality is what laws are based on", letter-to-the-editor, *The Star*, 5 November: 11.
————, 2004b. "Rape better than same-sex intercourse", letter-to-the-editor, *The Star*, 10 November: 9.
Khupiso, Victor, 2007. "'I wish they had hanged me'", *Sunday Times*, 21 January: 7.
Kifner, John, 2006. "Images of Muhammad, gone for good", *New York Times*, 12 February: WK4.
Kimmelman, Michael, 2006. "A startling new lesson in the power of imagery", *New York Times*, 8 February: E1, 8.
Kirby, Robert, 2003a. "Another triumph for the corporate bully boys", *Mail & Guardian*, 25 April: 39.
————, 2003b. "Using a steamroller to crush an ant", *Mail & Guardian*, 28 February: 28.
Kirk, Paul, 2006a. "Expect tourist deaths in 2010", *Citizen*, 27 June: 12.
————, 2006b. "Zuma case doomed: law prof", *Citizen*, 5 July: 4.
Kirkpatrick, David D., 2004. "A senator's call to 'Win this culture war'", *New York Times*, 1 September: 1, 6.
Khuzwayo, Wiseman, 2008. "Chinese are not fully black – Nafcoc", *Sunday Independent Business Report*, 21 June: 1.
Klein, Marcia, 2004a. "Clash of the beer titans", *Sunday Times Business*, 30 May: 3.
————, 2004b. "Nip 'n tuck for famous brew", *Sunday Times Business*,

8 August: 6.

Knox, Catherine, 1998. "Is this child porn?" *Cue*, 3 July: 6.

Kockott, Fred, 2004. "Are Indians safe in the Free State?", *The Star*, 1 May: 13.

Kombuis, Koos, 2006. "Afterword: Short drive to freedom", pp. 234–236 in Hopkins.

Konigkramer, Arthur, 1991. "The new censorship", pp. 19–24 in South African Institute of Race Relations.

Korber, Rose, 1982. "Gay art goes on exhibition", *Pretoria News*, 5 February.

Kors, Alan Charles, and Harvey A. Silvergate, 1998. *The shadow university: The betrayal of liberty on America's campuses*. New York: Free Press.

Kristof, Nicholas D., 2006. "China's cyberdissidents and the Yahoos at Yahoo", *New York Times*, 19 February: WK13.

Krog, Antjie, 2007. "De la Rey: Afrikaner absolution", *Mail & Guardian*, 30 March: 23.

Krouse, Matthew, 2005. "Beer ad brews bad spirits", *Mail & Guardian*, 17 June: 5.

Krüger, Franz, 2007. "When the media's voice is misheard", *Mail & Guardian*, 30 November: 31.

————, 2009. "Mystery of the missing film", *Mail & Guardian*, 12 June: 26.

Kupe, Tawana, 2007a. "Did the SA media cross the line over Manto?" *Weekender*, 18 August: 8.

————, 2007b. "The crisis of the SABC as a public broadcaster", *WitsReview*, September: 38–39.

Kurgan, Terry, 1998. "Mothers and others", pp. 1–3 in *Bringing up baby: Artists survey the reproductive body*. Cape Town: Bringing Up Baby Project.

Lacey, Marc, 2002. "Fiery zealotry leaves Nigeria in ashes again", *New York Times*, 29 November: A3.

LaFraniere, Sharon, 2005. "Women's rights laws and African custom clash", *New York Times*, 30 December: A1, 14.

Laganparsad, Monica, 2002. "Indian reporter forced to leave 'indigenous African' meeting", *Sunday Argus*, 23 June: 4.

La Grange, Zelda, 2007. "We are all protecting our interests", *The Star*, 31 January: 13.

Lamola, John, 2012. "'New' Africanness is lala-land", *City Press*, 10 June: 27.

Lamola, Tumelo, 2006. "Jacob Zuma, you have removed all doubt that you're a homophobe", letter-to-the-editor, *The Star*, 6 October: 20.

Landman, Andries, 2008. "David Bullard: What readers had to say", letter-to-the-editor, *Sunday Times*, 13 April: 17.

Laurence, Patrick, 2007. "Traits of an unbalanced paranoid", *The Star*, 24 July: 14.

————, 2008. "Patience of the poor stretched", *The Star*, 22 July: 12.

Leclerc-Madlala, Suzanne, 2001. "Virginity testing: Managing sexuality in a maturing HIV/AIDS epidemic", *Medical anthropology quarterly*, 15 (4): 533–552.

Ledimo, Moleleki Frank, 2004a. "Rites of passage: Refiguring initiation", pp. 128–137 in Bedford, ed.

———, 2004b. "Colbert Mashile", pp. 238–341, in Perryer, ed.

Leggett, Ted, 2004. "Race groups' views on safety differ", *Sunday Independent*, 14 January: 16.

Leithead, Alastair, 2005. "SA beer parody case to conclude", *BBC News*, 8 March. Downloaded 15 June 2005.

Lento, Mzukisi, 2012. "Democracy is a fine art", *Mail & Guardian*, 25 May: 32.

Leshilo, Thabo, 2007. "Enemies of the people? Counterpoint", *Mail & Guardian*, 7 September: 30.

Levin, Adam, 1998. "Cohen the barbarian", *Style*, April: 26–28.

Liphshiz, Cnaan, 2008. "Record-breaking year for returning Israeli citizens", *Haaretz*, 22 December: 1.

Local History Museums, 2001. *1949 Riots Durban*. Exhibition brochure.

Luirink, Bart, 2000. *Moffies: Gay life in Southern Africa*. Cape Town: David Philip.

Luker, Kristin, 1985. *Abortion and the politics of motherhood*. Berkeley: University of California Press.

Lyman, Rick, 2001. "At least for the moment, a cooling off in the culture wars", *New York Times*, 13 November: E1.

Mabuza, Ernest, 2008. "SA Chinese are black – court", *Business Day*, 19 June: 6.

Mabuza, Kingdom, 2003. "Jo'burg OKs backyard slaughter", *Citizen*, 26 June: 1.

Macdonald, Sharon, ed., 2006. *Blackwell companion to museum studies*. London: Blackwell.

McDowall, Patrick, 2007. "Afrikaners go 'Bok'", *Sunday Times*, 29 January, www.sundaytimes.co.za. Downloaded 27 May 2007.

Macfarlane, David, 2012. "Bunking Blade bust", *Mail & Guardian*, 1 7 August: 14.

McGreal, Chris, 2001. "Bard barred for being too boring", *Guardian* [London], 18 April: 1.

———, 2007. "Afrikaans singer stirs up controversy with war song", *Guardian* [London], 26 February: 23.

McLeod, Bruce, 2005. "Don't confuse me with Esther", letter-to-the-editor, *Mail & Guardian*, 8 April: 22.

McNeil, Donald G., Jr, 2002. "Killer songs", *New York Times*, 17 March.

Madlala, Bheko, 2002. "Racial tensions under scrutiny", *Independent* [Durban], 27 July: 2.

Mafela, Ndivhuho, Buyekezwa Makwabe, and Biénne Huisman, 2007a. "Yengeni turns to the ancestors", *Sunday Times*, 21 January: 6.

Mafela, Ndivhuho, Brendan Boyle, Paddy Harper, and Mpumelelo

Mkhabela, 2007b. "ANC's bullies ram through SABC board", *Sunday Times*, 16 September: 1.

Magill, R. Jay, Jr, 2007. "A cube, like Mecca's, becomes a pilgrim", *New York Times*, 15 April: AR29.

Mahlangu, Bongani, 2009. "Anti-Indian encore by music icon", *Sunday World*, 26 July: 4.

Mahomed, Nadima, 2006. "Do as the Prophet did", *Mail & Guardian*, 10 February: 22.

Maier, Karl, 1994. "South African elections: Gandhi's heirs fearful of black majority", *The Independent* [London], 27 April: 10.

Mail & Guardian, 2001. "Press clippings", 6 April: 29 [reprint of an article from the *Namibian,* 2 April 2001].

————, 2003. "Defenders of artistic freedom", 4 July: 24.

————, 2004. "Enormously bad ruling", 21 September: 14.

————, 2006a. "The constitution and the Qur'an", 10 February: 22.

————, 2006b. "With freedom comes responsibility", 10 February: 3.

————, 2007a. "A dirty war", 19 October: 24.

————, 2007b. "For crying out loud", 7 September: 26.

————, 2007c. "Nelson Mandela Rylaan? No, Dela Rylaan!" 26 June.

————, 2007d. "The full Manto", 17 August: 2–3.

————, 2008. "Towards a media tribunal", 1 February: 22.

Makgoba, Malegapuru, 2005. "Wrath of the dethroned white males", *Mail & Guardian*, 25 March, www.mg.co.za. Downloaded 14 September 2005.

Makhanya, Mondli, 2007. "We must delve into new wave of Afrikaner siege mentality", *Sunday Times*, 25 February: 28.

————, 2008. "Getting back our morality", *Sunday Times*, 9 July: 21.

Makoe, Abbey, 2006. "Let the darkies meet whenever they want to", *Saturday Star*, 29 July: 14.

Majavu, Mandisi, 2006. "The Native Club versus the status quo", *Mail & Guardian*, 7 July: 26.

Malala, Justice, 2008a. "A righteous firing", *Empire*, 1(6), 16 June: 29.

————, 2008b. "Victory for truth & independence", *Empire*, 1(5), 4 February: 20–21.

Malan, Pieter, 1996. "Row over exhibit of male nude studies", *The Star*, 23 November.

————, 1997. "Matie artists' show banned in Bellville", *Cape Argus*, 26 July, 1997: 3.

————, 1998. "Students cry foul as nude art removed", *Cape Argus*, 3 May: 11.

Malan, Rian, 2006. "South Africa: Not civil war but sad decay", *The Spectator* [UK], 14 October.

Maluleke, Elias, 2003. "Boeremag coup aimed to tie in with US terror attacks", *City Press*, 2 November: 6.

Mamaila, Khathu, 2003. "We can do without Rhodes' rands", *The Star*, 7 July: 8.

————, 2008. "Malema ploy spot on", *City Press*, 22 June: 22.

Mamdani, Mahmood, 1996. *Citizen and subject: Contemporary Africa and the legacy of late colonialism*. Princeton: Princeton University Press.

Mametse, Dikatso, 2003. "Pictures arouse stiff opposition", *Mail & Guardian*, 27 June: 5.

Mangcu, Xolela, 2007. "Prosecution may fuel Zuma", *Weekender*, 10 November: 5.

Mann, Chris, 2003. "Thuthula still causing a rumpus", *Sunday Independent*, 22 June: 11.

Mantshantsha, Sikonathi, 2006. "Born into the right family", *Finweek*, 4 May: 16.

Mason, Andy, 2006. "Bitterkomix 2002: Silent comics, critical noise and the politics of pielsuig", pp. 4–15 in Kannemeyer and Botes, eds.

Masood, Salman, 2006. "Pakistan's violent protests over cartoons taking political turn", *New York Times*, 16 February: A13.

Matshikiza, John, 2002. "A colonised intellect", *Mail & Guardian*, 17 May: 28–29.

————, 2004a. "The good, the bad and the ungrateful", *Mail & Guardian*, 20 August: 32.

————, 2004b. "Monkey me, monkey you", *Mail & Guardian*, 2 April: 42.

————, 2007a. "Die Bokke: another broken record", *Mail & Guardian*, 23 March: 31.

————, 2007b. "Even Confucius, he confused", *Mail & Guardian*, 1 June: 31.

————, 2007c. "Massaging race into cabbage", *Mail & Guardian*, 20 April: 30.

————, 2007d. "Sleaze: strictly for 'Chinese'", *Mail & Guardian*, 23 February: 29.

————, 2007e. "Unliked, unlikeable and unavailable", *Mail & Guardian*, 12 January: 26.

————, 2008. "Opening the door to 'blacks of convenience'", *Weekender*, 12 July: 8.

Matthews, Michelle, 2000. "Snipping flesh for art's sake: local artists are looking to surgery as a means of creation", *Mail & Guardian*, 20 October: 23.

Maughan, Karyn, 2003. "We'll laugh last, says T-shirt firm", *Cape Argus*, 22 April: 7.

————, 2006. "Why I wish that Zuma was dead", *The Star*, 6 July: 1.

————, and Gill Gifford, 2006. "Zuma legal action a cheap stunt, says Zapiro", *The Star*, 4 July: 1.

Mazwai, Thami, 1991. The present and future role of the press", pp. 11–18 in South African Institute of Race Relations.

Mbanjwa, Xolani, 2008. "R22m Ngema play raises row at ANC conference", *Sunday Independent*, 17 August: 3.

Mbeki, Thabo, 2007. "Facts, fiction and mini-skirts", *ANC Today*, 7 (29):

27 July, www.anc.org.za.

Mbita, Tarzan, 1999. "Artist Beezy Bailey threatened over Louis Botha", *Cape Argus*, 23 September: 3.

Mculu, Bandi, 2008. "To imagine that SA would have remained agrarian without colonisation is racist", letter-to-the-editor, *Saturday Star*, 19 April: 14.

Meer, Fatima, 1969. *Portrait of Indian South Africans*. Durban: Avon House.

Meer, Ismail, 2002. *A fortunate man*. Cape Town: Zebra Press.

Meiring, Jean, 2006. "Marriage for all", *Mail & Guardian*, 20 October: 38.

Memela, Sandile, 2006a. "Black brainpower", *Mail & Guardian*, 5 May: 19.

————, 2006b. "Commentators just replaceable pieces of human experience", letter-to-the-editor, *The Star*, 26 June: 24.

Merten, Marianne, 2004. "SAB won't Laugh it Off", *Mail & Guardian*, 19 November: 7.

————, 2012. "Cosatu says 'yes' to call to boycott Spear 'purveyors'", *Saturday Star*, 26 May: 3.

Michelsen, Anders, 1995. "Black looks, white myths", *Flash art*, 28 (183): 75.

Miles, William F.S., 2003. "*Shari'a* as de-Africanization: Evidence from Hausaland", *Africa today*, 50 (1): 51–75.

Miller, Andie, 2004. "Men on the brink", *Mail & Guardian*, 4 June.

Miller, Jonathan, 2005. "March of the conservatives: Penguin film as political fodder", *New York Times*, 13 September: 72.

Minnie, Jeanette, 2008. "Back to the future for SABC", *Mail & Guardian*, 27 June: 32.

Minty, Zayd, 2006. "Post-*apartheid* public art in Cape Town: Symbolic reparations and public space", *Urban studies*, 43 (2): 421–440.

Mjekula, Luvuyo, 2003. "Queen Thuthula a feminist hero?" *East Cape News*, 13 June.

Mkhabela, Mpumelelo, 2012. "President Zuma is under siege", *Sowetan*, 20 June: 13.

Mkhwanazi, Siyabonga, 2008. "'Kill for Zuma' gets life of its own as youths chant welcome", *The Star*, 30 June: 3.

Mngxitama, Andile, 2007. "The end of transformation?" *Weekender*, 27 October: 3.

Mofokeng, Lesley, 2006. "Well groomed", *Sunday Times Magazine*, 3 December: 8–9.

Mokoena, Eddie, 2002. "Murray's no walk in the park", *Sowetan*, 5 July.

Molefe, Russel, 2008. "The roots of Chinese in Africa date back 500 years", *City Press*, 22 June: 6.

Molele, Charles, 2007. "So how dangerous is the 'Queen of Racial Politics'?" *Sunday Times*, 30 September: 18.

Molema, Sonia, 2003. "Polygamy has many faces", *City Press*, 16 February: 3.

Molewa, Edna, 2006. "Let's give the Native Club a chance", *The Star*,

3 June: 20.

Moloto, Moloko, and Moffet Mofokeng, 2012. "Zuma won't quit power: Malema", *Sunday Independent*, 17 June: 1.

Molusi, Connie, 1991. "What hope political pluralism in South Africa? The nature of black fears and aspirations", pp. 25–28 in South African Institute of Race Relations.

Momberg, Eleanor, 2003. "JM Coetzee's honour sparks DA, ANC spat", *Citizen*, 4 October: 2.

———, 2007. "Scathing adverts in support of Manto unleash a can of worms", *Sunday Independent*, 23 September: 3.

Monageng, Gladwell, 2006. "No impotent minds required", *Mail & Guardian*, 15 May: 34.

Monare, Moshoeshoe, 2008. "Best way to deal with the likes of Bullard: just ignore them", *Sunday Independent*, 20 April: 8.

Moodie, T. Dunbar [with Vivienne Ndatshe], 1994. *Going for gold: Men, mines, and migration*. Berkeley: University of California Press.

Moolman, Athane, 1998. "No steps taken in 'porn' art debate", *Eastern Province Herald*, 7 July: 1.

Moreton, Cole, 2002. "Prejudices on parade", *Sunday Independent Sunday Life*, 15 December: 12.

Morrell, Robert, 2005. "White, male, democrat, African", *Mail & Guardian*, 1 April: 22.

Morris, Michael, 2006. "Strip teasers", pp. 47–51 in Kannemeyer and Botes, eds.

Morris, Mike, 2005. "It's my country and I'll whinge if I want to", *Mail & Guardian*, 8 April: 24.

Mothibi, Nano, 2003. "Racism charges erupt at sexuality conference", *The Star*, 26 June.

Motsei, Mmatshilo, 2007. *The kanga and the kangaroo court: Reflections on the rape trial of Jacob Zuma*. Johannesburg: Jacana.

Moya, Fikile-Ntsikelelo, 2005. "The virginity tester", *Mail & Guardian*, 23 September: 11.

———, 2006. "Publications Board boss slams 'media frenzy' over draft bill", *Mail & Guardian*, 1 September: 13.

———, 2007. "I'm like Oscar Wilde", *Mail & Guardian*, 26 January: 12.

Moyo, Simon, 2003. "Powell a disgraceful Uncle Tom", *Daily Dispatch*, 27 June: 19.

Mpanza, Horace, 2003. "'Disgrace' a disgrace", letter-to-the-editor, *Citizen*, 13 October: 11.

Mpofu, Dali, 2006. "Special public notice: SABC statement on withdrawal of President Thabo Mbeki's 'Unauthorised' documentary", *City Press*, 25 June: 33.

———, 2007a. "Enemies of the People? Point", *Mail & Guardian*, 7 September: 30.

———, 2007b. "SABC stands its ground, independently",

Mail & Guardian, 16 June: 24.

Msomi, S'thembiso, 2004. "His money's on the tokoloshe", *Sunday Times*, 10 October.

Mthembu, Bongani, 2005. "Zulu king slams gays", *Daily News*, 12 September: 1.

Mthethwa, Bongani, 2005. "Male virgin testing now a royal decree", *Sunday Times*, 11 September: 6.

———, 2007. "Zulu culture wears the pants", *Sunday Times*, 9 September: 7.

———, 2008. "Row over religion erupts at high school", *Sunday Times*, 24 February: 10.

Mthethwa, Buhle, 2008. "Are our Chinese black enough for empowerment?" *Sunday Times*, 29 June: 13.

Mtimkulu, Phil, 2006. "Native Club will inspire more black intellectuals", letter-to-the-editor, *The Star*, 13 June: 9.

Mtshali, Dr Mbuyiseni Oswald, 2007. "Freedom of expression should always prevail", letter-to-the-editor, *The Star*, 3 August: 11.

Mtshali, Nontobeko, 2012a. "'SA education worse than under apartheid'", *Pretoria News*, 23 March: 1

———, 2012b. "Shocking statistics on how education fails SA", *The Star*, 7 June: 2.

Muller, Sean, 2005. "An exercise in chest-thumping", letter-to-the-editor, *Mail & Guardian*, 15 April: 22.

Murinik, Tracy, 2004. "Interview with Churchill Madikida", pp. 80–85 in Enwezor et al., *op. cit.*

Musgrave, Amy, and Wyndham Hartley, 2006. "Gay marriage uproar", *Weekender*, 25 November: 2.

Naidoo, Kiru, 2003. "Romance and reality", *Sunday Times*, 23 November: 4.

Naidoo, Nalini, 2002. "Building bridges with words", *Natal Witness*, 30 July.

Naidoo, Prakash, 2006. "Between dignity and free speech", *Financial Mail*, 10 February: 24.

Naidoo, Subashni, 2008. "Mahatma's historic police cell converted into men's loos", *Sunday Times*, 20 July: 1.

Naidoo, T.P., and Rajendra Chetty, eds, 1981. *Indian annual: The settlers, 120th anniversary commemoration*. Durban: The Indian Academy of South Africa.

Naidu, Buddy, Simpiwe Piliso, and Ndivhuho Mafela, 2007. "Why bank chickened out of crime showdown with Mbeki", *Sunday Times*, 4 February: 1.

Naidu, Edwin, 2002. "The song of discord", *The Hindu*, 23 June.

———, 2008a. "Cast of clowns at the SABC is not raising a laugh from the public", *Sunday Independent*, 15 June: 8.

———, 2008b. "Concern over bid to control SABC", *Sunday Independent*, 17 August: 4.

———, 2008c. "Corridors of power a dangerous place to be at the SABC",

Sunday Independent, 20 April: 3.

————, 2008d. "Mpofu defends SABC turning its back on 'foreign, frigid freedoms'", *Sunday Independent,* 2 September: 1.

————, 2008e. "Press freedom will be under threat as long as the media is biased", *Sunday Independent,* 13 January: 8.

————, 2008f. "SABC teeters on the brink", *Sunday Independent,* 3 August: 4.

————, 2009. "Axed SABC head costs SABC R22m", *Sunday Independent,* 16 August: 4.

————, and Maureen Isaacson, 2006. "Mpofu launches internal probe into SABC blacklist row", *Sunday Independent,* 25 June: 1.

Naik, Sameer, 2012. "Kunene 'will pay thousands to burn Spear'", *Saturday Star,* 2 June: 5.

Naipaul, Shiva, 1980. *North of south.* Harmondsworth: Penguin.

The Namibian, 1997. "Alpheus comes out on gay issue", 24 January: 3.

Napo, Mphula, 2008. "Capitalists are trying to abuse BEE system", letter-to-the-editor, *City Press,* 29 June: 28.

Nare, Simon, 2006. "'Defamatory' Mbeki documentary scrapped", *Sowetan,* 15 June: 11.

Natal Witness, 2002. "IFP slams anti-Indian statement", 7 September.

Ncube, Japhet, 2006. "Makers of Mbeki documentary demand answers from SABC", *City Press,* 4 June: 8.

Ndletyana, Mondli, 2012. "We should be encouraging our artists to tell it like it is", *Sunday Times,* 3 June: 4.

Ndlovu, Nosimilo, 2007. "Tradition, stigma and piety", *Mail & Guardian,* 21 December: 24.

————, 2008. "The 21st-century pencil test", *Mail & Guardian,* 24 May.

Ndungane, Njongonkulu, 2004. "The church and gays", *Sunday Times,* 24 October: 21.

The News [Nigeria], 2002. "The killing fields of Kaduna", 9 December.

News24.com, 2007a. "Bok's *De la Rey* 'hijacked'", 6 February. Downloaded 27 February 2007.

————, 2007b, "Govt 'was wrong' to stop FNB", 5 February. Downloaded 7 May 2007.

————, 2007c. "Steve Hofmeyr in rape protest", 23 January. Downloaded 17 April 2007.

————, 2007d. "Tata-ma bullet", 8 February. Downloaded 5 March 2007.

————, 2008. "New Zuma claim against Rapport", 17 January.

New York Daily News, 2003. "'Prince Harry is a thief'", 21 August: 5.

New York Post, 2006. "15 die in Nigerian riots over Muhammad cartoons", 19 February: 6.

New York Times, 2002. "Rising nostalgia for apartheid", 12 December: A14.

Ngalwa, Sibusiso, 2008. "Jordan climbs into 'racist" Bullard and his ex-editor", *The Star,* 23 April: 11.

————, 2011. "Juju ridicules 'shower man'", *Sunday Times,*

18 December: 1.

Ngcakani, Anelisa, 2007. "Fury over same-sex marriages", *Daily Dispatch*, 4 January: 1.

Ngcobo, Nomzamo, 2012. "White private parts on display!" *Daily Sun*, 25 May: 2.

Ngobeni, Solani, 2006. "Black intellectuals must publish or be damned", *Sunday Times*, 19 October: 18.

Nixon, Nicholas, 1991. *Bearing witness: People with AIDS*. Boston: David B. Godine.

Noble, Kenneth, 1994. "Fearing domination by blacks, Indians of South Africa switch loyalties", *New York Times*, 22 April: A8.

Nocera, Joe, 2006. "Enough shame to go around on China", *New York Times*, 18 February: C1, 13.

Nolan, James L., Jr, ed., 1996. *The American culture wars: Current contests and future prospects*. Charlottesville: University Press of Virginia.

Noseweek, 2002. "'Hands off!' says Standard Bank", April (40): 40–41.

Nowbath, Ranji S., 1949a. *The Forum*, 29 January, pp. 209–211 in Bhana and Pachai, 1984.

————, 1949b. *Common Sense*, May, pp. 211–213 in Bhana and Pachai, 1984.

Ntsebeza, Lungisile, 2005. *Democracy compromised: Chiefs and the politics of the land in South Africa*. Boston: Brill.

Ntshangase, Ndela, 2006. "Ancient ceremonies help us to rediscover ourselves", *Sunday Times*, 17 December: 29.

Ntshingila, Futhi, 2006. "Animal rights vs Zulu culture", *Sunday Times*, 10 December: 5.

Ntuli, Fafa Sipho, 2003. "Gay culture taboo for blacks", *City Press*, 23 November: 26.

Nurse, Justin, and Chris Verridjt, eds, 2003. "Brand assassin: [interview with] Justin Nurse", *South African Youth Culture Annual*, 1: 32–35.

Nuttall, Sarah, and Liz McGregor, eds, 2007. *At risk: Writing on and over the edge of South Africa*. Johannesburg: Jonathan Ball.

Nxopo, Lulamile, 2012. "What you said on Facebook about …", *City Press*, 3 June: 30.

Oliphant, Andries Walter, 1991/1992. "The quest for appropriate representation", *Full frame: review of South African photography, Vrye Weekblad*, 13 December–10 January: 8–9.

Oliphant, Lumka, 2006. "Sex tourists crash Reed Dance", *Saturday Star*, 9 September: 3.

————, 2007. "When culture gets the chop", *Saturday Star*, 27 January: 10.

O'Neill, Tom, 1991. "Those circumcision photos: Arrogance or ignorance?" letter-to-the-editor, *Staffrider*, 9 (4): 149–150.

Oppelt, Phylicia, 2011. "Obscenely obese fat cats – literally and metaphorically", *Sunday Times*, 18 December: 5.

Orner, Peter, 2006. *The second coming of Mavala Shikongo*. New York: Little,

Brown and Company.

Osshar, Jonathan, 2007. "A whole lot of bull", letter-to-the-editor, *Mail & Guardian*, 8 February: 24.

O'Toole, Sean, 2004. "Churchill Madikida: From dubious beginnings to top of his class", *Business Day*, 5 March: 19.

———, 2008. "How to look & what to see", *Empire*, 1(3): 30–39.

Ottermann, Birgit, 2007. "*De la Rey* needs a girl", *News24.com*, 3 August. Downloaded 21 May 2007.

Outright SA, 2001. "Nujoma's Namibia", June/July: 38.

Owen, Therese, 2007. "Living her postmodern dream", *Star Tonight*, 8 August: 6.

———, 2008. "Enduring rebel of Afrikaans rock", *Star Tonight*, 20 August: 6–7.

Palmer, Riaaz, 2004. "The kiss of death for homophobia?" *Star Tonight*, 6 July: 10.

Pannick, David, 2005. "When is a joke a constitutional issue? When it's a brand of parody", *The Times* [London], 11 October: 4.

Parashar, Amita, 2004. "Where angels fear to tread", *Mail & Guardian*, 6 August: 37.

Parker, Richard, Regina Maria Barbosa, and Peter Aggleton, eds, 2000. *Framing the sexual subject: The politics of gender, sexuality, and power.* Berkeley: University of California Press.

Pelser, Waldimar, 2007. "Human rights versus Islam over sharia play", *City Press*, 11 November: 14.

———, 2008. "'Media played part in Kenya, SA's xenophobic violence'", *City Press*, 20 July: 16.

Perlman, John, 1989. "Beloofde Land: no consensus, but debate sure beat the scissors", *Weekly Mail*, 14 April: 23–24.

Perryer, Sophie, ed., 2004. *10 years 100 artists: Art in a democratic South Africa.* Cape Town: Bell-Roberts Publishing.

———, 2006. *Churchill Madikida.* Johannesburg: David Krut Publishing.

Petchesky, Rosalind, 2000. "Sexual rights: Inventing a concept, mapping an international practice", pp. 81–103 in Parker et al. eds.

Peters, Melanie, 2004. "New Afrikaner generation just wants to have a jol", *Saturday Star*, 14 August: 3.

———, and Candes Keating, 2007. "SPCA to charge Yengeni for animal cruelty", *Cape Argus*, 31 January.

Peters, Ralph, 2006. "Bigots on both sides", *New York Post*, 7 February: 31.

Petridis, Alexis, 2004. "Pride and prejudice", *The Guardian*, 10 December.

Pheko, Mohau, 2008. "Black judgment subjects Chinese to animosity, not equality", *Sunday Times*, 29 June: 23.

Philp, Rowan, 2003. "Chiefs slam historical Xhosa play as 'immoral'", *Sunday Times*, 15 June: 8.

Pienaar, Peet, 2000. "Work 'is not Xhosa ritual'", *Die Burger*, 9 August.

Piliso, Simpiwe, 2009. "The king's looking for a queen", *Sunday Times*,

26 July: 3.

Polgreen, Lydia, 2006. "Nigeria counts 100 deaths over Danish caricatures", *New York Times*, 24 February: A8.

———, 2007. "Nigeria turns from harsher side of Islamic law", *New York Times*, 1 December: A1, 6.

Pollak, Lloyd, 2000. "Cocking a snook at sacred cows", *Cape Times*, 31 May: 6.

Pollock, Barbara, 2003. "Circumcised, circumscribed", *Time Out New York*, 20 March.

Poovalingam, Pat, 2003. *Anand*. Durban: Madiba Publishers.

Popke, E. Jeffrey, 2000. "Violence and memory in the reconstruction of South Africa's Cato Manor", *Growth and change*, 30 (Spring): 235–254.

Potgieter, Deon, 2006. "Native Club is just like the Broederbond", letter-to-the-editor, *The Star*, 23 June: 15.

Powell, Anél, 2006. "Fringe visions revisited", *Cape Times*, 31 October: 4–5.

Powell, Ivor, 2007. "The anxiety of identity and *Some Afrikaners*", pp. 19–28 in Goldblatt.

Press Trust of India Limited, 2002a. "Indians attack song 'inciting' racism against them", 26 May.

———, 2002b. Mbeki condemns racial intolerance", 20 June.

———, 2002c. "SAfrican playwright accuses Indians of exploitation", 23 May.

Pressly, Donwald, 2007. "ANC wants 'black broederbond'", *The Star Business Report*, 26 June: 1.

Pretoria News, 1995. "Educational exhibit 'is pornographic'", 23 November.

Pretorius, Liesl, 2007. "*De la Gay* not such a hit ..." *Beeld*, 3 June.

Prince, Chandré, 2012. "Zuma forced to put out too many fires", *The Times*, 29 February: 2.

Quintal, Angela, 2006a. "Concern for SABC radio man's future", *The Star*, 22 June: 6.

———, 2006b. "Outrage over SABC's banning of some who have criticised Mbeki", *The Star*, 21 June: 14.

———, and Chiara Carter, 2007. "Mbeki wins control of SABC board", *Sunday Independent*, 16 September: 1.

Qunta, Christine, 2007. "Author's a colonial construction", *Star*, 9 May: 14.

Rademeyer, Julian, 1998. "Fate of controversial artworks known today", *Eastern Province Herald*, 8 July: 1.

———, 2005. "Poor of Asia find paradise in SA", *Sunday Times*, 7 August.

———, 2007a. "Press 'enemy of people' – SABC", *Sunday Times*, 2 September: 15.

———, 2007b. "Public had a 'need' to know the facts about the minister", *Sunday Times*, 2 September: 4.

Raghavan, Sudarsan, 1995. "Indians are wary of Mandela's ANC ... and their native land is beckoning", *Business Week*, 28 August.

Randall, Ina, 2003. "Play captures essence of Africa", *The Herald*, 1 July: 8.

Rank, Francois, 2008. "Young racists in cyberspace", *Sunday Times*,
      13 April: 7.

Rapetsoa, Dalton, 2006. "Clarity on Native Club needed", letter-to-the-
      editor, *The Star*, 5 June: 18.

Rapitso, Shadi, 2006. "Get some beef behind your lobola talks", *City Press*,
      22 October: 34.

Reid, Graeme, 2004. "Book review of Taxi book", *de arte*, 70: 62–64.

————, and Liz Walker, 2003. "Coming out of the closet: sex in Africa",
      Mail & Guardian, 23 December.

————, 2004. "Conference report: Sex and Secrecy: the 4th conference of
      the International Association for the Study of Sexuality, Culture and
      Society", *Sexuality research & social policy*, 1 (1): 98–103.

Reuters, Johannesburg, 2001. "Virginity tests on comeback trail in South
      Africa", *Jenda: A journal of culture and African women studies*, 1: 1

Richards, Colin, 2004. "Walking wounded", *Art South Africa*, 2 (4): 52–57.

————, 2006. "Inside out", pp. 25–79 in Perryer, ed.

Ritchie, Kevin, 2007a. "Hofmeyr won't join Mbeki's fight", *Saturday Star*,
      17 February: 6.

————, 2007b. "A song that answers a deep sadness", *Sunday Independent*,
      18 February, web.lexis-nexis.com. Downloaded 27 May 2007.

Roberts, Oliver, 2011. "Dis 'n lekker ou show", *Sunday Times Lifestyle*, 10
      July: 14–15.

————, 2012. "Heart of whiteness", *Sunday Times Lifestyle*, 24 June: 16–17.

Roberts, Ronald Suresh, 2007. "Circus not unlike the old days", *The Star*,
      16 August: 14.

————, 2008. "The making of a colonial creature", *Empire*, 1(6),
      16 June: 22–23.

Robertson, Delia, 2006. "Zuma rape trial impacts South Africa", *VOA
      News.com*, 6 May.

Rondganger, Lee, 2006. "Slanging match over Mbeki documentary",
      The Star, 15 June: 3.

————, 2008. "Minister's Chinese tirade", *The Star*, 25 June: 1.

Ronge, Barry, 2007. "Old faces, new look", *Sunday Times Magazine*, 8 April,
      www.sundaytimes.co.za. Downloaded 27 May 2007.

Roodt, Dan, 2003a. "Afrikaners are not free", letter-to-the-editor, *The Star*,
      30 July.

————, 2003b. "Afrikaners will still stand when SA falls", letter-to-the-
      editor, *The Star*, 8 August: 9.

————, 2005. "You can't have your banana and eat it", *Mail & Guardian*,
      1 April: 23.

————, 2007. "Wie sal ons nou lei? Nie Antjie nie", letter-to-the-editor,
      Mail & Guardian, 13 April: 22.

Roper, Chris, 1998a. "How not to get a head in art", *Mail & Guardian*,
      7 April: 4.

————, 1998b. "Villain or victim", *Mail & Guardian*, 15 May: 2.

———, 2002. "Art steps out", *Mail & Guardian Friday*, 22 March: 2.

———, 2007. "Bok van Blerk music review", www.news24.com. Downloaded 27 May 2007.

Rosen, Rhoda, 1992. "The documentary photographer and social responsibility", *de arte* 45: 4–14.

Rossouw, Mandy, 2008. "The Zuma factor", *Mail & Guardian*, 24 May.

Rossouw, Rehana, 2008."Understandable Afrikaner paranoia", *Weekender*, 8 March: 6.

Rostron, Bryan, 2008. "History makes its way to the present", *Weekender*, 28 June: 5.

Rothstein, Edward, 2006. "History illuminates the rage of Muslims", *New York Times*, 20 February: E1, 10.

Roup, Julian, 2004. *Boerejood*. Johannesburg: Jacana.

Roychoudhuri, Onnesha, 2004. "Paul Fusco: the story behind the photos", *Mother Jones*, 20 December.

Sachs, Albie, 1990. "Preparing ourselves for freedom", pp. 19–29 in De Kok and Press, eds.

———, 1991. "A Freedom Charter for South African artists", *Staffrider*, 9 (4): 45–50.

Salafranca, Arja, 2009. "How things have changed in 20 years", *Sunday Independent*, 14 June: 29.

Salamon, Julie, 2005. "Culture wars pull Buster into the fray", *New York Times*, 27 January: E1, 9.

Salzwedel, Ilse, 2007. "Bok van Blerk: unwilling icon", *De Kat*, Autumn: 48–49.

Sama Yende, Sizwe, 2005. "Gay marriage decision slammed", *News24.com*, 14 December. Downloaded 2 April 2006.

———, 2012. "2012: The year of over 300 protests", *City Press*, 17 June: 5.

Sassen, Robyn, 2004. "Christ with a 'disturbing twist'", *Sunday Times*, 1 August: 9.

Saturday Star, 2007. "Bloody welcome home for Yengeni", 20 January: 1.

Sawubona, 2006. "Empowering the value chain", August: 82–83.

Schmahmann, Brenda, 1999. "Censorship, censoriousness and a colourful ·commotion: The *Useful Objects* controversy, pp. 227–237 in Atkinson and Breitz, eds.

———, 1996. "Misquotation gave Kgositsile evidence in art/porn article", letter-to-the-editor, *The Star*, 20 August.

School Library Journal, 2007. "'And Tango makes three' prompts serious challenge in Massachusetts school", 8 May, schoollibraryjournal.com.

Schoonakker, Bonny, 2004. "Gordimer's supporters leap to her defence", *Sunday Times*,15 August: 6.

Schroeder, Fatima, and Estelle Ellis, 2003. "Laughs in court as lawyers get shirty", *Cape Times*, 21 February: 1.

Schuler, Catherine, 1990. "Spectator response and comprehension: the problem of Karen Finley's *Constant State of Desire*", *TDR* [*The Drama*

Review], 34 (1): 131–145.

Scott, Janny, 1997. "An Appomattox in the culture wars", *New York Times*, 25 May: WK1, 6.

Seeger, Dina, and Anthea Bristowe, 1998. "The skinhead and the drag queen", *Sunday Times*, 18 January: 1.

Sefara, Makhudu, 2008. "Living in fear of the mob", *City Press*, 20 July: 27.

———, and Jackie Mapiloko, 2008. "War talk moves up a gear", *City Press*, 10 August: 21.

Seme, Siyabonga, 2008. "Chinese did not suffer like blacks", letter-to-the-editor, *City Press*, 29 June: 28.

Serrao, Angelique, 2008. "Qwelane's anti-gay column breached code", *The Star*, 30 July: 3.

Sesanti, Simphiwe, 2003. "Setting record of a hero straight", *City Press*, 8 June: 26.

Sewchurran, Rowan, 2003. "Grey Street blues", *Tribune Herald* [Durban], 31 August: 4.

Sey, James, 1996. "Private acts and public rituals", *Mail & Guardian*, 13 September.

Shapshank, David, 1997. "That ashtray led to good", *Star Tonight*, 4 November: 8.

Shaw, Linda, 1993. "Steven frees his mind", *Sunday Times Metro Life*, 17 July: 7.

Sichel, Adrienne, 2002. "Unwrapping blanket covering secret lives of initiates", *Sunday Independent*, 8 September: 11.

———, 2005. "Mind-blowing Jomba! leads the other arts", *Sunday Independent*, 4 September: 10.

———, 2006. "Traditional dance turns contemporary", *Sunday Independent*, 3 September: 10.

Siegel, Fred, 2006. "Europe's new time of testing", *New York Post*, 7 February: 31.

Sikhakhane, Jabulani, 2008. "In a true democracy, black people can't stand on BEE crutches forever", *Saturday Star*, 12 July: 14.

Silverman, Melinda, and Sarah Charlton, 2004. "From Egoli to Egoati", *Mail & Guardian*, 1 October: 11.

Simpson, John, 2006. "Rioting Hamburglars: we're *not* loving it!" *New York Post*, 17 February: 38.

Slackman, Michael, 2006. "Beneath the rage in the Mideast", *New York Times*, 12 February: Sec. 4: 1, 4.

Smelser, Neil J., and Paul B. Baltes, eds, 2001. *International encyclopedia of the social and behavioural sciences*. Oxford, England: Pergamon.

Smith, Charlene, 2006. "Satyagraha centenary goes by unnoticed", *Sunday Independent*, 3 September: 5.

Smith, Janet, 2012. "Making the most of a forgiving crowd", *The Star*, 31 May: 19.

Sokana, Phumza, 2007a. "Mom fears for safety of her black Miss India teen as final draws near", *City Press*, 14 October: 3.

———, 2007b. "She's ready to die to keep family's chieftaincy", *City Press*, 28 October: 6.

———, 2008. "Vavi defends 'kill' rhetoric", *City Press*, 6 July: 2.

Sokupa, Vuyo, 2007. "Not in my Xhosa culture", *Mail & Guardian Classics*, June: 29.

———, and Zukile Majova, 2006. "Candidate of the left or the conservatives?" *Mail & Guardian*, 29 September: 4.

Sosibo, Kwanele, 2007. "Gay drama cut by several scenes", *Mail & Guardian*, 20 April: 6.

South African Art Times, 2008. "Artist too nude for learners", July: 13.

South African Institute of Race Relations, 1991. *Mau-mauing the media: New censorship for the new South Africa.* Johannesburg: South African Institute of Race Relations.

South African Press Association, 2001. "Namibian gays hit back at Nujoma", 21 March.

———, 2002a. "'AmaNdiya' inappropriate comment on racism, Mandela tells Ngema", 17 June.

———, 2002b. "Quotes of the week", 10 June.

———, 2004. "We hate hate speech", 1 December: 14.

———, 2007. "Anti-crime campaign gathers momentum", *Mail & Guardian*, 7 February.

South African Yearbook, 2007/2008. Pretoria: Government Communication and Information System, 15th edition.

Southey, Caroline, 1999. "Old faces, new places: Mafube publishing", *Financial Mail*, 5 February.

Sowaga, Dulile, 2004. "Gay kiss on TV 'wasn't the real thing'", *City Press*, 18 July: 2.

Sowetan, 2003. "Coverage of killing was 'unAfrican'", 26 June: 6.

Sparks, Allister, 1990. *The mind of South Africa: The story of the rise and fall of apartheid.* London: Heinemann.

———, 1994. *Tomorrow is another country: The inside story of South Africa's road to change.* Johannesburg: Struik.

Sparks, W., 2005. "Going ape", letter-to-the-editor, *Mail & Guardian*, 1 April: 20.

Spencer-Smith, Tony, 1982. "One for the boys! The art show with a different bent", *Sunday Tribune*, 31 January.

Spiegelman, Art, 2006. "Drawing blood: Outrageous cartoons and the art of outrage", *Harper's Magazine*, June: 43–52.

Spivak, Gayatri Chakravorty, 1998. "Cultural talks in the hot peace: revisiting the 'global village'", pp. 329–348 in Cheah and Robbins, eds.

Stanley, Alessandra, 2005. "A grim excursion to Rwanda's hell", *New York Times*, 18 March: WE1, 34.

The Star, 2002. "Indaba helps heal rift between Africans, Indians", 29 July: 2.

———, 2003. "Zim envoy calls death report 'un-African'", 26 June: 5.

———, 2004. "Station put in the box over gay broadcast", 5 October.

———, 2006. "Zuma fans made to leave Gandhi festival", 2 October: 2.

———, 2007a. "Banned memorabilia the hottest items", 18 December: 3.

———, 2007b. "DA says De la Rey isn't as subversive as 'Umshini Wam'", 8 February.

———, 2008. "Blogging a new way to beat censorship in Zim", 22 July: 15.

Steinberg, Jonny, 2008. *Sizwe's test: A young man's journey through Africa's AIDS epidemic*. New York: Simon & Schuster.

Stewart, Kathleen, and Susan Harding, 1999. "Apocalypsis", *Annual review of anthropology*, 28: 285–310.

Sulcas, Adele, 1998. "Landmark case separates art from porn", *Sunday Independent*, 2 August.

Sunday Times, 2003. "Journalists get life for inciting hatred", 7 December: 15.

———, 2006a. "Vandals hit Gandhi memorial second time", 14 May: 13.

———, 2006b. "Censorship alarm bells ring", 13 August: 20.

———, 2007a. "A victory for accountability", 2 September: 28.

———, 2007b. "Why bank chickened out of crime showdown with Mbeki", 4 February.

———, 2012. "When mob rule shouts down the rule of law", 4 June: 4.

Swarns, Rachel L., 2001. "A dispute over books unsettles Africa", *New York Times*, 23 April: A4.

———, 2002. "Beyond black and white", *New York Times*, 24 June: E5.

Swart, Werner, 2006. "SABC under siege", *Citizen*, 22 June: 1–2.

Taheri, Amir, 2006. "Rent-a-riot ABCs", *New York Post*, 9 February: 31.

Taylor, Jane, 1997. "Opening address [*Purity and Danger*]", *de arte*, 56 (September): 43–44.

Teale, Julia, 1996. "The nude made naked", *Mail & Guardian*, 18 October: 33.

Temple-Raston, Dina, 2002. "Journalism and genocide", *Columbia journalism review*, 41(3): 18–19.

Tepper, Steven J., 2011. *Not here! Not now! Not that! Protest over art and culture in America*. Chicago: University of Chicago Press.

Terreblanche, Christelle, 2003. "Farm attacks linked to crime, not politics", *The Star*, 26 September: 6.

———, and Deon de Lange, 2007. "ANC members allowed to wear only T-shirts with Mbeki's face", *The Star*, 29 October: 5.

———, and Janine Stephen, 2007. "Child porn law raises press freedom issues", *Sunday Independent*, 6 May: 4.

Thakali, Thabiso, and Justine Gerardy, 2008. "The 'sin' of a villager who would be chief", *Saturday Star*, 14 June: 8.

Thepa, Madala, 2012. "A piece for peace and the bandits triumph", *Sunday World*, 3 June: 10.

365Gay.com, 2006. "Mugabe threatens to arrest pro-gay clergy", 26 February.

www.365gay.com/Newscon06/02/022606mugabe.htm. Downloaded 31
March 2008.

Thorpe, Lindsey, 2006. "SA's top cartoonist sticks to his crayons", *Saturday
Star*, 8 July: 5.

Tilkin, Daniela, 2002. *Dislocación: Imagen & identidad, Sudáfrica*. Madrid:
PhotoEspaña.

The Times of India, 2002a. "Indian women murdered in Durban", 30 July.

————, 2002b. "S. Africans, Indians seek reconciliation over song",
28 July.

Tolsi, Niren, 2006. "Being gay and Zulu", *Mail & Guardian*, 13 October: 8.

————, 2007a. "'Child porn' film banned from the fest", *Mail & Guardian*,
22 June: 5.

————, 2007b. "Dancing to archaic rhythms", *Mail & Guardian*,
14 September: 8.

————, 2008a. "JZ's backers are like bad songs …" *Mail & Guardian*,
8 August: 3.

————, 2008b. "'Sarafina III' a hot potato", *Mail & Guardian*,
15 August: 3.

Trillin, Calvin, 2004. "Gadfly: The satirist Pieter-Dirk Uys adjusts to the
new South Africa", *New Yorker*, 10 May: 70–81.

Tromp, Beauregard, 2007. "Simmering settlement threatens more unrest",
The Star, 11 July: 2.

Tshabalala, Teddy, 2008. "Pledge simply imitates the West", *Sunday Times*,
24 February: 20.

Turner, Victor, 1969. *The ritual process: Structure and anti-structure*. Chicago:
Aldine.

————, 1974. *Dramas, fields, and metaphors: Symbolic action in human
society*. Ithaca: Cornell University Press.

Twiggs, Laura, 2000. "Slice of manhood contextualises limits of
masculinity", *Sunday Independent*, 22 September: 12.

Underhill, Glynnis, 2000. "Bart artist gleeful about heated debate over
statue", *Cape Argus*, 3 June: 15.

Vallie, Annaleigh, 2007a. "The surprising rise of Afrikaans music",
Weekender, 14 April: 1.

————, 2007b. "Taking art back home", *Weekender*, 25 August: 14.

Van Bosch, Cobus, 2000. "Circumcision debate important for local art
discourse", *Die Burger*, 31 July.

Van den Ende, Janine, 2004. *The ID of South African artists*. Amsterdam:
Stichting Art and Theatre.

Van der Merwe, André Carl, 2006. *Moffie*. Hermanus: Penstock.

Van der Westhuizen, Christi, 2007. "Identities are restless, not Afrikaners",
Business Day, 9 October.

Van Gass, Chris, 2006. "Makers of racist ring tone 'guilty of hate speech'",
Weekender, 22 July: 3.

Van Graan, Mike, 2004. "Art by invitation" *Mail & Guardian*, 26 March.

————, 2005. "Free speechless", *Mail & Guardian*, 3 June: 4.

Vanguard [Nigeria], 2002a. "A bloody pageant", 26 November.

————, 2002b. "Another Kaduna tragedy", 16 December.

Van Oostrum, Leendert, 2003. "Has Boer-bashing been institutionalised?" *The Star*, 8 August: 9.

Van Zyl, John, 1989. "Profound, beautiful, moving", *The Star*, 29 March.

Venezia, Todd, 2006. "Muslim madmen in mac attack", *New York Post*, 15 February: 13.

Venkatesh, Sudhir, 2008. *Gang leader for a day*. New York: Penguin Press.

Venter, Zelda, 2003a. "'Black music' is driving Boeremag to tears", *The Star*, 19 August: 3.

————, 2003b. "Boeremag 13 spared 'torturing music'", *Saturday Star*, 5 September: 2.

————, 2003c. "Plan was to create chaos for coup to succeed", *The Star*, 4 November: 2.

————, and Nano Mothibi, 2003. "Judge makes move to lessen 'black music torture'", *The Star*, 20 August: 2.

Viljoen, Buks, 2003. "Pupils chant 'Kill the Boer'", 23 July: 7.

Viljoen, Taslima, 2003. "Commission could silence funnymen", *Sowetan Sunday World*, 18 May: 7.

Vincour, John, and Dan Bilefsky, 2006. "Dane sees greed and politics in the crisis", *New York Times*, 10 February: A9.

Visser, Wessel, 2007. "Post-hegemonic Afrikanerdom and diaspora. Redefining Afrikaner identity in post-apartheid South Africa", paper presented at "Pax Africana: The continent and the diaspora in search of identity", Russian Academy of Sciences and Moscow State University, 12–14 September.

Vollgraaff, René, 2012. "SA doing well now but fear is lurking", *Sunday Times*, 6 May: 3.

Von Bonde, Jon, 2003. "Tradition not an excuse for cruelty", letter-to-the-editor, *The Herald* [Port Elizabeth], 5 July.

Von Stauss, Alexandra, 2004. "Representations and objections: Geert Van Kesteren and the 13th International Aids Conference, Durban, 2000", *Critical arts*, 18 (2): 45–62.

Wade, Jean-Philippe, 2006. "Abuse will surely backfire", letter-to-the-editor, *The Star*, 26 June: 24.

Wa ka Ngobeni, Evidence, 2000. "Aids conference bans 'graphic' photographs", *Mail & Guardian*, 7 July: 5.

Waldner, Mariechen, 2007a. "'De la Rey factor' alienates blacks at "Afrikaans' varsities", *City Press*, 30 September: 8.

————, 2007b. "Fighting bulls spell the end for whites, says Boeremag man", *City Press*, 7 October: 4.

————, 2007c. "Uproar over racist tendencies at universities", *City Press*, 30 September: 8.

Webb, Boyd, 2008. "Unrepentant Malema now claims he was misquoted",

The Star, 20 June: 6.

Weber, Bruce, 2004. "Poet brokers truce in culture wars", *New York Times*,
7 September: E1, 5.

Webster, E.C., 1977. "The 1946 [*sic*] Durban riots – a case-study in race and
class, pp. 1–54 in Bonner, ed.

Weekend Argus, 2006. "43 arrested for looting", 22 July.

Weekender, 2006. "SABC's problem is not so much bias as bungling",
17 June: 6.

————, 2007. "From a storybook start to turning a new page", 20 October:
6.

Wiechers, Riana, 2006. "Planet Fokofpolisiekar", *Sunday Times Lifestyle*,
17 September: 8–9.

Wieringa, Saskia, and Ruth Morgan, eds, 2005. *Tommy boys, lesbian men and
ancestral wives: Same-sex practices in Africa*. Johannesburg: Jacana.

Wierzycka, Aska, 1998. "Africa says 'eat my sculpture'", *Mail & Guardian*,
14 August.

Wilhelm, Peter, 1999. "Dead ducks in the mosh pit: the state we're in",
Financial Mail, 13 August.

Williams, Rhys H., ed., 1997. *Cultural wars in American politics: Critical
reviews of a popular myth*. New York: Aldine de Gruyter.

Williamson, Sue, 1989. *Resistance art in South Africa*. New York: St Martin's
Press.

————, 2000. "Cultural apartheid? Circumcision proposal provokes
questions", www.artthrob.com, July. Downloaded 4 April 2008.

Willoughby, Guy, 2005. "Shifting Geers", *Sunday Times Lifestyle*, 29 May: 6.

Wines, Michael, 2007. "Survivor is poised to lead South Africa", *New York
Times*, 20 December: A3.

Witthaus, Michele, 1989. "Statement and satire: two views of the volk",
Weekly Mail, 23 March: 27.

Wolfe, Alan, 1998. *One nation, after all: What middle-class Americans really
think about: God, country, racism, welfare, immigration, homosexuality,
work, the right, the left and each other*. New York: Viking.

Wolmarans, Riaan, 2007. "Mbeki doccie: red dress or black mini?" *Mail &
Guardian*, 19 July.

Woodward, Wendy, Patricia Hayes, and Gary Minkley, eds, 2002. *Deep
hiStories: Gender and colonialism in Southern Africa*. Amsterdam and New
York: Rodopi.

Woon, P., 2008. "Too stupid to see the difference", *Sunday Times*,
29 June: 20.

Wright, Robert, 2006. "The silent treatment", *New York Times*,
17 February: A23.

Wu, Chia-Chao, 2008. "Ruling on Chinese builds a bridge for attracting
investors", *Star Business Report*, 15 July: 2.

www.africancrisis.org, 2007. "Worries over song for a Boer leader",
26 January. Downloaded 27 February 2007.

www.english.ohmynews.com, 2007. "De la Rey: Afrikaner heritage".
   Downloaded 27 May 2007.

www.eProp.co.za, 2006. "Vivian Reddy's casino opens with a bang",
   11 December. Downloaded 19 February 2008.

www.rhodesian.server101.com/terrorontheveld.htm, 24 November 2003.
   Downloaded 3 March 2007.

www.stormfront.org/forum/showthread.php/plaasmoorde-farm-
   murders-271611.html, 18 February 2006. Downloaded 7 March 2007.

www.themuso.co.za, 2007. 19 February. Downloaded 27 February 2007.

www.wikipedia.org/wiki/One_Settler_One_Bullet.
   Downloaded 5 March 2007.

www.worldonline.co.za, 2001. "Mugabe's 'rubber penis' in court", 30 March.
   Downloaded 1 April 2001.

Xulu, Musa, 2007. "Zulu culture has been distorted to satisfy personal
   desire", *City Press*, 7 October: 27.

Yaqoob, Tanira, 2003. "Enid's books 'blighted' by PC police", *The Star*,
   11 December: 23.

Yeld, John, 2007. "Judge also finds controversial biographer to be
   'unlikeable'", *The Star*, 9 January: 2.

Zapasnik, Paul, 2006. "We, the people, demand to see 'Mbeki
   Unauthorised", *The Star*, 27 June: 15.

Zegeye, Abebe, ed., 2001. *Social identities in the new South Africa: After
   apartheid, volume 1*. Cape Town: Kwela Books.

Zondi, Mlungisi, 2007. "Gender politics swaying in the wind", *Business Day*,
   15 September: 1.

Zulu, Mandla, 2003. "Mbongeni Ngema fined a herd of 39 cows", *City Press*,
   2 February: 1.

Zvomuya, Percy, 2006. "Uganda's gays and lesbians outed", *Mail & Guardian*,
   16 September.